Racing & Football Outlook

JUMPS RACING GUIDE 2019-20

Interviews • Statistics • Results
Previews • Training centre reports

Contributors: Richard Birch, James Burn, Tom Collins, Graham Dench, Jack Haynes, Dylan Hill, Ben Hutton, Anthony Ive, Tony Jakobson, Andrew King, Justin O'Hanlon, Tom Ward, Nick Watts

Designed and edited by Nick Watts and Dylan Hill

Published in 2019 by Raceform Ltd
27 Kingfisher Court, Hambridge Road, Newbury RG14 5SJ

A catalogue record for this book is available from the British Library.

ISBN 978-1-83950-016-9

Printed by CPI Group (UK) Ltd, Croydon, CRO 4YY

RACING & FOOTBALL outlook

Contents

RACING & FOOTBALL outlook

Editor's introduction

THANK goodness for Tiger Roll. Not just for those who have followed our ante-post advice for the last two seasons and backed him at 50-1 and 20-1 to win the Grand National, but for the sake of the sport as a whole.

Coming into the National meeting at Aintree in April, jumps racing was in need of some good publicity. For all the brilliant racing, for all the front-page stories that followed Bryony Frost's stunning win on Frodon, in the media as a whole the aftermath of the Cheltenham Festival had been all about the hugely controversial National Hunt Chase and the sport was taking a hammering from ignorant people pushing their own misguided agenda.

One bad Grand National, one more high-profile fatality, even one more ill-conceived jockey ban, and we would have been forced to jump to the sport's defence even more vigorously than we already are in a climate of potential political interference into how it is run.

But then came Tiger Roll. The first back-to-back winner of the great race since Red Rum, he was simply magnificent once again at Aintree, writing himself into folklore and turning himself into a household name that put racing on the front pages of the national newspapers for all the right reasons for once.

And that wasn't the only feelgood story that came out of the end of the jumps season.

TIGER ROLL: second Grand National win was fantastic for the sport

RUBY WALSH: decided to go out on a high after Kemboy's Punchestown win

Some might question about feeling the good in arguably the greatest jumps jockey of all time, Ruby Walsh, hanging up his boots, but the fantastic news in that was that Walsh was able to go out on his own terms after an epic Grade 1 victory. And, for someone who had such an injury-prone career, that didn't always seem likely.

While Walsh can now put his feet up, the rest of us have to plough on, though, and we've been busy over the summer and autumn finding out just what's what ahead of the jumps really getting going again over the coming weeks.

We've been down in Wiltshire to catch up with a pair of Kings who had plenty to smile about last season. It was another solid campaign for Alan King, while at a lower level Neil King topped the trainers' standings for those who have 50 horses or fewer. Both will no doubt have plenty of success over the winter and you can read all about their best prospects in our stable tours.

Elsewhere across Britain and Ireland, our regional reporters have also been speaking to all the trainers in their area to bring you all the latest news on fresh arrivals and horses to follow from the rest of the leading names in the training ranks.

As well as all that, Nick Watts has picked out his 30 horses to follow from either side of the Irish Sea, while we have ante-post advice on the big betting races of the season, the views of RFO regulars Richard Birch and Tom Collins, a comprehensive guide to last season's big races by Dylan Hill and a rundown of the leading speed figures from last season.

Then there are reams of statistics that should help your punting, including figures for last season's top ten trainers broken down by month, jockey, race type and course plus lists of the leading trainers and jockeys for every course in Britain.

We have every angle covered to make it a profitable season, although to keep up to date make sure you also buy your copy of the RFO every Tuesday.

Profiles for punters
Alan King

ALAN KING: topped the £1 million mark in prize-money for the tenth time

Profile by Graham Dench

FEW trainers have been plying their trade at the top level for as long as Alan King, who topped the £1 million mark in prize-money for the tenth time in 13 seasons thanks to 91 winners during the last campaign.

That was King's second best total in a decade and it's a mark of the standards set by the Barbury Castle trainer that he still wasn't completely satisfied.

Asked to reflect upon the campaign, he immediately identifies where he came up short – and, perhaps more significantly, how he hopes to address it.

King says: "My novice hurdlers were no good last season and I basically knew that all year. We were very weak in that department, but we had a big clear-out and it's looking much stronger in that sphere this time.

"We had 11 or 12 individual bumper horses who are all coming through the system now and there will be nice horses coming off the Flat as well, like On To Victory, The Olympian and Trueshan, so I'm confident we are much stronger with our younger horses."

He adds: "Sceau Royal's Queen Mother third was an obvious thrill, and winning the bet365 Gold Cup at Sandown on the last day of the season was a great way to finish off. We'd already topped the £1m mark in prize-money again a few weeks earlier, so I was pleased on balance. As I said, we just needed a stronger batch of novices."

Talkischeap's victory in the bet365 Gold Cup, hugely impressive for a young novice and enough to fuel dreams of a Grand National tilt this season, wasn't the only way in which King signed off on a high. There was also a Grade 2 victory at the National meeting for bumper mare The Glancing Queen, who is the apple of the trainer's eye as she embarks on a novice hurdling campaign.

There were eight Graded or Listed victories, helping King to a haul of just over £1.25 million in prize-money.

However, King is no different to any other jumping trainer in that he loves a Grade 1 winner and he loves a winner at Cheltenham, so the feeling that last season was just missing something is inevitable, especially as he has become used to success on the biggest stage during a stellar career – 31 Grade 1 winners and 15 Cheltenham Festival winners is testament to that.

The first top-flight success came in his very first season with a licence in 1999 after he had taken over the training of the Stayers' Hurdle winner Anzum from his former boss David 'The Duke' Nicholson, guiding him to success in the Long Walk Hurdle when ridden by Richard Johnson, whose OBE was one of King's highlights of last season off the track.

"It was marvellous to hear that he'd been given an OBE, it was thoroughly deserved," King says. "Frighteningly, I've known him since he was a schoolboy and used to come to the Duke's during his holidays. You could see then that he had what it takes – he always had a lot of natural ability and he was so driven as well, with a great work ethic. And he hasn't changed one bit, that's the beauty of him. All the success hasn't altered him in the slightest."

It took a while for King to build on Anzum's initial success, but another Long Walk win with My Way De Solzen in 2005 was the trigger for the most successful period of his career, with My Way De Solzen and Voy Por Ustedes both then winning

MY WAY DE SOLZEN: brilliant dual Cheltenham Festival winner

at successive Cheltenham Festivals, including in 2007 when King also took the Champion Hurdle with Katchit.

More recently, he has turned himself into one of the outstanding dual-purpose trainers around. His name is not mentioned as often as it should be during such discussions, but we should not forget that he also had 38 winners on the Flat in 2018. He shouldn't be far off that total again in 2019, with a Northumberland Plate in the bag thanks to Who Dares Wins.

The ever-dependable Wayne Hutchinson leads the jockeys' line-up again, and Tom Cannon is no ordinary number two. Daryl Jacob rides the Simon Munir/Isaac Souede runners and there are plenty of others who ride successfully for the stable, including good conditionals.

With a string of around 130 horses in training all told, there is lots to look forward to for a man used to firing in plenty of big winners.

The horses

Alsa Mix 7yo mare
Al Namix – Lady Tsana

She won an Irish point-to-point, a bumper and her first two over hurdles, so she's a decent mare, but it was heavy ground for the last of those wins in a Grade 2 at Sandown and I think that took the edge off her as she was a bit disappointing on her last couple of starts. She's a big, powerful mare who has had a very good summer and the plan is to go novice chasing. She loves soft ground.

Azzerti 7yo gelding
Voix Du Nord – Zalagarry

He's taken a long time to grow up and used to get incredibly wound up before a race, but he was more relaxed with each run last year and he put up some good solid performances, winning a couple of novice chases. I'd imagine he'll at two and a half miles, but I could see him stepping up. I hope he'll progress again.

Ballywood 5yo gelding
Ballingarry – Miss Hollywood

He took very well to chasing last season, winning three out of five, and is still only five, so I'm hoping there's more improvement in him. He'll probably start off at two miles around Ascot or one of the decent tracks, but he might get two and a half. He likes goodish ground and although soft would probably be all right he certainly doesn't want it heavy.

Deyrann De Carjac 6yo gelding
Balko – Queyrann

He won only once over hurdles last season but was second to some pretty decent horses. We schooled him over fences in the spring and he was very good, so we gave him his chase debut at Cartmel at the end of May before putting him away and he bolted up. He's done very well and I think he could be an above-average novice.

AZZERTI (right): could progress again now he is becoming more relaxed

DINGO DOLLAR (left): has some smart form but you need to catch him right

Dingo Dollar 7yo gelding
Golden Lariat – Social Society

He ran very well when third in the Ladbrokes Trophy at Newbury last season and had one or two other good bits of form without winning. You just have to catch him right – he wants decent ground, and he's a better horse left-handed. We'll look at the Ladbrokes Trophy again, but there's a chance we might run him over the Aintree fences to just see if the National is an option. There will also be races at Doncaster for him again.

Edwardstone 5yo gelding
Kayf Tara – Nothingtoloose

He had three runs in bumpers and was second every time, beaten by a good one on each occasion. He's a big, powerful horse who will go straight over hurdles and ought to have a good future.

Elgin 7yo gelding
Duke Of Marmalade – China Tea

He progressed really well a couple of seasons ago, winning the Greatwood and the Kingwell. Unfortunately he then missed last season with a leg injury, but he came back into light training this summer. You won't see him until Christmas at the earliest, after which he'll go back down the conditions hurdles route.

Fidux 6yo gelding
Fine Grain – Folle Tempete

He's not very big and I couldn't believe how well he took to chasing this summer having just become up against it at the weights over hurdles. He won his first two over fences and, although it will get more difficult with penalties, his heart is in the right place. He's tough – a grand little horse.

Giving Glances 4yo filly
Passing Glance – Giving

She was a good filly on the Flat as a three-year-old and then won a couple over hurdles, including a Listed race at Doncaster. I think she'd gone on me by the spring as she'd been on the go all summer and then

HARAMBE: will stay hurdling and could be one for the Greatwood

all winter, so she's had a very good break. She could be better than her handicap mark. I think she'd like a bit of nice ground – not extremes.

Hacksaw Ridge **4yo gelding**
Stowaway – Erins Lass

He won a point-to-point in Ireland in the spring and I've been very happy with all I've seen from him. He's a big, fine horse who will go straight novice hurdling. I think he's above average.

Harambe **6yo gelding**
Malinas – Crystal Princess

He was a very good bumper horse, but it took a little while for things to click over hurdles after he was brought down on his debut and was then second to a potentially good horse of Ben Pauling's. He came good in the spring and won at Kempton and Market Rasen, and then we let him take his chance in a £100,000 novice handicap at Sandown at the end of the season, in which he ran very well in second. I think he'll stay hurdling this season and he could be one for the Greatwood.

Heart Of A Lion **4yo gelding**
Yeats – Lady Secret

He bolted up in a bumper at Southwell in the summer, but he's not really a summer horse. He ran there only because he'd been off for a while with a stress fracture and I was desperate to get a run into him because his work had been unbelievable. There's substance to the form, as the second and third both won next time, and I think he's a proper winter horse. He might stay down the bumper route for now, but he's exciting.

Hostile **5yo gelding**
Malinas – Skew

He's a half-brother to Valdez and finished second in a bumper at Warwick last season, doing all of his best work at the finish. He'd been a bit of a playboy and the penny took a while to drop, but I loved the way he finished. He'll go hurdling and he's schooled grand.

Lisp 5yo gelding
Poet's Voice – Hora

He had good form over hurdles and is now going novice chasing. We schooled him in the spring before turning him away and he really was excellent. He can be very fresh first time out, so he might have a run over hurdles to take the fizz out of him, but he's one I'm looking forward to in 2m novice chases. He's quite exciting.

Mahlermade 6yo gelding
Mahler – Double Concerto

He was a maiden for a very long time but then won a valuable handicap chase at Haydock in the spring. He's done really well since and when we schooled him on his return he was like a different horse, so I'm hoping he'll be winning again. He would be very ground-dependent though – he's had little issues with his wind and so he does want decent ground.

Midnightreferendum 6yo mare
Midnight Legend – Forget The Ref

She was a very good bumper mare and won her second start over hurdles. She was a bit disappointing after that, but we had her wind tidied up and she won her only race after that. She'll stay hurdling for now and could be well handicapped.

On To Victory 5yo gelding
Rock Of Gibraltar – Clouds Of Magellan

He's another good Flat horse owned by Henry Ponsonby and sent to us, like Who Dares Wins and Scarlet Dragon. He was rated 108 after finishing second in a 1m6f Listed race at Nottingham last year and he's as good a Flat horse as I've been sent for jumping.

MAHLERMADE (in front): like a different horse when he schooled on his return

SCARLET DRAGON: classy Flat horse can win a big handicap hurdle

Our Power 4yo gelding
Power – Scripture

He was a decent juvenile last season and was a bit unlucky not to finish closer than ninth in the Fred Winter, in which he got shuffled back and then stayed on. He's done very well over the summer and his first target will be the four-year-old handicap hurdle at Chepstow in October.

Outonpatrol 5yo mare
Stowaway – Burnt Oil Babe

She won an Irish point-to-point and hadn't been over here long when she ran a bit disappointingly at Uttoxeter in her bumper. I'm sure she's a lot better than that and she's quite a spectacular jumper, so I'm sure she'll be quite exciting now she goes novice hurdling.

Passing Call 6yo mare
Passing Glance – Call Me A Legend

She won three times over hurdles last summer and made a very pleasing chasing debut at Worcester in September. There's a black-type novice chase at Bangor early in November which will be her first main target.

Potterman 6yo gelding
Sulamani – Polly Potter

He's taken me by surprise somewhat with the summer he's had, because after winning a handicap hurdle at Warwick in May he went on to win three of his first four races over fences. I've been really pleased with his progress, but he's a proper good-ground horse so when the weather breaks – hopefully after Cheltenham in October – he'll have a winter holiday with a view to coming back for Aintree in the spring.

Scarlet Dragon 6yo gelding
Sir Percy – Welsh Angel

He finished fourth in the valuable novice handicap at Sandown in which Harambe was second and has run well on the Flat through the summer. We'll feel our way but there could be a big handicap hurdle in him as he's probably better in a better race. They'll go a good gallop and the jockey can settle him and also because he's one who could get into all sorts of trouble in a small field.

Sceau Royal 7yo gelding
Doctor Dino – Sandside

His Champion Chase third to Altior was a tremendous effort and among the highlights of last season. In fact he did well all season and his only poor effort came

TALKISCHEAP: has the Ladbrokes Trophy and the Grand National as his aims

in the Tingle Creek when the ground was bottomless. He kicked off by winning the Shloer Chase at Cheltenham and that will be his first target again this season. We'll then think about the Tingle Creek, although I wouldn't run him if the ground is like last year and he could step up to two and a half miles instead for the Peterborough Chase. We'll just feel our way again and hope to end back at Cheltenham in March, where I'd have thought his target would be the Champion Chase again.

Sheshoon Sonny **4yo gelding**
Youmzain – Minnie's Mystery

He improved with every run last season and ended up winning at Wetherby. We took him to Ayr for the bumper at the Scottish National meeting but it had dried out too much so he didn't run. He has a good engine in him and he'll go novice hurdling now. He'll love a bit of soft ground.

Talkischeap **7yo gelding**
Getaway – Carrigmoorna Oak

He had a very good first season over fences and ended up winning the bet365 Gold Cup at Sandown, in which he beat The Young Master in style under conditions that were perfect for him. He likes good, fastish ground and I think he's marginally better right-handed, though it's not essential. The first target this time is the Ladbrokes Trophy, with a prep run beforehand hopefully, and then in the second half of the season his owner is very keen to aim him at the Grand National.

The Glancing Queen **5yo mare**
Jeremy – Glancing

I think she's a bit special. She was a shade unlucky in the Champion Bumper at Cheltenham last season and then she was very, very good at Aintree, where she travelled easily and arrived on the scene still hard on the steel. She's schooled well over hurdles and will start off in mares' novice hurdles over two miles before we see how we go. She's pretty exciting – we don't come across one this good very often.

The Olympian 3yo gelding
Olympic Glory – Basira

He was a very good two-year-old last year, when he was second on his first two starts and then won at Newmarket in the autumn. JP McManus bought him afterwards and he had a good old break. He's back now and has schooled very well, so he could be a very exciting juvenile hurdle prospect. He got a mile and a quarter as a two-year-old, so there's no issue with stamina, and he'll love a bit of soft ground.

Timoteo 6yo gelding
Diamond Green – Goldnella

I've trained him for three years and I still don't know how good he is, but it's a nice problem to have. I was a little frustrated he couldn't win a race over hurdles, but when we schooled him over fences he was electric. He trotted up at Stratford on the Monday of Cheltenham week and then won again at Kempton on the Saturday. The ground dried up too much after that and we couldn't get another run into him before the sales, where he was bought back by Million In Mind. He's a novice until the end of October and then we'll go the handicap route.

Trueshan 3yo gelding
Planteur – Shao Line

He's a lovely big horse who improved fast on the Flat in August and September, winning his first two and then stepping up again to finish a good second in a valuable handicap at Haydock on his first try at 1m6f. There were only nine days between those last two runs and he'll have learned plenty. He has the scope to be good over hurdles.

Valdez 12yo gelding
Doyen – Skew

He was off for a long, long time and didn't win on his return last season, but he ran some excellent races in the spring when he was placed twice at Newbury. He's 12 now, but you wouldn't think it if you saw him on the gallops. He's run great around Newbury, but he'd be better going the other way as he's always gone a touch right at his fences. Hopefully we'll get a clear run with him and it will be very emotional if I can get his head in front again as I absolutely adore him.

Who Dares Wins 7yo gelding
Jeremy – Savigano

He had a very good season on the Flat and won the Northumberland Plate. As for the jumps, the plan is to go novice chasing. He hasn't schooled yet over fences, but he's always been a very good jumper of hurdles. He's a grand horse, but he is ground-dependent and has to have some give.

William H Bonney 8yo gelding
Midnight Legend – Calamintha

He won his first two last season and then the handicapper got hold of him. We haven't schooled him yet, but he might go over fences. He has his limitations but should win again.

Wynn House 4yo filly
Presenting – Glorious Twelfth

She won a bumper at Uttoxeter on her only start, when she was well on top at the finish and beat one who has won since. She might stay down the bumper route for now and we'll probably run her under a penalty and then look at the Listed bumper at Huntingdon in December. I've never had her off the bridle at home and she could be very smart.

Profiles for punters
Neil King

NEIL KING: did the best of any trainer in Britain with 50 horses or fewer

Profile by Dylan Hill

WHILE Paul Nicholls and Nicky Henderson continue their own personal battle this season, those slightly lower down the ladder have their own trainers' championship to compete for - and it was won last season by Neil King.

With 40 winners accruing over £470,000 in prize-money, King had the most successful small jumps yard in Britain – those housing 50 horses or fewer.

That made it his best ever jumps season and put him right back on track after a couple of quieter campaigns. During that time the yard was pretty much all about one horse - stable star Lil Rockerfeller - but now King has much more quality spread around.

"It was a fabulous year," he reflected. "The horses kept their form all through the season and we also have nicer, better young horses coming through now."

King picks out Farne and The Knot Is Tied as two at the top of that list, although they will have to go some way to match the achievements of Lil Rockerfeller, who had his finest hour in defeat when second to Nichols Canyon in the 2017 Stayers' Hurdle at the Cheltenham Festival and has since given King success at Glorious Goodwood.

JIM OLD: laid out King's gallops

"He's been such a great servant and has given us some wonderful days," said King. "I'm determined to give him more chances over fences this season as too much was made of his jumping last season, so hopefully we have more big days to come with him."

The current run of success rewards King for the bold decision he took to leave Newmarket in 2014 and set up base at Upper Herdswick Farm near Barbury Castle in Wiltshire.

Born and brought up in the Newmarket area, King had been successfully training jumpers since 2002, but he felt a move was needed to take his operation to the next level and purchased the former base of Jim Old upon the Champion Hurdle-winning trainer's retirement.

"We wanted to move somewhere with our own facilities that would allow us to expand," he explained. "Newmarket was a fantastic place to train and the natural place for me when I first started, but we wanted to try to get better horses and win better races.

"I can look to buy a different type of horse to go jumping with here. In Newmarket the best type of horse to be buying to try to win jumps races is ex-Flat horses. The place is set up for Flat horses with things like the gallops riding much faster. Now we can go out and buy more traditional types of horses such as the staying chasers as we have got very steep hills to work on and that makes a big difference. I don't need to be putting in so much fast work with the horses to get them fit as I was doing in Newmarket – and the more often you're asking a horse to go faster the more likely you are to have problems with them. The gallops here are totally different and allow us to train horses differently."

For that, King has Old to thank. Old designed and laid out the grass and all-weather gallops and trained from Upper Herdswick for 25 years, famously sending out Collier Bay to win the 1996 Champion Hurdle.

Aside from the gallops, Upper Herdswick is a stunning place to train all round, a 285-acre purpose-built establishment, and King has also invested heavily in upgrading all the facilities.

The aim now is to find more top horses to make use of the surroundings and King's bid to build on last season has begun well through the summer, although he concedes it will be hard to match.

"It's going to take some going to beat last season but we'll give it our best shot!" he said. "We had two new owners send us horses just this week, so things are going well."

Yet more good publicity from King's association with Bryony Frost can't hurt either. Frost was King's conditional rider before she struck the big time with Paul Nicholls and King continues to call on her services, the rider striking up a notably good partnership with veteran chaser Milansbar.

He said: "It's a big positive to have second call to Paul [Nicholls] for Bryony and she's a great asset. We all need enthusiasm in this game to pick us up on the dull days and she's got plenty of that.

"Horses run and jump for her and she rides very well. The owners love her riding for them and she gives plenty of thought into things before giving her feedback.

"If she has second thoughts on a horse she calls me on the way home and that's what you want as you have to work as a team to get the best results."

The horses

Brandon Castle 7yo gelding
Dylan Thomas – Chelsey Jayne

He came here from Archie Watson's yard last season and made a brilliant start over hurdles, winning his first three. I thought he was very impressive for the last of those at Plumpton as he won by nine lengths on his handicap debut off 130. Unfortunately the ground went against him after that – it was too soft when we ran him in the Supreme at Cheltenham and then it was rock-hard back at Plumpton for the Sussex Champion Hurdle. He'll stay hurdling and I'd like to think there's a nice race in him, although we'll start off low-key.

Canyon City 6yo gelding
Authorized – Colorado Dawn

He did brilliantly last season and went from strength to strength, going from 115 to 142 in the handicap with four wins. The last two wins came when we stepped him up in trip and I still think there's more to come from him in 3m hurdles. We'll test that route with him first, although he could go novice chasing later.

Cubswin 5yo mare
Zamindar – Moonlight Rhapsody

He's had a marvellous summer, winning on the Flat and over hurdles, and I'd like to think there's more to come. He's very ground-dependent, though, so we'll keep him going until the ground holds and then bring him back in the spring again.

Farne 5yo mare
Stowaway – Bonnies Island

I hold this mare in the highest regard and I think she could be outstanding. She's a 3m chaser in the making and was never meant to be a bumper horse, yet she was unlucky not to win a Listed bumper at Sandown and then she was fourth in a Grade 2 at Aintree behind The Glancing Queen. She jumps exceptionally well and I'm really looking forward to seeing her hurdling this season. She'll probably start off over

BRANDON CASTLE: in front in last season's Supreme Novices' Hurdle

LIL ROCKERFELLER: King feels too much was made of his "novicey" jumping

intermediate distances and then we'll step her up as the season goes on. She's a gorgeous mare and could be anything in the future.

Gateway To Europe 5yo gelding
Trans Island – Polly Doodle

He's a nice young horse. He's more of a summer horse as he likes good ground, but we'll keep him going through the winter and see what we can find for him. He started off over hurdles this summer and it took him a while to get off the mark, but that was my fault as I didn't place him very well and he kept bumping into one!

Lil Rockerfeller 8yo gelding
Hard Spun – Layounne

He's been a wonderful horse for us, finishing second in a Stayers' Hurdle and winning races at Ascot and Glorious Goodwood. We sent him novice chasing last season and he did really well to win his first three races, but he unseated his rider at Cheltenham and was only third at Ascot. We knew things would get even tougher in the top novice races after that, so it made sense to go back over hurdles and he wasn't beaten far in the National Spirit at Fontwell. He's been chasing again since then and we're going to stick to that route for the time being. I actually think too much was made of his jumping last season – yes, he was a bit novicey even when he was winning, but I've just said it – he was a novice! It was hard for him back over fences at Southwell as the trip was too sharp and he was flat to the boards the whole way round, but he jumped very nicely in the straight and stayed on to finish a close third. We'll step him up to three miles and I think that will help him. If it doesn't, we can always come back to staying hurdles.

Marienstar 8yo mare
Marienbard – Starofdonickmore

She was a big improver early last season and won three novice handicap chases, going up from 109 to 133. We then tried her in a Listed mares' chase, but she took a heavy fall at the last when beaten and took a knock so she's been off since then. She began cantering again this autumn and we'll look for more mares' chases for her as they can sometimes cut up and become quite ordinary races.

Milansbar 12yo gelding
Milan – Ardensbar

Last season he paid for having done so well the season before. He won the Classic Chase at Warwick, was second in the Midlands National and fifth in the Grand National, but he went up in the weights and we always knew last season would be tough. He's come down a bit now, though, and he looks an ideal candidate for veterans' chases. One of his big targets would be the veterans' final at Sandown at the start of January and he'd be much better on that proper winter ground.

Myplaceatmidnight 7yo gelding
Midnight Legend – Zahra's Place

I really like this horse. He won twice last season and I think he was unlucky not to win again as he was going well when he fell. He jumps for fun and will make a better chaser than hurdler, perhaps this season, but I'm keen to see what else he can do over hurdles first because I think there's more to come.

Nearly Perfect 5yo gelding
Malinas – The Lyme Volunteer

I'm looking forward to him this season. He hasn't won yet in seven runs in bumpers and hurdles, but he's been second three times and he's going to be a much better chaser. He was second to the Champion Bumper winner Envoi Allen in his point-to-point and he'll love running over 3m on soft ground.

Nordano 3yo gelding
Jukebox Jury – Navajo Queen

I got him at the Godolphin draft at the Ascot sales in July and I'm looking forward to running him in juvenile hurdles. He'll want a bit of cut in the ground and could do well through the winter.

Oh Land Abloom 9yo gelding
King's Theatre – Talinas Rose

He's a lovely fun horse who is very genuine and has been a model of consistency. He won at Uttoxeter last season and was second in a Pertemps qualifier at Warwick before giving his owners a great day out when mid-division in the final at Cheltenham. He'll go novice chasing.

Princeton Royale 10yo gelding
Royal Anthem – Shelikesitstraight

His big aim last season was the Challenger Series at Haydock and he won his qualifier at Ascot in March before finishing second in the final. His jumping wins him races as he's an absolutely brilliant jumper. I'd love to try him over the Grand National fences and the Becher Chase will be his target for the first half of the season.

The Knot Is Tied 4yo gelding
Casamento – Really Polish

He's a very, very exciting horse to have in the yard. He was crying out for a longer trip all last season, but your hands are tied with juvenile hurdlers. We finally got to step him up to 2m3f for a juvenile handicap at Newbury in March and he beat Legal History, who won a valuable handicap at Ascot the following week. I ride him myself at home and he's been giving me a good feel all autumn. He's a big, scopey horse with more to come, especially when he goes chasing.

Nick Watts' 30 horses to follow

A PLUS TARD 5 b g
Kapgarde – Turboka (Kahyasi)
2121-3

To win any Cheltenham Festival race by 16 lengths marks you down as something pretty special, and that is exactly what this exciting young horse did in March when taking the Close Brothers Novices' Handicap Chase. Although he couldn't follow up at Punchestown afterwards, the longer 3m trip may just have stretched him. He may get it in time, but it would be no surprise to see him stick at intermediate distances this season and target the Ryanair. He is seriously classy.

Henry De Bromhead, Co Waterford

ANDY DUFRESNE 5 b g
Doyen – Daytona Lily (Beneficial)
1/1-

This is a horse who is still much more about potential than actual form at this stage as he has only run twice – once in a point-to-point and once under rules. However, both of those races resulted in wins by wide margins and he was particularly impressive at Down Royal last Christmas when landing a bumper by ten lengths. His trainer then compared him favourably to all his top bumper performers. He wasn't seen again but should do well this season over hurdles and over a longer trip.

Gordon Elliott, Co Meath

ANGELS BREATH 5 gr g
Shantou – Mystic Masie (Turgeon)
1273-

Perhaps too much was expected of Angels Breath last season. His hurdle win at Ascot in December was good, but a lot of flights were missed out so it didn't give him much in the way of experience. It was clearly not enough for him to cope with the rigours of a Supreme Novices' Hurdle as he could finish only seventh, but he was better next time at Aintree over 2m4f when third in a Grade 1 behind Reserve Tank. He is likely to go chasing now and could easily fulfil his potential this season, with improvement likely as he steps up in trip.

Nicky Henderson, Lambourn

BALLYWOOD 5 b g

Ballingarry – Miss Hollywood (True Brave)

11214-

Ballywood wasn't an immediate hit after coming over from France, but after getting off the mark over fences at Taunton in December he never looked back. He won twice more after that and, although he was disappointing in a Grade 2 at Ayr's Scottish National meeting on his final start, he may have been over the top by then and it wouldn't pay to judge him too harshly on it. He loves good ground (missed Cheltenham as it was too soft) and distances of around 2m4f are likely to see him at his best. He could be one for a decent handicap on a sound surface.

Alan King, Wiltshire

BREWIN'UPASTORM 6 b g

Milan – Daraheen Diamond (Husyan)

14F42-

Already a point-to-point winner in Ireland, this is a horse who could excel over fences this season. His form over hurdles in his last campaign was of a high order – he wasn't beaten far in the Ballymore or at Aintree when a good second behind Reserve Tank. If he takes it to it he would be well up to contesting Graded novice chases and, although in time three miles might well suit, trips of around 2m4f could be better for him to start off with. There will be plenty of options for him whatever connections decide and he seems versatile regarding ground.

Olly Murphy, Wilmcote

BRIGHT FORECAST 5 b g

Arcadio – Check The Forecast (Shernazar)

1123-

An appropriate name for a horse who will carry the famous Aldaniti colours with distinction over fences this season. He was a surprise winner at Newbury on his return last season but went on to show it was no fluke with a series of good performances that culminated with a third-place finish in the Ballymore at Cheltenham in March behind City Leader. He was doing his best work at the end that day, suggesting that three miles should be within his remit at some point this season even if he starts off over shorter.

Ben Pauling, Gloucestershire

CAPTAIN CATTISTOCK 6 b g

Black Sam Bellamy – Pearl Buttons (Alflora)

F3131-

Not one of his stable's most obvious ones, maybe, but Captain Cattistock had a good campaign in handicap chases last term and could continue that progress this season. He won twice during the campaign – once at Exeter and then on his final start at Fontwell in first-time cheekpeices. He looks a thorough stayer and his handicap mark of 140 might be on the lenient side. It wouldn't be the biggest shock in the world if he went for the Badger Ales Trophy first up – a race his trainer excels in – before tackling other long-distance chases.

Paul Nicholls, Ditcheat

CHAMP 7 b g

King's Theatre – China Sky (Definite Article)

11121-

In many ways Champ needs little introduction. Only City Leader stopped him completing a perfect season, but he still managed to win two Grade 1 hurdles and the way he dismantled Emitom at Aintree was hugely impressive. That win highlighted the fact he was just at home over three miles as over 2m4f – and that gives his trainer more options when mapping out this season, which will presumably be over fences. Although he never ran in points, instead going straight into bumpers, there seems no reason why he won't excel over the larger obstacles.

Nicky Henderson, Lambourn

CROSSPARK 9 b g

Midnight Legend – Blue Shannon (Be My Native)

15312-

A worthy inclusion to this list as a potential Grand National contender. Connections wouldn't want his mark to drop much from his current perch of 146 with Aintree in mind, so he might be campaigned sparingly and over hurdles if that is the plan – his mark would ensure a run at the moment but any lower might spell difficulty. He was hugely consistent last season, winning the Eider Chase and finishing second in the Scottish National. He is tough, a good jumper and exactly the kind of horse who could excel at Aintree in April.

Caroline Bailey, Northants

DEFI DU SEUIL 6 b g

Voix Du Nord – Quarvine Du Seuil (Lavirco)

1211-2

It's difficult to remember now how poor this horse was on his chase debut at Cheltenham last November. He was beaten 25 lengths by Lalor and you wouldn't have supported him for anything on the back of that. However, his trainer did a fantastic job of rebuilding him and he looked the finished article when he took the JLT at Cheltenham in March. The obvious route for him now is the Ryanair, especially after losing out to Chacun Pour Soi down in trip at Punchestown, but he doesn't lack speed and the Champion Chase would still be a worthy alternative.

Philip Hobbs, Somerset

DICKIE DIVER 6 b g

Gold Well – Merry Excuse (Flemensfirth)

1/214-

Dickie Diver could easily be one for long-distance novice chases this season. He had a brief hurdling campaign around the turn of the year – he just got beaten by Lisnagar Oscar on his return at Chepstow and then won at the same track in February, thus booking his ticket for the Albert Bartlett. He excelled himself in that race for one so inexperienced, finishing fourth behind Minella Indo, and he was wisely put away afterwards to recover from those exertions. He stays very well and anything from three to four miles should suit.

Nicky Henderson, Lambourn

DISCORAMA 6 b g

Saddler Maker – Quentala (Lone Bid)

15F2-2

While the four-miler at Cheltenham last season caused quite a bit of controversy, there could be no faulting the performance or application of this stayer, who did everything right in the race and only just failed to beat Le Breuil. He must be tough as he went to Punchestown after that gruelling race and ran just as well to finish second behind Delta Work, with A Plus Tard back in third. He may be a bit young for Aintree, but there seems no reason why he couldn't have a crack at the Irish Grand National instead.

Paul Nolan, Co Wexford

FELIX DESJY 6 ch g

Maresca Sorrento – Lamadoun (Smadoun)

2151-2

This horse is a bit of a tearaway, but a Grade 1-winning one at that, and he could be an exciting proposition if he goes chasing this season, which seems likely. He was really consistent in his last four runs of the season and put up another good effort at Punchestown on his final start when beating all bar Klassical Dream in a Grade 1 event. He likes to get on with things and can make the odd error, but he did win a point-to-point back in 2017 and if he takes to the job he could easily be good enough for an Arkle bid.

Gordon Elliott, Co Meath

IF THE CAP FITS 7 b g

Milan – Derravaragh Sayra (Sayarshan)

21321-

If The Cap Fits started off last season in the Elite Hurdle at Wincanton over two miles and ran over that trip again in the Christmas Hurdle two starts later – on both occasions he was beaten by Verdana Blue. But on what we know of him now, he never had a prayer against that mare as she is all speed while he is all stamina. He proved that when stepped up to three miles for a Grade 1 hurdle on Grand National day when he beat Roksana in an absolute thriller. He stays hurdling and he has to be a contender for the Stayers' Hurdle.

Harry Fry, Seaborough

JANIKA 6 b g

Saddler Maker – Majaka (Kapgarde)

1/2224-

It seems very unfair that Janika has not yet won in Britain since his move from France. He went close on two occasions and will be sick of the sight of Siruh Du Lac, who was his conqueror both times. On the first of those at Cheltenham's January meeting there was only a head in it, while in the Plate in March there was only three-quarters of a length that separated the two. A fourth in the Topham on his final start highlighted what a great jumper he is and, although up to a mark of 162 now for not winning, he could be up to Graded level this season.

Nicky Henderson, Lambourn

KILDISART 7 b g

Dubai Destination – Princess Mairead (Blueprint)

21141-

Now rated 156, it will be interesting to see how Kildisart is campaigned this season and whether he is up to that mark – I think he might be. His win in an Aintree handicap on Grand National day over 3m1f was very impressive and the longer trip seemed to bring about a good jolt of improvement. He was good over shorter anyway, winning an informative novice handicap at Cheltenham in January over 2m4½f before finishing fourth in the JLT. I could easily see him running a big race in the Ladbrokes Trophy or Welsh National in the first half of the season – possibly both.

Ben Pauling, Gloucestershire

LA BAGUE AU ROI 8 b m

Doctor Dino – Alliance Royale (Turgeon)

11112-

It must be a long time since a mare has won the King George, but when you have course figures of 11 and those wins came in Listed and Grade 1 company you have to sit up and take notice. La Bague Au Roi was brilliant last season and her defeat of Topofthegame and Santini on Boxing Day was impressive. She followed that up with another Grade 1 win at Leopardstown before her only defeat of the season at Aintree. She does seem to be at her best earlier in the season, which makes Kempton a realistic aim, and she shouldn't be taken lightly.

Warren Greatrex, Lambourn

MALONE ROAD 5 b g

Kalanisi – Zaffarella (Zaffaran)

1/11-

Gordon Elliott won the 2019 Champion Bumper at Cheltenham anyway with Envoi Allen, so it didn't matter so much that this horse was sidelined during the spring just when his name could, and possibly would, have been up in lights. He looked sensational in the only two starts he managed last season, both of which came well before Christmas. He won at Down Royal and then Punchestown by an aggregate margin of 16 lengths – and he wasn't beating rubbish either. He will go hurdling this season and let us hope he can make up for lost time and show what he can do.

Gordon Elliott, Co Meath

McFABULOUS 5 b g

Milan – Rossavon (Beneficial)

1711-

A half-brother to Waiting Patiently, McFabulous wasn't ready for Cheltenham's November meeting and could only manage seventh in the bumper there. However, after that he was left off until March so he could grow and develop, and it paid instant dividends with a win at Newbury. Things then got even better as he landed the Grade 2 bumper at Aintree, beating Thebannerkingrebel by a length. He should be a high-class novice hurdler this season. He will be effective at two miles but may well stay a bit further.

Paul Nicholls, Ditcheat

MUSICAL SLAVE 6 b g
Getaway – Inghwung (Kayf Tara)
6511-1

Musical Slave didn't have the greatest start to last season and was well beaten in novice hurdles at Exeter and Ffos Las. However, he couldn't have ended it much better as he proceeded to then win three handicaps in a row, including on his final start at the Punchestown festival. That win came over 2m5f, the furthest trip he has run over, and while he could still stay over hurdles with his mark only 131 it would make more sense to get him over fences as he does jump very well according to his trainer. If he's not an immediate hit, handicaps could be his best option again.

Philip Hobbs, Somerset

ORNUA 8 ch g
Mahler – Merry Heart (Broken Hearted)
22F1-P

Although he was pulled up at Punchestown on his final start, that shouldn't be held against Ornua as he had endured an awfully long campaign that began in May 2018 and didn't finish until a whole year later. In that time, he won and was placed in another two Grade 1s, including when second to Dynamite Dollars in the Henry VIII at Sandown's Tingle Creek meeting. Despite his stout breeding, blazing away at the front over two miles seems to suit him well and he may well help fill the void left by his trainer's similar type – Special Tiara.

Henry De Bromhead, Co Waterford

RESERVE TANK 5 b g
Jeremy – Lady Bellamy (Black Sam Bellamy)
7111-1

Last season was a tale of two halves for Reserve Tank. The first bit was moderate as he finished third in a bumper and seventh in a novice hurdle at Newbury. However, from that point on he never looked back as he won four races in succession, culminating in a Grade 1 festival double at Aintree and Punchestown. He got the better of some fair horses on both occasions and was rated 151 by the end of the season. His attentions will now be turned to fences and he could be this season's Lostintranslation for the Tizzard team. His best trip is 2m4f.

Colin Tizzard, Dorset

SALDIER 5 b g
Soldier Hollow – Salve Evita (Monsun)
1531/F-

Saldier could be the dark horse in the Champion Hurdle market. He was probably going better than Espoir D'Allen when he fell at the last in a Grade 3 hurdle at Naas on his only start of last season and apparently he is flying again now. A Grade 1-winning hurdler at Punchestown previously, he could be the real deal this season if fully over his fall. Sadly Espoir D'Allen is no longer around, but that does leave the field clear for something to emerge in the two-mile hurdling division and it might well be this five-year-old.

Willie Mullins, Co Carlow

SANTINI 7 b g

Milan – Tinagoodnight (Sleeping Car)

31/132-

For a horse who was held up before the Cheltenham Festival and whose participation was in considerable doubt at one stage, Santini ran an absolute stormer in the RSA Chase, jumping well and leading over the last only to succumb close home to Topofthegame. He still beat Delta Work comfortably enough and, on only his third chase start and first since Boxing Day, it was a great effort. The Gold Cup is the big race on his calendar for this season and, assuming he gets a trouble-free run, there is no horse I would rather be on.

Nicky Henderson, Lambourn

SIXSHOOTER x b g

Well Chosen – Lobinstown Girl (Luso)

1-1

Sixshooter won two out of two bumpers last season and did it at the big tracks – Leopardstown and Punchestown – so he must be useful at the very least. On the latter occasion he was the 8-1 outsider of the whole field but surpassed expectations to just get the better of the odds-on favourite The Big Getaway (mentioned opposite). He handles good ground well and is one to look forward to over hurdles. His trainer described him as being "very green" last season so he did well to win twice and it bodes well for his chances this season.

Noel Meade, Co Meath

SNUGSBOROUGH HALL 8 b g

Beneficial – Saddlers Arc (Saddlers' Hall)

311C-1

Unluckily carried out when looking dangerous at Fairyhouse in April, this rapidly improving gelding made no mistake at the Punchestown festival on his next start, beating Impact Factor by 11 lengths. It was extraordinarily easy and indicates that he might have a future in better races than handicaps. He is now rated 142 so still has a way to go, but he did win three of his last four starts and has formed a really good rapport with Denis O'Regan, who rides him quietly before pouncing late on. He should be coming into his prime now and is exciting.

Liam Cusack, Co Laois

SOME DETAIL 5 b g

Getaway – You Should Know Me (Oscar)

22317-

An unheralded horse from an unheralded yard maybe, but this five-year-old still showed some useful form in bumpers last season and could be an under-the-radar type who can win a few novice hurdles this season. He failed to win a point-to-point and was beaten in his opening two bumpers. However, it did get better after that as he won at Chepstow – beating a Paul Nicholls-trained runner into second – and then finished an excellent seventh of 14 in the Champion Bumper behind Envoi Allen. That was a great effort and one that bodes well for novice hurdles.

Nigel Hawke, Devon

THE BIG DOG 6 b g

Mahler – Saddlers Leader (Saddlers' Hall)

4219-2

A lightly raced sort who, on occasions, showed some really useful form last season. He won a maiden hurdle at Gowran Park in January and was second behind Zero Ten on his final start of the season at Punchestown. Unfortunately, in between he didn't make much impression in a Leopardstown Grade 1, but he was only 13-2 to win that so he was fancied. He is likely to go chasing this season and, with experience from points to call upon, he should do well at it. He stays well and likes soft ground.

Peter Fahey, Co Kildare

THE BIG GETAWAY 5 b g

Getaway – Saddlers Dawn (Saddlers' Hall)

1/2-2

The Big Getaway was a bit of a letdown in bumpers last season. He ran in two, was sent off odds-on in both, and was beaten in both. However, all is by no means lost. He was beaten only half a length on his second outing by Sixshooter – who has earned himself a place in this list – and he really is a chaser in the making rather than a hurdler. He won his sole point-to-point start by a whopping 30 lengths and it'll be interesting to see if he is sent chasing immediately or goes in long-distance hurdles. He is still useful.

Willie Mullins, Co Carlow

THE GLANCING QUEEN 5 b m

Jeremy – Glancing (Kayf Tara)

1/1351-

The Glancing Queen did very well in bumpers last season and, although she won a Grade 2 mares' bumper at Aintree in April, she was also able to mix it with the boys when required. She was fifth to Envoi Allen in the big one at Cheltenham in March and was also placed in a Listed event at Ascot in a traditionally hot bumper just before Christmas. We are used to Willie Mullins dominating mares' races, but she beat a hot favourite of his – Minella Melody – at Aintree and if she takes to hurdling then a return to Cheltenham next March for the mares' novice is a definite possibility.

Alan King, Wiltshire

Top ten horses

Andy Dufresne
Bright Forecast
Defi Du Seuil
Janika
La Bague Au Roi
Malone Road
McFabulous
Saldier
Santini
The Big Getaway

RACING & FOOTBALL outlook

Ante-post preview by Dylan Hill, Nick Watts and Anthony Ive

King George

THE head of the market for this year's King George has a most unusual look to it, featuring two horses who have never run over the trip and are highly unlikely to have done so before lining up.

In fact the favourite, **Altior**, has never run beyond two and a quarter miles and it was back in November 2016, when winning at Kempton on his chasing debut, that he tackled even that trip. Every run since then has been over shorter.

He has won them all but didn't look as impressive last season as he had in the past, often getting himself out of trouble with his trademark power-packed finishes, and it's for that reason that a step up in trip seems more likely this term.

King George — Kempton, December 26

	Bet365	*Betfair*	*Betfred*	*Coral*	*Hills*	*Lads*	*P Power*	*Skybet*
Altior	5-2	5-2	5-2	5-2	**11-4**	5-2	5-2	5-2
Cyrname	**5**	**5**	**5**	**5**	**5**	**5**	**5**	9-2
Clan Des Obeaux	**11-2**	5	**11-2**	**11-2**	5	**11-2**	5	**11-2**
Kemboy	5	**8**	5	11-2	-	5	**8**	**8**
Lostintranslation	**12**	8	10	10	10	9	8	10
Min	**14**	**14**	-	-	-	-	**14**	**14**
La Bague Au Roi	**16**	**16**	14	**16**	14	**16**	**16**	**16**
Frodon	12	**16**	-	12	**16**	14	**16**	**16**
Al Boum Photo	**16**	**16**	-	-	-	10	**16**	14
Might Bite	20	14	14	16	**25**	14	14	20
Waiting Patiently	20	**25**	12	14	16	16	**25**	20
Presenting Percy	20	**25**	16	20	-	20	**25**	**25**
Native River	**33**	**33**	20	25	**33**	20	**33**	20
Bristol De Mai	**33**	**33**	-	**33**	-	**33**	**33**	**33**

each-way 1/5 odds, 1-2-3

Others on application, prices correct at time of going to press

ALTIOR: favourite for the King George – but how likely is he to run?

But as churlish as it might be to question a horse who has never been beaten over obstacles, I just wonder whether we have seen the best of Altior.

It was a weak 2m division that he dominated last season and he won't get away with jumping out to his left as violently as he did at times, notably at right-handed Ascot. I'll be very keen to take him on if he turns up.

That's another question for ante-post punters to consider and it wouldn't surprise me at all if Nicky Henderson decided to skip Kempton. Henderson can be quite conservative in placing his horses, which is no criticism at all as his record speaks for itself, but I suspect it wouldn't take much on his likely return at Ascot to put Henderson off this bold route despite his bullishness through the autumn.

At least we can be more confident **Cyrname** will line up at Kempton.

The way he demolished his rivals in the Grade 1 Ascot Chase certainly put the King George in mind. Looking at the way he went away from his rivals again in the straight having forced the pace throughout, it's hard to believe he wouldn't stay this longer trip and his front-running style seems tailormade for Kempton, which is one of the best tracks for front-runners in Britain.

He hasn't been missed in the market, though, for a horse who has only looked in this class on one occasion – perhaps two – and the Ascot Chase seemed to fall apart, with several below-par performances behind him. The fragile pair Waiting Patiently and Fox Norton are hardly the most reliable horses in the places.

Continuing the theme of horses stepping up in trip, **Min** seems more likely to make the trip for Willie Mullins than **Kemboy**, who won the Savills Chase at Leopardstown at this time of year last season.

Min's owner, Susannah Ricci, has previous in the race having finished second with Champagne Fever and Vautour, so we know he likes a crack at it, and Min is a similar type having shown top-class form

BRISTOL DE MAI: fell in last season's King George but can make amends

over shorter trips. This would be a leap into the unknown for a horse who can be too keen, though.

Clan Des Obeaux gives Nicholls a strong hand and will surely return to defend his crown, although that won't affect Cyrname's participation.

Indeed, Clan Des Obeaux wasn't even the stable's number one hope last year, with Politologue going off a shorter price before fading into a non-staying fourth.

Politologue wasn't the only horse below his best that day as Might Bite went wrong and Native River proved totally unsuited by the track, while Bristol De Mai fell and brought down Waiting Patiently, so all in all it was a pretty messy contest and the form is hard to take seriously.

It still might be the case that Clan Des Obeaux is much better on this sort of track than he is at Cheltenham, where he failed again in the Gold Cup, but I'd expect him to come up short in a stronger renewal.

The one to bear in mind from 12 months ago might be **BRISTOL DE MAI**, who has yet to quite match his phenomenal Betfair Chase form elsewhere but didn't really have the chance to do so here last year given his early departure. He went on to finish third in the Gold Cup and can be forgiven his Aintree fourth given how hard it is to back up so soon after a hard run in that race.

Bristol De Mai still seems underappreciated to me. He is a dual Betfair Chase winner and, while he has often struggled to build on his early-season form, he went a long way to putting that right last season with his run in the Gold Cup, appearing to be much more consistent after a breathing operation.

Bookmakers have him at 33-1 and I can't see how he's so much bigger than the overhyped **Waiting Patiently** or the declining **Might Bite**.

I'd rather trust that sort of proven quality in this race than the potential of second-season chasers like **Lostintranslation** and **La Bague Au Roi**. Might Bite and Thistlecrack won this early in their chasing careers, the latter even as a novice, but youngsters have a much better record in the Gold Cup, giving them an extra two and a half months to catch up. [DH]

Champion Hurdle

THE cupboard is pretty bare in terms of genuine Champion Hurdle prospects going into the season and that makes **BUVEUR D'AIR** a solid ante-post bet to regain his title following the sad news of Espoir D'Allen's death.

Nicky Henderson's dual champion was an early faller when going for the hat-trick last season, although some of his other performances – a narrow defeat to Verdana Blue over Christmas and his second to Supasundae in the Aintree Hurdle – suggested he would have struggled to beat Espoir D'Allen anyway.

However, he finished off in style with an easy victory at Punchestown and, while he will be nine by the time we get to March, that's not impossible to overcome, as Hurricane Fly has shown most recently.

I can see him mopping up all the main trials in Britain and going off much shorter than his current 7-1 on the day.

The market is headed by the Willie Mullins-trained **Klassical Dream**, an impressive winner of the Supreme Novices' Hurdle last season.

Once again, the master trainer took a horse with hurdles experience as a three-year-old in France to Cheltenham glory. A perfect four from four in novice company since he made his stable debut over Christmas, he looked to be getting better with each run during the season and victories on good and soft ground underlined his versatility.

My issue is that I am not entirely convinced the novice division was a great one and he needs to overcome the fact that no Supreme winner has ever won the Champion Hurdle the following year. He looks too short at this stage.

In fact it's hard to see how Klassical Dream can be so much shorter than some of last season's other leading novices.

Elixir De Nutz, a 33-1 shot, missed the Supreme last season after a late setback but had been progressive, winning the Tolworth on his most recent start, and will be trained with the Champion Hurdle in mind according to Colin Tizzard.

At similar odds, **Itchy Feet** would be interesting if Olly Murphy sounded a bit more keen on keeping to hurdles. He was beaten only a length and a quarter by Elixir De Nutz at Cheltenham in December when

Champion Hurdle

Cheltenham, March 10

	Bet365	*Betfair*	*Betfred*	*Coral*	*Hills*	*Lads*	*P Power*	*Skybet*
Klassical Dream	**7-2**	3	3	3	**7-2**	3	3	3
Buveur D'Air	6	6	**7**	6	6	6	6	6
Pentland Hills	**10**	8	**10**	**10**	9	**10**	8	**10**
Fusil Raffles	**16**	12	**16**	10	**16**	12	12	14
Saldier	**20**	14	16	**20**	16	**20**	14	16
Apple's Jade	20	20	-	16	**25**	20	20	25
Melon	**25**	**25**	**25**	20	-	**25**	**25**	**25**
Fakir D'Oudairies	**33**	25	25	25	25	25	25	25
Thomas Darby	25	**33**	**33**	25	-	25	**33**	**33**
Laurina	**33**	25	20	20	25	16	25	16
City Island	20	25	-	16	**33**	16	25	20
Elixir De Nutz	**33**	25	-	**33**	**33**	**33**	25	**33**
Itchy Feet	33	-	**40**	-	-	-	-	33
Band Of Outlaws	**40**	33	33	25	25	25	33	33

each-way 1/5 odds, 1-2-3

Others on application, prices correct at time of going to press

SALDIER: in front of Espoir D'Allen when he took this fall and off the track since

conceding 5lb and I would fancy him to turn around that form should the pair meet again. Although no match for Klassical Dream in the Supreme, he broke blood vessels and was still beaten only five lengths, while the soft ground wouldn't have been in his favour either.

Murphy plans on starting Itchy Feet over hurdles before probably going novice chasign, but he already has his Supreme runner-up **Thomas Darby** for fences and it wouldn't be the biggest surprise if Itchy Feet did enough to change his mind on his reappearance.

The up-and-comers of **Pentland Hills** and **Fusil Raffles** gave Nicky Henderson a spring festival treble in the four-year-old division last season.

Pentland Hills went from a Class 5 handicap at Hamilton for Chris Wall in September to winning at both the Cheltenham and Aintree festivals, while Fusil Raffles made his stable debut in the Adonis Hrdle at Kempton, winning in spectacular style, before success at the Punchestown festival ahead of **Fakir D'Oudairies**.

Both horses are undoubtedly promising, but only Espoir D'Allen and Katchit have won the Champion Hurdle as five-year-olds since the brilliant See You Then in 1985 and will need to make a huge amount of progress over the season to be a real threat to the likes of Buveur D'Air.

On a line though Espoir D'Allen, the positive news from Willie Mullins regarding **Saldier** is more than welcome.

His only run in the 2018-19 season was a final-flight fall at Naas in November. Espoir D'Allen took the victory that day, but it would have been a fascinating finish, with Ruby Walsh looking confident and poised to run the subsequent Champion Hurdle winner close. He stays over hurdles this year and could have a lively chance if he turns up fit and healthy in March.

With Klassical Dream and Saldier as his Champion Hurdle horses, it is hard to see Mullins aiming **Laurina** at this race again and the same goes for **Benie Des Dieux**, while fellow mare **Apple's Jade** will surely find an alternative target as well.

Chasing looks like Aintree winner **Felix Desjy**'s game and the chances are this race will comprise another small field with Buveur D'Air very much to the fore in the market once again. [AI]

Champion Chase

ALTIOR maintained his unbeaten record over obstacles last season and a 14th successive win over fences, achieved at Sandown in April, equalled the legendary Sprinter Sacre.

That run includes the last two editions of this race and Nicky Henderson's star could now attempt to become only the second horse to win three in a row following Badsworth Boy.

If we could be sure he would end up going for it then the current 5-1 would be huge, but he has increasingly looked like he could do with further than the minimum trip and I'd rather look elsewhere.

Next in the market is the Willie Mullins-trained Chacun Pour Soi.

The seven-year-old was spoken of as a potential Arkle horse when he arrived from France in 2016, but injury setbacks meant that his stable debut was delayed for two years. After a very easy success at Naas in March, though, he followed up with victory in the Grade 1 Ryanair Novice Chase at Punchestown, beating 2019 Cheltenham Festival winners Duc Des Genievres and Defi Du Seuil. It was an impressive performance for a horse with only two chase starts to his name.

However, the decision of Paul Townend to ride **Duc Des Genievres** in the race, coupled with the fact that **Defi Du Seuil** has not won over 2m or 2m1f since 2017, raises too many questions about the form. The horse is clearly talented and could be a star, but his price looks an overreaction.

Duc Des Genievres was clearly below his best that day, but it could be that 2m on a quicker surface simply isn't for him. The ground was soft when he won the Arkle and conditions would have to be similar for him to have any chance over this trip.

Similarly, it's likely that longer distances are now needed for stablemate **Min**.

While disappointing in this race last year, he would probably still be seen as the best two-miler around but for Altior, finishing second to him in the 2016 Supreme and the 2018 Champion Chase.

However, his record beyond 2m1f is 1211, with the defeat by a neck against Politologue in the 2018 Melling Chase, form he emphatically reversed in that race last season.

Champion Chase

Cheltenham, March 11

	Bet365	*Betfair*	*Betfred*	*Coral*	*Hills*	*Lads*	*P Power*	*Skybet*
Altior	4	7-2	3	7-2	**5**	7-2	7-2	7-2
Chacun Pour Soi	**7**	7-2	6	6	5	6	7-2	6
Min	**12**	**12**	**12**	**12**	8	**12**	**12**	10
Sceau Royal	16	16	**20**	16	12	16	16	12
Duc Des Genievres	12	**20**	8	14	14	12	**20**	16
Defi Du Seuil	-	**20**	10	10	14	10	**20**	16
Le Richebourg	-	**20**	-	16	**20**	16	**20**	**20**
Cilaos Emery	**20**	16	-	14	**20**	**20**	16	**20**
A Plus Tard	**25**	**25**	20	20	25	16	**25**	**25**
Kalashnikov	16	**25**	-		**25**	-	**25**	16
Douvan	**33**	20	-	20	25	25	20	-
Politologue	25	20	-	25	**33**	20	20	20
Dynamite Dollars	33	33	-	33	**40**	33	33	**40**
Lalor	**66**	50	-	-	**66**	-	50	-

each-way 1/5 odds, 1-2-3

Others on application, prices correct at time of going to press

Min stepping up in trip would make it more likely the legendary **Un De Sceaux** runs in this race, but he will be 12 come March and would need soft ground.

Cilaos Emery, who has run only once over fences but is a fascinating long-term prospect, is also a possibility for Mullins, while **Le Richebourg** is another interesting contender.

However, the member of last season's novice crop to interest me most is the forgotten horse **LALOR**.

Kayley Woollacott's Grade 1-winning hurdler won only once over fences last season, but it was the manner of the success that still stands out. His seven-length victory at Cheltenham in November looked good at the time, jumping fluently and cruising home, and was made to look even better when both Dynamite Dollars and Defi Du Seuil won subsequent Grade 1 chases.

The time that Lalor clocked in that performance was also seriously quick – so quick it was in line with the Arkle successes of Captain Chris and the brilliant Sprinter Sacre on similar ground. Only two horses in the last ten years have won the Arkle in quicker times than Lalor ran that day.

While he won at Aintree over hurdles in soft ground, he looks far better on good ground and a wet winter last season didn't suit him at all.

He has been written off as a 66-1 shot on the back of that, but a good-ground festival would give the son of It's Gino a real chance.

Those conditions would also suit **SCEAU ROYAL** more than the soft ground on which he was a fine third to Altior in this race last season.

He has been one of the most consistent 2m chasers in the last two seasons, finishing out of the first three only once in his chase career, and a repeat of his Celebration Chase performance at Sandown in April, when second to Altior, would give him a great chance should his old rival head elsewhere.

This is his obvious target, as Alan King has confirmed, and 20-1 looks big. [AI]

LALOR: spectacular winner at Cheltenham last season and worth sticking with

Stayers' Hurdle

THIS race is a hard one to predict – even more so from an ante-post perspective – as the make-up of the field is the least certain out of the big four Cheltenham events.

You can easily get failed chasers parachuting back into this division mid-way through the season whom you just wouldn't have considered at the start of the campaign.

Add in the fact that Paisley Park is a very solid favourite – his running style bears more than a passing resemblance to the great Big Buck's – and any value is hard to achieve.

Therefore it is probably best to play the percentages and stick to a couple of horses who, injury permitting, will definitely be aimed at the race.

First up is **IF THE CAP FITS**, Harry Fry's eight-year-old who improved as he stepped up in trip last season.

He has yet to race at Cheltenham, but that's more by accident than design as he missed a run at the festival in 2018 due to injury.

He looks to have the perfect blend of speed and staying power you need for this race. He even mixed it with Verdana Blue a couple of times last season – placed at Grade 1 level over two miles – but how he managed to do that is hard to ascertain for such a strong stayer.

That stamina is evident from the fact he won a 3m Grade 1 event at Aintree's

IF THE CAP FITS: looks the obvious one from an each-way perspective

Stayers' Hurdle

Cheltenham, March 12

	Bet365	*Betfair*	*Betfred*	*Coral*	*Hills*	*Lads*	*P Power*	*Skybet*
Paisley Park	**3**	**3**	5-2	5-2	5-2	**3**	11-4	**3**
Benie Des Dieux	6	8	-	8	**10**	7	8	7
If The Cap Fits	10	10	**12**	10	**12**	10	10	**12**
Minella Indo	10	**14**	12	-	-	-	**14**	**14**
Champ	10	-	-	-	**14**	-	-	**14**
Penhill	14	**16**	12	14	14	14	**16**	14
City Island	**16**	**16**	12	14	14	**16**	**16**	14
Apple's Jade	16	**20**	-	14	-	14	**20**	12
Next Destination	**20**	**20**	-	-	-	-	**20**	-
Allaho	20	25	-	-	-	-	25	**33**
Roksana	-	**33**	-	16	-	14	**33**	16
Bapaume	**33**	20	16	-	25	-	20	**33**
Emitom	20	**33**	-	-	25	-	**33**	**33**
Sam Spinner	25	25	**33**	**33**	25	**33**	25	20

each-way 1/5 odds, 1-2-3

Others on application, prices correct at time of going to press

PENHILL: won in 2018 and his price has doubled now despite staying in his box

Grand National meeting in April, beating Roksana and Apple's Jade in a thriller.

There are caveats to the form. Winners of the Liverpool Hurdle have a mixed record at Cheltenham because, while Big Buck's won the Aintree race four times and Thistlecrack took it, more often it seems to be won by a Yanworth, an Identity Thief or a Whisper – high-class stayers on their day but not up to this race.

Beating Apple's Jade last spring can't be held up as a beacon of top-class staying form either as she was well below-par for some reason in the later months of the season.

It is still worth taking a positive view, however, as it was a huge hike in trip for If The Cap Fits – the longest previous distance he had run over was 2m3½f.

Furthermore, it was just the 11th run of his career – he has won eight of them – so there are precious few miles on the clock.

I hope Fry gets a full season into him this winter over proper staying trips and we see him take on Paisley Park in the Long Walk Hurdle at Ascot over Christmas. That would be a great spectacle and give us an early indicator of what might happen at Cheltenham. I would hope If The Cap Fits measures up well – he is already a Grade 2 winner at the Berkshire venue – and the 12-1 ante-post seems by far the best option to take at this stage.

But if you wanted another string to your bow why not consider the 2018 champion **PENHILL**?

He is available at 16-1 this season in several places whereas he was half that a year ago. That seems bizarre given he has done nothing wrong other than pick up an injury and miss the season.

Injuries are always a concern with Penhill as he is fragile and barely runs anyway, but it is safe to assume that if he makes it he will not go off anything like 16-1 bearing in mind his brilliant festival record that saw him win the Albert Bartlett as a novice before seeing off the big boys a year later.

That 2018 Stayers' Hurdle became known as a very messy renewal with loads of horses in with a chance at the last, but the runner-up Supasundae has won two Grade 1 races since then, and the fifth, Sam Spinner, finished a great second in this race last season, so it's not bad form by any means.

If Penhill can make it through the winter unscathed there's no reason why he couldn't win it again as a nine-year-old in a race that favours older horses – Inglis Drever, Big Buck's and Solwhit have all won it at that age. [NW]

Gold Cup

LAST year's Gold Cup highlighted what a strange game racing can be. Willie Mullins launched a four-pronged assault in his bid to win the race for the first time, but by the time they had reached the tenth fence three of his party – Kemboy, Bellshill and, fatally, Invitation Only – had already departed.

His hopes thus rested with **Al Boum Photo**, a horse who was beaten when he fell in the RSA Chase the previous season and had had only one run as a warm-up for Cheltenham – at Tramore on New Year's Day but somehow proved good enough on the day.

He was, in my opinion, an unlikely hero and is now an even more unlikely one to follow up. Best Mate was the last to do it and such are the demands of the race it's not a given he even makes it to the 2020 renewal.

Native River made it back last year but showed just how hard it was to do the double as he was never quite the same horse all season and could only plug on into fourth on the big day.

So it is best to look for some fresh blood when analysing this race – but we can bend the rules where **Kemboy** is concerned bearing in mind he exited at the first fence in March.

AL BOUM PHOTO: will struggle to retain his Gold Cup crown this season

SANTINI (near): put in a great performance in the RSA after a poor preparation

His win in the Savills Chase at Leopardstown wasn't accepted by many at the time (myself included) due to the strange nature of the race – a funereal opening before he took the race by the scruff of the neck and went clear. It didn't look to be a serious examination of his staying credentials, but in fairness to the horse, after his Gold Cup blip, he proved us all wrong. He thrashed Clan Des Obeaux by nine lengths over 3m1f and for good measure beat Al Boum Photo in the Punchestown Gold Cup afterwards.

I am a believer now, but then so are many others, which is why he sits at the top of the market at around the 5-1 mark. It goes without saying he has a big chance, but with so many months between now and the race he looks short enough.

SANTINI is a strong alternative at a slightly bigger price.

He managed just three runs over fences last season and won only once, but it would be unfair to crab him for that.

He won at Newbury on his chase debut in a Grade 2 and was then sent off to Kempton for the Kauto Star, in which he performed with credit to finish third to La Bague Au Roi and Topofthegame, closing all the way to the line.

It looked like the track didn't suit him and that he would be able to get his revenge in the RSA – his next destination.

However, his preparation was awful. He was affected by the outbreak of equine flu and the travel restrictions which followed and he also pulled off a shoe when schooling at Newbury.

Bearing that in mind, he ran a tremendous race to lead over the last before succumbing by only half a length to Topofthegame with Delta Work well beaten in third.

You would expect and hope for more improvement in his second season as he gets more experienced and battle-hardened and, with Cheltenham form figures of 132, it is clear he enjoys the place. There is plenty of 10-1 around for him and he is a good place to start.

For a more speculative suggestion it may be worth considering the 50-1 available about **FOOTPAD**.

Last season did not go according to plan at all for him but that can happen sometimes and it doesn't mean he has become a bad horse. He just appeared to be on the back foot ever since he injured himself on his seasonal return at Naas.

Being given a summer off could make all the difference to him and maybe now is the time to try him over much longer trips.

He is unlikely to be kept at two miles anymore and, while it is questionable what trip he would get, don't forget he was placed in a 3m Grade 1 hurdle at the Punchestown festival in 2017.

He has won a Grade 1 over 2m3½f in very soft conditions so we know he stays at least that far – and with a few more years on his back since then it's not impossible that staying trips over fences will be within his remit.

If 2018-19 was a mere blip, he could be a dangerously big price. [NW]

FOOTPAD: missed out last season

Cheltenham Gold Cup

Cheltenham, March 13

	Bet365	Betfair	Betfred	Coral	Hills	Lads	P Power	Skybet
Kemboy	6	**13-2**	6	5	5	6	6	6
Al Boum Photo	**8**	7	**8**	7	**8**	6	7	7
Santini	**10**	**10**	8	9	**10**	**10**	**10**	9
Lostintranslation	**11**	10	10	10	10	10	10	9
Delta Work	**14**	12	**14**	12	12	**14**	12	**14**
Altior	**14**	**14**	12	10	12	12	**14**	**14**
Presenting Percy	14	**20**	16	14	16	14	**20**	16
Clan Des Obeaux	16	**20**	16	16	16	16	**20**	**20**
Tiger Roll	16	**25**	12	16	20	16	**25**	16
Native River	20	**25**	20	16	20	20	**25**	20
Cyrname	20	**33**	-	20	20	20	**33**	16
Anibale Fly	25	**33**	**33**	25	**33**	25	**33**	20
Frodon	25	**33**	**33**	**33**	25	25	**33**	25
Footpad	40	**50**	-	-	33	-	**50**	-

each-way 1/5 odds, 1-2-3

Others on application, prices correct at time of going to press

TIGER ROLL: will be back at Aintree to bid for an incredible third National win

Grand National

TIGER ROLL has been tipped in this column to win the Grand National for the last two seasons. So why change a winning formula?

Unfortunately, though, antepost betting is all about getting on at the right price and the goalposts have moved so far they're not even on the pitch now. Gordon Elliott's superstar was 50-1 at this stage two years ago and still a very reasonable 20-1 last year; now you won't get any better than 6-1.

Of course, there's a good reason for that. It's hard to remember any horse in recent history taking to Aintree quite like Tiger Roll, whose performances last season suggested he is even getting better with age and is on the cusp of Grade 1 level.

Those happy to lump on at 6-1 can also point to the fact he is bound to go off considerably shorter should he get there on the day, pretty much regardless of what happens to him between now and then. I doubt we'll have seen a gamble like it in years.

But that just means Tiger Roll would be becoming even worse value than he is now because, for all of the positives above, there is a glaring negative this time around.

For all that there have been more great weight-carrying performances in this race in recent times than was once the case, most notably by Many Clouds in 2014, weight is still a massive factor in the Grand National, with just 12 horses carrying 11st or above finishing in the first 11 in the last seven years.

Tiger Roll didn't have it easy with 11st 5lb last year, but it will be a whole different game with 11st 10lb on his back, especially as he will also surely be the highest-rated top-weight for many years, leaving the rest of the field on much nicer racing weights.

That would be particularly good news for my main fancy **BEWARE THE BEAR**, whose mark of 158 would have looked higher than ideal in other seasons but could be fine this time around.

Nicky Henderson's nine-year-old has long looked the sort of thorough stayer who would be well suited to this sort of race, but it just hasn't happened for him when tried over marathon distances so far. His jumping went to pieces in the 2017 National Hunt Chase and he's been pulled up in the Soottish National and the bet365 Gold Cup in the last two seasons.

But apart from his poor run at Sandown, he seemed to turn a corner last season following a wind operation, winning a couple of good handicaps at Cheltenham including the Ultima, in which he powered up the hill to again suggest a longer trip would bring out even more in him.

The issue at Sandown was the ground, as if often has been in the spring before, as he needs plenty of cut. That shouldn't be such a problem for Aintree, where officials are aware of the need to create a safe racing surface, and I can see him finding a rhythm off the pace before coming home strongest of all.

Others for the shortlist include **Le Breuil**, who has always had class and showed unexpected reserves of stamina to win a gruelling National Hunt Chase, which has been a great trial in recent times, and **Mister Malarky**, who could progress over this sort of distance this season and ran an eyecatching race over Aintree's Mildmay fences in April. [DH]

Betting advice

King George

Bristol De Mai 1pt 33-1
(generally available)

Champion Hurdle

Buveur D'Air 2pts 7-1
(Betfred)

Champion Chase

Lalor 1pt 66-1
(bet365, Hills)

Sceau Royal 1pt 20-1
(Betfred)

Stayers' Hurdle

If The Cap Fits 1pt 12-1
(Betfred, Skybet)

Penhill 1pt 16-1
(Betfair, Paddy Power)

Gold Cup

Santini 1pt 10-1
(generally available)

Footpad 1pt 50-1
(Betfair, Paddy Power)

Grand National

Beware The Bear 1pt 66-1
(Betfair, Paddy Power)

Grand National

Aintree, April 4

	Bet365	*Betfair*	*Betfred*	*Coral*	*Hills*	*Lads*	*P Power*	*Skybet*
Tiger Roll	5	**6**	**6**	5	**6**	5	**6**	5
Burrows Saint	16	**20**	16	14	**20**	12	**20**	14
Anibale Fly	**33**	**33**	**33**	**33**	**33**	25	**33**	25
Talkischeap	**33**	**33**	-	-	**33**	-	**33**	25
Native River	**33**	25	**33**	25	-	25	25	25
Magic Of Light	25	**33**	-	25	25	20	**33**	25
Rathvinden	25	**33**	**33**	20	25	25	**33**	25
Mister Malarky	**40**	33	33	-	-	-	33	25
Cadmium	**40**	33	33	33	25	33	33	20
Vintage Clouds	**40**	**40**	33	33	**40**	33	**40**	33
Le Breuil	**40**	**40**	33	33	**40**	**40**	**40**	25
Beware the Bear	40	**66**	50	33	50	33	**66**	33

each-way 1/4 odds, 1-2-3-4

Others on application, prices correct at time of going to press

KLASSICAL DREAM: looks every inch a Champion Hurdle contender in 2020

Ireland by Jerry M

LAST season's Cheltenham Festival could hardly have been more of a mixed bag for *WILLIE MULLINS*, but the upshot is that he starts this season with an even stronger hand than might have looked the case back at the start of March.

Victory in the first two races at Cheltenham was followed by a couple of crushing blows on the opening day, but the week certainly ended on a high as Mullins finally won the Gold Cup after numerous near misses.

Al Boum Photo won the race like a horse who could go on and win a couple more. Whether the campaign he had of just one run and win in a New Year's Day chase at Tramore was by accident or design, it certainly paid off and there must be every chance that a winning formula won't be tampered with.

It is unfortunate for his connections that the main danger to him lies in another box at Closutton.

Mullins has not had a stronger hand at Gold Cup level for some time and the main danger to Al Boum Photo lies in another box at Closutton.

Kemboy had a busier campaign and seemingly had to go on proving himself all season. Some commentators seemed happy to dismiss his impressive success in the Savills Chase at Leopardstown over Christmas for whatever reason, but while his Gold Cup challenge ended ignominiously at the first fence, he made up for that with a convincing success in the Betway Bowl at Aintree and when beating Al Boum Photo to send Ruby Walsh into retirement in the Punchestown Gold Cup.

The Mullins team for the novice events at Cheltenham certainly seemed to lack the strength and the depth of previous years. But how wrong we were as Klassical Dream and Duc Des Genievres took the Sky Bet Supreme Novices' Hurdle and the Racing Post Arkle respectively with real conviction.

Klassical Dream went on to prove his worth with an even more convincing success at the Punchestown festival. Given he looks to be a cracking prospect over fences in time, it is noteworthy that Mullins is keen to put that off and go down the Champion Hurdle route.

Duc Des Genievres looks likely to be campaigned over further this season as Mullins will unleash potentially one of the most exciting 2m chasers in recent seasons in **Chacun Pour Soi**.

This French-bred had not seen a racecourse for three years before making his Irish debut in a 2m beginners' chase at Naas on the Sunday before Cheltenham, when he put in a spectacular display of jumping and galloping.

He showed that impression to be far from misleading when he was thrown in at the deep end in the Grade 1 Ryanair Novice Chase at Punchestown, dismissing the challenge of JLT winner Defi Du Seuil with Duc Des Genievres 20 lengths behind him.

If Altior stays at 2m this season, what a race we could be in store for if and when these two meet.

The presence of Chacun Pour Soi means that Mullins can step **Min** up in trip permanently.

His most impressive performance was when bolting up in the Grade 1 Melling Chase at Aintree and it would not even be much of a surprise if Mullins tried him over 3m, maybe even in the King George at Kempton, with the Ryanair Chase at Cheltenham being his main target.

And then there's always jump racing's iron horse, **Un De Sceaux**. Pickings might be slimmer for him this season, but don't expect him to go winless.

Mullins will have his usual strong hand in mares' races this season.

Benie Des Dieux and **Laurina** provided the big disappointments for him at Cheltenham last season, but Benie Des Dieux bounced back from her final-flight fall to win at Punchestown and Auteuil. She could go back over fences this season, with the Ladbrokes Trophy a possibility.

It will also be very interesting to see how Laurina is campaigned. She was below-par when only fourth in the Champion Hurdle and remains very exciting.

GORDON ELLIOTT had another fine season with 176 domestic winners, but his disappointments made as many headlines as his successes and of course the question arose of what the future holds in years to come if Gigginstown House Stud do indeed wind down over the next five years, a move they announced in May.

For the coming season, though, there is plenty to look forward to, especially with a reputation to be redeemed during **Samcro's** novice chase season.

Campaigning him for a Champion Hurdle bid last season turned out to be a mistake, but he is certainly good enough to be a top campaigner over fences this season.

Over hurdles, **Apple's Jade** can come back from her failures in the spring to be a factor again in domestic Grade 1 races, with the likelihood of the Mares' Hurdle or the Stayers' Hurdle being her Cheltenham target. Perhaps there is even an argument for skipping Cheltenham altogether as she has never really been at her best around there.

Last season's top bumper performer **Envoi Allen** is an obvious early candidate as a potential top-notch novice hurdler, while **Battleoverdoyen** has the tools to be a real novice chase prospect.

However, no other horse in the yard,

DELTA WORK: he has to be a big player in all the top staying chases

Samcro included, might be getting Elliott more excited this season than **Delta Work**.

He won four of his five starts over fences and perhaps if Davy Russell could have the ride back in the RSA Chase, in which he finished third to Topofthegame, he would still be unbeaten over fences going into this season.

Be that as it may, the real Delta Work turned up in the Grade 1 at Punchestown and produced his best performance of the season to beat Discorama by 12 lengths. To be at his best at the end of a tough campaign showed the constitution he has and he should be a big player in the top staying chases this season.

And then there is **Tiger Roll**. This diminutive performer won his second consecutive Grand National in April, which brought him firmly into people's champion territory.

After initial reticence about going for the three-in-a-row, owner Michael O'Leary has confirmed that is the direction he will be heading in, with the Boyne Hurdle at Navan in February and the Cross Country Chase at Cheltenham being his warm-up races. It is a prospect to savour.

HENRY DE BROMHEAD has established himself now as the third major power in the training ranks after saddling 98 domestic winners last season and his partnership with Rachael Blackmore was one of the stories of the season.

The horse the Knockeen trainer is most looking forward to is the Ken Alexander-owned mare **Honeysuckle**.

She enjoyed an unbeaten novice hurdle campaign last season, culminating in a most impressive success in a Grade 1 at Fairyhouse over Easter, and it will be very interesting to see how she is campaigned.

Minella Indo's improvement in the spring was quite rapid. He was a 50-1 shot when giving Blackmore her first Grade 1 success when landing the Albert Bartlett Novices' Hurdle at Cheltenham but showed that was no fluke when he went on to win the 3m Grade 1 novice hurdle at Punchestown.

He is a point-to-point winner already and chances are that he could well make a leading staying novice chaser this season.

JOSEPH O'BRIEN saddled two Cheltenham winners last season in **Band Of Outlaws** and **Early Doors**, which was some achievement given his stable star missed the gig.

Le Richebourg didn't make it to any of the spring festivals after a setback, but his quality was obvious in his novice chase campaign last season when his only defeat came when beaten half a length by

Delta Work in the Drinmore at Fairyhouse.

Also worth noting is the unexposed **Darasso**, winner of a Grade 3 hurdle and a Grade 2 chase in a short campaign last season and with his best probably ahead of him.

Presenting Percy and his media-shy trainer *PAT KELLY* were never far from the headlines last season thanks to the unorthodox campaign given to the Gold Cup favourite.

It backfired, though, and while he looked a potential Gold Cup winner as a novice more evidence is needed this season as to whether that remains the case.

Two more names to note this season are **Sixshooter**, a winner of both bumper starts last season for *NOEL MEADE* and a fine novice hurdle prospect, and *PETER FAHEY'S* mare **Gypsy Island**, who was quite spectacular in victory in bumpers at Fairyhouse and Punchestown in the spring and could be anything.

Finally, a word on *GAVIN CROMWELL*, who suffered an awful blow when his Champion Hurdle winner Espoir D'Allen met a tragic end after a freak accident at home in August.

Cromwell's star will continue on the rise this season, but you would have to wonder if he will ever have one as good as this again. This horse could have dominated the division for years to come.

Invincible Irish

Delta Work

Min

Minella Indo

BAND OF OUTLAWS (right): a Cheltenham Festival winner for Joseph O'Brien

Berkshire by Downsman

THE major question facing *NICKY HENDERSON* this autumn is whether the mighty **Altior** steps up in trip after four successive wins over the minimum trip at the Cheltenham Festival.

A second successive Champion Chase completed Altior's festival four-timer in March, but that wasn't the only time when he looked in trouble before his stamina let him pull a race out of the fire.

The 1965 Chase at Ascot in November appears the most likely launchpad to the King George VI Chase, but do not be surprised if the Tingle Creek is once again on the record-breaking chaser's agenda.

Altior has had a wind operation over the summer and is expected to prove hard to beat again, regardless of trip.

Henderson, who has memorably patched up See You Then, Binocular and Sprinter Sacre, has not given up on **Might Bite**, the 2017 King George hero, after a thorough MOT.

However, RSA Chase second **Santini** is potentially the stable's principal staying chaser this season. He might head for the Ladbrokes Trophy at Newbury before being prepared for the Gold Cup, the same route taken by the trainer's 2013 Gold Cup hero Bobs Worth.

That late November weekend will be a big one for the yard as **Buveur D'Air**, twice the Champion Hurdle king, will go to Newcastle for the Fighting Fifth, which he has won for the last two years. He should continue to be a leading player in that division.

Star juveniles **Fusil Raffles** and **Pentland Hills** will also be trained with the Cheltenham crown in mind, while **Angels Breath**, **Mister Fisher** and **Clarendon Street** might have unfinished business over hurdles as well.

MIGHT BITE: things didn't go his way last year but don't give up on him

Henderson's novice chase department seems formidable with **Birchdale**, **Champ**, **Champagne Platinum**, **Dickie Diver**, **Downtown Getaway**, **Precious Cargo** and **Rathhill** on the teamsheet.

Chantry House could also come into that equation, although he has the option of novice hurdling, as do the exciting quartet of **Arturus**, **Shishkin**, **Mister Coffey** and **Jack Sharp**.

If the five-time champion trainer is to end his Grand National hoodoo, **Beware The Bear** might be the answer to that particular puzzle.

The King George on Boxing Day is the main objective for *WARREN GREATREX*'s star mare **La Bague Au Roi**, who could start her campaign in Wetherby's Charlie Hall Chase.

The Cotswold Chase or Irish Gold Cup might then tee up the dual Grade 1 winner for the Cheltenham Gold Cup, although the trainer is conscious she can lose her form in the spring. However, he reports her to be looking as well as ever.

Santa Adelia, who showed a good level of form as a juvenile hurdler in France, is fancied to make a splash over fences, while **Miss Honey Ryder**, who has taken time but has always had plenty of ability and looks amazing, is another mare expected to take high rank, as a novice hurdler in her case.

The West Yorkshire Hurdle at Wetherby and Newbury's Long Distance Hurdle are the plan for the promising **Emitom**, whom Greatrex adores and thinks the world of. His ultimate aim is the Stayers' Hurdle at Cheltenham.

Keeper Hill is on a fair chase mark, while **Bob Mahler**, who landed two decent races before the trainer – in his words – got greedy, might run in the Ladbrokes Trophy and could even develop into a National contender.

Aintree is the intention for last year's Kim Muir winner **Missed Approach**, who will not be out before Christmas.

The world's most famous chase might one day be a goal for the honest and straightforward **Trio For Rio**, who goes over fences for new owner Trevor Hemmings.

Capable hurdler and Miss Honey Ryder's half-brother **Western Ryder** is another novice chaser to note and the talented but fragile **Portrush Ted** is thought attractively handicapped for hurdles.

Kemble's Cascade and **Sunny Express** are well-regarded youngsters who should prove hard to stop in bumpers before going novice hurdling.

HARRY WHITTINGTON has big hopes for flagbearer **Saint Calvados**, a six-year-old who has summered brilliantly and is close to filling his imposing frame.

Still only six but successful in seven of his 12 starts, he has had a breathing operation and is due to appear in Exeter's Haldon Gold Cup.

The Old Roan Chase at Aintree is the aim for **Bigmartre**, who could also take in the Grand Sefton and Topham over the National fences and should be winning when back in the low 140s, while the Durham and London Nationals are on **Vinnie Lewis**'s agenda.

Rouge Vif schooled satisfactorily over fences this autumn and is a strong, powerful sort who has thrived over the summer. He may be an Arkle contender.

Khage, who could begin in a novice handicap chase in mid-October, is another to look forward to and Whittington is also keen to see **Charlemar**, who has had just one outing since March 2017, over fences.

Captain Tommy is set to stay over hurdles and might end up a Pertemps horse, while Whittington is excited about a trio of novice hurdlers. **Rebel Leader** should come on for a September appearance at Newton Abbot, **Young Bull** could be handy over a trip and **Stick With Bill** has some solid bumper form.

JAMIE SNOWDEN is on course for his best season after a fruitful summer and his emerging stable star **Thebannerkingrebel** ran a huge race when second in the Grade 2 bumper at Aintree in April after a lengthy absence. He is being targeted at Cheltenham's Grade 2 novice hurdle in November and is reckoned to be a Supreme challenger.

Pacify, unbeaten in four as a jumper, will be allowed to fly as high as he can over hurdles.

MORNEY WING: there is more to come from Charlie Mann's chaser

Alrightjack is pencilled in for the Pertemps route and could start in Chepstow's Silver Trophy this month, a meeting that might also host the return of **Some Day Soon**, who will seek to complete a five-timer in the Persian War Novices' Hurdle.

A decent handicap should be within **Chapmanshype**'s reach this autumn, while Belgium Grand National fifth **Fact Of The Matter** is booked for a Cheltenham cross-country campaign and the useful **Monbeg Theatre** goes novice chasing, as does **Thistle Do Nicely**, whose long-term goal is the Cheltenham Festival race Snowden won with Present View in 2014.

Mares **Oneofthesenights** and **Shantewe** are set for novice chase and hurdle programmes, while staying trips over hurdles could be the making of **Thomas Macdonagh**.

Less familiar names worth a mention include **Exod'ela**, **Barrowlands**, **Kiltealy Briggs**, **Minella Beat**, **Mustang Alpha** and **First Maltaix**, while **Frankadore**, a Frankel gelding out of a Grade 1-winning Flat mare in the US, is an interesting recruit who has taken to jumping enthusiastically.

OLIVER SHERWOOD had his most prolific campaign for 20 years last season and hopes he can unearth a headline act.

That could easily be **Severano**, who had some rock-solid hurdles form and remains a novice for 2019-20, although as a strapping type fences ought to be the making of him. He was perhaps on the weak side last season and Sherwood still rates him highly.

What's Occurring is also due to go novice chasing and likes better ground, so could be one for early autumn, especially as he goes well fresh.

The National-winning trainer has always liked **Tarada**, who runs in the Hemmings silks ill-fated stable favourite Many Clouds carried at Aintree. He is another possible to make the move from hurdling.

The 135-rated **Papagana** will stick in that discipline and is believed to have a good race in her on appalling ground.

Makety, who ran with credit at Newbury on her last start, and point winner **Wheesht** are other mares to track in novice hurdles.

CHARLIE MANN could do well in handicap chases and the biggest of them all is the dream for **Like The Sound** at Aintree.

There should be more to come from **The Dubai Way**, **Morney Wing** and **Fixed Rate**, while **The Lion Dancer** might have a nice staying race in him on bad ground.

Zen Master catches the eye at home and Mann has not lost faith after a wind operation, while **Ivilnoble** is an individual in the old-fashioned mould and one to follow over fences.

Prabeni, who wants further than two miles, and **Capone**, thought way better than a 127-rated animal, are second-season hurdlers forecast to shine having performed with credit last term.

Top Up The Fashion, **Financial Conduct**, **Robaddan**, **Commit Or Quit** and **Jack Thunder** are under-the-radar names who can make an impact.

JO DAVIS is optimistic she has a fair bunch of horses and they include **The Big Yin**, a proper soft-ground galloper who was green on his debut last season. He can win a bumper before going hurdling.

Davis is drooling about the unraced **Saggazza**, who could be anything according to the trainer and is the most talented she has had.

Cronins Hill is a promising signing from the point-to-point sphere.

ALI STRONGE could exploit small-field 2m handicap chases on testing conditions with **Ardmayle**, who has improvement in him, while **Blu Cavalier** is not easy to keep sound but has an engine.

The unraced **Ocean Wind** could be a dark horse for the yard and was picked up cheaply from a Godolphin dispersal. He is said to work nicely at home and may go for a juvenile bumper before a possible switch to the Flat.

MARK BRADSTOCK and his wife Sara can often be relied on to ready one and their 2018 bet365 Gold Cup winner **Step Back** has another big pot in him going right-handed on soft ground, while **Eglantier** looked useful when landing a heavy-ground Fontwell bumper on his debut in March.

Best of Berkshire

La Bague Au Roi
Thebannerkingrebel
Severano

STEP BACK: a good chaser for the Bradstocks but must go right-handed

CYRNAME: brilliant going right-handed but can he go the other way round?

The West by Hastings

EVEN *PAUL NICHOLLS* could barely believe he emerged as champion jumps trainer for the 11th time last April and has likened the outcome to an episode from the old TV series 'Tales Of The Unexpected'.

It will not be a shock if he makes it 12 this time around as he can now call on a potent mix of established stable stars and a raft of potentially very smart newcomers assembled at Ditcheat over the summer months.

Nicholls would dearly love to clinch his fifth success in the Cheltenham Gold Cup as it has been ten long years since jumping's Blue Riband went back to Manor Farm Stables and was gutted to see his main hope **Topofthegame** ruled out through injury in September as his other top staying chasers might not necessarily be Cheltenham types.

Indeed, Nicholls faces something of a conundrum with **Cyrname**, who is obviously out of the top drawer but has yet to prove himself going left-handed as all his impressive victories have been going the other way at circuits such as Ascot and Kempton.

His three attempts left-handed have ended in defeat, which makes any thoughts of Cheltenham glory somewhat dubious, and Nicholls certainly intends to keep him right-handed, at least for the first half of this season.

Cyrname's main target before Christmas will be the King George VI Chase at Kempton on Boxing Day and there is every chance that he will warm up for the step up to three miles by making his seasonal bow in the 1965 Chase at his beloved Ascot in November.

That plan puts him on a collision course with stablemate **Clan Des Obeaux**, who landed the King George last year and, not surprisingly, again has the Christmas feature at the top of his early-season agenda.

He is also only a seven-year-old and still progressive but seems to save his better efforts for flat tracks as Cheltenham's undulations do not seem to play to his strengths.

He looks the ideal type for the the JNWine Champion Chase at Down Royal in November as he wants decent underfoot conditions .

There is a wealth of young talent at the yard and, if there is a superstar among the novice hurdlers, it might well be **McFabulous**, who suffered from sore shins when suffering his only defeat at Cheltenham in November but came back strongly in the spring and won the Grade 2 bumper at Aintree.

One of last year's exciting novices, **Getaway Trump**, is now set to go over fences and is a fine prospect in that sphere, while **Grand Sancy** and **Posh Trish** are among the other talented hurdlers to be sent novice chasing.

For a bit more value, certainly in their early outings, it might be better to focus on some darker types and you could do a lot worse than making a note of Brewers Project, Skatman and Trevelyn's Corn.

Brewers Project is well regarded at home and was in training last year before picking up a minor injury and the decision was taken to put him away with this season in mind. He has thrived for the enforced break and it will be a surprise if he is not winning shortly.

Skatman is a real looker and is the type who could end up in the top-class bumpers next spring as he has shown plenty of pace in his provisional work at home, while **Trevelyn's Corn** was a shell of a horse last term but has really strengthened up in the meantime.

One of the strongest lines of form to emerge from last season's festival was the victory of **Defi Du Seuil** over Lostintranslation in the Grade 1 JLT Novices' Chase and *PHILIP HOBBS*'s six-year-old is one to follow again this time around.

Obviously the decision by Hobbs and owner JP McManus to switch the former Triumph Hurdle winner's attentions to chasing last term was spot on as he seemed to progress with each outing and he was given a particularly brilliant ride by Barry Geraghty to win at the festival.

The switch back to 2m did not work at Punchestown in May, but he lost little in defeat and Hobbs will be thinking in terms of the Ryanair Chase as the target next spring as the 2m4½f trip is tailormade for his charge. He deserves his place near the ante-post market for that contest.

After undergoing a virus-stricken time the previous season, last year Hobbs found himself back where he belongs with more than 100 winners on the board and £1 million in prize-money and that will be again the benchmark he sets himself again this term.

Among the youngsters, one who could help him towards that target is **Umndeni**, who ended last season with a clearcut victory over hurdles at Taunton and is likely to be sent over fences this autumn.

He is the type of horse who can do much better over fences as he tended to show scant regard for hurdles on occasions whereas the bigger obstacles are likely to keep his mind on the job

COLIN TIZZARD finally threw caution to to the wind with his potential stable star **Lostintranslation** at Aintree and the ploy worked to perfection as he romped home in the Grade 1 Mildmay Novices' Chase and put himself in place to play a leading role in this season's Gold Cup.

He had previously been duelling with Defi Du Seuil over 2m4f, with the result being 2-1 in the latter's favour, and on each occasion he gave the distinct impression that a step up in distance would have the desired effect. That was given greater clarity as he beat a below-par Topofthegame at Aintree.

Lostintranslation now lodges in the box

formerly occupied by Tizzard flagbearer Cue Card and all roads will lead to Cheltenham next March with options such as the Charlie Parker Intermediate Chase at Carlisle or the Charlie Hall Chase around Wetherby as his seasonal first port of call.

Tizzard also has former Gold Cup hero **Native River** in his care and many good judges at the Dorset yard are convinced it is too soon to write him off.

He never really got his conditions last term but still managed to finish a staying-on fourth in last season's festival showpiece.

He remains very much of interest when the mud is flying and, if given a little help from the handicapper, a race like the Grand National might even be on his radar at some point. He is surely capable of winning another decent staying prize.

While Tizzard is used to housing top-class staying chasers – he also has the 2016 King George hero **Thistlecrack** coming back for more and is leaning towards sending dual Grade 1 novice hurdle winner **Reserve Tank** down the fences route – it is most unusual for him to have a serious Champion Hurdle horse on his hands.

However, the trainer feels that might well be the case with **Elixir De Nutz**, who went from strength to strength last winter and won the Tolworth when last seen in January. The setback that saw him miss the Supreme means he is unlikely to return to the track before December, but he will then be built up towards a Champion Hurdle bid and, while needing to improve, Tizzard feels he might well prove up to it in an open division.

DAVID PIPE endured a quiet time of things last season by his own high stand-

ELIXIR DE NUTZ (far side): missed Cheltenham and now stays over hurdles

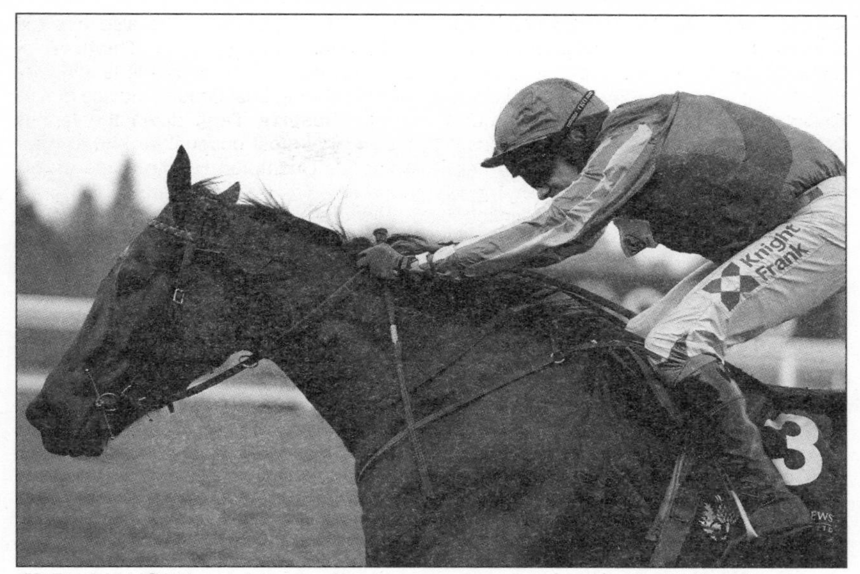

EDEN DU HOUX: could go to the top over hurdles for the David Pipe team

ards, but punters ignoring anyone in racing with the surname Pipe do so at their own risk as he has also been busy building a team of quality horses for the year ahead.

Pipe was left with something of a poisoned chalice on the retirement of his legendary father Martin as emulating his exploits were always going to prove an uphill battle and it has not been easy for him in the last couple of years.

However, with the likes of Eden Du Houx and Umbrigado ready to fly the flag for Pond House over the coming months, he now has something to look forward to

Eden Du Houx could go to the top in novice hurdle company as he was impressive in a couple of bumpers, while three-times hurdle winner **Umbrigado** has the make and shape for jumping fences and will be even better when sent chasing.

HARRY FRY thought he had a Champion Hurdle contender on his hands in the shape of **If The Cap Fits** at this stage 12 months ago, but as the season progressed it became apparent that he was suited by further and he ended last term by landing the Grade 1 Ryanair Stayers Hurdle at Aintree.

The victory pointed to a crack at the Stayers' Hurdle at Cheltenham next March as the way forward for the Paul and Clare Rooney-owned seven-year-old and he will be campaigned with that prize very much in mind.

Things have definitely not worked out for **Bullionaire** since a very impressive bumper debut success at Newbury two and a half years ago as he has gone from one issue to another and has been seen in public only twice since, but he should be able to get his career back on track and could be a forgotten horse.

Western wonders

Brewers Project
Defi Du Seuil
Topofthegame

The North by Borderer

LAST season confirmed *PHIL KIRBY* as the latest northern jumps trainer who can be a force in the big Saturday races, with a notable treble at Wetherby on Charlie Hall Chase day and a seasonal total of 43 that comprehensively eclipsed his previous best of 28.

Star mare **Lady Buttons** was responsible for four of those wins, mixing hurdles and fences, with the highlight the Grade 2 Yorkshire Rose Mares' Hurdle at Doncaster in January.

The nine-year-old should be tough to beat in similar races this time around, possibly starting with the Listed mares' hurdle she won at Wetherby last November.

Richmond trainer Kirby is gaining a reputation for doing very well with recruits from other yards and the ex-Nicky Henderson **Top Ville Ben** had an excellent first chasing campaign last season, winning three of his six starts.

The seven-year-old twice made all with plenty to spare at Wetherby and an early-season target could be the Charlie Hall Chase over the same course and distance, in which he would be capable of a bold bid against rivals who will be using the race as a stepping stone to bigger targets further down the line.

Another cast-off from a big stable, the ex-Godolphin **December Second**, has proved to be another excellent buy, with

LADY BUTTONS (right): might start off again at Wetherby in November

two bumper wins in the spring and a Flat victory at Haydock in August. The five-year-old will be an exciting novice hurdle prospect.

Whoshotthesheriff is another young horse who is going places for the Kirby stable. He was two from two for the yard in novice hurdles in spring having moved from Gordon Elliott and he can make his mark in handicaps this term.

There was another blank for the north at the Cheltenham Festival but there was a welcome return to form for *JEDD O'KEEFFE*'s **Sam Spinner** in the Stayers' Hurdle, with a fine second place to Paisley Park.

The seven-year-old endured a patchy campaign but that Grade 1 effort suggests he could pop up and win a big race at some stage in the campaign, while there will also be nice prizes to be won if his connections send him over fences.

Without Beware The Bear the north would have been celebrating a fantastic one-two-three in the Ultima Chase at Cheltenham, with Vintage Clouds finishing second ahead of Lake View Lad and Big River.

Vintage Clouds is trained by *SUE SMITH* and the nine-year-old, who has been placed in a Welsh and a Scottish National and at the last two Cheltenham Festivals, always warrants respect in the top staying races. Hopefully this season will be the one in which he picks up the sort of big prize that his talent and tenacity deserves.

The stable's **Midnight Shadow** took his form to the next level last season, winning the Grade 2 Relkeel Hurdle at Cheltenham on New Year's Day, and chasing is likely to be on the agenda at some stage.

Smith's horses usually make better chasers than hurdlers and therefore the six-year-old is very much one to look forward to when he makes the switch.

There are quite a few young horses from the Bingley stable who should be set for progressive campaigns, headed by **Hill Sixteen**.

Trevor Hemmings' six-year-old may have won just one of his six hurdle starts but this point winner should be a different

VINTAGE CLOUDS: has to be given respect in all the staying chases

proposition when he goes over fences.

Two others to keep an eye on are **Joke Dancer**, who retains potential and could do well over fences, and **Informateur**, who enjoyed a solid novice hurdle campaign and is open to further improvement.

NICK ALEXANDER trains **Lake View Lad** and enjoyed a fantastic campaign with the grey, picking up the Rehearsal and Rowland Meyrick Chases prior to that big Cheltenham Festival run. He is unexposed beyond 3m and the step up to marathon trips could bear further fruit.

It is an exciting time for the Kinneston trainer as he has two very useful prospects coming through in **Ebony Jewel** and **Elvis Mail**.

Ebony Jewel was an easy winner of an

Ayr bumper on his debut for the stable in March and should enjoy plenty of success in novice hurdles, while Elvis Mail won two novice hurdles at Kelso last season and should continue to improve, whether that be in handicap hurdles or over fences.

The mare **Off The Hook** is another who can continue to go the right way for Alexander. Her campaign concluded with a good fourth in the mares' novice handicap hurdle final at Newbury in March and there is the firm feeling that she will get even better when stepped up to 3m.

Fellow Perth and Kinross trainer *LUCINDA RUSSELL* saddled the Ultima fourth **Big River**, who should be a serious player this season in races such as the Welsh National or the Haydock marathons.

Having got outpaced, he stayed on really well over 3m1f on soft ground at the Cheltenham Festival and also seemed to be lacking the necessary speed when tackling 4m on good going in the Scottish National. There is a big staying prize in him on slow ground this season.

It was a heartwarming sight to see 2017 Grand National winner **One For Arthur** in contention in last season's renewal, following a pair of unseats, and Aintree is likely to be the aim once more.

Granted a smooth preparation, unlike last time around, he could well be a major force in April.

Russell is renowned for her staying chasers and her next stable star is likely to be **Highland Hunter**, a point and bumper winner who achieved a useful level of form over hurdles last season.

The six-year-old is one of the north's top prospects and he can be expected to go to the next level when sent over fences.

Waiting Patiently could not find his very best form for *RUTH JEFFERSON* last season, but the eight-year-old has plenty of time to get back on track and add to his sole Grade 1 win.

The mare **Mega Yeats** won three of her five starts for the yard last season and her only defeats were a second place in a Listed bumper at Cheltenham and a third place in a Listed hurdle at Haydock.

As was the case with her late father Malcolm, Jefferson brings her horses along steadily and Mega Yeats is likely to continue to progress this term, with fences an option for this point winner.

As a hurdler **Buster Valentine** had his limitations exposed, but he still showed plenty of promise and this lightly raced point winner is one to follow when he goes over fences.

Return Ticket also did well in novice hurdles, in the same Richard Collins colours at Waiting Patiently, and is another one to look forward to in novice chases.

The *NICKY RICHARDS* yard is another stable best known for their chasers and took the Scottish National in April with the ten-year-old **Takingrisks**, whose jumping became more fluent when he got cheekpieces.

Things might not be easy off his revised mark although Richards is particularly adept at keeping these old-timers sweet, as evidenced by the continued good form of stable stalwarts Simply Ned and Duke Of Navan.

Admirable duo **Guitar Pete** and **Looking Well** can pick up races and the mares **Glittering Love** and **My Old Gold** can continue the good work that saw them win six races between them last season.

The Greystoke trainer also has a promising battalion waiting to step up and provide him with his next rank of big-race winners.

Reivers Lad won his one and only chase start in December, while **Uncle Alastair** bumped into the classy Vinndication on his sole outing over fences at Carlisle in November.

Two who bring plenty of potential from bumpers are **Ribble Valley**, in particular, and **Marown**.

BRIAN ELLISON picked up some big prizes last autumn with **Definitly Red** in the Charlie Hall and Nietzsche in the Greatwood and the early-season Wetherby Grade 2 could well be on Definitly Red's agenda once more.

He followed up in the Grade 2 Many Clouds Chase at Aintree next time out and can put up a solid show in similar events this season.

Nietzsche has made a promising transition to fences this summer and there could be a nice handicap chase in him at some stage.

Forest Bihan failed to score last season but was fourth in the Grand Annual and, clearly suited by strongly run races in big fields, he will be an each-way player back at Cheltenham in March.

Chti Balko, for *DONALD McCAIN*, also endured a blank 2018-19 but he contested some hot handicap hurdles and has been given a major chance by the handicapper ahead of this season.

The seven-year-old should be winning sooner rather than later.

Cloudy Dream, formerly with Ruth Jefferson, ran just once for McCain last season, but it was a fine third in the Old Roan Chase at Aintree in October and he is a likely player in that 2m4f Grade 2 handicap once again having finished second in the same race in 2017.

Seeyouatmidnight has been retired and has left some very big shoes to fill in the *SANDY THOMSON* stable, but the Lambden trainer has some promising types who could take on a share of that mantle.

Dimple and **Geronimo** could well build on their productive 2018-19 campaigns, while we may not yet have seen the best of **Donna's Delight** and **Seemorelights**.

Angels of the north

Lady Buttons
One For Arthur
Vintage Clouds

CHTI BALKO: drew a blank last season but is now well treated

The South by Southerner

MANY were surprised to learn that **Paisley Park**'s win in the Long Walk Hurdle at Ascot was a first at Grade 1 level for trainer *EMMA LAVELLE*.

It was not the last, though, for Paisley Park was on a steep upward curve and went on to add the Cleeve Hurdle at Cheltenham before justifying short odds in style in the Stayers' Hurdle at the festival for a second Grade 1 success.

There will be no easy pickings this time for the seven-year-old, who started last season in handicaps off 140 and ended it rated 169, but if all goes well he can add another two or three wins at the top level.

Lavelle told me: "Paisley Park summered at the Kingwood Stud and did really well. He'll be starting later this time, and that means we can hopefully extend the campaign at the other end to include Punchestown.

"He'll start in the Long Distance Hurdle at Newbury. He'll have a penalty, because it's Grade 2, but the track is perfect for him. All things being equal it will then be Ascot again, the Cleeve, the Stayers' and then hopefully Punchestown, which we felt we couldn't ask him to run in last season as he'd been on the go since October.

"The beauty with him is that he doesn't care if he goes left-handed or right-handed, or if it's good ground or soft ground, so conditions make no difference and we know where we are going."

Lavelle, still part of the Southerner contacts list despite her successful move to Marlborough a few years ago, reports that Paisley Park's success has led to more new horses and new owners than might have been expected otherwise.

The arrival of an unraced Black Sam Bellamy four-year-old and a six-year-old point-to-point winner called **Thoor Castle**

PAISLEY PARK: Emma Lavelle's first Grade 1 winner. Surely there'll be more

for Trevor Hemmings could prove particularly significant.

Lavelle is proud to point out that even if Paisley Park had never set foot outside the yard she would still have beaten the previous season's prize-money haul, thanks to horses like **De Rasher Counter**.

She said: "The plan with De Rasher Counter is to give him a run over hurdles in order to maintain his chase mark of 149 for the Ladbrokes Trophy. Second-season novices have a good record there and he's at the right end of the handicap. He's got a lot of strings to his bow as he's not a slow horse but has stamina too. He's a lot more grown up now and might be a National horse one day."

Lots of the other established handicappers are back and Lavelle is hopeful the likes of **Flemcara** and **Enniscoffey Oscar**, for example, will pay their way. She also has nice novices coming through, particularly over fences.

She said: "**Fontsanta** was big and backward last season but got better with each run and beat a decent one of Dan Skelton's in a novice hurdle at Hereford without coming off the bridle. He'll go chasing and has a lot of untapped potential.

"**Down The Highway** won a nice novice hurdle at Lingfield very easily and is a big, strong horse who could be pretty smart, as could **Old Rascals**, an impressive hurdles winner at Wincanton."

Among the novice hurdlers we should look out for are dual bumper second **Thunderstruck**, "a natural over hurdles who could be quite sharp"; **Eclair Surf**, a very impressive point-to-point winner in Ireland who was bought at the sale at Cheltenham Festival sale and is "a big galloper who finds everything very easy"; and **Hang In There**, by Yeats and second of 24 in a maiden hurdle at Fairyhouse.

There are plenty of other nice youngsters and one to note for bumpers this time is **Hoi Polloi**.

GARY MOORE has long been regarded as the pre-eminent dual-purpose trainer in the south of England and he had a particularly good first half to last season, winning the Sodexo Gold Cup at Ascot with Traffic Fluide and the BetVictor Gold Cup

BARON ALCO: out around Christmas

with Baron Alco. The season also ended well too, when Larry won a valuable novice handicap chase at Sandown.

Baron Alco has had a good break and won't be out much before Christmas, but Moore has major targets mapped out already for the other two.

He said: "**Traffic Fluide** will be trained for the National. He won't run until after Christmas and I'm not sure whether to run him over hurdles or go for the trial at Haydock. We got him qualified last season by winning a three-mile chase and then he unfortunately met with a slight setback.

"**Larry** is one I'm really looking forward to and his first big target will be the Ladbrokes Trophy at Newbury. He had top weight when he won at Sandown, so that was a good effort, and he's still hopefully on a reasonable mark after being raised 4lb to 143."

Another with a big early target is **Knocknanuss** as Moore revealed: "He's being aimed at the BetVictor Gold Cup. We think he's ready for two and a half miles now and he could still be on a reasonable mark. He's not a bad horse for that sort of race."

That race, and races like it, could also be the target for **Not Another Muddle**.

ERAGON DE CHANAY: one of Gary Moore's who will go novice chasing

Others for some of the better handicap chases include **Darebin**, a stable stalwart, **Dell Oro**, who trained off after winning at Huntingdon but is thriving under a different regime, and **Diakali**, who also lost his way a bit but is back looking really well again.

There is a good team ready to go novice chasing, among them **Ar Mest**, whom Moore reckons should do well, **Eragon De Chanay**, who won a couple of nice handicap hurdles, and **Not Never**, who put up a decent performance when winning over fences at Fontwell in June and was put away soon afterwards.

Sussex Ranger is also going novice chasing and Moore hopes the switch might rekindle his appetite, because he disappointed after winning at Fontwell over Christmas.

We are advised also to keep an eye out for **Full Back**, "a very, very nice four-year-old who was second in an Irish point-to-point to a horse that fetched £375,000 shortly afterwards".

Botox Has, second in a Listed hurdle at Auteuil in the spring, is a juvenile to look forward to and Moore is hoping **Goshen**, who won two Flat handicaps by huge margins, is another who will do well in that sphere.

Touchthesoul, a Flat winner in France who finished second on his hurdles debut at Auteuil, is another for novice hurdles and Moore is also looking forward to hurdling **Quloob**, a 90-rated stayer. A darker one to look out for is **Donnytwobuckets**.

CHRIS GORDON regularly turns out 25-30 winners a season, but that is not enough for his liking as a fiercely competitive streak underlies the fun-loving prankster you often see when interviewed.

The quality of the string is improving all the time and Gordon hopes he has a realistic candidate for some of the bigger handicap chases this season in **Highway One O One**.

Gordon said: "The plan is for Highway One O One to have a prep run at Chepstow, weather permitting, and then have a crack at the BetVictor Gold Cup, where his mark of 144 should put him in on a nice weight. He'll be campaigned at around two and a half miles and there are some nice prizes over the trip through the season, at Cheltenham in particular."

Remiluc, one of many who has done well for the stable after being bought privately from Paul Nicholls, is back after missing a season with a leg problem. He has yet to win in three tries over fences, but his Newbury second to Saint Calvados two seasons ago looked very much better by the end of that season.

Gordon said: "Remiluc has won at Cheltenham and been second twice there, including at the festival, so it's great to have him back. We'll look after him, but if it came up heavy the Betfair Hurdle would be the sort of race for him. I'm hoping the handicapper will drop him a few pounds for his absence and he's lower over fences in any case."

The stable has several strong candidates for novice chasing, all of them rated around 130 over hurdles.

He said: "**Baddesley Knight**, **Commanche Red** and **On The Slopes** are among the best novice chase prospects I've had, all of them big, strong chasing types for whom their wins in bumpers and over hurdles were genuinely a bonus. They are just the type of nice young horse I'm trying to get more of."

Asked for one youngster to look out for, he nominated **Baddesley**, who races for the same owners as Baddesley Knight.

Gordon said: "I don't ready my horses for bumpers like some, so I was delighted when Baddesley was second at Plumpton first time out. He'll stay in bumpers to begin with because I'm pretty sure he can win one."

Baddesley was second at Plumpton to **Strike The Flint**, a mare Lewes trainer *SUZY SMITH* has high hopes for.

Smith said: "I think Strike The Flint is decent as it was the manner of her win as much as anything. She won in a canter really. We also have her older half-sister, **Rosy World**, who won a bumper at the same stage and then got off the mark over hurdles at Plumpton in the spring. They are from the Material World family that get better with age."

Cracker Jak improved fast in the spring and won handicap hurdles at Newbury and Exeter. He's only five, so he will stay hurdling for another season and is expected to continue improving.

Point-to-point winner **Debestyman** had "a little niggle" after he won a Plumpton novice hurdle in January but Smith is looking forward to him again.

She also suggested two dark ones to look out for, adding: "We bought a horse called **Oscarsman** in March. We didn't have time to run him, but I think he'll be a nice horse. We've also got the first foal of Aimigayle, called **Counteract**, and although it's too early to say how good he is I'm hoping he'll prove useful."

NICK GIFFORD is looking forward to having another go over fences with **The Mighty Don**, who followed a handicap hurdle win at Cheltenham with a Grade 2 third at Newbury and then ran into Paisley Park on all his three subsequent starts.

He confirmed: "We are going to have a proper go at chasing again. He went back over hurdles after an aborted try last season, when Leighton [Aspell] was unseated at Fontwell, but my sister Tina [Cook, an Olympic silver medallist] will be doing a lot of schooling with him to see if we can improve his technique. With a hurdles rating of 147 he ought to be decent if he takes to it this time."

Ascot hurdles winner **Belargus**, who is owed by JP McManus, is another Gifford is looking forward to for novice chases, saying: "He's only four, so he gets those allowances, and he's a big, scopey type who loved jumping hurdles, so I've high hopes he'll enjoy chasing even more."

Didtheyleaveuoutto, also owned by McManus, will stay over hurdles. Gifford said: "When we ran him over three miles at Galway he plainly didn't stay, and he couldn't cut it in good races over two, so hopefully he'll win a decent handicap at two and a half miles on good ground."

Cheltenham bumper winner **Mystic Dream** is a mare he likes, although she's very much a stayer and might need three miles to be seen to advantage.

Theo's Charm has had a little wind op and is down to a mark he could win off on soft ground, but unfortunately Glen Rocco, who looked so good at Kempton in January, is out for the season.

Southern stars

Fontsanta

Larry

Paisley Park

Midlands by John Bull

WARWICKSHIRE trainer *OLLY MURPHY* continues to boost his burgeoning reputation and is eyeing a tilt at the Arkle with Supreme Novices' Hurdle second **Thomas Darby**.

The Diana Whateley-owned six-year-old didn't finish out of the first three during his novice hurdle campaign, culminating in finishing a four-and-a-half length runner-up to Klassical Dream in the Cheltenham Festival opener, and hopes are high for a stellar novice chase season.

The good-looking son of Beneficial is set to start off in a novice chase towards the end of October having reached an official mark of 151 over hurdles last season.

Murphy, who enjoyed a career-best 82 winners last season, said: "We have a little plan with him and he will start off in a beginners' or novices' chase at Market Rasen in the third week of October as long as ground conditions are fine for him.

"He handled soft ground at Cheltenham but I've always thought better ground brings out the best in him. We're taking it one race at a time, but obviously we hope he progresses and can become a live contender for the Arkle."

Itchy Feet finished one place behind Thomas Darby at the festival but failed to trouble the principals when fourth in the Top Novices' Hurdle at the Grand National meeting.

The Kate and Andrew Brooks-owned five-year-old is another likely smart novice chaser but is set to start off in good company over hurdles.

Murphy said: "Itchy Feet could return in the Welsh Champion Hurdle at Ffos Las or a Listed hurdle at Kempton in mid-October and if he runs well we have the option of staying over hurdles.

"He could easily go chasing as I've always considered that would be his future, but we're keeping plans fluid until after he has run."

Murphy has always held **Brewin'Upastorm** in high regard and the imposing six-year-old should come into his own over fences this season.

Brewin'Upastorm, owned by Barbara Hester, finished fourth in the Ballymore Novices' Hurdle at Cheltenham before filling the runner-up spot behind Reserve Tank in the Mersey Novices' Hurdle at Aintree.

The trainer said: "He's a lovely horse and did everything but win a Grade 1 last season. He's had a little wind operation over the summer as he wasn't really seeing it out over 2m5f because of his breathing.

"He'll now be tried over fences in the middle of October – there's a 2m novice chase at Warwick – and after that we have the choice of stepping him back up in trip if necessary."

The Grade 3 handicap hurdle winner **Hunters Call** provided Murphy with his first big-race success at Ascot in 2017 but was sidelined with a tendon injury last season. He is set to return this campaign and is worth following in valuable handicap hurdles.

Murphy said: "Hunters Call is back in full training and could be one to keep an eye out for in another decent handicap hurdle as I still think he's well handicapped.

"We have to play it one day at a time with him because of his problem, but he will be ready to run later in the autumn."

John Hales and Tim Syder are among the new owners at Murphy's yard this season, with the trainer pinpointing **I K Brunel** as a novice hurdler to follow after his Carlisle bumper success and promising effort behind Elixir De Nutz at Cheltenham.

Gunsight Ridge, **Finawn Bawn**, **Dun-**

THOMAS DARBY: he will be going novice chasing this season for Olly Murphy

drum Wood and **Fusionice** are other names to note from the yard brimmed with quality and quantity and it is likely to prove another great season for a trainer destined for the top.

Roksana proved to be an exceptionally smart mare for *DAN SKELTON* last season with victory in the OLBG Mares' Hurdle at the Cheltenham Festival and a narrow runner-up effort in the Stayers' Hurdle at Aintree.

She can be the leading light once again for the Alcester trainer with a similar route likely to be taken.

Fellow Cheltenham Festival winner **Ch'tibello** is another worth following at the big meetings after a County Hurdle victory and fine third in the Aintree Hurdle.

Skelton has two fine novice chase prospects in **Beakstown**, a Grade 2 novice hurdle winner at Warwick in January, and the imposing **Ardlethen**, who is simply built for fences.

Imposing mare **Molly The Dolly** progressed nicely through the ranks over fences last season, culminating in victory at Ayr in April, and can make an impact in Listed and potentially Graded company this campaign, while big-money recruit **Interconnected** is another worth following.

Foxtrot Racing have bought into 2m chaser **Marracudja**, trained by Skelton, and are preparing a double attack at the £125,000 handicap chase at Ascot in November that they landed with *RICHARD NEWLAND*'s **Caid Du Lin** last year.

Dan Abraham, who runs Foxtrot Racing, said: "We will target all the big meetings with Marracudja and he's a very exciting horse for us. He's likely to be our Cheltenham Festival horse and will initially be aimed at the valuable handicap chase at Ascot, with Caid Du Lin heading back there too.

"Caid Du Lin is getting better with time since coming over from France and he goes particularly well at right-handed tracks, so hopefully we have two strong chances for the Ascot race."

Foxtrot Racing have been big supporters

HUNTSMAN SON: a spring campaign awaits this improving chaser

of Newland, who has moved to a top-of-the-range yard in Worcestershire ahead of the winter.

Whoshotwho proved extremely consistent for the owners last season, while Abraham nominated **Witness Protection**, third on debut in a bumper for Martin Keighley, as a novice hurdler to follow.

Abraham said: "Whoshotwho was arguably too consistent for his own good! He ran a fantastic race in the Tommy Whittle and relishes soft ground so hopefully he can continue his progression this season.

"Witness Protection ran really well when third in a good-ground bumper at Worcester and has a good mix of speed, stamina and a tremendous attitude. He wants three miles and soft ground and is a nice prospect.

"We had an excellent season in 2019-20 with a quarter of our horses winning and 49 per cent finishing first or second. We believe this is our best group of horses for this campaign with a good mix of young and old jumpers."

Swinton Hurdle scorer **Le Patriote**, owned by Canard Vert Racing Club, climbed the handicap hurdle ranks in impressive style last season and is another to keep on your side for Newland.

ALEX HALES enjoyed a fruitful end to the summer and hopes to carry on his form into the depths of winter with novice chase prospects **Florrie Knox** and **Rough Night** likely to lead the way.

The lightly raced Florrie Knox boasts some eyecatching form over hurdles and is well regarded by the Edgcote trainer, as is Rough Night, who did well in his first season in Britain and is built for chasing.

Huntsman Son flew the flag for Hales last season with victory at Newbury and runner-up efforts on three of his other five starts over fences.

He is pencilled in for a spring campaign in the leading 2m handicap chases, while **Millers Bank** and **Flow Away** are worth noting in novice hurdles.

Three others who should go into your notebook for the winter from our region are **First Assignment**, the star of the *IAN WILLIAMS* yard; **Zakharova**, trained by *LAURA MORGAN*; and **Indefatigable**, a ten-length winner at Cheltenham in April for *PAUL WEBBER*.

Midlands magic

Roksana

Thomas Darby

Whoshotwho

Newmarket by Aborigine

AMY MURPHY has quickly established herself on the Newmarket scene and hit the headlines when saddling **Kalashnikov** to win the Grade 1 Manifesto Novices Chase at Aintree's Grand National meeting in the spring.

Murphy had worked wonders with him in his novice hurdle season, saddling him to win three of his six starts, al though his best effort was in defeat – it was only in the closing stages of the Supreme Novices' at the 2018 Cheltenham Festival that he succumbed to Summerville Boy by a neck.

It was always clear that this fine, strong individual would be even more of a force over fences and Murphy gave him a low-key introduction to the larger obstacles with wins at Warwick and Plumpton.

His next two starts were slightly disappointing and at Cheltenham the luck did not go his way as he was hampered and unseated his rider at the sixth fence in the Racing Post Arkle.

Much to her credit, Murphy did not lose faith in her star and he rewarded her well-placed belief in him at the big Aintree meeting. It was still not without incident as he made a mistake two out, but Jack Quinlan managed to keep him going forward and at the line he had a length and three quarters spare over La Bague Au Roi.

The six-year-old Kalanisi gelding had a midsummer holiday, coming back to the yard in August, and the trainer is delighted with his condition.

He is being aimed at the Old Roan Chase at Aintree towards the end of October, with a return to Cheltenham on the agenda for March.

Among the other jumpers in her yard, Murphy picked **Mercian Prince** for a favourable mention.

After winning well at Kempton in January,

KALASHNIKOV: had bad luck in the Arkle but still managed to win at Aintree

he may have found the rarefied atmosphere of both Newbury's Greatwood Gold Cup at Newbury and Aintree's Topham Chase rather too daunting.

Dropped in class and fitted with cheekpieces for the first time, he bounced back in style at Plumpton in April, winning the Sussex Champion Chase by three lengths from Romain De Senam.

Murphy has not yet organised a race for his return but will place this safe, reliable jumper to good advantage in her father Paul's colours.

Another likely moneyspinner is **Logan Rocks**, who had five runs in bumpers, signing off with a highly creditable Listed fourth to House Island at Newbury. Top novice hurdles beckon.

LUCY WADHAM has her usual strong team of jumpers and the evergreen **Le Reve** soldiers on at the age of 11.

While he occasionally puts in a bad jump, he stays well and has a particularly good record at Sandown, where he will have the valuable veterans' chase final in January and the Grand Military Gold Cup on his agenda.

Also on the staying chase front, **Potter's Legend** is well worth following as he comes back from a year off through tendon trouble. At his best he's quite capable of picking up a valuable staying handicap.

Keep **Movie Legend** on your side as well. He has had a couple of wind operations to help his soft palate, but the indications are that the sparkle is still there and he figures on a weight that will give him a chance in top company.

RICHARD SPENCER is aiming **Outlander** at the Grand National again.

The 11-year-old won some decent races for Gordon Elliott in Ireland before Spencer bought him at the pre-National sales this spring. He gave his new connections a good run for their money by finishing ninth to his former stablemate Tiger Roll.

Spencer is pleased with the way he has done over the summer months and, although no plans have yet been firmed up, he reckons a tilt at the Cross Country Chase at the Cheltenham Festival could be the way to go before a return visit to

MOVIE LEGEND: his sparkle is still there according to Lucy Wadham

Aintree for the National.

The up-and-coming Spencer also rates his progressive hurdler **Thistimenextyear** very highly.

That is understandable in view of the form he showed last season. The gelded grey son of New Approach won a modest race at Fakenham but his best efforts undoubtedly came in defeat in good company in the spring.

It was cruel to see him beaten a head by the Irish raider Chief Justice at Aintree as he was making up ground quickly on the run to the line.

It was even crueller next time out in the valuable Swinton Hurdle at Haydock because he was strongly fancied only to see his chances disappear in the straight through no fault of his own as a horse capsized in front of him, almost bringing him almost standstill. It is to his credit that he regained momentum, finishing strongly but too late to make the prize-money.

The five-year-old confirmed his versatility with a second back on the Flat at Haydock in June and Spencer then decided to give him the rest of the summer off after his very busy campaign.

He tells me he will not be rushing back but that the target will be the big Haydock race once again. There is a possibility he will be allowed to take his chance in other valuable handicap hurdles, including the Imperial Cup, beforehand.

Spencer is also enthusiastic about **Its'afreebee**, whom he reckons is currently on a favourable handicap mark and will win a decent handicap hurdle or two.

The Royal Ascot-winning trainer also made mention of his eight-year-old **Sir Jack Yeats**, who still retains his zest for racing. The plan is to find a small race for him as a confidence booster on his way to another tilt at the Foxhunters' at Aintree, in which he finished a creditable sixth to Top Wood in the spring.

JAMES EUSTACE is mainly Flat-oriented but has a good record with the horses he keeps on the move over jumps.

It should pay to keep a weather eye open for **Peripherique**, whom he bought as a dual-purpose type.

Her best effort on the Flat this summer was a staying-on sixth to Champagne Marengo at Chelmsford back in July.

This daughter of Champs Elysees was catching the eye in the loose school before jumping the practice hurdles on the Links like a natural.

It is easy to see why Eustace believes she will make her mark over timber under Jack Quinlan, who rides most of the stable's jumpers.

Two other novices whom Eustace feels will be worth following are **Captain Felix** and **See The City**.

There is also a lot to like about the way **Glendun** has been shaping and he now figures on what may prove to be a favourable handicap mark.

Incidentally, Eustace reports that his hurdle winner Apache Song has been retired due to injury but has been tested in foal to the brilliant jumping stallion Kayf Tara. The offspring will be worth watching.

JOHN RYAN has a top-notch hurdler in **Normal Norman**, who won two of his seven starts over timber last season.

His promise was revealed in his previous campaign when he readily landed a bumper at Market Rasen and it was on the same course he registered his first hurdling success.

That was in a novice hurdle in October and he stepped up on that effort, running seventh to Red Hot Chilly in a competitive handicap hurdle at Cheltenham.

The five-year-old son of Shamardal then won a handicap hurdle at Musselburgh on New Year's Day before his season ended disappointingly when he was pulled up three out in the Supreme Novices'.

He has thrived since then, returning in good form on the Flat, and the prime jumping objective is the Hogmaneigh Handicap Hurdle that he won at Musselburgh early this year. Remember that he needs good ground to produce his best form.

Hot off the Heath

Logan Rocks

Normal Norman

Peripherique

Hunter chasers by Nick Watts

PACHA DU POLDER finally relinquished his Cheltenham crown in 2019 after two years on the top step of the podium. He failed to complete the course as Hazel Hill romped to victory, and the latter will surely be going for his own repeat in 2020 – but will he manage it?

Hazel Hill will now surely be going for his own repeat in 2020, but I doubt he can match Pacha Du Polder's achievement. Not because he isn't capable but because I marginally prefer the claims of a younger horse who may have Cheltenham on his mind – **Caryto Des Brosses**.

He will be just eight in 2020 but as already compiled a pretty decent record under rules and between the flags. What is more, he has only a neck to make up with Hazel Hill on their running at Cheltenham's hunter chase meeting in May.

On his most recent start, Caryto Des Brosses was sent off at 8-13 to win what used to be known as the Horse and Hound Gold Cup at Stratford – an influential contest that normally goes to one of the highflyers in this sphere.

He couldn't quite get the job done, going down by a neck to Wonderful Charm, but looking back it wasn't that disappointing.

Wonderful Charm is a very good operator on his day for one thing and the time of year – this race was run on Oaks day – means it is possible for any National Hunt horse who has been on the go through the winter to run slightly below par.

It doesn't alter the fact that he is a high-class, improving hunter chaser who should come back and do even better this season.

The Richard Spencer-trained **Sir Jack Yeats** has been around a little bit longer but he is also one to keep on your side.

FENNO'S STORM: a hat-trick bid in the Tetratema Cup next year awaits

ROAD TO RICHES (background, right): still capable despite advancing years

He ran a great race in the Aintree Foxhunters' when sixth of 27 behind Top Wood and had won at Fakenham prior to that. Although you have to forgive a subsequent 1-5 defeat at Fakenham on his latest start, that did come only 18 days after his trip to Liverpool.

He has formed a good alliance with James King and if you see him jocked up on Sir Jack Yeats next spring that is a definite tick in the box.

Of the older brigade, **Road To Riches** should still have a few more wins in him for the effervescent David Maxwell.

The former Cheltenham Gold Cup third will be 13 next season, so is obviously well into the veteran stage, but other teenagers have performed well in hunter chases down the years so it doesn't preclude further success.

He was, of course, a top-class chaser back in the day for Gigginstown and Noel Meade. While those heroics are over, he still managed a win, two seconds and a third last spring, with the third coming at Aintree behind Top Wood.

Given that he had previously finished sixth in the 2018 Grand National, it is obvious that the big fences suit him very well indeed, so don't be surprised to see him line up for the big one again next April, with a few runs beforehand to put him right.

In Ireland, **Stand Up And Fight** was supposed to be the next big thing, but he disappointed where it mattered most and another of his compatriots, **Fenno's Storm**, might be one to follow instead.

He has been a prolific winner in point-to-points and, while he was a bit disappointing when beaten 30 lengths by Caid Du Berlais at Punchestown in May, it is still very much early days for him under rules.

Prior to that, at Gowran Park in March he had annexed the Tetratema Cup when wearing a first-time visor, so he does have potential, particularly when the ground gets testing – pretty much a given during the Irish winter.

He is another up-and-comer in terms of age as he will only be a nine-year-old in 2020 and, when the emphasis is put on stamina, that is when he wil come to the fore.

Whatever happens, a return to the Tetratema in March in very likely as he will be bidding for a hat-trick in that and I would not want to bet against him.

Tipping Point with Tom Collins

Five to note as we Roll with it once more

LAST year was all about the story surrounding Tiger Roll. Gordon Elliott's exceptional Flat-bred nine-year-old proved that size matters little but determination, grit and heart means most by landing a second consecutive Grand National at Aintree.

Winner of all three starts at the start of 2019 – once over hurdles, once over the cross-country fences at Cheltenham and the other in the National – Tiger Roll wrote himself into the history books for the umpteenth time and it was fantastic to read in September that owners Gigginstown Stud have decided to go for racing's showpiece event again this season. Let's hope he can continue his winning ways.

The other of the sport's biggest prizes, the Cheltenham Gold Cup, was memorable on a more personal level after Al Boum Photo, put forward as one to follow for the season in this column last year, rewarded those who retained the faith come March.

In a pointer to the future, he was partnered by Paul Townend, who now faces an almighty task in replacing Ruby Walsh as the number one rider for the Willie Mullins team. Those are big boots to fill because Walsh was certainly the best jumps jockey of my lifetime.

While the Grand National and the Gold Cup went to Ireland, Paul Nicholls' fabulous season at a slightly lower level saw him land a remarkable 11th trainers' title, becoming just the third trainer to rack up 3,000 winners along the way.

In recent times, though, the bigger stars have come from Nicky Henderson's yard and it will be fascinating to see what the Seven Barrows maestro does with Altior this season. He has proved unbeatable at the minimum trip but could always step up in distance, potentially putting him on a collision course with the enigma that is Nicholls' Cyrname.

There will be plenty more thrills, spills and news stories that will shock racing fans this year and here are five potential superstars who might just be the headline writers.

Blue Sari **4yo gelding**
12- (Willie Mullins)

This half-brother to Grade 3-winning mare Sancta Simona is far from the most impressive-looking horse you will see all

BLUE SARI (left): Supreme hope was a fine second in the Champion Bumper

year, but he is with top connections and surprised everyone with a phenomenal debut effort when winning a Gowran Park bumper by 11 lengths.

That race was run at a steady pace but he quickened up in exhilarating fashion, something you need to be top class over two miles, and the runner-up subsequently boosted the form with a fine victory in a 25-runner contest at Punchestown.

Blue Sari looked likely to maintain his unbeaten record when looming up to challenge in the Champion Bumper at the Cheltenham Festival but bumped into an exceptional talent in Envoi Allen, who just fended him off in the final furlong.

Mullins doesn't often run four-year-olds in that race, which underlines the high regard in which he is held, and a good season is predicted now he is sent hurdling, hopefully capped with a victory in the Supreme Novices' Hurdle.

Faustinovick 5yo gelding
2- (Colin Tizzard)

One who could fly under the radar in Colin Tizzard's talent-laden yard is Faustinovick, a son of Black Sam Bellamy who was bought at the Aintree horses-in-training sale from Ellmarie Holden last year.

His sole start for Holden was promising to say the least, a six-length second to the unbeaten Andy Dufresne, who was described by his trainer Gordon Elliott as "as nice a bumper horse as we have".

Having been well backed before the off, Faustinovick, who is a big horse who will need a staying trip and fences in time, filled the same berth on his debut for Tizzard at Newbury in March, rallying well under pressure after being hampered.

The winner that day, McFabulous, is the talk of Ditcheat and followed up at Aintree, so the form looks strong. Keep an eye on Faustinovick.

Geordie B 6yo gelding
6211- (Venetia Williams)

An unexposed gelding who needs soft ground, much like most of Venetia Williams' runners, Geordie B could prove prolific during the winter months.

GYPSY ISLAND: has all the talent in the world and handles all types of ground

He clearly struggled with the trip and ground when sixth of seven on his return last season but built on that with a narrow second at Hereford in December before being stepped up dramatically in distance.

That proved the key to him as he won both starts over 2m7f to end his season, beating smart novices Samburu Shujaa and Tidal Flow in decisive fashion.

Those two performers are rated above 130 and recorded four wins between them last campaign, so the future looks bright for Geordie B, who is a chaser through and through – anything he did over hurdles was a bonus.

Gypsy Island 5yo mare
1211-1 (Peter Fahey)

Gypsy Island won a weak bumper in fine style last August before suffering her only loss on her hurdling debut when her jumping when awry.

In hindsight, though, a length beating by Put The Kettle On looks strong form as that runner has subsequently won a further four times and Gypsy Island didn't take long to get back to winning form, racking up three consecutive victories to end her campaign, including at Grade 3 and Listed level.

They all came in bumpers, so she still needs to prove her jumping capabilities, but she clearly has all the talent in the world and she handles all kinds of ground.

She has been off since May and will probably be kept under wraps in the early part of the season, but further Graded victories will be just around the corner.

Pic D'Orhy 4yo gelding
21U220- (Paul Nicholls)

Seldom do you see a horse garner Paul Nicholls' attention and praise so early in his career without having achieved great status on the track.

However, that is the case with Pic D'Orhy, who moved to Ditcheat on the back of a Grade 1 second – by far his career-best effort – for former trainer Francois Nicolle at Auteuil and finished down the field, beating just four home, on his only start for Nicholls in the Triumph Hurdle.

French imports often take time to acclimatise and you can only assume that he will leave that Cheltenham effort some way behind.

Given time to get over those exertions, he is reported to have come to himself over the summer and I would expect a glittering season for the imposing gelding.

Richard Birch

Read Birchy every week in the RFO

Profit from this group of under-the-radar horses

WITH each passing year the jumps season becomes more and more focused around four days in March – no doubt it will soon be five - at Cheltenham.

While I love watching the likes of Buveur D'Air, Altior and Native River as much as anyone, we all know everything there is to know about those horses.

Here's a list of ten less exposed, less high-profile jumpers to follow throughout the 2019-20 season which will hopefully lead to a decent profit.

We kick off with **Bafana Blue**, trained by Maurice Barnes.

He is is no star, but he simply adores Hexham and I expect him to be placed to win multiple staying handicap chases there next spring and early summer. He's an out-and-out stayer who takes time to hit full stride, which is why the testing Northumberland track suits him so well.

After wins at Hexham and Wetherby last term, the eight-year-old will start off on a stiff enough mark of 112. Hopefully it will be down to around 105 before those Hexham opportunities in early 2020.

Burn Baby Byrne, trained by Evan Williams, is a dual point-to-point winner who enjoyed a successful first campaign over hurdles last season, landing two good-ground handicaps at Ludlow over 2m5f.

Isabel Williams, whose riding has improved considerably this summer, has built up an excellent rapport with the six-year-old mare, who appears likely to take her form to another level when sent over regulation fences.

Ignore her disappointing final run at Haydock where she was probably over the top, and focus instead on the potential for her to improve her mark of 121 when tackling handicap chases.

Williams's **Peterborough** is probably the darkest horse in this list.

A £60,000 purchase, he looked a well-handicapped young horse when romping to a five-length Exeter success last November. His canny trainer immediately stressed another summer at grass would be the making of this six-year-old and in two subsequent starts he failed to cut much ice.

The obvious plus is he starts the new season off just 108. I'll be amazed if he isn't a 130+ horse by this time next year.

Suzy Smith's **Cracker Jak**, a big, chasing type with abundant physical scope, went straight to the top of my list of horses to follow when landing a 3m handicap hurdle at Newbury in March off a lowly 94.

The five-year-old clearly appreciated the big, galloping track that day and followed up off an 8lb higher mark the following month at Exeter.

He possesses a huge stride, good cruising speed and a likeable attitude off the bridle. It was all a learning curve for him last year and I expect him to make further progress this term off an opening 109. He could be some weapon in novice handicap chases over the winter.

Earth Leader, formerly of the Paul Nicholls yard, disappointed in a short hurdle campaign for Nicholls during the 2017-18 season, but a switch to Rose Loxton's pointing operation last year saw the six-year-old make startling progress.

The strong-travelling gelding won three points and two hunter chases, including on his final start at Stratford in May when value for ten times the winning margin of two and three-quarter lengths.

He jumps beautifully and presumably will return to Nicholls to exploit a mark of 117. A sequence beckons – don't be surprised if he is rated 140 by the end of the season.

Glittering Love proved the undoubted star of my 2018-19 RFO ten to follow list, going through the winter unbeaten in four handicap chases in the north for Nicky Richards.

His mark soared from 92 to 125 as a result, but the best is still to come as this highly progressive stayer has yet to tackle trips in excess of 3m. He looks the type who will stay longer than the mother-in-law and the step up to 3m4f-plus will clearly open up plenty more opportunities. I wonder if he could emulate former stable companion Baywing by landing the Eider?

On A Promise, another from Grey-

GLITTERING LOVE: can emulate former stablemate Baywing and win the Eider

YALLTARI (right): could win a valuable handicap chase for Venetia Williams

stoke, missed the entire 2018-19 season, which was most frustrating since I had been banking on him landing a few novice handicap chases in the north.

The seven-year-old won three of his four races in handicap hurdles the previous campaign, his rating going up from 91 to 120. The manner in which he breezed to success on his final start at Market Rasen suggests he will still have the handicapper endeavouring to play catch-up when he goes over fences. I can't wait to see him back in action.

Musical Slave made it three wins from three starts for Philip Hobbs since graduating to handicaps when posting an impressive success at the Punchestown festival. While her rider, Jonjo O'Neill jr, rightly received plenty of plaudits, we should not forget that the reason he was able to shine was because of the engine underneath him.

Musical Slave, who also scored at Ludlow and Market Rasen, is reportedly going novice chasing and the six-year-old remains emphatically one to follow on soft ground. If there is a Cheltenham horse in this list, it is him.

Some Can Dance of Sam Drinkwater's is one to pay close attention to whenever he is sent on the long journey north from deepest Gloucestershire to Carlisle.

Two trips last season paid maximum dividends in handicap hurdles and this relentless stayer is perfectly suited to the demands of one of the stiffest tracks in Britain.

The six-year-old will improve further when switched to fences and will play a big part in my punting operation this season.

Finally, Venetia Williams' **Yalltari** is capable of winning a valuable 3m handicap chase or two in the mud this season.

The strapping grey took extremely well to fences last term and simply couldn't have been more impressive at Chepstow in December off a mark of 137.

He's 8lb higher now, but I feel there's still plenty of mileage in his rating. He's a real good horse.

Good luck, everyone!

RACING & FOOTBALL outlook

Time Test

Photo tops list but Gold Cup can leave its mark

AL BOUM PHOTO produced the top performance of the season against the clock with his rousing success in the Cheltenham Gold Cup and, if the figures are to be taken literally, he will be the horse to beat in the top staying chases again this season.

The seven-year-old powered home in a strongly run race at Cheltenham, earning a rating of 92, with **Anibale Fly** and **Bristol De Mai** also producing fine efforts to fill the places.

The worry is that recent history tells us that returning to Gold Cup-winning form is a difficult task, as evidenced by the winless seasons of **Native River** and **Might Bite**, who also topped the Time Test list last season after epic Gold Cup runs.

That means we have something of a conundrum in the staying division because there's no obvious sign of where the next big thing might be coming from.

Many will look to the RSA Chase, in which **Santini** and **Delta Work** were placed behind the crocked **Topofthegame** in a thrilling clash, but the winner's display was worth a Time Test figure of just 69.

In fact, the best performance by a staying novice last season came from **Talkischeap** (74), who hacked up in the bet365 Gold Cup. He could still be ahead of the handicapper and it's no wonder his connections have the Ladbrokes Trophy and the Grand National on their agenda.

The RSA Chase of 2018 had been won by **Presenting Percy** and, while he can be forgiven last season's damp squib of a campaign when he ran only once over fences, the reservations expressed in this column last season still apply. He has yet to record an eyecatching Time Test figure over fences and his championship claims rest more on his hurdling form, with his victory in the 2017 Pertemps Final the best by a staying hurdler that season.

Three-time Grade 1 winner **Kemboy** finds himself in a similar boat as another who hasn't yet registered a meaningful Time Test figure. He won three Grade 1 chases last season, but all came in slowly run races in which he was pretty much allowed to do his own thing and it remains to be seen what he can produce in a truer test.

Clan Des Obeaux is far more solid, his King George victory worthy of a Time Test figure of 82 before he failed to replicate that form at Cheltenham.

It's fantastic news that dual Grand National winner **Tiger Roll** has had a historic bid for a third Grand National confirmed as his primary target this season, but at the same time it's a shame that his route to Aintree will be as low-key as last season because a cohesive argument could be made that racing's most familiar name would have a leading chance in top Grade 1 chases. The mark of 88 he achieved at Aintree was well up to that standard.

There's certainly scope for new names to come through, so it's perhaps timely that the two highest-rated chasers of last season on official marks, **Altior** and **Cyrname**, might soon be plying their trade over longer trips.

The pair's proximity on ratings last season caused controversy in some quarters and it's worth pointing out that they aren't nearly as close on Time Test figures, with Altior some way ahead of his rival. While he might not have been as easy on the eye last season as in previous campaigns, his performances in winning the Clarence House Chase at Ascot and a second successive Champion Chase at Cheltenham were the two best of his career according to the clock.

In contrast, while Cyrname's performances took the breath away, the clock sounds a more cautionary note. His peak Time Test figure of 77 is decent but leaves him with a bit to find against the very best.

With Altior's dominance of the 2m landscape potentially put on hold, that division looks very weak. **Min**'s victory in the Melling Chase was exceptional and leaves him at the top of the pack, although he could also stick to intermediate trips, and **Duc Des Genievres** is more interesting for the Champion Chase.

The Racing Post Arkle is traditionally a strong guide to the following season's championship and Duc Des Genievres posted easily the best performance by a novice chaser last season when winning it.

Willie Mullins' gelding was a long way behind stablemate **Chacun Pour Soi** at Punchestown, but he was a long way below his best that day and is much preferred at this stage.

Among the hurdlers, it was remarkable that the top ten times of last season were all clocked at 2m, with the ill-fated **Espoir D'Allen** (81) leading the way.

PRESENTING PERCY: lots to prove

His unfortunate passing leaves a hole at the head of the division and it's one that **Klassical Dream** is expected to fill.

A superb winner of a truly run Supreme Novices' Hurdle, Klassical Dream achieved a Time Test figure of 75 and is open to further improvement given his progressive profile, making him a hugely exciting prospect.

That mark was matched by **Apple's Jade** as the second best over hurdles last season behind Espoir D'Allen. She remains an outstanding mare, but her targets this season will surely be over greater distances or mares' races.

As with last season's novice chasers, the juvenile brigade attempting to make the step up into open company have plenty to find of the figures. **Fusil Raffles** and **Pentland Hills**, both trained by Nicky Henderson, ended the season as Grade 1 winners but are quite some way off the top of the division against the clock and need to improve significantly. Henderson might still find more joy with his dual Champion Hurdle winner **Buveur D'Air** (72), who will be back for more.

Paisley Park's moderate figures suggest he had little to beat in what was a poor staying hurdle division last season and he could face competition from a rejuvenated **Penhill**. His Stayers' Hurdle win in 2018 came in a very slowly run race, but his Albert Bartlett win the year before was won in a much better time than anything Paisley Park has ever achieved.

With promising novice **Reserve Tank** likely to go novice chasing and Albert Bartlett winner **Minella Indo** a long way off on Time Test figures, it could well be **Sire Du Berlais**, an impressive winner of the Pertemps Final in March, who gives Paisley Park the most to think about of those coming from lower down the ranks.

One horse belatedly stepping up in trip this season, albeit over fences, will be **Samcro**, who was a bitter disappointment last term. However, his first run of the season at Down Royal was a hugely encouraging one and, assuming it was physical problems affecting him later, he remains one to follow. Look out for him in the top novice chases.

Top chasers of 2018-19

	Horse	*Speed rating*	*Distance in furlongs*	*Going*	*Track*	*Date achieved*
1	**Al Boum Photo**	**92**	**26**	**GS**	**Cheltenham**	**Mar 15**
2	Anibale Fly	89	26	GS	Cheltenham	Mar 15
3	Tiger Roll	88	34	GS	Aintree	Apr 6
4	Bristol De Mai	85	26	GS	Cheltenham	Mar 15
5	Altior	84	16	SFT	Cheltenham	Mar 13
6	Frodon	83	21	GS	Cheltenham	Mar 14
6	Min	83	20	SFT	Aintree	Apr 5
8	Aso	82	21	GS	Cheltenham	Mar 14
8	Clan Des Obeaux	82	24	GS	Kempton	Dec 26
8	Native River	82	26	GS	Cheltenham	Mar 15
8	Politologue	82	16	SFT	Cheltenham	Mar 13

Top hurdlers of 2018-19

	Horse	*Speed rating*	*Distance in furlongs*	*Going*	*Track*	*Date achieved*
1	**Espoir D'Allen**	**81**	**16**	**SFT**	**Cheltenham**	**Mar 12**
2	Apple's Jade	75	16	GY	Leopardstown	Feb 2
2	Klassical Dream	75	16	SFT	Cheltenham	Mar 12
4	Buveur D'Air	72	16	GS	Kempton	Dec 26
5	Thomas Darby	70	16	SFT	Cheltenham	Mar 12
6	Itchy Feet	69	16	SFT	Cheltenham	Mar 12
6	Old Guard	69	16	GD	Cheltenham	Nov 18
8	Samcro	68	16	GD	Down Royal	Nov 2
9	Mohaayed	67	16	SFT	Ascot	Dec 22
9	Reserve Tank	67	20	GY	Punchestown	May 3
9	Sams Profile	67	20	GY	Punchestown	May 3
9	Verdana Blue	67	16	GD	Cheltenham	Nov 18

Big-race review by Dylan Hill

1 JNwine.com Champion Chase (Grade 1) (3m)

Down Royal IRE November 3 (Good To Yielding)

1 **Road To Respect** 7-11-10 Sean Flanagan
2 **Woodland Opera** 8-11-10 Robbie Power
3 **Outlander** 10-11-10 Jack Kennedy
6/4F, 13/2, 6/1. 16l, 1¾l. 6 ran. 6:04
(Noel Meade).

Road To Respect would continue to come up frustratingly short against the very best, but he easily took advantage of this straightforward opening at the top level with his main rivals well below their best. Always going well as he made his ground from the rear, Road To Respect was much too good for **Woodland Opera** and the regressive **Outlander**, while it was 25l back to **Balko Des Flos** and **Sub Lieutenant**.

2 BetVictor Gold Cup (Handicap Chase) (Grade 3) (2m4f44y)

Cheltenham November 17 (Good)

1 **Baron Alco** 7-10-11 Jamie Moore
2 **Frodon** 6-11-12 Bryony Frost
3 **Guitar Pete** 8-10-2 Brian Hughes
8/1, 16/1, 12/1. 2l, 8l. 18 ran. 4:55
(Gary Moore).

A strange renewal of this fiercely competitive handicap with only six getting round and the first two holding those positions virtually throughout, but with this proving to be Ryanair Chase hero **Frodon**'s only defeat all season **Baron Alco**'s effort in victory might have been underestimated. Baron Alco produced an outstanding round of jumping as he made all the running ahead of the gallant Frodon and had excuses for his only subsequent defeat in the Caspian Caviar Gold Cup, missing the rest of the season after he returned sore. Still, the pair were fortunate to avoid carnage behind, with **Willie Boy**'s fall four out bringing down **Rather Be** and badly hampering **Ballyandy**, who were both going well, while **Kings Socks** fell three out when close up. It left **Guitar Pete** to pick up the pieces in third ahead of **Mister Whitaker**, who won the Silver Trophy at the track in April off just 3lb lower, and subsequent Cheltenham Festival fourth **Eamon An Cnoic**.

3 Unibet Morgiana Hurdle (Grade 1) (2m40y)

Punchestown (IRE) November 18 (Good)

1 **Sharjah** 5-11-10 Paul Townend
2 **Faugheen** 10-11-10 R Walsh
3 **Tombstone** 8-11-10 Rachael Blackmore
7/2, 2/5F, 20/1. 7½l, 10l. 4 ran. 3:47
(W P Mullins).

Punters got this one badly wrong as **Faugheen**, ludicrously short at 2-5 in hindsight given he would prove to no longer have anything like the speed for 2m, was well beaten by an underrated rival in **Sharjah**. Having already improved on an ultimately disappointing novice campaign with a win in the Galway Hurdle, Sharjah had far too much speed for Faugheen, who was at least able to pull clear of **Tombstone** and **Wicklow Brave**.

4 Betfair Chase (Grade 1) (registered as the Lancashire Chase) (3m1f125y)

Haydock November 24 (Good)

1 **Bristol De Mai** 7-11-7 Daryl Jacob
2 **Native River** 8-11-7 Richard Johnson
3 **Thistlecrack** 10-11-7 Tom Scudamore
13/2, 5/2, 10/1. 4l, 1¾l. 5 ran. 6:28

(Nigel Twiston-Davies).

Bristol De Mai proved plenty of doubters wrong last season, kicking off by managing a second Betfair Chase win in hugely contrasting conditions to his heavy-ground romp a year earlier. Facing a much stronger field on good ground, Bristol De Mai locked horns with **Native River** up front from an early stage, always travelling nicely, and drew clear for a tremendous win before again finishing in front of the runner-up when third in the Gold Cup. Native River showed his stamina reserves to stay on well for second ahead of **Thistlecrack** and **Clan Des Obeaux**, who would come on most for the run. **Might Bite** jumped tentatively and was a poor fifth to set the tone for his bitterly disappointing season.

5 Christy 1965 Chase (Grade 2) (2m5f8y)

Ascot November 24 (Good To Soft)
1 **Politologue** 7-11-7 Sam Twiston-Davies
2 **Charbel** 7-11-1 David Bass
3 **Gold Present** 8-11-5 James Bowen
5/4F, 5/2, 15/2. ½l, 10l. 6 ran. 5:13
(Paul Nicholls).

A terrific performance from **Politologue** to concede 6lb to a classy and in-form rival in **Charbel**, although he was perhaps a shade fortunate as the runner-up made a significant number of mistakes. The Champion Chase second had already proved equally comfortable over this longer trip and had excuses when unable to win a second Melling Chase in the spring, so to still come so close to winning underlined Charbel's largely unfulfilled potential, as would his subsequent Peterborough Chase victory, especially as there were big gaps back to **Gold Present** and **Benatar**.

6 Ladbrokes Trophy Chase (Handicap) (Grade 3) (3m1f214y)

Newbury December 1 (Soft)
1 **Sizing Tennessee** 10-11-3 T Scudamore
2 **Elegant Escape** 6-11-10 Harry Cobden
3 **Dingo Dollar** 6-11-3 Wayne Hutchinson
12/1, 4/1, 10/1. 10l, 7l. 12 ran. 6:37
(Colin Tizzard).

It's rare that this race is won by a ten-year-old – it hadn't happened since 1981 – and that might have unfairly caused the lukewarm reception that followed it as **Sizing Tennessee**'s victory was franked time and time again, suggesting this was a top-class display. Sizing Tennessee travelled and jumped notably well, led four out and powered clear of his rivals, who were well strung out, making it a huge shame for connections that he had to miss the rest of the season after a setback. Welsh National winner **Elegant Escape** stayed on for second ahead of **Dingo Dollar**, who never got soft ground again all season, with subsequent dual Cheltenham winner **Beware The Bear** in fourth.

7 BetVictor Fighting Fifth Hurdle (Grade 1) (2m98y)

Newcastle December 1 (Soft)
1 **Buveur D'Air** 7-11-7 Barry Geraghty
2 **Samcro** 6-11-7 Jack Kennedy
3 **Vision Des Flos** 5-11-7 Robbie Power
11/8, 6/5F, 14/1. 8l, 13l. 5 ran. 3:57
(Nicky Henderson).

This was billed as an epic clash between dual Champion Hurdle winner **Buveur D'Air** and young pretender **Samcro**, but Buveur D'Air surely achieved far less in victory than it appeared at the time. Buveur D'Air cantered all over the front-running Samcro and scooted clear on the run-in despite flattening the last, making the runner-up look distinctly laboured, but that was perhaps explained by Samcro's lung infection after another defeat at Leopardstown. The pair still pulled well clear of the disappointing **Vision Des Flos** and **Summerville Boy**, who was later found to have a hairline fracture of his leg.

8 baroneracing.com Hatton's Grace Hurdle (Grade 1) (2m4f)

Fairyhouse (IRE) December 2 (Good)
1 **Apple's Jade** 6-11-3 Jack Kennedy
2 **Supasundae** 8-11-10 Robbie Power
3 **Limini** 7-11-3 R Walsh
4/6F, 9/2, 11/2. 20l, 2l. 9 ran. 4:49
(Gordon Elliott).

A third successive win in the race for **Apple's Jade**, who again looked invincible over this trip, although her rivals made things even harder for themselves by sitting well off what was only a modest gallop. Apple's Jade was the only horse to race within touch of the early leader **Wicklow Brave** and took over after the third-last, eventually easing home 20l clear of **Supasundae**, who won a tight battle for second, with **Limini**, **Bapaume**, **Early Doors** and **Farclas** all within just over 6l of him.

9 Betfair Tingle Creek Chase (Grade 1) (2m119y)

Sandown December 8 (Soft)
1 **Altior** 8-11-7 Nico de Boinville
2 **Un De Sceaux** 10-11-7 R Walsh
3 **Saint Calvados** 5-11-7 Gavin Sheehan
8/13F, 7/2, 8/1. 4l, 15l. 4 ran. 4:03
(Nicky Henderson).

Altior kicked off yet another unbeaten season with what was probably his best performance, coming through a tough test with conditions ideal for the evergreen **Un De Sceaux**. Benefiting from getting a good lead, Altior jumped well after an early mistake and typically hit top gear from the final fence to pull clear of Un De Sceaux, who proved as good as ever during a light campaign. **Saint Calvados** had his limitations exposed in third, while **Sceau Royal** was unsuited by the ground.

10 Betway Many Clouds Chase (Grade 2) (3m210y)

Aintree December 8 (Soft)

1 **Definitly Red** 9-11-6 Danny Cook
2 **Double Shuffle** 8-11-0 Jonathan Burke
3 **Acdc** 8-11-0 Liam Quinlan
1/2F, 11/4, 28/1. 4½l, 34l. 4 ran. 6:47
(Brian Ellison).

Definitly Red won his fourth Grade 2 chase across the last two seasons as he comfortably saw off **Double Shuffle**. With four of those wins coming on soft or heavy ground – all bar his victory in a weak Charlie Hall Chase – Definitly Red was in his element in the conditions and duly made all, though he faced only one serious rival in Double Shuffle, who would come close to his best form only once all season when second back at his beloved Kempton in a handicap off 154 in February, and the winner would continue to come up short at the top level.

11 Tattersalls Ireland Edredon Bleu Chase (registered as the Peterborough Chase) (Grade 2) (2m3f189y)

Huntingdon December 9 (Good To Soft)

1 **Charbel** 7-11-0 Noel Fehily
2 **God's Own** 10-11-6 Paddy Brennan
3 **Tea For Two** 9-11-0 Lizzie Kelly
13/8F, 6/1, 13/2. 8l, 4l. 9 ran. 4:52
(Kim Bailey).

Charbel showed his true capability when putting in a clean round of jumping as he stormed to an impressive victory. Much better at his fences than at any other time all

APPLE'S JADE: won a third straight Hatton's Grace over surely her best trip

BRAIN POWER: more and more of an enigma but still showed his quality

season, perhaps helped by more prominent tactics, Charbel made most of the running and was eased down as he thrashed the veteran **God's Own**, who had proved he was no back-number by winning the Haldon Gold Cup but was weighed down by a 6lb penalty.

12 John Durkan Memorial Punchestown Chase (Grade 1) (2m4f40y)

Punchestown (IRE) December 9 (Yielding)

1 **Min** 7-11-10 R Walsh
2 **Shattered Love** 7-11-3 Jack Kennedy
3 **Balko Des Flos** 7-11-10 R Blackmore
EvensF, 5/2, 5/1. 1½l, 2½l. 5 ran. 5:17
(W P Mullins).

In a field largely made up of stayers, a moderate gallop played into the hands of class act **Min**, who had far too much speed for his rivals and made a comfortable winning return. Min cruised into the lead after the second-last and was always holding **Shattered Love**, who stayed on past **Balko Des Flos** into second with **The Storyteller** a close fourth.

13 Caspian Caviar Gold Cup (Handicap Chase) (Grade 3) (2m4f127y)

Cheltenham December 15 (Good)

1 **Frodon** 6-11-12 Bryony Frost
2 **Cepage** 6-10-5 Charlie Deutsch
3 **Guitar Pete** 8-10-0 Ryan Day
7/1, 12/1, 13/2. 1¼l, 15l. 12 ran. 5:11
(Paul Nicholls).

One of the great weight-carrying performances of recent times from **Frodon**, who ran his rivals ragged under 11st 12lb with only **Cepage** able to get close, pointing to his big breakthrough at Grade 1 level in the Ryanair Chase in March. Frodon jumped superbly and was in command after a magnificent leap at the second-last, gamely holding off the strong-staying Cepage as the pair pulled 15l clear of **Guitar Pete**. BetVictor Gold Cup winner **Baron Alco** returned sore after managing only fourth, while **Rather Be**, sent off favourite having looked unlucky that day, was never travelling as well and proved disappointing subsequently.

14 Unibet International Hurdle (Grade 2) (2m1f179y)

Cheltenham December 15 (Good To Soft)

1 **Brain Power** 7-11-0 Nico de Boinville
2 **Silver Streak** 5-11-4 Barry Geraghty
3 **Western Ryder** 6-11-0 Richard Johnson
7/1, 9/2, 4/1F. 1¾l, 2¼l. 8 ran. 4:05
(Nicky Henderson).

It was a strange season for **Brain Power**, who was reverting to hurdles after not quite hitting the heights anticipated over fences and was then pulled up on both subsequent runs in the spring, but he gave a reminder of his quality with this win in a competitive race. Brain Power was always going well and held off **Silver Streak**, who was the best horse at the weights and would go on to prove an underrated rival with his Champion Hurdle third, while **Western Ryder** was third. The ill-fated **We Have A Dream** was next ahead of **Vision Des Flos**, who would thrive when stepped up in trip after taking fifth, and **Old Guard**.

15 JLT Hurdle (registered as the Long Walk Hurdle) (Grade 1) (3m97y)

Ascot December 22 (Soft)

1 **Paisley Park** 6-11-7 Aidan Coleman
2 **West Approach** 8-11-7 Harry Cobden
3 **Top Notch** 7-11-7 James Bowen
8/1, 40/1, 10/1. 2l, 3¾l. 11 ran. 6:03
(Emma Lavelle).

A breakthrough win for **Paisley Park** but without much hint of the fireworks to come as he just got the better of a fairly ordinary bunch behind. Perhaps unsuited by a more modest gallop than twice subsequently at Cheltenham, Paisley Park got on top only after the last when his stamina kicked in, taking him past **West Approach**. However, the first five were covered by less than 8l and there was a 100-1 shot, **Garo De Juilley**, in sixth, with West Approach's Cleeve Hurdle second the only time any of Paisley Park's nearest rivals were placed again over hurdles all season. **Call Me Lord** looked a non-stayer in seventh ahead of **Younevercall**, while the reluctant **Sam Spinner** unseated his rider at the second and **Unowhatimeanharry** fell at the eighth.

16 32Red King George VI Chase (Grade 1) (3m)

Kempton December 26 (Good To Soft)

1 **Clan Des Obeaux** 6-11-10 Harry Cobden
2 **Thistlecrack** 10-11-10 Tom Scudamore
3 **Native River** 8-11-10 Richard Johnson
12/1, 15/2, 9/2. 1½l, 12l. 10 ran. 5:59
(Paul Nicholls).

A thrilling battle between rising star **Clan Des Obeaux** and veteran **Thistlecrack**, who were effectively the last two standing in an incident-packed race. If that led to misgivings over the form they would have been reinforced by Clan Des Obeaux managing to win only a Denman Chase subsequently, but he had excuses for his Cheltenham and Aintree defeats and certainly travelled like a class act, cantering all over Thistlecrack before being pushed clear from the last. Thistlecrack, back at the scene of his 2016 King George win, in turn pulled 12l clear of **Native River** with the likes of Kempton specialists **Tea For Two** and **Double Shuffle** a long way behind, although the 2018 Gold Cup winner was totally unsuited by this tight track, doing really well to rally after being run off his feet throughout, and it was a huge shame that **Bristol De Mai** couldn't instead represent the Betfair Chase form, falling at the ninth and bringing down **Waiting Patiently**. **Politologue** didn't quite get home in fourth, hindered by a couple of notable jumping errors, while **Might Bite** was found to have bled from the nose after finishing last of the seven finishers.

17 Unibet Christmas Hurdle (Grade 1) (2m)

Kempton December 26 (Good To Soft)

1 **Verdana Blue** 6-11-0 Nico de Boinville
2 **Buveur D'Air** 7-11-7 Barry Geraghty
3 **If The Cap Fits** 6-11-7 Noel Fehily
11/2, 1/4F, 7/1. shd, 6l. 5 ran. 3:46
(Nicky Henderson).

The first sign of vulnerability in **Buveur D'Air**, who suffered his first defeat since going hurdling nearly two years earlier at the hands of stablemate **Verdana Blue**, who won with more authority than the narrow margin suggests having quickened up under only hands and heels from the last to get up quite cosily. Still, having blundered three out and hit the front earlier than ideal, Buveur D'Air probably wasn't far off his best conceding 7lb to a mare who would go on to romp home in the Scottish Champion Hurdle off 154 and proved in her element on sharp, flat tracks having also landed the Elite Hurdle. **If The Cap Fits** was outpaced in third but stuck on far better than **Global Citizen**, who did too much in front.

18 Coral Welsh Grand National (Handicap Chase) (Grade 3) (3m5f110y)

Chepstow December 27 (Soft)

1 **Elegant Escape** 6-11-8 Tom O'Brien
2 **Ramses De Teillee** 6-11-1 David Noonan
3 **Yala Enki** 8-11-11 Charlie Deutsch
3/1F, 10/1, 12/1. 1¼l, 4l. 20 ran. 7:48
(Colin Tizzard).

A really classy renewal of this great race as two horses at the top of the weights dominated, split by a rapid improver in second, with **Elegant Escape** leading the way. The Ladbrokes Trophy runner-up had ample stamina for this even more searching test and beat **Ramses De Teillee**, a course specialist who also franked the form by finishing a closer second in the Grand National Trial at Haydock off 5lb higher, although he didn't win with quite enough authority to put himself in genuine Gold Cup contention. Indeed, **Yala Enki** came out similarly at the weights, being beaten just over 5l carrying 3lb more, and arguably deserves extra credit having gone for home a long way out. The leading trio were 11l clear of **Rons Dream**, with another 8l back to defending champion **Raz De Maree**.

19 Paddy's Rewards Club "Sugar Paddy" Chase (Grade 1) (2m1f) Leopardstown (IRE) December 27 (Good)

1 **Simply Ned** 11-11-12 Mark Walsh
2 **Footpad** 6-11-12 R Walsh
3 **Ordinary World** 8-11-12 R Blackmore
16/1, EvensF, 25/1. ½l, 4¾l. 7 ran. 4:02 (Nicky Richards).

Simply Ned had won this race 12 months earlier on the rightful disqualification of Min to show his love of Leopardstown and he claimed another major scalp in **Footpad**. Unbeaten as a novice when winning the 2018 Racing Post Arkle, Footpad had suffered a nasty overreach when disappointing first time out and that setback seemed to catch him out as he tied up in the final 100 yards having done everything right, although another setback when only eighth in the Ryanair still leaves him with plenty to prove in open company. Simply Ned was only third at the last, but **Great Field** fell when seemingly beating a retreat and he finished strongly to cut down the runner-up, with the pair 4¾l clear of **Ordinary World** and **Castlegrace Paddy**.

20 Savills Chase (Grade 1) (3m) Leopardstown (IRE) December 28 (Good)

1 **Kemboy** 6-11-10 David Mullins
2 **Monalee** 7-11-10 Noel Fehily

SIMPLY NED (left): runs down Footpad in a thriller at Leopardstown

3 **Road To Respect** 7-11-10 S Flanagan
8/1, 11/2, 9/4F. 7½l, hd. 11 ran. 6:06
(W P Mullins).

A breakthrough performance from **Kemboy**, who was helped by a smart tactical ride but still ran out a remarkably easy winner of a slowly run race and would prove it was no fluke with his wins at Aintree and Punchestown. With no early pace on, Kemboy made rapid headway to go to the front just before halfway and dictated the race from then on, quickening clear superbly from the second-last as the rest finished in a heap behind. **Road To Respect** rallied well after a stumble after the third-last had ended his chances, almost getting up for second ahead of **Monalee**, with **Bellshill** also better than the bare form after a good return from eight months out. **Outlander** was fifth ahead of **The Storyteller** and **Coney Island**, with **Balko Des Flos** and **Shattered Love** well below their best.

21 Squared Financial Christmas Hurdle (Grade 1) (3m)

Leopardstown (IRE) December 28 (Good To Yielding)

1 **Apple's Jade** 6-11-3 Jack Kennedy
2 **Early Doors** 5-11-10 Mark Walsh
3 **Bapaume** 5-11-10 Noel Fehily
8/13F, 22/1, 8/1. 26l, 3¼l. 7 ran. 6:01
(Gordon Elliott).

Apple's Jade hadn't really convinced when winning this race 12 months earlier on her only previous run over 3m and this proved nothing new about her ability at the trip as she was gifted a clear lead by all bar **Faugheen**, who fell two out when still holding every chance. Apple's Jade came home strongly enough from that point to suggest Faugheen would have done well to beat her, but she was never seriously tested with nothing else ever put into the race, coming home 26l clear of **Early Doors** and **Bapaume** despite clocking only a modest time.

22 Ryanair Hurdle (Grade 1) (2m)

Leopardstown (IRE) December 29 (Good To Yielding)

1 **Sharjah** 5-11-10 Mr P W Mullins
2 **Supasundae** 8-11-10 Robbie Power
3 **Tombstone** 8-11-10 Davy Russell
6/1, 7/2, 66/1. 3¾l, 1¾l. 6 ran. 3:55
(W P Mullins).

A second Grade 1 victory for **Sharjah**, who saw off a much deeper field than he had faced in the Morgiana, albeit one without a real star once **Samcro**'s early-season struggles had come to a head with his tame fifth followed by the diagnosis of a lung infection. Held up in rear, Sharjah made smooth headway and ran on well to beat **Supasundae**, who was outpaced before staying on past **Tombstone** into second. The below-par **Melon** was only fourth ahead of Samcro and **Petit Mouchoir**.

23 Dornan Engineering Relkeel Hurdle (Grade 2) (2m4f56y)

Cheltenham January 1 (Good To Soft)

1 **Midnight Shadow** 6-11-6 Danny Cook
2 **Wholestone** 8-11-6 Daryl Jacob
3 **Old Guard** 8-11-6 Harry Cobden
8/1, 6/4F, 7/2. 2¼l, ½l. 6 ran. 4:58
(Sue Smith).

An impressive victory for **Midnight Shadow**, who comfortably saw off several solid performers for the grade. Running over 2m4f for only the second time – with his first run also working out well as he beat subsequent County Hurdle winner Ch'Tibello at Aintree – Midnight Shadow looked a stayer of some potential as he quickened up well to beat **Wholestone** and **Old Guard**, with **Thomas Campbell** and **Clyne** next.

24 The New One Unibet Hurdle (registered as the Champion Hurdle Trial) (Grade 2) (2m144y)

Haydock January 19 (Good To Soft)

1 **Global Citizen** 7-11-8 David Bass
2 **Silver Streak** 6-11-8 Adam Wedge
3 **Western Ryder** 7-11-4 Richard Johnson
3/1, 5/2J, 5/2J. 3l, 9l. 5 ran. 3:44
(Ben Pauling).

A great clash between two progressive hurdlers in **Global Citizen** and **Silver Streak**, with Global Citizen's superior jumping probably making the difference as the runner-up paid for a couple of late errors. Global Citizen benefited from less aggressive tactics than those employed in the Christmas Hurdle and ran out a ready winner, although Silver Streak would have gone close but for a couple of late errors and proved much the best of the pair when they were thrust into the Champion Hurdle, franking this form with a fine third. It was 9l back to **Western Ryder** with another 10l to **Mohaayed**, that pair struggling to reproduce high-class handicap form in Graded company.

25 Matchbook Clarence House Chase (Grade 1) (2m167y)

Ascot January 19 (Good To Soft)

1 **Altior** 9-11-7 Nico de Boinville
2 **Fox Norton** 9-11-7 Robbie Power

3 **Diego Du Charmil** 7-11-7 Harry Cobden
1/10F, 10/1, 16/1. 7l, 34l. 3 ran. 4:06
(Nicky Henderson).

Easy pickings for **Altior**, who had scared off most meaningful opposition and duly strolled home despite some worrying signs as he jumped markedly left at times. Victorious at 1-8 in the Desert Orchid Chase at Kempton since his Tingle Creek win, Altior was even shorter at 1-10 and anyone taking such odds never had any cause for concern as he made all the running to beat **Fox Norton**, having his first run in more than a year, and the outclassed **Diego Du Charmil**.

26 BetBright Trial Cotswold Chase (Grade 2) (3m1f56y)

Cheltenham January 26 (Good To Soft)

1 **Frodon** 7-11-6 Bryony Frost
2 **Elegant Escape** 7-11-4 Tom O'Brien
3 **Terrefort** 6-11-3 Daryl Jacob
9/4, 2/1F, 4/1. ¾l, 2¼l. 6 ran. 6:35
(Paul Nicholls).

Another front-running masterclass from **Frodon**, who had too much speed for **Elegant Escape** and just about lasted home on this step up in trip. Jumping superbly in front, Frodon was pushed clear two out and had enough in hand to hold off Elegant Escape, although he didn't see it out well enough to persuade connections to stick to their original plan to go for the Gold Cup – a wise rethink! Elegant Escape was outpaced before staying on again past **Terrefort**, who got back on track after a poor reappearance without being good enough to build on his strong novice campaign.

27 galliardhomes.com Cleeve Hurdle (Grade 2) (2m7f213y)

Cheltenham January 26 (Good To Soft)

1 **Paisley Park** 7-11-6 Aidan Coleman
2 **West Approach** 9-11-0 Tom Scudamore
3 **Black Op** 8-11-3 Noel Fehily
100/30F, 20/1, 11/2. 12l, 2l. 12 ran. 5:59
(Emma Lavelle).

Paisley Park had flopped in the Albert Bartlett as a novice, but returning to Cheltenham's seriously stiff test and getting a strong gallop to run off saw him move on to the next level in stunning fashion. Paisley Park faced a deeper field than at Ascot, albeit one lacking another proper Grade 1 stayer with **Sam Spinner** still feeling his way back to form, and this time he annihilated the opposition. Nudged along briefly after the third-last, Paisley Park soon got into overdrive and powered away from his old rival **West Approach** in the straight, with **Black Op**, back over hurdles after an aborted chase campaign, in third and another 10l back to Sam Spinner and **Lil Rockerfeller**. **Midnight Shadow** was already struggling to make an impression and looked booked for sixth when badly hampered at the last by **Unowhatimeanharry**, who broke a blood vessel, with **Aux Ptits Soins** and **Wholestone** also well beaten.

28 BHP Insurance Irish Champion Hurdle (Grade 1) (2m)

Leopardstown (IRE) February 2 (Good To Yielding)

1 **Apple's Jade** 7-11-3 Jack Kennedy
2 **Supasundae** 9-11-10 Robbie Power
3 **Petit Mouchoir** 8-11-10 R Blackmore
8/11F, 4/1, 12/1. 16l, 5l. 6 ran. 3:44
(Gordon Elliott).

Apple's Jade showed her versatility by successfully dropping back to the minimum trip and produced a sensational performance as she thrashed old rival **Supasundae**. Apple's Jade made all the running yet again, but this time her main rivals were much closer approaching the home turn and were simply blown away from that point by the mare's relentless galloping, with an excellent Time Test figure adding substance. Supasundae finished a tired second ahead of **Petit Mouchoir** and the below-par **Melon**.

29 Ladbrokes Dublin Chase (Grade 1) (2m1f)

Leopardstown (IRE) February 2 (Good)

1 **Min** 8-11-10 R Walsh
2 **Ordinary World** 9-11-10 R Blackmore
3 **Saint Calvados** 6-11-10 Gavin Sheehan
4/9F, 12/1, 4/1. 6l, 6l. 5 ran. 4:00
(W P Mullins).

A race overshadowed by a fatal injury suffered by **Special Tiara**, which made this an even more straightforward task for **Min**. With **Castlegrace Paddy** falling at the first, Min was left with just two rivals and easily mastered the front-running **Saint Calvados**, with **Ordinary World** running on to finish a never-threatening second.

30 Unibet Irish Gold Cup (Chase) (Grade 1) (3m)

Leopardstown (IRE) February 3 (Good)

1 **Bellshill** 9-11-10 R Walsh
2 **Road To Respect** 8-11-10 S Flanagan
3 **The Storyteller** 8-11-10 Davy Russell
2/1, 5/6F, 8/1. shd, 7½l. 4 ran. 6:06
(W P Mullins).

Just four runners and none of them neces-

BELLSHILL: Irish Gold Cup winner – but in a moderate four-runner race

sarily the cream of Irish staying chasers, but this still produced a terrific finish as **Bellshill** got up to deny **Road To Respect**. Sharper for his comeback run in the Savills Chase, Bellshill jumped more fluently than Road To Respect and that helped him to come out on top with a powerful late run as the pair pulled 7½l clear of **The Storyteller**, with **Outlander** behind.

31 Betfair Ascot Chase (Grade 1) (2m5f8y)

Ascot February 16 (Good To Soft)

1 **Cyrname** 7-11-7 Harry Cobden
2 **Waiting Patiently** 8-11-7 Brian Hughes
3 **Fox Norton** 9-11-7 Robbie Power
3/1, 11/8F, 6/1. 17l, 1¼l. 6 ran. 5:10 (Paul Nicholls).

An extraordinary performance from **Cyrname**, who had won a handicap over course and distance by 21l four weeks earlier and delivered another demolition job in top-class company. Cyrname set searching fractions in front and achieved an impressive Time Test figure for the second time – it was telling that both placed horses had been ridden in the last two places early on, whereas those ridden closest to Cyrname folded – yet he was able to pull away again once pressed in the straight for a sensational victory. **Waiting Patiently** admittedly failed to frank the form after plugging on for a distant second ahead of **Fox Norton**, while **Politologue** was below his best in fourth and **Charbel** paid the price for trying to go with Cyrname as he dropped out in fifth ahead of **Aso**.

32 Betfair Hurdle (Handicap) (Grade 3) (1m7f152y)

Ascot February 16 (Good To Soft)

1 **Al Dancer** 6-11-8 Sam Twiston-Davies
2 **Magic Dancer** 7-10-3 Richard Patrick
3 **Blu Cavalier** 9-11-2 Jonjo O'Neill Jr
5/2F, 20/1, 100/1. 3¾l, 2½l. 14 ran. 3:44 (Nigel Twiston-Davies).

Run the week after its original date at Newbury, this race was still feeling the effects of the equine flu problems with several contenders ruled out having not had up-to-date vaccinations, but **Al Dancer** was still a good winner. The eighth novice to win in ten years but the joint-second highest-rated to do so in that time – below only My Tent Or Yours – Al Dancer did really well to find a smart turn of

BEWARE THE BEAR: suited by big emphasis on stamina in the Ultima

foot from the last having raced more keenly than ideal in rear. That said, the fact that **Magic Dancer**, without a win all season, and 100-1 shot **Blu Cavalier** chased him home suggests this wasn't as competitive as usual and fourth-placed **Getaway Trump** was given too much to do.

33 Betfair Denman Chase (Grade 2) (2m7f180y)

Ascot February 16 (Good To Soft)

1 **Clan Des Obeaux** 7-11-6 Harry Cobden
2 **Terrefort** 6-11-3 Nico de Boinville
3 **Ballyhill** 8-11-4 Sam Twiston-Davies
2/5F, 5/2, 25/1. 11l, 25l. 4 ran. 5:59
(Paul Nicholls).

Clan Des Obeaux added a bit more substance to his campaign as he produced a similarly strong-travelling display to the one that had seen him win the King George, albeit in a much weaker race. In receipt of 3lb and entitled to come on for his run in the Cotswold Chase, the front-running **Terrefort** could still never get Clan Des Obeaux off the bridle and the 2-5 favourite effortlessly eased clear from the last in hugely impressive fashion.

34 NetBet Casino National Spirit Hurdle (Grade 2) (2m3f49y)

Fontwell February 24 (Good To Soft)

1 **Vision Des Flos** 6-11-5 Tom Scudamore
2 **If The Cap Fits** 7-11-9 Noel Fehily
3 **Lil Rockerfeller** 8-11-9 Bryony Frost
7/2, 13/8F, 8/1. 1½l, 2¼l. 6 ran. 4:50
(Colin Tizzard).

A strong race for the grade fought out by two horses who would prove Grade 1 stayers when stepped up in trip, most notably **If The Cap Fits**, who was felt to be below his best by his trainer after a recent flu jab but still only narrowly failed to concede 4lb to **Vision Des Flos**. Not for the first time, If The Cap Fits didn't travel particularly well even over this longer trip – he had done much of his previous racing over just 2m – and having got up close home in the Ascot Hurdle against **Old Guard**, he couldn't pull off the same feat against a classier rival in Vision Des Flos, who relished the distance having also come up short several times over 2m. **Lil**

Rockerfeller was a close third, with a 13l gap back to the below-par Old Guard.

35 Ultima Handicap Chase (Grade 3) (3m1f)

Cheltenham March 12 (Soft)

1 **Beware The Bear** 9-11-8 J McGrath
2 **Vintage Clouds** 9-11-1 Danny Cook
3 **Lake View Lad** 9-11-12 Henry Brooke
10/1, 16/1, 25/1. 1¼l, 2l. 24 ran. 6:39
(Nicky Henderson).

Having both made the frame 12 months earlier, **Beware The Bear** and **Vintage Clouds** stepped forward to fight out the finish this time as a huge emphasis on stamina perhaps suited more battle-hardened types. Beware The Bear had often found things happening too quickly in top races, including when staying on into fourth in 2018, but he had been sharpened up by headgear and a wind operation earlier in the season and just outstayed Vintage Clouds, who had been in front three out on his first run after wind surgery. Rowland Meyrick winner **Lake View Lad** was next ahead of **Big River** as proven staying chase form very much came to the fore, while Grand National runner-up **Magic Of Light** didn't quite jump well enough in seventh.

36 Unibet Champion Hurdle Challenge Trophy (Grade 1) (2m87y)

Cheltenham March 12 (Soft)

1 **Espoir D'Allen** 5-11-10 Mark Walsh
2 **Melon** 7-11-10 Paul Townend
3 **Silver Streak** 6-11-10 Adam Wedge
16/1, 20/1, 80/1. 15l, nk. 10 ran. 3:59
(Gavin Cromwell).

A major anti-climax as the three standout runners beforehand all failed to make the first three, with dual champion **Buveur D'Air** even falling at the third, but it was still no mean feat for **Espoir D'Allen** to beat what was left by a record winning margin of 15l. A tragic loss over the summer, Espoir D'Allen had taken a big leap forward after progressing quietly at a lower level earlier in the season, travelling strongly and cruised into the lead two out before roaring up the hill ahead of 2018 runner-up **Melon**, whose switch to prominent tactics at least sparked a partial return to form, and solid yardstick **Silver Streak**. **Laurina** did best of the big three but, having looked outstanding in mares' company, she was still a disappointment in fourth, with **Verdana Blue** only fifth after the ground went against her. It was just a shame that neither **Apple's Jade** nor Buveur D'Air could run to their best to really test the winner, with a mystifying performance from Apple's Jade in sixth explained later by a dirty scope and Buveur D'Air's early fall also bringing down the luckless **Sharjah**. **Global Citizen** was last of the seven finishers, with **Brain Power** pulled up.

37 OLBG Mares' Hurdle (registered as the David Nicholson Mares' Hurdle) (Grade 1) (2m3f200y)

Cheltenham March 12 (Soft)

1 **Roksana** 7-11-5 Harry Skelton
2 **Stormy Ireland** 5-11-5 Paul Townend
3 **Good Thyne Tara** 9-11-5 R Blackmore
10/1, 7/1, 25/1. 2¼l, 2l. 14 ran. 5:00
(Dan Skelton).

Huge drama as red-hot favourite **Benie Des Dieux** fell at the last with the race at her mercy, handing her crown to **Roksana**. Having scrambled home in the race in 2018, Benie Des Dieux had travelled far more strongly this time and looked set for an impressive win, still going easily in a 3l lead, when she crumpled on landing at the final flight. Roksana was the one to take advantage and would prove herself a top-class mare in her own right when going down by just a head in open Grade 1 company at Aintree, with Benie Des Dieux's stablemates **Stormy Ireland** and **Good Thyne Tara** the only mares in a deep field to finish within 16l of her.

38 Coral Cup (Handicap Hurdle) (Grade 3) (2m5f)

Cheltenham March 13 (Soft)

1 **William Henry** 9-11-10 Nico de Boinville
2 **Wicklow Brave** 10-11-12 Mr P W Mullins
3 **Ballyandy** 8-11-7 Sam Twiston-Davies
28/1, 28/1, 14/1. shd, ½l. 25 ran. 5:08
(Nicky Henderson).

A tough race in which experience of these big-field handicaps was key, with **William Henry** improving on his close fourth in the race in 2018. Having had an awful lot to do turning for home, William Henry produced a withering late run to get up on the line at the expense of former County and Betfair Hurdle winners in **Wicklow Brave** and **Ballyandy**, but this probably took less winning than most major handicaps and his limitations were exposed in Grade 1 company at Aintree. **Brio Conti** was fourth ahead of **Canardier** and **Apple's Shakira**, whose sixth is particularly noteworthy as the only horse younger than seven to finish in the top half of the field from nine to try.

39 Betway Queen Mother Champion Chase (Grade 1) (1m7f199y)

Cheltenham March 13 (Soft)

1 **Altior** 9-11-10 Nico de Boinville
2 **Politologue** 8-11-10 Harry Cobden
3 **Sceau Royal** 7-11-10 Daryl Jacob
4/11F, 11/1, 16/1. 1¾l, 1¾l. 9 ran. 3:58 (Nicky Henderson).

Altior retained his title with one of his least impressive performances as he got himself out of self-inflicted trouble to beat **Politologue** and **Sceau Royal**. In a bizarre race tactically, every horse bar the front-running **Saint Calvados** started a long way behind Altior, gifting him a possibly decisive head-start but seemingly affecting his concentration as he made a hash of the water jump and made several other errors, including at the second-last after being left in front three out. Joined on both sides at that point and even headed by Sceau Royal at the last, Altior finally delivered in trademark fashion up the hill as he asserted in the final 100 yards to beat Politologue, who bounced back to form with a huge run in second at a track where he had never run to his best previously, and Sceau Royal, who proved a revelation in third. It was 6l back to **Hell's Kitchen** and the disappointing **Min**, who appeared to resent being ridden with more restraint than usual, while **God's Own** would also have finished close to that pair but for going wrong between the last two. **Castlegrace Paddy** was sixth ahead of Saint Calvados and **Ordinary World**.

40 Pertemps Network Final (Handicap Hurdle) (Grade 3) (2m7f213y)

Cheltenham March 14 (Good To Soft)

1 **Sire Du Berlais** 7-11-9 Barry Geraghty
2 **Tobefair** 9-11-0 Tom Bellamy
3 **Not Many Left** 6-11-5 Mark Walsh
4/1F, 40/1, 16/1. nk, 1¼l. 24 ran. 5:52 (Gordon Elliott).

The successful conclusion of a year-long plan with **Sire Du Berlais**, who had caught the eye in fourth in the 2018 Martin Pipe and made amends 12 months later having been laid out for this longer race, proving sufficiently ahead of his mark to win a red-hot handicap. Sire Du Berlais was done no favours when squeezed up three out and had plenty to do turning for home, but he showed class and stamina to just deny another fast finisher in **Tobefair**, who won well at the track the following month despite a 6lb rise. Stronger travellers like **Not Many Left** and

FRODON: receiving deserved acclaim after his Ryanair Chase victory

Cuneo were perhaps delivered too early, with Not Many Left going on to run well at Grade 1 level at Punchestown.

41 Ryanair Chase (registered as the Festival Trophy) (Grade 1) (2m4f127y)

Cheltenham March 14 (Good To Soft)
1 **Frodon** 7-11-10 Bryony Frost
2 **Aso** 9-11-10 Charlie Deutsch
3 **Road To Respect** 8-11-10 S Flanagan
9/2, 33/1, 9/2. 1¼l, 1¾l. 12 ran. 5:09
(Paul Nicholls).

A fiercely competitive renewal with several leading contenders from other Grade 1 races rerouted here and **Frodon** dispelled any doubts about whether his form in handicaps put him in this league, producing another thrilling win. Frodon again made nearly all the running with an exhibition display of jumping and fought back superbly when headed by **Aso**, forging clear in the final 100 yards. Aso had also produced his best form in handicaps, winning at Newbury and Cheltenham earlier in the season, but behind the pair were proven Grade 1 performers in **Road To Respect**, **Monalee** and **Un De Sceaux**, the last-named finding this trip just beyond his optimum on soft ground while the other two continued to come up just short in the top races regardless of distance. It was 5l back to **Coney Island**, with **Balko Des Flos** and **Footpad**, who broke blood vessels, the only others to finish, while **Charbel**, **The Storyteller** and **Terrefort** were pulled up.

42 Sun Racing Stayers' Hurdle (Grade 1) (2m7f213y)

Cheltenham March 14 (Good To Soft)
1 **Paisley Park** 7-11-10 Aidan Coleman
2 **Sam Spinner** 7-11-10 Joe Colliver
3 **Faugheen** 11-11-10 R Walsh
11/8F, 33/1, 4/1. 2¾l, 4l. 18 ran. 5:53
(Emma Lavelle).

The culmination of a remarkable campaign for **Paisley Park**, who had started it rated just 140 but ended it with a fifth successive win, repeating his Cleeve Hurdle heroics on the biggest stage. This was a remarkably similar performance as Paisley Park came off the bridle coming down the hill but stormed home in the straight, not even a bad mistake at the last able to knock him off his stride. **Sam Spinner** ran a tremendous race in second, bouncing back to the form of his 2017 Long Walk Hurdle victory as he helped to force a solid gallop and went down valiantly, while the veteran **Faugheen** ran his best race of

SIRUH DU LAC: hugely progressive

the season in third and just finished ahead of younger stablemate **Bapaume**. That quartet pulled 11l clear of **Wholestone**, **Bacardys** and **Supasundae**, with **West Approach**, **Kilbricken Storm**, **Top Notch** and **Black Op** among the disappointments further back.

43 Brown Advisory & Merriebelle Stable Plate (Handicap Chase) (Grade 3) (2m4f127y)

Cheltenham March 14 (Good To Soft)
1 **Siruh Du Lac** 6-10-8 Lizzie Kelly
2 **Janika** 6-11-12 Daryl Jacob
3 **Spiritofthegames** 7-11-3 Harry Skelton
9/2, 3/1F, 6/1. ¾l, 2¼l. 22 ran. 5:14
(Nick Williams).

A thrilling finish served up by two of the most progressive chasers of the season as **Siruh Du Lac** and **Janika**, first and second in a course-and-distance handicap in January, filled the same places again. Both were higher in the weights as a result, but they still looked to be keeping well ahead of the handicapper as they dominated what appeared a quality race with the first four in the market filling first four places and pulling clear, Siruh Du Lac again leading the way as he made virtually all the running and held on gamely. Janika pushed him all the way ahead of **Spiritofthegames** and **Eamon An Cnoic**, with 8l back to **Didero Vallis**.

44 Randox Health County Handicap Hurdle (Grade 3) (2m179y)

Cheltenham March 15 (Good To Soft)

1 **Ch'Tibello** 8-11-5 Harry Skelton
2 **We Have A Dream** 5-11-11 Daryl Jacob
3 **Countister** 7-10-6 Barry Geraghty
12/1, 14/1, 18/1. 1½l, hd. 24 ran. 4:04
(Dan Skelton).

Class came to the fore as two proven Graded performers finished first and second in a strong renewal, with **Ch'Tibello** proving better-handicapped than **We Have A Dream**. Still good enough to finish a close third in the Aintree Hurdle yet able to run off a mark of just 146 after dropping 11lb in little over a year, Ch'Tibello made smooth headway from the rear and ran on well to beat We Have A Dream, who ran a cracker under a big weight but sadly died on the gallops soon after, and the inexperienced mare **Countister**, with the trio 4½l clear of a strong chasing pack. There were several solid handicappers behind, including the 2018 winner **Mohaather** in seventh off a 14lb higher mark after another big handicap win and the 2018 Triumph Hurdle runner-up **Mr Adjudicator**, who went on to win big races at Punchestown and Auteuil.

45 Magners Cheltenham Gold Cup Chase (Grade 1) (3m2f70y)

Cheltenham March 15 (Good To Soft)

1 **Al Boum Photo** 7-11-10 Paul Townend
2 **Anibale Fly** 9-11-10 Barry Geraghty
3 **Bristol De Mai** 8-11-10 Daryl Jacob
12/1, 22/1, 18/1. 2½l, 3¾l. 16 ran. 6:39
(W P Mullins).

A wide-open Gold Cup with doubts about many of the leading contenders which all came to fruition, helping **Al Boum Photo** to win what may well prove to have been a slightly sub-standard renewal. Al Boum Photo was at least progressive and unexposed, running for only the second time since his novice campaign as he made good headway to lead turning for home and stayed on strongly to beat the 2018 third **Anibale Fly**, who managed to get closer in what was probably a slightly weaker race. **Bristol De Mai** ran a fine race in third ahead of **Native River**, who was slowly away and had to expend more energy than ideal in getting to the front as he was rousted along virtually throughout, though he still rallied bravely to reclaim fourth from **Clan Des Obeaux**, who finished slightly tamely after travelling strongly to the straight. It was 15l back to **Elegant Escape** and **Yala Enki**, while **Presenting Percy**, on the back of a remarkable preparation that had seen him run in only a single race over hurdles all season, faded badly and finished lame, beating only **Shattered Love** of the nine finishers. **Might Bite** raced prominently for a long way but was pulled up after weakening quickly, as were **Bellshill**, whose jumping fell apart, and **Thistlecrack**. **Kemboy** unseated his rider at the first, while **Invitation Only** sadly suffered a fatal fall at the tenth when bringing down **Definitly Red**.

46 Johnny Henderson Grand Annual Challenge Cup (Handicap Chase) (Grade 3) (2m62y)

Cheltenham March 15 (Good To Soft)

1 **Croco Bay** 12-10-12 Kielan Woods
2 **Bun Doran** 8-11-7 Paddy Brennan
3 **Brelan D'As** 8-10-9 Bryony Frost
66/1, 11/1, 8/1. 1½l, 2½l. 19 ran. 4:05
(Ben Case).

A remarkable victory for 12-year-old **Croco Bay**, who had run only once since finishing fifth in the race two years earlier, although he probably dropped lucky in a weak renewal with the first four all well beaten in similar handicaps at subsequent spring festivals and fifth-placed **Not Another Muddle** doing well to finish so close after a string of errors. Croco Bay was always prominent in a race strongly favouring those up with the pace, with **Theo** and **Whatswrongwithyou** the best of those held up off an unusually steady gallop.

47 Betway Bowl (Chase) (Grade 1) (3m210y)

Aintree April 4 (Good To Soft)

1 **Kemboy** 7-11-7 R Walsh
2 **Clan Des Obeaux** 7-11-7 Harry Cobden
3 **Balko Des Flos** 8-11-7 R Blackmore
9/4F, 11/4, 20/1. 9l, hd. 6 ran. 6:35
(W P Mullins).

Falling at the first in the Gold Cup proved a blessing in disguise for **Kemboy**, who was much fresher than chief rivals **Clan Des Obeaux** and **Bristol De Mai**, though his

SUPASUNDAE (near): won this head-to-head with a disappointing Buveur D'Air

subsequent Punchestown success suggests he might have been the best horse in the race anyway. Making the running at a much more even tempo than he had done at Leopardstown, Kemboy jumped well and was still on the bridle at the final fence before scooting clear for a resounding triumph. However, Clan Des Obeaux and Bristol De Mai had had infinitely harder races at Cheltenham and seemed to struggle to back that up given they were split by **Balko Des Flos**, who would probably have even hung on for second but for a mistake at the last. It was another 5l back to **Road To Respect**, while **Elegant Escape** was well beaten after jumping repeatedly to his right.

48 Betway Aintree Hurdle (Grade 1) (2m4f)

Aintree April 4 (Soft)

1 **Supasundae** 9-11-7 Robbie Power
2 **Buveur D'Air** 8-11-7 Barry Geraghty
3 **Ch'Tibello** 8-11-7 Harry Skelton
15/2, 5/6F, 14/1. 1 1/4l, ½l. 7 ran. 5:10
(Mrs John Harrington).

This race rather fell apart and **Supasundae**, hugely consistent but far more often the bridesmaid at the top level, managed to take advantage at the expense of the disappointing **Buveur D'Air**. With **Faugheen** pulled up suffering from an irregular heartbeat and **Melon** falling when holding a narrow lead three out, Supasundae was left to gamely hold off Buveur D'Air, who was hampered by Melon's fall but didn't lose enough ground or momentum for that to be a real excuse, perhaps finding this longer trip just too much of a test. The County Hurdle winner **Ch'Tibello** was just ½l further back before a 31l gap to the disappointing **Summerville Boy** and **Silver Streak**, who looked a patent non-stayer.

49 JLT Chase (registered as the Melling Chase) (Grade 1) (2m3f200y)

Aintree April 5 (Soft)

1 **Min** 8-11-7 R Walsh
2 **Politologue** 8-11-7 Harry Cobden
3 **Waiting Patiently** 8-11-7 Brian Hughes
2/1F, 5/2, 9/4. 20l, 9l. 6 ran. 5:02
(W P Mullins).

A runaway victory for **Min**, who had been outstayed in the race 12 months earlier after racing keenly but proved in his element over the trip when given his head in front. Min jumped superbly in front and cruised clear from the second-last, appearing to surpass even his very best 2m form as an outstanding time lent substance to the performance. That said, the race rather fell apart behind him with **Politologue** a clear second despite being found to have bled from the nose. **Waiting Patiently** failed to build on his return at Ascot in third despite having the ground in his favour, while **Hell's Kitchen** and **God's Own** were well beaten and **Top Notch** was pulled up.

50 Randox Health Topham Handicap Chase (Grade 3) (2m5f19y)
Aintree April 5 (Soft)
1 **Cadmium** 7-11-2 Paul Townend
2 **Sub Lieutenant** 10-11-5 R Blackmore
3 **Doitforthevillage** 10-10-4 Tom O'Brien
8/1, 25/1, 25/1. 6l, 3¼l. 27 ran. 5:31
(W P Mullins).

A notable performance from **Cadmium**, who was the third-youngest winner of what is often a brutal test all century that had also seen no winner rated any higher in that time. Cadmium again managed to leave his useful small-field form behind when running in a handicap for only the second time since a devastating 8l triumph at Punchestown in 2018, winning with similar ease as he jumped superbly in front and made virtually all the running. **Sub Lieutenant**, down to a good mark on his best form, showed plenty of his old spark in second, while **Janika** could never quite land a blow in fourth.

51 Ryanair Stayers Hurdle (registered as the Liverpool Hurdle) (Grade 1) (3m149y)
Aintree April 6 (Good)
1 **If The Cap Fits** 7-11-7 Sean Bowen
2 **Roksana** 7-11-0 Harry Skelton
3 **Apple's Jade** 7-11-0 Jack Kennedy
7/1, 10/1, 5/6F. hd, nk. 15 ran. 5:58
(Harry Fry).

Connections finally got the trip right for **If The Cap Fits**, who had looked every inch a stayer in the making earlier in the season and took a big step forward on his first run over 3m to beat the mares **Roksana** and **Apple's Jade**. Travelling strongly between the last two, If The Cap Fits made a terrible blunder at the final flight and did really well to get up close home, winning with a little more in hand than the bare form. Roksana seemed to improve on her Mares' Hurdle win going back up in trip, whereas Apple's Jade, who made a bold bid to make nearly all the running, just seemed to have her stamina shortcomings exposed, though she wasn't helped by being hassled up front by **Sam Spinner**. That trio pulled 11l clear of Coral Cup winner **William Henry**, with another progressive handicapper, **Lord Napier**, and **West Approach** next and Sam Spinner a below-par eighth. **Wholestone**, **Unowhatimeanharry** and **Kilbricken Storm** were among those further back.

52 Randox Health Grand National (Handicap Chase) (Grade 3) (4m2f74y)
Aintree April 6 (Good To Soft)
1 **Tiger Roll** 9-11-5 Davy Russell
2 **Magic Of Light** 8-10-11 Paddy Kennedy
3 **Rathvinden** 11-11-0 R Walsh
4/1F, 66/1, 8/1. 2¾l, 2¼l. 40 ran. 9:01
(Gordon Elliott).

History for **Tiger Roll**, who became the first horse since Red Rum to win back-to-back Nationals and did it off a mark just 1lb lower than Many Clouds, who was one of only two winners since Red Rum to carry more weight to victory. Having travelled remarkably smoothly through the race and seen out the trip much better than 12 months earlier on this quicker surface, Tiger Roll was also a much easier winner than Many Clouds, suggesting this was a performance of Grade 1 standard to underline the apparent improvement he had shown in winning over hurdles and Cheltenham's cross-country course earlier in the season. The proximity of **Magic Of Light** in second is the only reason to question the form as she ploughed through many of the fences and still had the strength to stay on into second, though that might be a testament to the mare's quality given third-placed **Rathvinden** was a leading fancy off a mark 5lb ahead of the handicapper and the trio pulled 11l clear of Becher Chase winner **Walk In The Mill** and Gold Cup runner-up **Anibale Fly**, with 2017 winner **One For Arthur** next. The hard-luck stories came at the fourth-last, with **Ballyoptic** and **Pleasant Company** both departing when firmly in contention.

53 Coral Scottish Grand National (Handicap Chase) (Grade 3) (3m7f176y)
Ayr April 13 (Good)
1 **Takingrisks** 10-10-1 Sean Quinlan
2 **Crosspark** 9-10-8 Harry Skelton
3 **Cloth Cap** 7-10-0 Richie McLernon
25/1, 10/1, 9/1. 4l, nse. 23 ran. 8:02
(Nicky Richards).

With a ten-year-old winning at 25-1, it would be easy to write off this race as a fluke result, but that might well turn out to underestimate **Takingrisks**. Totally unexposed over mara-

VERDANA BLUE: hard to beat when granted good ground and a flat track

thon trips and with his form over shorter earlier in the season working out well, Takingrisks did really well to overcome a significant blunder at the first as he crept into contention and saw out the trip really well having led four out. **Crosspark** had won the Eider on his previous start but was still just outstayed, clinging on to third ahead of youngsters **Cloth Cap** and **Blue Flight**. Those four pulled 13l clear of **Big River**, who kept on well having got too far back, with **Vintage Clouds** sixth.

54 CPMS Scottish Champion Hurdle (Limited Handicap) (Grade 2) (2m)

Ayr April 13 (Good)

1 **Verdana Blue** 7-11-3 Connor Brace
2 **Dino Velvet** 6-10-4 Paddy Brennan
3 **Equus Amadeus** 6-10-2 Stan Sheppard
4/1F, 14/1, 16/1. 7l, 1¼l. 14 ran. 3:39
(Nicky Henderson).

A tremendous performance from **Verdana Blue**, who backed up her Christmas Hurdle defeat of Buveur D'Air when back on a flat track and suitable ground. Held up early, Verdana Blue eased through to lead after the second-last and quickened clear in hugely impressive fashion, readily defying a mark upwards of 10lb higher than all her rivals bar the bitterly disappointing **Brain Power**.

55 BoyleSports Irish Grand National (Extended Handicap Chase) (Grade A) (3m5f)

Fairyhouse (IRE) April 22 (Good To Yielding)

1 **Burrows Saint** 6-10-8 R Walsh
2 **Isleofhopendreams** 12-10-7 D Mullins
3 **Acapella Bourgeois** 9-11-0 J Burke
6/1F, 20/1, 18/1. 1¾l, 5½l. 30 ran. 7:47
(W P Mullins).

Only three horses mattered from a long way out, all trained by Willie Mullins in a remarkable show of dominance, as **Burrows Saint** beat stablemates **Isleofhopendreams** and **Acapella Bourgeois**. A novice running for only the fourth time over fences, Burrows Saint defied his inexperience with a tremendous performance as he travelled supremely well to lead on the bridle three out and just pulled out enough under pressure. Isleofhopendreams had stopped in front when looking set to win in 2018, but he saw out the trip better on quicker ground to take second again ahead of Acapella Bourgeois, who was back to form having taken time to come to hand following a move to the Mullins yard.

KEMBOY: produced probably the best performance by a staying chaser all season when he saw off Gold Cup hero Al Boum Photo at Punchestown

The rest were well strung out, with a 21l gap back to **Snugsborough Benny**.

56 bet365 Gold Cup (Handicap Chase) (Grade 3) (3m4f166y)

Sandown April 27 (Good)

1 **Talkischeap** 7-10-11 Wayne Hutchinson
2 **The Young Master** 10-10-5Mr S W-Cohen
3 **Step Back** 9-10-11 Nico de Boinville
7/1, 8/1, 10/1. 10l, 9l. 15 ran. 7:15
(Alan King).

A stunning performance from **Talkischeap**, who relished a stiff test of stamina as he stormed to a resounding victory over two past winners with what looked a strong field well strung out. Only four horses – all from the first seven in the market – finished within 30l of the winner, emphasising the strong gallop, yet the first three were up with the pace throughout and, having tracked the leaders, Talkischeap quickened clear in hugely impressive fashion from the last, making a mockery of the mark of 145 he had earned when beaten in good novice races early in the season. **The Young Master**, back to form earlier in the season but still 6lb lower than when winning the race in 2016, was a fine second ahead of 2018 winner **Step Back**, who ran his best race of the campaign, with another 10l gap back to **Give Me A Copper** in fourth.

57 bet365 Celebration Chase (Grade 1) (1m7f119y)

Sandown April 27 (Good)

1 **Altior** 9-11-7 Nico de Boinville
2 **Sceau Royal** 7-11-7 Daryl Jacob
3 **God's Own** 11-11-7 Paddy Brennan
1/6F, 100/30, 20/1. 2½l, 3l. 5 ran. 3:50
(Nicky Henderson).

A record 19th successive victory over jumps for **Altior** as he beat the mark set by Big Buck's, albeit with a performance rather in keeping with his slightly underwhelming second half of the season. Forced to make the running, Altior jumped boldly in front – albeit to his right again – but came off the bridle and was challenged by **Sceau Royal** before finally asserting up the hill. **God's Own** and **Vosne Romanee** also finished within 7½l.

58 bet365 Oaksey Chase (Grade 2) (for the Menorah Challenge Trophy) (2m6f164y)

Sandown April 27 (Good)

1 **Black Corton** 8-11-3 Bryony Frost
2 **Gold Present** 9-11-4 Jeremiah McGrath
3 **San Benedeto** 8-11-4 Harry Cobden
15/8F, 10/1, 5/1. 11l, 5l. 7 ran. 5:39
(Paul Nicholls).

Black Corton had endured a somewhat frustrating campaign, finishing second in four of his five races and exposing his level as just below his best given he was realistically campaigned, but this proved a good opportunity in a weak race for the grade. Always prominent, Black Corton led three out and drew clear of **Gold Present** and **San Benedeto**, with **Charbel**'s jumping falling apart in sixth as his campaign tailed off disappointingly.

59 bet365 Select Hurdle (Grade 2) (2m5f110y)

Sandown April 27 (Good)

1 **Younevercall** 8-11-0 David Bass
2 **On The Blind Side** 7-11-3 N de Boinville
3 **Thomas Campbell** 7-11-4 James Bowen
9/4F, 11/4, 12/1. 9l, 12l. 7 ran. 5:16
(Kim Bailey).

An unusual Grade 2 with few of the horses having competed at that level elsewhere during the campaign and most with plenty to prove, but the first two managed to pull well clear, led by **Younevercall**. Progressive in handicaps prior to finishing eighth in the Long Walk and given a wind operation since then, Younevercall gradually wound up the pace in front and drew clear from the second-last, with **On The Blind Side**, back over hurdles after a poor chasing campaign, in turn pulling away from **Thomas Campbell** and **Black Op**.

60 BoyleSports Champion Chase (Grade 1) (2m)

Punchestown (IRE) April 30 (Yielding)

1 **Un De Sceaux** 11-11-12 Paul Townend
2 **Min** 8-11-13 R Walsh
3 **Castlegrace Paddy** 8-11-12 Davy Russell
11/4, 8/13F, 20/1. 4l, 38l. 6 ran. 4:09
(W P Mullins).

A heartwarming victory for **Un De Sceaux**, who defied his advancing years to claim his second successive win in the race in typically exuberant fashion. Un De Sceaux perhaps benefited from a much lighter campaign than odds-on favourite **Min**, who couldn't quite live up to his billing in second, but Un De Sceaux had nonetheless set a solid gallop that led to him coming home upwards of 40l clear of **Castlegrace Paddy**, **Great Field** and **Hell's Kitchen**.

61 Coral Punchestown Gold Cup (Chase) (Grade 1) (3m120y)

Punchestown (IRE) May 1 (Yielding To Soft)

1 **Kemboy** 7-11-10 R Walsh
2 **Al Boum Photo** 7-11-10 Paul Townend
3 **The Storyteller** 8-11-10 Davy Russell
13/8F, 7/4, 25/1. 2l, 22l. 8 ran. 6:25
(W P Mullins).

This race was overshadowed by Ruby Walsh immediately announcing his retirement, but the battle between **Kemboy** and **Al Boum Photo** shouldn't be forgotten either as the Aintree and Cheltenham winners served up a cracker. Kemboy again made much of the running and, though joined briefly by Al Boum Photo two out, he proved just the strongest from that point, managing a third Grade 1 win with probably the best performance by a staying chaser all season. Al Boum Photo went down fighting and had good horses a long way behind him, with a 22l gap back to **The Storyteller** and **Bellshill**, whose jumping let him down again. **Definitly Red** and **Sub Lieutenant** were behind and **Monalee** was also struggling when pulled up.

62 Ladbrokes Champion Stayers Hurdle (Grade 1) (3m)

Punchestown (IRE) May 2 (Good To Yielding)

1 **Unowhatimeanharry** 11-11-10 M Walsh
2 **Bacardys** 8-11-10 Mr P W Mullins
3 **Bapaume** 6-11-10 Paul Townend
16/1, 8/1, 9/4F. 3l, hd. 10 ran. 6:01
(Harry Fry).

With top mares Apple's Jade and Benie Des Dieux heading elsewhere at Punchestown, this exposed the shortcomings of Ireland's male staying hurdlers as the veteran **Unowhatimeanharry** managed to claim what may well prove one last hurrah. Unowhatimeanharry had looked out of sorts since winning a weak Long Distance Hurdle at Newbury early in the season, but he bounced back under more prominent tactics and stayed on strongly. Another British raider, **Vision Des Flos**, might well have chased him home but for a bad mistake at the last, allowing **Bacardys** to run on into second ahead of **Bapaume**, **Killultagh Vic** and **Aux Ptits Soins**.

63 Betdaq Punchestown Champion Hurdle (Grade 1) (2m)

Punchestown (IRE) May 3 (Good To Yielding)

1 **Buveur D'Air** 8-11-12 Davy Russell
2 **Supasundae** 9-11-12 Robbie Power
3 **Wicklow Brave** 10-11-12 Mr P W Mullins
2/1J, 9/2, 16/1. 2½l, 1¼l. 7 ran. 3:54
(Nicky Henderson).

Buveur D'Air managed to end a disappointing campaign on a high as he proved too strong for a fairly modest Irish defence with Espoir D'Allen and Sharjah absent and **Apple's Jade** below her best. With most of his rivals better over further, Buveur D'Air was able to put the race to bed quickly with a smart turn of foot before the last and was a comfortable winner as **Supasundae** stayed on into second ahead of Coral Cup runner-up **Wicklow Brave** and **Petit Mouchoir**, who had been stepped up in trip since his Irish Champion Hurdle third. Apple's Jade never looked like confirming that form, unusually being ridden just off the pace and keeping on for a one-paced fifth ahead of **Summerville Boy** and the disappointing **Melon**.

64 Irish Stallion Farms EBF Annie Power Mares Champion Hurdle (Grade 1) (2m4f)

Punchestown (IRE) May 4 (Good To Yielding)

1 **Benie Des Dieux** 8-11-7 Paul Townend
2 **Stormy Ireland** 5-11-7 Robbie Power
3 **Good Thyne Tara** 9-11-7 Danny Mullins
2/5F, 7/2, 8/1. 9½l, 15l. 5 ran. 4:49
(W P Mullins).

Redemption for **Benie Des Dieux**, who again looked a better mare than the one who had won this prize more narrowly 12 months earlier, albeit in a race that lacked much depth, and would back up that impression with a brilliant French Champion Hurdle win at Auteuil. So unlucky to fall at Cheltenham, Benie Des Dieux had no such mishaps this time as she comfortably mastered **Stormy Ireland**, who again ran her race from the front yet was beaten much further than at Cheltenham, just like third-placed **Good Thyne Tara**. Disappointingly, there was just one British challenger as **With Discretion** finished a distant fourth on her first run in more than a year.

BENIE DES DIEUX: made amends for her Cheltenham disaster

Big-race index

All horses placed or commented on in our big-race review section, with race numbers

ROAD TO RESPECT: Grade 1 winner but came up short in the very top races

Novice review by Dylan Hill

1 Racing Post Arkle Trophy Trial Novices' Chase (registered as the November Novices' Chase) (Grade 2) (1m7f199y) Cheltenham November 18 (Good)
1 **Lalor** 6-11-2 Richard Johnson
2 **Dynamite Dollars** 5-11-2 Harry Cobden
3 **Claimantakinforgan** 6-11-2 J McGrath
11/2, 3/1, 11/8F. 7l, 4l. 5 ran. 3:50
(Kayley Woollacott).

A hugely impressive chasing debut from **Lalor**, enough to see him go off favourite for the Arkle despite being beaten in his only run in between, although he may just have been flattered by some below-par runs among the opposition. Subsequent Grade 1 winners **Dynamite Dollars** and **Defi Du Seuil** were up against Lalor, but connections reflected they hadn't made enough use of Dynamite Dollars and Defi Du Seuil looked more in need of the experience on his first run over fences. In contrast, Lalor jumped superbly and was always in charge, but his poor performances after this leave him with plenty to prove.

2 Sky Bet Supreme Trial Novices' Hurdle (registered as the Sharp Novices' Hurdle) (Grade 2) (2m87y) Cheltenham November 18 (Good)
1 **Elixir De Nutz** 4-11-0 Harry Cobden
2 **Itchy Feet** 4-11-5 Gavin Sheehan
3 **Seddon** 5-11-0 A P Heskin
5/1, 5/1, EvensF. 1¼l, 3l. 5 ran. 3:51
(Colin Tizzard).

An early clash between two of the very best 2m novice hurdlers in Britain, with Tolworth winner **Elixir De Nutz** beating Supreme third **Itchy Feet**. Elixir De Nutz made all the running and ran on strongly to beat Itchy Feet, whose effort conceding 5lb to the winner was clearly underrated given he went off at 25-1 when running his mighty race at Cheltenham. **Seddon** was sent off favourite but lacked the pace of the first two.

3 baroneracing.com Drinmore Novice Chase (Grade 1) (2m4f) Fairyhouse (IRE) December 2 (Good)
1 **Delta Work** 5-11-10 Davy Russell
2 **Le Richebourg** 5-11-10 Barry Geraghty
3 **Jetz** 6-11-10 Robbie Power
100/30, 11/4F, 9/1. ½l, 8l. 11 ran. 5:00
(Gordon Elliott).

This race brought together the best staying novice chaser in Ireland and the dominant force over 2m from the first half of the season, with **Delta Work** too good for **Le Richebourg** over the intermediate trip. Delta Work was always going well and would have won more comfortably but for a bad mistake at the last, doing well to rally past Le Richebourg, though he didn't have to match the level of his top-class 3m form with the runner-up below his best. **Jetz** was 8l back in third, while **Discorama** needed to go up in trip after a tame fifth.

4 randoxhealth.com Henry VIII Novices' Chase (Grade 1) (1m7f119y) Sandown December 8 (Soft)
1 **Dynamite Dollars** 5-11-2 Harry Cobden
2 **Ornua** 7-11-2 Dylan Robinson
3 **Lalor** 6-11-2 Richard Johnson
9/2, 9/1, 8/11F. 1¾l, 10l. 6 ran. 3:59
(Paul Nicholls).

A rematch between **Lalor** and **Dynamite Dollars** with a very different outcome, this one looking a far more reliable formline as

ANGELS BREATH: still has quite a reputation but form didn't work out last term

Dynamite Dollars saw off subsequent Grade 1 winner **Ornua** and would go on to win a pair of Grade 2 races under a penalty, notably against Kalashnikov at Kempton, before his season was ended early by injury. Ridden more prominently than at Cheltenham and challenging Ornua from the third-last, Dynamite Dollars finally wore down the front-running second in the final 100 yards, doing really well to beat an opponent who would last home under the same tactics in the Grade 1 novice at Aintree in April. Lalor seemed run off his feet in a disappointing third.

5 Sky Bet Supreme Trial Novices' Hurdle (registered as the Kennel Gate Novices' Hurdle) (Grade 2) (1m7f152y)
Ascot December 21 (Soft)

1 **Angels Breath** 4-11-0 Nico de Boinville
2 **Danny Kirwan** 5-11-0 Harry Cobden
3 **Seddon** 5-11-0 Paddy Brennan
6/4F, 6/1, 11/4. 4½l, 3½l. 9 ran. 3:54
(Nicky Henderson).

This performance saw **Angels Breath** hold favouritism for the Supreme for much of the winter, but there was little substance to the race and he would get found out subsequently. Angels Breath drew clear of his rivals in impressive fashion, but four hurdles had been omitted anyway and the eight runners went on to win just one out of 21 races between them – a Class 4 novice at Kelso – later in the season.

6 32Red Kauto Star Novices' Chase (Grade 1) (3m)
Kempton December 26 (Good To Soft)

1 **La Bague Au Roi** 7-11-0 Richard Johnson
2 **Topofthegame** 6-11-7 Harry Cobden
3 **Santini** 6-11-7 Nico de Boinville
8/1, 5/1, 11/10F. 1½l, 2l. 7 ran. 6:01
(Warren Greatrex).

A top-class contest with subsequent RSA Chase one-two **Topofthegame** and **Santini** beaten by **La Bague Au Roi**. The brilliant mare is probably best at this trip, but she also showed the speed to be effective over 2m4f several times during the season – even winning an admittedly sub-standard Flogas at Leopardstown for a second Grade 1 win

– and that was a massive weapon as Santini, in particular, looked short of toe around this sharp track. That said, Topofthegame managed to travel just as strongly as he would later at Cheltenham and it appeared to be La Bague Au Roi's terrific battling qualities that saw her come out on top of that desperately tight duel as she rallied gamely in a thriller. Santini stayed on really well in third, with the leading trio 11l clear of **Red Indian** and **Bags Groove**, whose trainer felt the race came too soon after a win just two weeks earlier.

7 Coral Finale Juvenile Hurdle (Grade 1) (2m11y)

Chepstow December 27 (Soft)

1 **Quel Destin** 3-11-0 Sam Twiston-Davies
2 **Adjali** 3-11-0 Daryl Jacob
3 **Arverne** 3-11-0 Aidan Coleman
7/4, 4/6F, 10/1. nk, 22l. 5 ran. 4:01
(Paul Nicholls).

Quel Destin proved dominant among the British-trained juveniles in the first half of the season and gained a deserved Grade 1 victory in the middle of a five-race winning streak. Quel Destin made all the running and showed real tenacity to hold off the persistent challenge of **Adjali**, although he was put in his place when only fifth in the Triumph and the shortcomings of this form were also shown by the runner-up's struggles in similar races.

8 Betway Challow Novices' Hurdle (Grade 1) (2m4f118y)

Newbury December 29 (Good To Soft)

1 **Champ** 6-11-7 Barry Geraghty
2 **Getaway Trump** 5-11-7 Harry Cobden
3 **Kateson** 5-11-7 Tom Scudamore
EvensF, 10/1, 9/2. 2½l, ¾l. 7 ran. 5:10
(Nicky Henderson).

A really strong renewal won in terrific fashion by **Champ**, who was much too sharp for his rivals in a slowly run race despite looking every inch a three-miler when he won the Sefton and facing a serious rival in **Getaway Trump** who would subsequently thrive over shorter. Champ quickened away from Getaway Trump, who went on to win a good novice handicap at Sandown when back at 2m, while **Brewin'upastorm** also franked the form with several fine efforts after his close fourth and the well-beaten **Coolanly** and **Alsa Mix** had already won Grade 2 races before being outclassed in this stronger company. **Kateson** struggled to build on his third and was perhaps flattered by being ridden handiest of the four principals.

9 Unibet Tolworth Novices' Hurdle (Grade 1) (1m7f216y)

Sandown January 5 (Soft)

1 **Elixir De Nutz** 5-11-7 Tom O'Brien
2 **Grand Sancy** 5-11-7 Sam Twiston-Davies
3 **Southfield Stone** 6-11-7 Harry Cobden
3/1, 4/1, 6/1. ½l, 3¼l. 5 ran. 4:05
(Colin Tizzard).

Another terrific all-the-way win from **Elixir De Nutz**, which might have been underrated at the time but saw him become an increasingly strong candidate for the Supreme until ruled out by injury as the form was franked more than once. Jumping notably well in front, Elixir De Nutz gamely held off **Grand Sancy**, who went on to win a Grade 2 in open company in an admittedly modest Kingwell Hurdle, with the pair pulling clear of **Southfield Stone**, who claimed the scalp of Angels Breath in the Dovecote when in receipt of 5lb. There was another 8l back to the disappointing favourite **Rathhill**.

10 Lawlor's of Naas Novice Hurdle (Grade 1) (2m4f)

Naas (IRE) January 6 (Good)

1 **Battleoverdoyen** 6-11-10 Jack Kennedy
2 **Sams Profile** 5-11-7 B J Cooper
3 **Getareason** 6-11-10 Noel Fehily
2/1F, 16/1, 12/1. 2¾l, 2l. 8 ran. 4:43
(Gordon Elliott).

This was a desperately weak Grade 1 and, while **Battleoverdoyen** marked himself a fine prospect with a comfortable victory, there was nothing in the form to justify him being anything like the 3-1 favourite he was made when flopping at Cheltenham. Battleoverdoyen was always going well and stayed on strongly, but little over 8l covered the first six, of whom **Sams Profile** was unlucky not to get much closer – he made several mistakes and was badly short of room at a key stage – and only First Approach did anything else for the form subsequently among the rest. Battleoverdoyen's market rival **Tornado Flyer** was badly out of sorts and pulled up.

11 McCoy Contractors 2019 Construction News Award Finalist Hampton Novices' Chase (Listed) (3m)

Warwick January 12 (Good)

1 **Ok Corral** 9-11-0 Mr Derek O'Connor
2 **Secret Investor** 7-11-0 Harry Cobden
3 **Rocky's Treasure** 8-11-5 David Bass
11/4, 100/30, 6/5F. 6l, 8l. 4 ran. 5:56
(Nicky Henderson).

A quality line-up for a Listed race and **Ok Corral** ran out a hugely impressive winner.

With crack amateur Derek O'Connor in the plate as connections plotted what proved a fruitless plan for the National Hunt Chase at Cheltenham, Ok Corral looked perfectly at home over this shorter trip as he travelled strongly and had mastered **Secret Investor** even before that horse made a hash of the last. **Rocky's Treasure**, who had a 17l Grade 2 win at Doncaster and a second to Santini as his previous two runs, seemed to run his race in third behind two classier horses.

12 Ballymore Novices' Hurdle (registered as the Classic Novices' Hurdle) (Grade 2) (2m4f56y)

Cheltenham January 26 (Good To Soft)

1 **Birchdale** 5-11-5 Barry Geraghty
2 **Buster Valentine** 6-11-5 Leighton Aspell
3 **Jarveys Plate** 6-11-10 Paddy Brennan
2/1, 16/1, 5/2. 18l, ½l. 5 ran. 5:04
(Nicky Henderson).

Connections probably opted for the wrong target at Cheltenham with **Birchdale**, who didn't appear to stay in the Albert Bartlett but showed he was much better than that with this victory. It's still hard to be sure Birchdale would have won without **Brewin'upastorm** falling at the last, but he was only narrowly behind and staying on strongly against a rock-solid yardstick – and subsequent Ballymore fourth – at the time. Birchdale was left to come home 18l clear of **Buster Valentine** and Ballymore ninth **Jarveys Plate**.

13 888Sport Scilly Isles Novices' Chase (Grade 1) (2m4f10y)

Sandown February 2 (Soft)

1 **Defi Du Seuil** 6-11-4 Barry Geraghty
2 **Lostintranslation** 7-11-4 Richard Johnson
3 **Vinndication** 6-11-4 David Bass
7/2, 2/1, 11/8F. ¾l, 2½l. 5 ran. 5:12
(Philip Hobbs).

Defi Du Seuil and **Lostintranslation** served up one of the best rivalries of the whole season and this first showed Defi Du Seuil's superiority over this trip as he reversed the form of a narrow defeat in the Dipper at Cheltenham on New Year's Day. Outstayed in their previous clash after hitting the front two out, Defi Du Seuil was ridden with more restraint this time and put his greater speed to better use, allowing his rival a lead until after the last when he produced a fine turn of foot to win a top-class race. **Vinndication** lost his unbeaten record but surpassed anything he had previously achieved by coming third in much the strongest race he had contested, with a 24l gap back to **Mulcahys Hill**.

14 Frank Ward Solicitors Arkle Novice Chase (Grade 1) (2m1f)

Leopardstown (IRE) February 2 (Good)

1 **Le Richebourg** 6-11-10 Mark Walsh
2 **Us And Them** 6-11-10 J J Slevin
3 **Mengli Khan** 6-11-10 Jack Kennedy
11/10F, 11/1, 5/1. 7l, 13l. 6 ran. 4:00
(Joseph Patrick O'Brien).

A Grade 1 double for **Le Richebourg**, who proved dynamite when down in trip after his near miss in the Drinmore before unfortunately being ruled out of the Racing Post Arkle through injury. With Cheltenham winner Duc Des Genievres absent and fellow top novice Chacun Pour Soi yet to get going, Le Richebourg was up against only the same set of rivals he had beaten over Christmas, but he won really well off a good gallop and had taken the measure of subsequent Ryanair Gold Cup winner **Voix Du Reve** when that one fell at the last. From that point Le Richebourg quickened away from Arkle runner-up **Us And Them** on the run-in, with a 13l gap back to **Mengli Khan** in third.

15 Nathaniel Lacy & Partners Solicitors 50,000 Cheltenham Bonus For Stable Staff Novice Hurdle (Grade 1) (2m6f)

Leopardstown (IRE) February 2 (Good To Yielding)

1 **Commander Of Fleet** 5-11-8 J Kennedy
2 **Rhinestone** 6-11-10 Mark Walsh
3 **Gallant John Joe** 6-11-10 Barry Browne
13/2, 10/1, 33/1. ½l, 6l. 16 ran. 5:20
(Gordon Elliott).

A tight battle between **Commander Of Fleet** and **Rhinestone**, with the subsequent Albert Bartlett runner-up proving a really strong stayer as he got on top close home. Rhinestone ran a stormer in defeat, showing himself to be a high-class novice as well despite going wrong at Cheltenham, with the pair pulling 6l clear of **Gallant John Joe** and the progressive **First Approach**, who was sharpened up by first-time cheekpieces. Champion Bumper winner **Relegate**, expected to relish going up in trip, certainly did that but had got too far back before staying on strongly into a close fifth, with an 11l gap back to the rest.

16 Chanelle Pharma Novice Hurdle (Grade 1) (2m)

Leopardstown (IRE) February 3 (Good)

1 **Klassical Dream** 5-11-9 R Walsh
2 **Aramon** 6-11-10 Paul Townend
3 **Vision D'Honneur** 5-11-9 Jack Kennedy
9/4F, 5/2, 3/1. hd, 6l. 7 ran. 3:48

(W P Mullins).

The closest **Klassical Dream** came to defeat all season as he scrambled home from **Aramon**. Klassical Dream lacked the brilliance he would show at Cheltenham and Punchestown, but he showed terrific battling qualities to rally after being headed on the run-in and still beat a high-class opponent in Aramon, who had won a course-and-distance Grade 1 over Christmas by 10l and ran another fine race in second. The pair pulled 6l clear of **Vision D'Honneur**.

17 Albert Bartlett Prestige Novices' Hurdle (Grade 2) (3m58y)

Haydock February 16 (Good)

1 **Lisnagar Oscar** 6-10-12 Sean Bowen
2 **Ask Ben** 6-11-1 Kielan Woods
3 **Stoney Mountain** 6-10-12 Andrew Tinker
6/1, 6/1, 6/1. 10l, 4l. 9 ran. 6:08
(Rebecca Curtis).

A terrific performance from **Lisnagar Oscar**, who was probably better than he managed to show at Cheltenham and Aintree as he relished this quicker surface. Much improved since finishing second to **Rockpoint** in a Grade 2 at Cheltenham on just his second run over hurdles, Lisnagar Oscar led two out and drew clear of **Ask Ben** and **Stoney Treasure**, who had been a much closer to Beakstown in another Grade 2 at Warwick. Rockpoint was a well-beaten sixth this time, with Challow Hurdle third **Kateson** a below-par seventh.

18 888Sport Pendil Novices' Chase (Grade 2) (2m4f110y)

Kempton February 23 (Good)

1 **Bags Groove** 8-11-5 Noel Fehily
2 **Castafiore** 6-10-12 Paul O'Brien
3 **Good Man Pat** 6-11-0 Wayne Hutchinson
7/4, 10/1, 5/1. 1½l, 3¾l. 4 ran. 5:02
(Harry Fry).

Some of the most solid form at this level all season was represented in this race and **Bags Groove**, who had excuses for two failures in Grade 1 races, proved himself a smart horse with a second Grade 2 win. Bags Groove was too good for **Castafiore**, who had also won at this level when beating a good yardstick in Jerrysback at Haydock more easily than Scilly Isles third Vinndication had managed previously at Ascot, while

LE RICHEBOURG: dynamite when dropped back in trip

DUC DES GENIEVRES: task made easier by early carnage in the Arkle

Secret Investor was let down by his jumping in fourth as he finished behind Bags Groove for a second time.

19 Sky Bet Supreme Novices' Hurdle (Grade 1) (2m87y)

Cheltenham March 12 (Soft)

1 **Klassical Dream** 5-11-7 R Walsh
2 **Thomas Darby** 6-11-7 Richard Johnson
3 **Itchy Feet** 5-11-7 Gavin Sheehan
6/1, 28/1, 25/1. 4½l, ½l. 16 ran. 3:59 (W P Mullins).

What had looked a fiercely competitive race was turned into a procession by **Klassical Dream**, who stormed to a comprehensive success. Klassical Dream was always to the fore, leading four out and taking command in the straight, and while there might have been questions about the form at the time – most of those behind had excuses and soft ground had been expected to suit the winner more than most – Klassical Dream's subsequent win at Punchestown suggested it would be harsh to hold that against him. That said, **Thomas Darby** (lame) and **Itchy Feet** (broke blood vessels) came home with physical issues after filling the places ahead of **Fakir D'Oudairies**, who went on to prove himself a top-class juvenile but couldn't take advantage of the weight allowance as he plugged on into fourth. **Felix Desjy** was badly affected by the standing start, meaning he was unable to adopt his preferred front-running role, and finished fifth ahead of **Aramon**, who didn't get home on the soft ground having moved into third two out. Those six were 11l clear of **Angels Breath** and **Mister Fisher**, with **Vision D'Honneur** and Betfair Hurdle winner **Al Dancer** among those further back.

20 Racing Post Arkle Challenge Trophy Novices' Chase (Grade 1) (1m7f199y)

Cheltenham March 12 (Soft)

1 **Duc Des Genievres** 6-11-4 Paul Townend
2 **Us And Them** 6-11-4 J J Slevin
3 **Articulum** 9-11-4 David Mullins
5/1, 14/1, 25/1. 13l, 3¾l. 12 ran. 3:58 (W P Mullins).

A remarkably comfortable victory for **Duc Des Genievres**, though what had already looked a poor renewal was made significantly weaker at the sixth when subsequent Aintree winners **Ornua** and **Kalashnikov** departed and Duc Des Genievres's subsequent third at Punchestown raised further doubts about just how much he achieved. The field contained just one runner who had won a Graded race last time out (**Glen Forsa** in a three-runner race in which his only serious rival, Kalashnikov, flopped) and none had been rated higher than 152 over hurdles, but Duc Des Genievres at least proved head and shoulders above what was left, drawing clear from the second-last after a fine round of

KLASSICAL DREAM: turned the Supreme into a procession

jumping. In contrast, **Us And Them** jumped far too ponderously before managing to run through into second past **Articulum** and **Clondaw Castle**, with **Knocknanuss** and **Paloma Blue** next ahead of **Hardline**. The 2018 Supreme runner-up Kalashnikov, whose reputation had taken a hit with two below-par efforts going right-handed, was at least travelling much better when brought down by the front-running Ornua, while Glen Forsa, who had thrashed him at Sandown in the rearranged Kingmaker, had already unseated his rider by then at the fourth.

21 Close Brothers Novices' Handicap Chase (Listed) (2m4f44y)

Cheltenham March 12 (Soft)

1 **A Plus Tard** 5-11-5 Rachael Blackmore
2 **Tower Bridge** 6-11-3 J J Slevin
3 **Ben Dundee** 7-11-3 Keith Donoghue
5/1F, 6/1, 33/1. 16l, 4½l. 20 ran. 5:13
(Henry De Bromhead).

A stunning performance from **A Plus Tard**, one that might even have left connections regretting not going for the JLT as he stormed to a 16l victory. A Plus Tard certainly proved a long way ahead of his mark of 144, staying on strongly after he hit the front turning for home, and he is better than his subsequent third behind the brilliant Delta Work at Punchestown having appeared to find that longer trip beyond him. In a race run at an unusually steady gallop, the hold-up horses found plenty of trouble and **Tower Bridge**, having lost a good early pitch, did well to come from a long way back into second ahead of **Ben Dundee**. **The Russian Doyen** did best of the British-trained runners in fourth ahead of **Springtown Lake**.

22 National Hunt Challenge Cup (Amateur Riders' Novices' Chase) (Grade 2) (3m7f147y)

Cheltenham March 12 (Soft)

1 **Le Breuil** 7-11-6 Mr J J Codd
2 **Discorama** 6-11-6 Mr B O'Neill
3 **Jerrysback** 7-11-6 Mr D G Lavery
14/1, 9/2, 16/1. ½l, 47l. 18 ran. 8:42

DEFI DU SEUIL (left): got the better of old rival Lostintranslation

(Ben Pauling).

Controversy understandably followed this race, which became a serious war of attrition as a suicidal gallop in tough conditions led to just four horses getting round, two of them out on their feet, with **Le Breuil** and **Discorama** the last ones standing. Le Breuil proved just the strongest, showing tremendous courage to battle back after the more patiently ridden Discorama had looked likely to win on the run-in, though it's hard to know just what to make of the form in such a uniquely bruising race. **Jerrysback**, up markedly in trip having shown solid form at around 2m4f, travelled particularly well to the home turn even after being brought to a standstill and losing lots of ground when badly hampered with a circuit to go, eventually staggering home in third ahead of **Clondaw Cian**. **Atlanta Ablaze** was running a cracker in a close third when falling two out, but **Ok Corral** was always struggling in rear and was pulled up.

23 Ballymore Novices' Hurdle (Grade 1) (registered as the Baring Bingham Novices' Hurdle) (2m5f)

Cheltenham March 13 (Soft)

1 **City Island** 6-11-7 Mark Walsh
2 **Champ** 7-11-7 Barry Geraghty
3 **Bright Forecast** 5-11-7 Nico de Boinville
8/1, 9/2, 25/1. 2l, 2¼l. 16 ran. 5:06 (Martin Brassil).

This race didn't have a huge amount of strength to it, especially with the form of favourite **Battleoverdoyen** flopping, but the first four pulled clear even off a moderate gallop as **City Island** was just too good for **Champ**. The pair were always close enough to the pace and had the race between them from the second-last, with City Island, first past the post in all three previous runs over hurdles but yet to run at Graded level, doing well to see off his older, more experienced rival. **Bright Forecast** and **Brewin'upastorm** deserve plenty of credit for coming from further back, especially Bright Forecast as he stayed on well into third, and it was 9l back to **Sams Profile** and **Galvin**, with **Seddon** and **Jarveys Plate** among those behind. Battleoverdoyen was never travelling well – he was later reported to have lost a shoe – and was pulled up, as was **Beakstown**.

24 RSA Insurance Novices' Chase (Grade 1) (3m80y)

Cheltenham March 13 (Soft)

1 **Topofthegame** 7-11-4 Harry Cobden
2 **Santini** 7-11-4 Nico de Boinville
3 **Delta Work** 6-11-4 Davy Russell
4/1, 3/1, 15/8F. ½l, 1¾l. 12 ran. 6:17

(Paul Nicholls).

A vintage renewal featuring three hugely exciting young chasers who were locked together at the last and pulled well clear of their rivals, with **Topofthegame** brilliantly seeing off **Santini** and **Delta Work**. In front too soon when second to La Bague Au Roi at Kempton, Topofthegame had his challenge delayed much longer this time and showed no signs of stopping up the hill as he beat old rival Santini, who relished a stiffer track and ran a stormer considering he had had a nightmare preparation, missing an intended run in the Reynoldstown and suffering a late injury scare. Delta Work was on a par with the British pair, looking unlucky to get squeezed out at the last and finishing best of all once reorganised, and would underline his quality by brilliantly landing a third Grade 1 win at Punchestown soon after. The trio came 16l clear of a high-class yardstick in **Mister Malarky**, who had won the Reynoldstown and extended that superiority over **Now McGinty** before finishing second off 147 in a competitive handicap at Aintree, while **Mortal**, second to Delta Work in a 3m Grade 1 at Leopardstown over Christmas, also ran a solid race in fifth ahead of **Drovers Lane**, who travelled well but looked a non-stayer. **Top Ville Ben** was an early faller.

25 Boodles Juvenile Handicap Hurdle (registered as the Fred Winter) (Grade 3) (2m87y)

Cheltenham March 13 (Soft)

1 **Band Of Outlaws** 4-11-8 J J Slevin
2 **Coko Beach** 4-11-3 Jack Kennedy
3 **Ciel De Neige** 4-11-1 R Walsh
7/2F, 14/1, 17/2. 2l, 1¾l. 21 ran. 3:57
(Joseph Patrick O'Brien).

Joseph O'Brien's huge strength in depth in the juvenile department – he also housed the Triumph and Supreme favourites as well as the Triumph third – allowed him to save a potential Grade 1 horse for this race and **Band Of Outlaws** duly proved different class even under 11st 8lb. Having travelled supremely well as he made headway from the rear, Band Of Outlaws quickened clear from the last for a really impressive triumph and, while the first two both disappointed at Grade 1 level subsequently, the manner of victory in such a competitive handicap suggests he will prove a lot better than he showed at Aintree. **Coko Beach** and **Ciel De Neige** were next, with **King D'Argent** best of the British runners in fourth.

26 Weatherbys Champion Bumper (A Standard Open National Hunt Flat Race) (Grade 1) (2m87y)

Cheltenham March 13 (Soft)

1 **Envoi Allen** 5-11-5 Mr J J Codd
2 **Blue Sari** 4-10-11 Barry Geraghty
3 **Thyme Hill** 5-11-5 Richard Johnson
2/1F, 7/2, 20/1. ¾l, 1¾l. 14 ran. 3:55
(Gordon Elliott).

The smallest field in the history of this race contributed to an unusually pedestrian gallop and it bodes well for **Envoi Allen**, an archetypal chasing type, that he was still able to prevail in such a test of speed when pushed all the way by chief market rival **Blue Sari**. Envoi Allen was always going well and made strong headway to lead 3f out before holding off Blue Sari, who also ran a cracker having come from further back. **Abacadabras**, who had run out when challenging Envoi Allen in a Grade 2 at Leopardstown, was fourth this time after racing keenly, splitting leading British runners **Thyme Hill** and **The Glancing Queen**, the latter a notable fifth as the only mare in the field. **Sempo** was sixth, with a 9l gap back to the rest.

27 JLT Novices' Chase (Grade 1) (registered as the Golden Miller Novices' Chase) (2m3f168y)

Cheltenham March 14 (Good To Soft)

1 **Defi Du Seuil** 6-11-4 Barry Geraghty
2 **Lostintranslation** 7-11-4 Robbie Power
3 **Mengli Khan** 6-11-4 Jack Kennedy
3/1F, 4/1, 9/1. 2¼l, 7l. 10 ran. 4:59
(Philip Hobbs).

A second Cheltenham Festival victory for 2017 Triumph Hurdle winner **Defi Du Seuil**, completing a brilliant renaissance after a disastrous following campaign as he beat old rival **Lostintranslation**. The form of the pair's previous clashes proved red-hot as they pulled clear of a strong field – with Lostintranslation himself a subsequent Grade 1 winner at Aintree to frank it further – and Defi Du Seuil beat Lostintranslation more convincingly this time, storming up the hill after a mistake at the second-last had briefly threatened to derail him. Lostintranslation ran another fine race from the front and was 7l clear of **Mengli Khan**, who got much closer to Kalashnikov and La Bague Au Roi when third again at Aintree. **Kildisart** also franked the form at that meeting, winning a big handicap off 148, albeit when helped by the step up to 3m1f having found this trip on the sharp side as he got up for fourth on the line ahead of **Vinndication**, who acquitted himself well after a bad mistake. Those five pulled clear of subsequent Punchestown winner **Real Steel**, with **Castafiore** next, while **Voix Du Reve** unseated his rider three out when creeping into contention.

28 National Hunt Breeders Supported By Tattersalls Mares' Novices' Hurdle (Grade 2) (registered as the Dawn Run Mares' Novices' Hurdle) (2m179y)

Cheltenham March 14 (Good To Soft)

1 **Eglantine Du Seuil** 5-11-2 Noel Fehily
2 **Concertista** 5-11-2 Danny Mullins
3 **Tintangle** 6-11-5 Jack Kennedy
50/1, 66/1, 40/1. shd, 1¾l. 22 ran. 4:02
(W P Mullins).

Willie Mullins had won the previous three runnings of this race with short-priced favourites and struck again even without having a star in the division this time, although he was indebted to the absence of subsequent Fairyhouse winner Honeysuckle. The race proved wide-open and eminently winnable in her absence, with the first six covered by less than 6l and none of them shorter than 25-1, with 50-1 shot **Eglantine Du Seuil** producing a storming run from the rear to get up to beat 66-1 stablemate **Concertista**. **Tintangle**, carrying a penalty, was just the best horse at the weights in third ahead of **Black Tears** and leading British mare **Indefatigable**, while **Elfile** was also close in sixth and would reverse the form with the first, third and fourth at Fairyhouse having been ridden much more prominently than that trio here. **Epatante** and **Posh Trish** were the most notable disappointments as a fancied British challenge came to nothing.

29 JCB Triumph Hurdle (Grade 1) (2m179y)

Cheltenham March 15 (Good To Soft)

1 **Pentland Hills** 4-11-0 Nico de Boinville
2 **Coeur Sublime** 4-11-0 Davy Russell
3 **Gardens Of Babylon** 4-11-0 B Geraghty
20/1, 20/1, 9/1. 3l, 3¾l. 14 ran. 4:04
(Nicky Henderson).

A race overshadowed by the death of red-hot favourite **Sir Erec**, who had looked by far the best juvenile in Ireland, and that means **Pentland Hills** was probably underrated initially given he was only third favourite when following up at Aintree. A winner at Plumpton on his only previous start, Pentland Hills was seemingly just left to pick up the pieces with the second-string Irish contenders coming up short and the form of the established British candidates not up to much, but it was no mean feat for such an inexperienced horse to overcome a significant first-flight blunder and he was much the best in the race as he travelled strongly and quickened clear. The form behind was modest, though, with Irish pair **Coeur Sublime** and **Gardens Of Babylon** placed despite being 0-8 between them in Graded races by the end of the season. **Quel Destin** was only fifth, splitting 66-1 and 100-1 shots in **Nelson River** and **Ecco**, and he looked to have no excuses given his Grade 1 win at Chepstow had already been let down by Fakir D'Oudairies thrashing **Adjali** at Cheltenham in January, with Adjali only seventh here ahead of the below-par **French Made**.

30 Albert Bartlett Novices' Hurdle (Grade 1) (registered as the Spa Novices' Hurdle) (2m7f213y)

Cheltenham March 15 (Good To Soft)

1 **Minella Indo** 6-11-5 Rachael Blackmore
2 **Commander Of Fleet** 5-11-5 J Kennedy
3 **Allaho** 5-11-5 R Walsh
50/1, 4/1F, 8/1. 2l, 7l. 20 ran. 5:57
(Henry De Bromhead).

A surprise result but a top-class winner in **Minella Indo**, who hadn't looked a superstar when second to **Allaho** at Clonmel on his previous start but took a massive step forward to win what looked a strong renewal at 50-1. Minella Indo raced keenly and tanked his way to the front three out, but he still found remarkable reserves to hold off the persistent threat of **Commander Of Fleet** as the pair pulled clear of the rest and he would underline the strength of the form when following up at Punchestown. Allaho, close enough turning for home, was left behind from that point but stayed on well enough to take third ahead of **Dickie Diver**, with a couple of rock-solid yardsticks in Grade 2 winners **Lisnagar Oscar** and **Derrinross** next. **Ask Ben**, **First Approach** and **Rockpoint** were among those well beaten but at least got round, unlike **Rhinestone** and the patent non-stayer **Birchdale**, who were both pulled up.

31 Devenish Manifesto Novices' Chase (Grade 1) (2m3f200y)

Aintree April 4 (Good To Soft)

1 **Kalashnikov** 6-11-4 Jack Quinlan
2 **La Bague Au Roi** 8-10-11 R Johnson
3 **Mengli Khan** 6-11-4 Jack Kennedy
4/1, 7/4F, 7/1. 1¼l, 1¾l. 6 ran. 5:05
(Amy Murphy).

Hitherto disappointing over fences, **Kalashnikov** finally got things right as he had too much class for a stronger stayer in **La Bague Au Roi**. Much better going left-handed and avoiding the ill fortune that befell him in the Arkle, Kalashnikov produced a smart turn of foot between the last two to put the race to bed and just hung on despite tying up on the run-in. La Bague Au Roi proved a sitting duck in front but was still a creditable second ahead of **Mengli Khan**, who ran a fine race to finish a close third, with 27l back to **Bags Groove**, who was unsuited by heavy rain turning the ground increasingly soft, and **Spiritofthegames**. **Glen Forsa** had thrashed Kalashnikov in the rerouted Kingmaker at Sandown, but that was only a three-runner race and his jumping fell apart in a tougher test, leading to him being pulled up.

32 Doom Bar Anniversary 4YO Juvenile Hurdle (Grade 1) (2m209y)

Aintree April 4 (Good To Soft)

1 **Pentland Hills** 4-11-0 Nico de Boinville
2 **Fakir D'Oudairies** 4-11-0 Mark Walsh
3 **Christopher Wood** 4-11-0 Harry Cobden
11/4, 5/2, 10/1. nk, 6l. 9 ran. 4:13
(Nicky Henderson).

Pentland Hills followed up his Triumph Hurdle victory in a terrific battle with **Fakir D'Oudairies**, whose better-fancied stablemate **Band Of Outlaws** trailed home a disappointing fifth. Only third in the market despite his Cheltenham success, Pentland Hills proved there was no fluke about that victory as he wore down the front-running Fakir D'Oudairies in a terrific battle, with Fakir D'Oudairies in turn pulling 6l clear of the rest as he seemed to step up on his Supreme fourth under front-running tactics that brought his stamina to the fore. Band Of Outlaws was perhaps unsuited by such a test of stamina – especially with heavy rain leading the going to be changed to 'soft' soon after –and faded into fifth behind **Christopher Wood** and **Adjali**.

33 Betway Top Novices' Hurdle (Grade 1) (2m103y)

Aintree April 5 (Soft)

1 **Felix Desjy** 6-11-4 Jack Kennedy
2 **Aramon** 6-11-4 R Walsh
3 **Rouge Vif** 5-11-4 Daryl Jacob
7/2, 3/1F, 9/1. 1½l, 7l. 7 ran. 4:02
(Gordon Elliott).

A fascinating race fought out by two horses seemingly much improved from Cheltenham, notably **Felix Desjy**, who benefited from a return to his preferred front-running tactics and made all the running in fine style. In contrast,

PENTLAND HILLS: Aintree win proved he deserved far more credit

Aramon was ridden far more patiently than at Cheltenham and came home much better as a result, but he was unable to reel in Felix Desjy, who set a solid gallop and just held on despite tiring from the final flight. The pair pulled 7l clear of Grade 2 winner **Rouge Vif** and **Itchy Feet**, who failed to get close to the level of his Supreme third, while **Southfield Stone** trailed home last of seven.

34 Betway Mildmay Novices' Chase (Grade 1) (3m210y)

Aintree April 5 (Soft)

1 **Lostintranslation** 7-11-4 Robbie Power
2 **Topofthegame** 7-11-4 Harry Cobden
3 **Top Ville Ben** 7-11-4 Sean Quinlan
3/1, 10/11F, 14/1. 6l, ½l. 6 ran. 6:31
(Colin Tizzard).

Stepping up to 3m for the first time, **Lostintranslation** landed a thoroughly deserved maiden Grade 1 win after two fine efforts behind Defi Du Seuil as he comfortably saw off **Topofthegame**. With the RSA winner clearly below his best, Lostintranslation didn't necessarily need to improve on his high-class 2m4f form, but he certainly saw out the longer trip well as he eased past the long-time leader **Top Ville Ben** and quickly came clear when shaken up at the last. Topofthegame was always struggling but stuck on dourly to get up for second close home, with **Mr Whipped** fourth ahead of **Chris's Dream**.

35 Doom Bar Sefton Novices' Hurdle (Grade 1) (3m149y)

Aintree April 5 (Soft)

1 **Champ** 7-11-4 Mark Walsh
2 **Emitom** 5-11-4 Gavin Sheehan
3 **Lisnagar Oscar** 6-11-4 Sean Bowen
9/4F, 5/1, 11/2. 3l, 7l. 12 ran. 6:17
(Nicky Henderson).

Champ successfully stepped up to 3m for the first time in hugely impressive fashion, although he was perhaps favoured by a slow pace in what may prove a sub-standard renewal. Champ travelled with typical panache and just had to be ridden out having hit the front at the second-last, coming clear with **Emitom**, who was also going beyond around 2m4f for the first time. Stronger stayers behind were perhaps inconvenienced, most notably **Lisnagar Oscar**, who also failed to pick up as well as anticipated on the softest ground he had encountered since his hurdling debut. **Walk Away**, **Arthur Mac** and **Champagne Well** were the only others to finish within 38l of the winner.

36 Betway Mersey Novices' Hurdle (Grade 1) (2m4f)

Aintree April 6 (Good)

1 **Reserve Tank** 5-11-4 Robbie Power
2 **Brewin'upastorm** 6-11-4 R Johnson
3 **Angels Breath** 5-11-4 Nico de Boinville
20/1, 100/30, 11/4F. 3¼l, 2¼l. 9 ran. 4:50
(Colin Tizzard).

A weak race with just one top-six finisher from Cheltenham, but **Reserve Tank** still produced a smart performance to beat form horses **Brewin'upastorm** and **Angels Breath** and would follow up at Punchestown. Stepping up to Grade 1 level after winning his last two in a much lower grade, Reserve Tank was always prominent and, having led three out, he stayed on much too strongly for Brewin'upastorm, who ran another solid race in second. Angels Breath was typically keen as he stepped up in trip and could only keep at one pace in a dead-heat for third with **One For Rosie**, who had been a short-head second in the EBF Final at Sandown off 138 and ran to a similar level. **Kateson** was a disappointing seventh, albeit beaten only 11l.

37 Doom Bar Maghull Novices' Chase (Grade 1) (1m7ff176y)

Aintree April 6 (Good)

1 **Ornua** 8-11-4 Davy Russell
2 **Us And Them** 6-11-4 J J Slevin
3 **Destrier** 6-11-4 Harry Skelton
3/1J, 3/1J, 7/1. 1¾l, 1¼l. 7 ran. 3:50
(Henry De Bromhead).

Ornua became the second horse at Aintree to gain compensation for failing to get round in the Arkle as he got the better of Cheltenham runner-up **Us And Them** in a race that confirmed Ireland's dominance among the 2m novice chasers. Ornua made all the running, jumping superbly, and gamely held off Us And Them, who rallied well having struggled to keep tabs on the winner throughout. By no means the leading lights in the division in Ireland, Ornua and Us And Them were seriously challenged by only one of the British runners as **Destrier**, stepping up in class after two wins at a much lower level, finished a fine third and pulled 20l clear of **Clondaw Castle**, with **Knocknanuss** and **Lalor** behind.

38 Jordan Electrics Ltd Future Champion Novices' Chase (Grade 2) (2m4f110y)

Ayr April 13 (Good)

1 **Secret Investor** 7-11-0 Harry Cobden
2 **Louis' Vac Pouch** 7-11-0 J McGrath
3 **Monbeg Legend** 9-11-0 Nico de Boinville

CHAMP: favoured by a steady gallop when stepping up to 3m for the first time

2/1F, 12/1, 1½. 3¾l, 8l. 7 ran. 4:56 (Paul Nicholls).

Beaten at 11-10 and 6-4 at this level earlier in the season, Persian War Novices' Hurdle winner **Secret Investor** finally got things right over fences in good style. Let down by his jumping previously, Secret Investor was much better in that department and, having moved to the front five out, he stayed on well to beat **Louis' Vac Pouch,** who also did well to pull 8l clear of **Monbeg Legend** and **Ballywood**. **Castafiore** disappointed in fifth but was dismounted and appeared lame after the line.

39 Ryanair Gold Cup (Novice Chase) (Grade 1) (2m4f)

Fairyhouse (IRE) April 21 (Good To Yielding)

1 **Voix Du Reve** 7-11-10 R Walsh
2 **Real Steel** 6-11-10 Paul Townend
3 **Winter Escape** 8-11-10 Mark Walsh

9/4, 2/1F, 4/1. 5½l, 25l. 5 ran. 5:03 (W P Mullins).

Still in contention when departing in the JLT, **Voix Du Reve** gained rich compensation by winning a fairly soft Grade 1 in which the sole top-five finisher from Cheltenham, **Mengli Khan**, disappointed. **Real Steel**, sixth in the JLT and a winner at Punchestown after this race, still set a useful standard but couldn't get close to Voix Du Reve, who led four out and stayed on strongly for a decisive success. The pair pulled 25l clear of **Winter Escape** and Mengli Khan, who seemed to find it a race too far.

40 Irish Stallion Farms EBF Mares Novice Hurdle Championship Final (Grade 1) (2m4f)

Fairyhouse (IRE) April 21 (Good To Yielding)

1 **Honeysuckle** 5-11-7 Rachael Blackmore
2 **Elfile** 5-11-7 Jonathan Burke

MINELLA INDO: puts in a fine leap on the way to completing a Grade 1 double

3 **Eglantine Du Seuil** 5-11-7 R Walsh
6/4F, 20/1, 4/1. 5½l, 3l. 16 ran. 4:52
(Henry De Bromhead).

Honeysuckle had missed Cheltenham when her trainer wasn't happy with her but returned to make it four out of four over hurdles and proved herself the best novice mare by some distance, easing clear having jumped and travelled well throughout just off the pace. Cheltenham sixth **Elfile** ran a fine race in second and reversed form with **Eglantine Du Seuil**, **Tintangle** and **Black Tears**, although Tintangle did well to get close at all in fourth after some poor jumping.

41 Herald Champion Novice Hurdle (Grade 1) (2m100y)
Punchestown (IRE) April 30 (Yielding)

1 **Klassical Dream** 5-11-12 R Walsh
2 **Felix Desjy** 6-11-12 Jack Kennedy
3 **Mister Blue Sky** 5-11-12 Danny Mullins
8/13F, 11/2, 16/1. 5½l, 11l. 6 ran. 4:00
(W P Mullins).

This was a serious test for **Klassical Dream**, who had to hunt down Aintree winner **Felix Desjy** on much quicker ground than he had faced at Cheltenham, and he came through it with flying colours, arguably running out an even more impressive winner. Felix Desjy kept up a solid gallop that saw none of his other four rivals finish within 11l of him, yet Klassical Dream was able to ease up to him at the second-last and quickened into a decisive lead around the home turn before appearing to idle from the last as Felix Desky rallied. **Mister Blue Sky**, coming off a Grade 2 win at Fairyhouse, was a fair third, but **Aramon** perhaps found this one race too many as he trailed home last.

42 Dooley Insurance Group Champion Novice Chase (Grade 1) (3m)
Punchestown (IRE) Apr 30 (Yielding To Soft)

1 **Delta Work** 6-11-10 Davy Russell
2 **Discorama** 6-11-10 B J Cooper
3 **A Plus Tard** 5-11-5 Rachael Blackmore
13/8F, 12/1, 9/4. 12l, 2¼l. 8 ran. 6:41
(Gordon Elliott).

A stunning performance from **Delta Work**, who proved much too good for a decent field including runaway Cheltenham winner **A Plus Tard.** That horse clearly failed to stay this longer 3m trip despite only a moderate gallop as he faded between the last two, but Delta Work always had his measure throughout anyway, travelling strongly as he took up the running three out and powering on to a bloodless victory. National Hunt Chase runner-up **Discorama** ran a cracker in second, staying on strongly from the rear, with **Drovers Lane** the only other horse to finish having run well for a long way in fourth. **Articulum**, **Getabird**, **Winter Escape** and **Chris's Dream** were all pulled up.

43 Irish Daily Mirror Novice Hurdle (Grade 1) (3m)

Punchestown (IRE) May 1 (Yielding)

1 **Minella Indo** 6-11-10 Rachael Blackmore
2 **Allaho** 5-11-10 R Walsh
3 **Carefully Selected** 7-11-10 Paul Townend
5/1, 11/4F, 9/2. 2l, 1½l. 12 ran. 6:02
(Henry De Bromhead).

A tremendous double for **Minella Indo**, who was again underrated in the market against old rival **Allaho** but confirmed the Cheltenham form in style. Connections attempted a change of tactics with Allaho, who made the running this time at a steady pace and had Minella Indo being pushed along in second as he increased the tempo three out, but Minella Indo again proved strongest in the straight. Less than 6l covered the first five as Allaho held on for second ahead of **Carefully Selected**, the 2018 Champion Bumper runner-up running for only the second time over hurdles, with **First Approach** and **Go Another One** next. **Commander Of Fleet** went lame and was pulled up early on.

44 Ryanair Novice Chase (Grade 1) (2m)

Punchestown (IRE) May 2 (Yielding)

1 **Chacun Pour Soi** 7-11-10 Robbie Power
2 **Defi Du Seuil** 6-11-10 Richard Johnson
3 **Duc Des Genievres** 6-11-10 P Townend
3/1, 9/4F, 5/2. 4¼l, 16l. 7 ran. 4:07
(W P Mullins).

Two Cheltenham Festival winners and two other Grade 1 winners were put in their place in remarkable fashion by **Chacun Pour Soi**, who had been coming off a three-year layoff when winning his first chase at Naas in March yet bridged the gap to the top level with ease. Understandably seen as the Willie Mullins second string with Arkle hero **Duc Des Genievres** in the field but still sent off just 3-1, Chacun Pour Soi crept into the race to lead two out and had more speed than **Defi Du Seuil**, who was perhaps unsuited by the drop to 2m but still ran a fine race in second. The pair pulled 16l clear of the disappointing Duc Des Genievres, while **Voix Du Reve** couldn't back up his Ryanair Gold Cup win in fourth, **Ornua** was pulled up after jumping poorly and **Us And Them** unseated his rider early.

CHACUN POUR SOI: electrifying

45 Alanna Homes Champion Novice Hurdle (Grade 1) (2m4f)

Punchestown (IRE) May 3 (Good To Yielding)

1 **Reserve Tank** 5-11-10 Robbie Power
2 **Sams Profile** 5-11-10 Davy Russell
3 **Eglantine Du Seuil** 5-11-3 J Burke
13/2, 6/1, 14/1. ½l, 1¾l. 11 ran. 4:50
(Colin Tizzard).

With Ballymore winner **City Island** well below his best, this was another fairly inviting opportunity for **Reserve Tank** and he duly completed a Grade 1 double. Having beaten the Cheltenham fourth Brewin'upastorm at Aintree, Reserve Tank was pushed closer by the fifth, **Sams Profile**, this time but was perhaps just idling after a mistake by the runner-up at the last had secured a decisive lead. **Eglantine Du Seuil** had been found out by a better mare in Honeysuckle at Fairyhouse yet managed to finish a clear third, pulling 6½l

FUSIL RAFFLES: saw off two high-class opponents at Punchestown

ahead of **Tornado Flyer** with City Island a bitterly disappointing sixth.

46 EMS Copiers Novice Handicap Chase (Grade A) (2m5f)

Punchestown (IRE) May 3 (Good To Yielding)

1 **Real Steel** 6-11-10 Paul Townend
2 **Hardline** 7-11-10 Mr R James (7)
3 **Poker Party** 7-10-11 Rachael Blackmore
5/2F, 7/1, 8/1. 6½l, 12l. 12 ran. 5:31
(W P Mullins).

Grade 1 form came to the fore as **Real Steel** and **Hardline**, the highest-rated horses in the field, managed to concede weight to a field of more unexposed novices. Real Steel led the way in terrific fashion off 151, leading four out and easily coming clear. Hardline ran well in second, especially after being hampered four out, but was no match for the winner off level weights (even before taking into account his jockey's claim that took him down to 11st 3lb), underlining the fact that his win in a soft Grade 1 at Limerick over the disappointing Getabird wasn't up to the level shown by Real Steel in defeat in similar contests.

47 AES Champion Four-Year-Old Hurdle (Grade 1) (2m)

Punchestown (IRE) May 4 (Good To Yielding)

1 **Fusil Raffles** 4-11-0 Daryl Jacob
2 **Fakir D'Oudairies** 4-11-0 Mr D O'Connor
3 **French Made** 4-10-7 Paul Townend
13/8F, 7/4, 100/30. 2¾l, 5l. 5 ran. 3:51
(Nicky Henderson).

An easy winner of a weak renewal of the Adonis at Kempton on his British debut, **Fusil Raffles** was just as impressive in a much stronger race as he saw off two high-class opponents in **Fakir D'Oudairies** and **French Made**. Fusil Raffles had missed the Triumph Hurdle through injury in between but made up for lost time in style, comfortably reeling in the front-running Fakir D'Oudairies, who ran yet another fine race from the front but had no answer to the winner's turn of foot. French Made, only eighth in the Triumph, had reversed that form with Coeur Sublime and Gardens Of Babylon when winning a Grade 2 at Fairyhouse and again ran well as she stayed on into third. **Coko Beach** was a disappointing fifth.

Novice index

All horses placed or commented on in our novice review section, with race numbers

SECRET INVESTOR: landed a Grade 2 chase win at the third attempt at Ayr

Trainer Statistics

By race type

	Overall			Chases			Hurdles		
	W-R	%	£1	W-R	%	£1	W-R	%	£1
Graded	5-60	8	0.00	0-25	0	-25.00	5-33	15	+27.00
Handicap	132-634	21	+13.72	63-262	24	+34.29	69-372	19	-20.57
Novice	64-276	23	+18.31	29-103	28	+35.84	35-173	20	-17.53

By jockey

	Overall			Chases			Hurdles			Bumpers		
	W-R	%	£1	W-R	%	£1	W-R	%	£1	W-R	%	£1
Harry Skelton	172-696	25	+32.31	60-228	26	+10.81	103-430	24	+34.28	9-38	24	-12.78
B Andrews	22-175	13	-55.51	10-50	20	+25.63	9-110	8	-76.64	3-15	20	-4.50
William Marshall	7-51	14	-10.38	3-8	38	+14.50	4-38	11	-19.88	0-5	0	-5.00
Mr T Durrell	1-3	33	+0.25	0-0	-	0	0-1	0	-1.00	1-2	50	+1.25
Noel Fehily	1-3	33	+1.50	1-2	50	+2.50	0-1	0	-1.00	0-0	-	0
David England	1-16	6	-14.27	1-5	20	-3.27	0-11	0	-11.00	0-0	-	0
Conor Shoemark	1-33	3	-31.09	1-10	10	-8.09	0-23	0	-23.00	0-0	-	0
Adam Wedge	0-1	0	-1.00	0-1	0	-1.00	0-0	-	0	0-0	-	0
Charlie Poste	0-1	0	-1.00	0-1	0	-1.00	0-0	-	0	0-0	-	0
Lorcan Williams	0-1	0	-1.00	0-0	-	0	0-1	0	-1.00	0-0	-	0

By month

	Overall			Chases			Hurdles			Bumpers		
	W-R	%	£1	W-R	%	£1	W-R	%	£1	W-R	%	£1
May	30-99	30	+25.62	10-29	34	-2.67	19-67	28	+24.78	1-3	33	+3.50
June	17-69	25	+0.36	7-24	29	+3.08	9-43	21	-3.34	1-2	50	+0.63
July	24-61	39	+6.78	9-18	50	+11.58	14-42	33	-5.30	1-1	100	+0.50
August	11-55	20	-24.30	4-14	29	-3.53	5-39	13	-21.20	2-2	100	+0.43
September	6-44	14	-23.98	3-14	21	-2.43	3-30	10	-21.55	0-0	-	0
October	15-99	15	-4.62	7-32	22	+24.25	8-59	14	-20.87	0-8	0	-8.00
November	18-132	14	-47.31	8-52	15	-5.19	9-73	12	-39.63	1-7	14	-2.50
December	17-105	16	+36.80	6-33	18	+16.25	10-64	16	+24.80	1-8	13	-4.25
January	12-56	21	-2.50	4-15	27	+4.00	7-38	18	-8.50	1-3	33	+2.00
February	7-61	11	-33.72	2-18	11	-11.09	5-40	13	-19.63	0-3	0	-3.00
March	24-113	21	-11.82	5-33	15	-11.17	16-68	24	+2.36	3-12	25	-3.00
April	24-94	26	-9.49	11-28	39	+12.00	11-55	20	-14.16	2-11	18	-7.33

By horse

	Wins-Runs	%	£1 level stakes	Win prize	Total prize
Roksana	1-3	33	+8.00	£70,562.58	£111,971.58
Mohaayed	1-6	17	+11.00	£85,425.00	£92,821.50
Ch'tibello	1-6	17	+7.00	£56,270.00	£90,488.50
Molly The Dolly	3-4	75	+14.50	£79,946.72	£83,073.47
Virgilio	2-4	50	+8.00	£57,764.50	£70,241.16
Born Survivor	3-5	60	+6.58	£55,566.92	£59,856.42
Aux Ptits Soins	2-4	50	+14.00	£57,677.50	£58,882.00
Peppay Le Pugh	6-15	40	+4.65	£37,753.38	£55,594.67
Cobra De Mai	3-10	30	+6.60	£32,015.77	£38,220.99
Spiritofthegames	1-5	20	+3.00	£16,465.00	£35,720.25
Hatcher	6-9	67	+0.88	£33,551.82	£35,154.54
Desirable Court	3-5	60	+6.50	£30,665.82	£33,179.82
Gortroe Joe	3-8	38	+1.75	£27,270.18	£32,154.66

Dan Skelton

All runners

	Wins-Runs	%	Win prize	Total prize	£1 level stakes
2018-19	205-988	21	£1,516,810.62	£2,301,456.88	-88.19
2017-18	156-801	19	£1,065,531.87	£1,738,235.26	-153.35
2016-17	118-698	17	£789,125.19	£1,329,107	-259.57
2015-16	104-529	20	£732,806.31	£1,255,803.76	-156.34

By course - last five seasons

	Overall			Chases			Hurdles			Bumpers		
	W-R	%	£1	W-R	%	£1	W-R	%	£1	W-R	%	£1
Aintree	15-111	14	-1.95	5-37	14	-2.25	10-66	15	+8.30	0-8	0	-8.00
Ascot	4-63	6	-24.25	2-27	7	-9.00	2-32	6	-11.25	0-4	0	-4.00
Ayr	15-54	28	+5.07	8-23	35	+9.08	6-29	21	-5.76	1-2	50	+1.75
Bangor-on-Dee	27-106	25	-6.82	10-29	34	+16.63	16-70	23	-20.78	1-7	14	-2.67
Carlisle	5-24	21	+0.03	0-10	0	-10.00	5-11	45	+13.03	0-3	0	-3.00
Cartmel	1-13	8	-10.13	1-3	33	-0.13	0-10	0	-10.00	0-0	-	0
Catterick	8-33	24	-11.61	2-12	17	-1.75	5-19	26	-9.77	1-2	50	-0.09
Cheltenham	19-194	10	-40.29	5-61	8	-22.67	14-127	11	-11.63	0-6	0	-6.00
Chepstow	11-90	12	-10.50	3-22	14	+10.00	6-54	11	-22.50	2-14	14	+2.00
Doncaster	11-82	13	-45.29	3-22	14	-13.50	7-54	13	-29.04	1-6	17	-2.75
Exeter	5-27	19	-3.96	1-4	25	-2.43	4-23	17	-1.53	0-0	-	0
Fakenham	16-72	22	-17.42	6-24	25	-8.33	9-46	20	-14.09	1-2	50	+5.00
Ffos Las	4-41	10	-20.00	2-11	18	+0.50	2-26	8	-16.50	0-4	0	-4.00
Fontwell	22-105	21	-20.46	11-27	41	+8.69	9-64	14	-24.40	2-14	14	-4.75
Haydock	7-77	9	-40.13	1-20	5	-17.13	6-57	11	-23.00	0-0	-	0
Hereford	6-32	19	-2.56	3-11	27	+10.38	3-19	16	-10.93	0-2	0	-2.00
Hexham	4-11	36	-3.19	1-2	50	-0.50	3-9	33	-2.69	0-0	-	0
Huntingdon	24-153	16	-55.38	6-36	17	-8.25	16-96	17	-35.23	2-21	10	-11.90
Kelso	1-5	20	0.00	1-2	50	+3.00	0-3	0	-3.00	0-0	-	0
Kempton	10-133	8	-99.46	3-36	8	-29.43	7-87	8	-60.03	0-10	0	-10.00
Leicester	12-40	30	+12.17	7-18	39	+13.42	5-22	23	-1.25	0-0	-	0
Lingfield	5-17	29	+9.00	2-4	50	+8.50	3-13	23	+0.50	0-0	-	0
Lingfield (AW)	1-3	33	+0.75	0-0	-	0	0-0	-	0	1-3	33	+0.75
Ludlow	29-129	22	-14.76	3-21	14	-6.75	23-93	25	-12.01	3-15	20	+4.00
Market Rasen	57-209	27	+18.29	18-60	30	+13.84	33-131	25	+3.89	6-18	33	+0.56
Musselburgh	1-9	11	-6.63	0-2	0	-2.00	1-7	14	-4.63	0-0	-	0
Newbury	10-91	11	-36.63	3-22	14	-3.50	6-65	9	-32.63	1-4	25	-0.50
Newcastle	4-22	18	-13.29	1-10	10	-8.71	2-11	18	-5.38	1-1	100	+0.80
Newton Abbot	10-77	13	-45.92	4-27	15	-14.78	6-50	12	-31.15	0-0	-	0
Perth	5-14	36	+3.84	2-8	25	-0.50	3-6	50	+4.34	0-0	-	0
Plumpton	9-41	22	-18.08	2-8	25	-3.77	7-32	22	-13.31	0-1	0	-1.00
Sandown	1-58	2	-53.00	1-17	6	-12.00	0-38	0	-38.00	0-3	0	-3.00
Sedgefield	17-63	27	-11.04	5-18	28	+4.82	12-41	29	-11.85	0-4	0	-4.00
Southwell	37-173	21	-32.92	16-41	39	+10.88	20-109	18	-25.30	1-23	4	-18.50
Southwell (AW)	1-1	100	+0.50	0-0	-	0	0-0	-	0	1-1	100	+0.50
Stratford	29-157	18	-58.49	10-44	23	-12.60	17-102	17	-45.89	2-11	18	0.00
Taunton	11-63	17	-29.53	0-5	0	-5.00	9-53	17	-27.53	2-5	40	+3.00
Towcester	9-37	24	-13.39	2-7	29	-3.97	6-25	24	-8.42	1-5	20	-1.00
Uttoxeter	68-216	31	+46.86	20-68	29	+0.44	46-134	34	+54.92	2-14	14	-8.50
Warwick	46-204	23	-34.82	17-52	33	+4.78	23-125	18	-40.34	6-27	22	+0.75
Wetherby	37-118	31	+9.50	12-37	32	+7.64	22-72	31	+1.83	3-9	33	+0.04
Wincanton	8-47	17	-11.25	2-14	14	-5.00	6-31	19	-4.25	0-2	0	-2.00
Worcester	34-178	19	-34.03	12-53	23	+10.94	20-112	18	-35.95	2-13	15	-9.01

By race type

	Overall			Chases			Hurdles		
	W-R	%	£1	W-R	%	£1	W-R	%	£1
Graded	21-115	18	+1.62	7-51	14	-31.25	14-64	22	+32.87
Handicap	33-206	16	+42.26	12-86	14	-2.74	21-120	18	+45.00
Novice	60-205	29	-59.09	23-70	33	-19.81	37-135	27	-39.28

By jockey

	Overall			Chases			Hurdles			Bumpers		
	W-R	%	£1	W-R	%	£1	W-R	%	£1	W-R	%	£1
N de Boinville	67-235	29	+29.83	20-76	26	-25.18	44-135	33	+72.90	3-24	13	-17.89
James Bowen	20-80	25	-1.15	7-20	35	+23.92	7-46	15	-27.88	6-14	43	+2.81
Barry Geraghty	15-30	50	+0.48	2-2	100	+1.47	12-27	44	-1.61	1-1	100	+0.62
J McGrath	13-79	16	-26.38	7-31	23	-4.29	5-42	12	-18.00	1-6	17	-4.09
Daryl Jacob	7-42	17	-17.28	2-19	11	-14.13	5-22	23	-2.15	0-1	0	-1.00
Aidan Coleman	5-9	56	+3.72	2-3	67	+1.48	3-6	50	+2.24	0-0	-	0
Ned Curtis	4-23	17	-0.38	0-1	0	-1.00	4-19	21	+3.63	0-3	0	-3.00
Mr S W-Cohen	2-7	29	-3.63	0-0	-	0	2-6	33	-2.63	0-1	0	-1.00
Alan Doyle	2-12	17	+4.50	0-1	0	-1.00	2-9	22	+7.50	0-2	0	-2.00
Mark Walsh	1-1	100	+2.25	0-0	-	0	1-1	100	+2.25	0-0	-	0

By month

	Overall			Chases			Hurdles			Bumpers		
	W-R	%	£1	W-R	%	£1	W-R	%	£1	W-R	%	£1
May	19-49	39	+12.81	4-6	67	+3.73	13-31	42	+17.18	2-12	17	-8.09
June	5-17	29	-1.67	0-4	0	-4.00	4-12	33	-0.67	1-1	100	+3.00
July	6-16	38	+3.87	2-3	67	+1.44	3-11	27	+2.70	1-2	50	-0.27
August	7-13	54	+3.57	2-4	50	-1.14	3-7	43	+2.63	2-2	100	+2.08
September	4-11	36	+11.37	4-4	100	+18.37	0-7	0	-7.00	0-0	-	0
October	6-27	22	-14.05	2-14	14	-11.52	4-13	31	-2.54	0-0	-	0
November	17-60	28	-10.01	9-25	36	-7.90	7-32	22	-0.56	1-3	33	-1.56
December	24-89	27	+22.06	7-34	21	+10.44	17-50	34	+16.62	0-5	0	-5.00
January	20-60	33	-14.14	8-23	35	-1.00	12-34	35	-10.14	0-3	0	-3.00
February	14-45	31	-12.69	2-9	22	-4.90	12-32	38	-3.79	0-4	0	-4.00
March	12-83	14	+13.40	2-19	11	-6.64	6-52	12	+20.75	4-12	33	-0.72
April	7-74	9	-29.26	1-23	4	-21.83	6-43	14	+0.57	0-8	0	-8.00

By horse

	Wins-Runs	%	£1 level stakes	Win prize	Total prize
Altior	5-5	100	+1.37	£537,285.00	£537,285.00
Verdana Blue	4-6	67	+10.62	£190,782.50	£208,271.07
Buveur D'Air	2-5	40	-1.43	£79,914.50	£161,470.50
Champ	5-6	83	+7.15	£116,521.80	£143,021.80
Pentland Hills	3-3	100	+25.25	£130,586.24	£130,586.24
Beware The Bear	2-4	50	+11.50	£77,372.00	£90,697.00
Brain Power	1-4	25	+4.00	£78,846.00	£82,821.00
Santini	1-3	33	-0.63	£22,780.00	£70,580.00
William Henry	1-3	33	+26.00	£56,270.00	£65,756.00
We Have A Dream	1-5	20	-3.75	£18,768.00	£59,206.00
Valtor	1-3	33	+31.00	£56,950.00	£56,950.00
Janika	0-4	-	-4.00	£0.00	£53,066.00
Monbeg Legend	3-7	43	+3.00	£23,301.00	£41,964.84

Nicky Henderson

All runners

	Wins-Runs	%	Win prize	Total prize	£1 level stakes
2018-19	141-544	26	£2,149,852.63	£2,908,079.57	-14.75
2017-18	141-524	27	£2,612,359.32	£3,477,604.29	-76.49
2016-17	154-618	25	£1,883,034.9	£2,846,487.333	-113.50
2015-16	81-414	20	£1,066,034.86	£1,614,347.54	-101.03

By course - last five seasons

	Overall			Chases			Hurdles			Bumpers		
	W-R	%	£1	W-R	%	£1	W-R	%	£1	W-R	%	£1
Aintree	28-143	20	+8.11	7-47	15	-14.09	19-85	22	+16.19	2-11	18	+6.00
Ascot	33-158	21	-6.26	12-45	27	+27.19	19-100	19	-30.36	2-13	15	-3.09
Ayr	6-48	13	-27.86	2-18	11	-10.00	2-27	7	-20.09	2-3	67	+2.23
Bangor-on-Dee	7-45	16	-30.47	1-7	14	-5.56	5-26	19	-14.92	1-12	8	-10.00
Carlisle	1-1	100	+0.91	0-0	-	0	1-1	100	+0.91	0-0	-	0
Catterick	3-6	50	+2.73	3-4	75	+4.73	0-2	0	-2.00	0-0	-	0
Cheltenham	44-378	12	-109.86	12-126	10	-75.39	31-239	13	-28.48	1-13	8	-6.00
Chepstow	9-41	22	-9.94	2-11	18	-1.90	7-28	25	-6.04	0-2	0	-2.00
Doncaster	26-78	33	-1.46	9-24	38	0.00	17-45	38	+7.55	0-9	0	-9.00
Exeter	6-28	21	-7.04	1-6	17	+5.00	5-17	29	-7.04	0-5	0	-5.00
Fakenham	13-38	34	-11.33	2-7	29	-4.31	7-25	28	-9.16	4-6	67	+2.15
Ffos Las	12-33	36	-9.69	1-5	20	-3.60	9-21	43	-4.59	2-7	29	-1.50
Fontwell	12-43	28	-9.55	3-9	33	-3.59	8-25	32	+1.24	1-9	11	-7.20
Haydock	10-44	23	-13.59	3-11	27	-3.36	6-31	19	-11.97	1-2	50	+1.75
Hereford	4-10	40	-1.38	1-3	33	-1.50	3-7	43	+0.13	0-0	-	0
Hexham	2-4	50	-0.97	1-1	100	+0.20	1-3	33	-1.17	0-0	-	0
Huntingdon	31-105	30	-21.26	8-19	42	-2.46	21-64	33	-0.36	2-22	9	-18.44
Kelso	5-8	63	+5.70	1-1	100	+2.25	3-4	75	-0.05	1-3	33	+3.50
Kempton	64-238	27	-25.31	21-69	30	-9.47	36-143	25	-13.09	7-26	27	-2.76
Kempton (AW)	1-4	25	+1.00	0-0	-	0	0-0	-	0	1-4	25	+1.00
Leicester	4-22	18	-6.31	1-9	11	-7.86	3-13	23	+1.55	0-0	-	0
Lingfield	4-6	67	-0.25	1-1	100	+0.40	3-5	60	-0.65	0-0	-	0
Lingfield (AW)	3-9	33	-1.56	0-0	-	0	0-0	-	0	3-9	33	-1.56
Ludlow	31-101	31	-11.19	6-22	27	-4.70	16-56	29	-6.68	9-23	39	+0.19
Market Rasen	22-73	30	-2.38	3-13	23	+2.10	14-47	30	-10.61	5-13	38	+6.13
Musselburgh	7-21	33	-5.96	0-2	0	-2.00	7-18	39	-2.96	0-1	0	-1.00
Newbury	42-199	21	-39.33	5-46	11	-29.99	33-124	27	+2.29	4-29	14	-11.63
Newcastle	7-8	88	+5.39	1-1	100	+2.75	6-7	86	+2.64	0-0	-	0
Newton Abbot	13-34	38	+6.65	2-6	33	-2.73	9-25	36	+8.40	2-3	67	+0.98
Perth	1-13	8	-11.93	0-4	0	-4.00	1-8	13	-6.93	0-1	0	-1.00
Plumpton	9-23	39	+1.89	4-6	67	-0.20	5-14	36	+5.08	0-3	0	-3.00
Sandown	44-161	27	+4.83	12-50	24	-17.98	31-108	29	+22.81	1-3	33	0.00
Southwell	18-55	33	-6.32	1-8	13	-6.71	8-31	26	-9.74	9-16	56	+10.13
Stratford	8-45	18	-22.91	5-14	36	+1.86	2-22	9	-17.10	1-9	11	-7.67
Taunton	12-36	33	+0.62	1-3	33	-1.56	10-30	33	+3.18	1-3	33	-1.00
Towcester	16-37	43	+5.32	2-5	40	-1.27	12-20	60	+13.20	2-12	17	-6.60
Uttoxeter	21-75	28	-22.52	6-24	25	-9.12	13-43	30	-11.17	2-8	25	-2.22
Warwick	28-86	33	+17.64	7-10	70	+15.33	16-49	33	+14.78	5-27	19	-12.48
Wetherby	6-16	38	-4.17	2-6	33	-3.39	3-8	38	-2.53	1-2	50	+1.75
Wincanton	8-43	19	-5.20	3-13	23	-6.00	5-25	20	+5.80	0-5	0	-5.00
Worcester	25-83	30	+0.93	5-16	31	-2.43	14-48	29	-3.72	6-19	32	+7.08

By race type

	Overall			Chases			Hurdles		
	W-R	%	£1	W-R	%	£1	W-R	%	£1
Graded	23-123	19	-8.67	15-69	22	+7.52	7-51	14	-16.19
Handicap	47-285	16	-15.34	31-167	19	-13.84	16-118	14	-1.50
Novice	56-186	30	+2.27	21-71	30	-6.11	35-115	30	+8.38

By jockey

	Overall			Chases			Hurdles			Bumpers		
	W-R	%	£1	W-R	%	£1	W-R	%	£1	W-R	%	£1
Harry Cobden	84-322	26	-9.37	31-129	24	-4.52	43-160	27	-6.70	10-33	30	+1.85
Bryony Frost	18-71	25	+31.88	11-31	35	+25.23	5-32	16	+8.90	2-8	25	-2.25
Lorcan Williams	11-68	16	-31.01	2-21	10	-17.06	6-41	15	-18.45	3-6	50	+4.50
S T-Davies	9-34	26	-7.64	4-15	27	+1.58	4-17	24	-8.89	1-2	50	-0.33
Sean Bowen	3-15	20	-1.83	2-10	20	+1.50	1-4	25	-2.33	0-1	0	-1.00
Daryl Jacob	2-5	40	+6.10	1-2	50	+0.10	1-3	33	+6.00	0-0	-	0
Mr Jody Sole	1-1	100	+2.00	0-0	-	0	1-1	100	+2.00	0-0	-	0
Mr S W-Cohen	1-2	50	-0.09	1-2	50	-0.09	0-0	-	0	0-0	-	0
Mr W Biddick	1-3	33	-1.00	1-3	33	-1.00	0-0	-	0	0-0	-	0
Miss N Parker	1-4	25	-2.50	1-3	33	-1.50	0-1	0	-1.00	0-0	-	0

By month

	Overall			Chases			Hurdles			Bumpers		
	W-R	%	£1	W-R	%	£1	W-R	%	£1	W-R	%	£1
May	6-42	14	-22.67	2-19	11	-15.17	3-19	16	-6.50	1-4	25	-1.00
June	1-12	8	-6.50	1-6	17	-0.50	0-6	0	-6.00	0-0	-	0
July	1-14	7	-12.39	0-9	0	-9.00	1-5	20	-3.39	0-0	-	0
August	0-1	0	-1.00	0-1	0	-1.00	0-0	-	0	0-0	-	0
September	0-1	0	-1.00	0-0	-	0	0-1	0	-1.00	0-0	-	0
October	13-45	29	+7.68	5-19	26	-0.13	5-23	22	-3.20	3-3	100	+11.00
November	21-95	22	-16.73	9-46	20	-2.22	9-41	22	-17.26	3-8	38	+2.75
December	26-92	28	+44.16	11-41	27	+29.13	13-43	30	+18.37	2-8	25	-3.33
January	8-53	15	-29.93	4-22	18	-10.40	4-26	15	-14.53	0-5	0	-5.00
February	25-89	28	+21.54	11-33	33	+2.26	11-49	22	+17.83	3-7	43	+1.45
March	17-81	21	-16.98	6-32	19	+0.23	10-41	24	-12.71	1-8	13	-4.50
April	17-64	27	-18.38	7-27	26	-10.95	7-30	23	-8.83	3-7	43	+1.40

By horse

	Wins-Runs	%	£1 level stakes	Win prize	Total prize
Frodon	4-5	80	+17.25	£372,532.00	£406,718.66
Clan Des Obeaux	2-5	40	+9.40	£170,850.00	£240,295.00
Politologue	1-5	20	-2.75	£39,865.00	£199,420.00
Topofthegame	1-4	25	+1.00	£98,472.50	£145,986.50
Cyrname	2-4	50	+5.00	£132,345.00	£135,555.00
Quel Destin	5-7	71	+4.78	£102,652.90	£107,962.22
Getaway Trump	4-8	50	+10.43	£80,809.18	£97,896.19
Black Corton	1-6	17	-3.13	£31,322.50	£92,134.66
Grand Sancy	4-8	50	+7.42	£67,901.50	£90,855.50
Dynamite Dollars	4-5	80	+8.50	£81,872.90	£89,292.90
Secret Investor	4-7	57	+5.98	£58,475.71	£72,576.61
Capeland	3-11	27	-3.15	£36,926.70	£61,588.90
Old Guard	0-7	-	-7.00	£0.00	£60,575.00

Paul Nicholls

All runners

	Wins-Runs	%	Win prize	Total prize	£1 level stakes
2018-19	135-589	23	£2,211,224.1	£3,307,171.58	-52.21
2017-18	127-576	22	£1,612,108.45	£2,513,233.47	-132.84
2016-17	171-673	25	£1,733,593.6	£2,529,250.45	-78.39
2015-16	122-568	21	£1,505,433.62	£2,439,740.26	-73.23

By course - last five seasons

	Overall			Chases			Hurdles			Bumpers		
	W-R	%	£1	W-R	%	£1	W-R	%	£1	W-R	%	£1
Aintree	17-148	11	-49.63	11-92	12	-29.88	4-47	9	-16.75	2-9	22	-3.00
Ascot	35-179	20	+22.42	21-95	22	-1.46	12-74	16	+28.13	2-10	20	-4.25
Ayr	10-48	21	+12.21	5-27	19	+10.75	4-19	21	-2.54	1-2	50	+4.00
Bangor-on-Dee	5-17	29	-1.28	4-12	33	+1.47	1-5	20	-2.75	0-0	-	0
Carlisle	5-10	50	+3.35	4-9	44	+0.85	1-1	100	+2.50	0-0	-	0
Cartmel	0-3	0	-3.00	0-3	0	-3.00	0-0	-	0	0-0	-	0
Catterick	1-5	20	-2.50	1-2	50	+0.50	0-2	0	-2.00	0-1	0	-1.00
Cheltenham	41-354	12	+11.84	24-192	13	+37.48	14-152	9	-26.13	3-10	30	+0.50
Chepstow	35-154	23	-23.24	7-52	13	-21.42	20-85	24	-9.31	8-17	47	+7.48
Doncaster	18-70	26	-13.95	10-39	26	-4.80	7-29	24	-8.82	1-2	50	-0.33
Exeter	45-142	32	-7.69	15-49	31	-11.78	28-81	35	+7.09	2-12	17	-3.00
Fakenham	5-22	23	-7.40	3-12	25	-3.27	2-10	20	-4.13	0-0	-	0
Ffos Las	3-14	21	-0.43	1-3	33	-1.43	2-8	25	+4.00	0-3	0	-3.00
Fontwell	37-91	41	+8.13	24-45	53	+16.64	12-43	28	-8.76	1-3	33	+0.25
Haydock	16-70	23	-18.45	10-26	38	+5.48	6-42	14	-21.92	0-2	0	-2.00
Hereford	3-14	21	-1.83	1-7	14	0.00	2-7	29	-1.83	0-0	-	0
Hexham	2-2	100	+2.40	2-2	100	+2.40	0-0	-	0	0-0	-	0
Huntingdon	6-24	25	+3.75	4-13	31	+6.38	1-9	11	-6.13	1-2	50	+3.50
Kelso	9-23	39	-1.44	6-16	38	-2.66	3-7	43	+1.23	0-0	-	0
Kempton	42-196	21	-24.28	25-95	26	+4.89	15-91	16	-23.99	2-10	20	-5.18
Kempton (AW)	1-6	17	+5.00	0-0	-	0	0-0	-	0	1-6	17	+5.00
Leicester	4-9	44	-0.93	3-7	43	-1.80	1-2	50	+0.88	0-0	-	0
Lingfield (AW)	0-1	0	-1.00	0-0	-	0	0-0	-	0	0-1	0	-1.00
Ludlow	15-59	25	-14.08	8-31	26	-4.41	6-24	25	-8.29	1-4	25	-1.38
Market Rasen	7-32	22	-3.51	5-23	22	+2.66	2-8	25	-5.17	0-1	0	-1.00
Musselburgh	10-26	38	+6.72	6-10	60	+4.45	4-16	25	+2.27	0-0	-	0
Newbury	23-151	15	-13.18	14-84	17	+11.75	8-62	13	-23.43	1-5	20	-1.50
Newcastle	3-8	38	+3.88	0-3	0	-3.00	3-5	60	+6.88	0-0	-	0
Newton Abbot	43-149	29	-45.35	24-81	30	-26.46	18-63	29	-16.64	1-5	20	-2.25
Perth	4-9	44	+2.66	3-7	43	+3.30	1-2	50	-0.64	0-0	-	0
Plumpton	7-23	30	-1.93	3-9	33	-0.87	4-14	29	-1.07	0-0	-	0
Sandown	25-191	13	-44.55	16-111	14	-22.46	9-76	12	-18.09	0-4	0	-4.00
Sedgefield	1-2	50	-0.82	1-1	100	+0.18	0-1	0	-1.00	0-0	-	0
Southwell	3-5	60	+2.30	1-2	50	0.00	2-3	67	+2.30	0-0	-	0
Stratford	8-32	25	-11.88	2-16	13	-11.58	5-15	33	-4.31	1-1	100	+4.00
Taunton	60-194	31	-14.90	14-50	28	-8.21	42-128	33	-3.20	4-16	25	-3.50
Towcester	0-1	0	-1.00	0-1	0	-1.00	0-0	-	0	0-0	-	0
Uttoxeter	0-18	0	-18.00	0-15	0	-15.00	0-3	0	-3.00	0-0	-	0
Warwick	12-55	22	-18.79	8-28	29	-3.91	3-23	13	-14.63	1-4	25	-0.25
Wetherby	4-15	27	-0.93	1-9	11	-7.09	3-6	50	+6.16	0-0	-	0
Wincanton	99-298	33	-5.10	28-94	30	-7.98	62-169	37	+2.69	9-35	26	+0.19
Worcester	15-53	28	-10.87	7-25	28	-6.99	7-27	26	-6.64	1-1	100	+2.75

By race type

	Overall			Chases			Hurdles		
	W-R	%	£1	W-R	%	£1	W-R	%	£1
Graded	3-36	8	-17.50	3-22	14	-3.50	0-13	0	-13.00
Handicap	56-332	17	-54.10	29-155	19	-3.96	27-177	15	-50.14
Novice	35-155	23	+41.83	12-60	20	+4.15	23-95	24	+37.68

By jockey

	Overall			Chases			Hurdles			Bumpers		
	W-R	%	£1	W-R	%	£1	W-R	%	£1	W-R	%	£1
R Johnson	53-262	20	-48.17	20-84	24	+3.15	30-155	19	-40.57	3-23	13	-10.75
Tom O'Brien	16-78	21	+12.72	4-19	21	+8.50	11-53	21	+6.97	1-6	17	-2.75
Micheal Nolan	11-78	14	-6.05	5-29	17	-4.92	6-42	14	+5.86	0-7	0	-7.00
Mr D Maxwell	9-32	28	+30.25	4-20	20	-6.56	5-12	42	+36.82	0-0	-	0
Barry Geraghty	6-21	29	+8.05	3-9	33	+9.50	3-12	25	-1.45	0-0	-	0
Mr Ben Jones	3-14	21	-0.67	0-6	0	-6.00	3-7	43	+6.33	0-1	0	-1.00
Connor Brace	2-3	67	+7.25	0-0	-	0	2-3	67	+7.25	0-0	-	0
James Best	2-6	33	+9.00	1-3	33	+6.00	1-2	50	+4.00	0-1	0	-1.00
Sean Houlihan	2-37	5	-32.00	1-9	11	-6.50	1-22	5	-19.50	0-6	0	-6.00
Sean Bowen	1-1	100	+2.25	0-0	-	0	1-1	100	+2.25	0-0	-	0

By month

	Overall			Chases			Hurdles			Bumpers		
	W-R	%	£1	W-R	%	£1	W-R	%	£1	W-R	%	£1
May	4-47	9	-33.13	3-11	27	0.00	1-33	3	-30.13	0-3	0	-3.00
June	2-14	14	-1.25	1-7	14	-3.25	1-6	17	+3.00	0-1	0	-1.00
July	3-9	33	-2.75	1-4	25	-1.38	2-3	67	+0.63	0-2	0	-2.00
August	0-6	0	-6.00	0-3	0	-3.00	0-1	0	-1.00	0-2	0	-2.00
September	6-10	60	+17.98	3-6	50	+14.13	3-4	75	+3.85	0-0	-	0
October	10-60	17	-28.02	2-12	17	-8.55	6-38	16	-15.97	2-10	20	-3.50
November	19-96	20	+53.73	8-32	25	+9.25	11-51	22	+57.48	0-13	0	-13.00
December	22-93	24	+62.83	10-38	26	+68.28	11-51	22	-7.45	1-4	25	+2.00
January	8-55	15	-23.30	2-14	14	-5.00	6-40	15	-17.30	0-1	0	-1.00
February	4-39	10	-7.75	1-14	7	-9.50	3-23	13	+3.75	0-2	0	-2.00
March	22-86	26	-4.92	7-31	23	-8.81	14-50	28	+5.89	1-5	20	-2.00
April	6-45	13	-21.79	1-16	6	-7.00	5-25	20	-10.79	0-4	0	-4.00

By horse

	Wins-Runs	%	£1 level stakes	Win prize	Total prize
Defi Du Seuil	3-5	60	+13.50	£136,144.84	£144,495.84
Ozzie The Oscar	2-7	29	-0.50	£37,510.50	£61,917.00
Leapaway	5-9	56	+5.98	£53,095.36	£61,324.52
War Sound	1-4	25	+2.50	£49,520.00	£49,775.00
Imperial Presence	3-5	60	+5.88	£37,424.90	£45,379.90
Beau Du Brizais	2-8	25	+7.00	£27,421.56	£37,252.91
Rock The Kasbah	1-5	20	+5.00	£33,762.00	£34,589.14
Jerrysback	1-5	20	+46.00	£6,108.12	£34,091.14
Little Miss Poet	2-8	25	-2.13	£15,563.70	£30,896.28
Sternrubin	2-8	25	-3.55	£17,284.68	£28,789.48
Cotswold Way	4-6	67	+9.86	£25,407.18	£26,323.18
Crooks Peak	3-5	60	+5.87	£23,512.98	£23,927.97
Scoop The Pot	2-8	25	-1.80	£17,280.90	£23,822.88

Philip Hobbs

All runners

	Wins-Runs	%	Win prize	Total prize	£1 level stakes
2018-19	106-560	19	£905,087.31	£1,305,373.66	+5.63
2017-18	63-460	14	£363,185.51	£709,991.93	-161.95
2016-17	111-593	19	£1,004,400.1	£1,502,991.03	-92.03
2015-16	113-523	22	£909,949.12	£1,386,467.83	-64.73

By course - last five seasons

	Overall			Chases			Hurdles			Bumpers		
	W-R	%	£1	W-R	%	£1	W-R	%	£1	W-R	%	£1
Aintree	8-84	10	-41.05	4-38	11	-6.00	4-39	10	-28.05	0-7	0	-7.00
Ascot	10-90	11	-19.59	4-45	9	-15.50	4-40	10	-12.09	2-5	40	+8.00
Ayr	1-16	6	-5.00	0-7	0	-7.00	1-9	11	+2.00	0-0	-	0
Bangor-on-Dee	3-27	11	+31.50	1-10	10	+41.00	2-14	14	-6.50	0-3	0	-3.00
Carlisle	1-7	14	-5.17	1-2	50	-0.17	0-4	0	-4.00	0-1	0	-1.00
Cartmel	2-5	40	+0.88	1-2	50	+1.50	1-3	33	-0.63	0-0	-	0
Catterick	3-7	43	-2.51	2-3	67	-0.18	1-3	33	-1.33	0-1	0	-1.00
Cheltenham	27-231	12	-57.88	16-120	13	-28.00	8-93	9	-24.76	3-18	17	-5.13
Chepstow	35-167	21	-10.07	14-67	21	-1.33	20-82	24	+6.02	1-18	6	-14.75
Doncaster	5-26	19	-9.90	2-10	20	-1.25	3-16	19	-8.65	0-0	-	0
Exeter	51-238	21	-49.59	14-91	15	-23.14	33-130	25	-19.73	4-17	24	-6.72
Fakenham	2-6	33	-2.44	1-3	33	-1.27	0-1	0	-1.00	1-2	50	-0.17
Ffos Las	8-43	19	-2.42	2-12	17	+3.00	5-23	22	+0.08	1-8	13	-5.50
Fontwell	17-67	25	-20.98	6-19	32	-2.98	10-43	23	-16.25	1-5	20	-1.75
Haydock	5-58	9	-26.00	2-23	9	-13.50	3-31	10	-8.50	0-4	0	-4.00
Hereford	6-32	19	-13.24	2-8	25	-1.50	3-21	14	-15.74	1-3	33	+4.00
Hexham	4-7	57	+1.85	1-2	50	0.00	2-3	67	+0.35	1-2	50	+1.50
Huntingdon	8-58	14	-22.59	1-12	8	-4.50	5-38	13	-15.25	2-8	25	-2.84
Kelso	1-4	25	-2.33	0-2	0	-2.00	1-2	50	-0.33	0-0	-	0
Kempton	12-100	12	-63.53	3-36	8	-23.00	9-54	17	-30.53	0-10	0	-10.00
Leicester	12-27	44	+14.50	5-10	50	+5.87	7-17	41	+8.63	0-0	-	0
Lingfield	1-10	10	-6.75	1-4	25	-0.75	0-6	0	-6.00	0-0	-	0
Ludlow	29-114	25	+18.87	10-40	25	+5.79	18-65	28	+13.58	1-9	11	-0.50
Market Rasen	9-40	23	-10.40	1-13	8	-10.25	6-21	29	+0.98	2-6	33	-1.13
Musselburgh	4-5	80	+3.93	2-2	100	+2.53	2-3	67	+1.40	0-0	-	0
Newbury	26-144	18	+65.76	10-65	15	-18.04	15-71	21	+82.80	1-8	13	+1.00
Newcastle	0-4	0	-4.00	0-2	0	-2.00	0-1	0	-1.00	0-1	0	-1.00
Newton Abbot	30-143	21	-22.16	5-46	11	-27.95	20-83	24	+4.93	5-14	36	+0.86
Perth	6-13	46	+5.01	2-8	25	-2.13	4-5	80	+7.13	0-0	-	0
Plumpton	4-18	22	-10.50	0-3	0	-3.00	4-15	27	-7.50	0-0	-	0
Sandown	16-97	16	-16.15	10-53	19	-2.88	6-39	15	-8.28	0-5	0	-5.00
Sedgefield	2-7	29	-3.00	0-2	0	-2.00	2-5	40	-1.00	0-0	-	0
Southwell	6-29	21	-8.97	1-4	25	+1.50	4-17	24	-4.84	1-8	13	-5.63
Stratford	17-71	24	+25.28	12-46	26	+17.08	5-23	22	+10.19	0-2	0	-2.00
Taunton	17-132	13	-63.98	1-25	4	-19.00	13-96	14	-46.61	3-11	27	+1.63
Towcester	1-11	9	-7.25	0-2	0	-2.00	1-7	14	-3.25	0-2	0	-2.00
Uttoxeter	18-111	16	-36.96	5-39	13	-25.37	11-64	17	-16.97	2-8	25	+5.38
Warwick	23-109	21	-9.04	8-32	25	-3.25	8-54	15	-10.44	7-23	30	+4.65
Wetherby	10-30	33	+4.89	4-16	25	+6.08	6-14	43	-1.19	0-0	-	0
Wincanton	21-177	12	-66.63	8-51	16	-18.63	9-103	9	-65.25	4-23	17	+17.25
Worcester	34-122	28	+54.47	11-46	24	+12.44	20-69	29	+36.28	3-7	43	+5.75

By race type

	Overall			Chases			Hurdles		
	W-R	%	£1	W-R	%	£1	W-R	%	£1
Graded	4-51	8	-21.75	2-14	14	-3.75	1-33	3	-20.00
Handicap	27-222	12	-99.38	10-67	15	-26.06	17-155	11	-73.32
Novice	30-155	19	-61.00	10-46	22	-20.69	20-109	18	-40.31

By jockey

	Overall			Chases			Hurdles			Bumpers		
	W-R	%	£1	W-R	%	£1	W-R	%	£1	W-R	%	£1
W Hutchinson	68-315	22	-43.00	13-65	20	-19.65	44-206	21	-44.08	11-44	25	+20.73
Tom Cannon	10-65	15	-28.25	1-10	10	-7.75	7-48	15	-22.50	2-7	29	+2.00
Daryl Jacob	6-20	30	-7.70	1-6	17	-3.75	5-13	38	-2.95	0-1	0	-1.00
James Bowen	2-4	50	+0.75	0-0	-	0	2-3	67	+1.75	0-1	0	-1.00
Tom Bellamy	2-41	5	-33.93	0-7	0	-7.00	2-27	7	-19.93	0-7	0	-7.00
Oakley Brown	1-4	25	-2.00	0-0	-	0	0-1	0	-1.00	1-3	33	-1.00
Barry Geraghty	1-9	11	-7.20	0-1	0	-1.00	1-8	13	-6.20	0-0	-	0
A P Heskin	1-10	10	-4.00	0-2	0	-2.00	1-7	14	-1.00	0-1	0	-1.00
Fergus Gregory	0-1	0	-1.00	0-0	-	0	0-1	0	-1.00	0-0	-	0
Mr Alex Edwards	0-1	0	-1.00	0-0	-	0	0-0	-	0	0-1	0	-1.00

By month

	Overall			Chases			Hurdles			Bumpers		
	W-R	%	£1	W-R	%	£1	W-R	%	£1	W-R	%	£1
May	9-33	27	+1.08	0-4	0	-4.00	7-22	32	+3.08	2-7	29	+2.00
June	4-21	19	-14.94	1-3	33	-1.56	3-15	20	-10.38	0-3	0	-3.00
July	5-14	36	+0.04	0-1	0	-1.00	4-11	36	+1.68	1-2	50	-0.64
August	7-14	50	+2.26	1-1	100	+1.63	6-13	46	+0.63	0-0	-	0
September	3-9	33	-1.04	0-0	-	0	2-8	25	-1.38	1-1	100	+0.33
October	4-29	14	-13.59	0-1	0	-1.00	4-27	15	-11.59	0-1	0	-1.00
November	18-85	21	-11.84	1-10	10	-7.75	15-67	22	-17.59	2-8	25	+13.50
December	11-90	12	-40.00	4-19	21	-1.50	6-61	10	-32.83	1-10	10	-5.67
January	4-45	9	-33.50	1-12	8	-10.50	2-25	8	-18.25	1-8	13	-4.75
February	6-49	12	-21.73	2-12	17	-9.07	3-30	10	-10.00	1-7	14	-2.67
March	12-66	18	-16.29	3-20	15	-12.90	5-32	16	-14.00	4-14	29	+10.62
April	8-44	18	-6.77	2-10	20	+4.50	5-26	19	-9.27	1-8	13	-2.00

By horse

	Wins-Runs	%	£1 level stakes	Win prize	Total prize
Sceau Royal	1-5	20	-2.75	£42,202.50	£137,469.50
Talkischeap	2-6	33	+3.50	£89,018.58	£102,679.28
Lisp	1-5	20	-1.00	£7,216.20	£52,905.20
Cracker Factory	4-8	50	-0.33	£35,865.82	£46,841.82
Fidux	2-7	29	+5.50	£40,408.08	£44,843.68
Dino Velvet	2-7	29	+5.00	£19,753.92	£43,907.44
The Glancing Queen	2-4	50	+19.00	£37,700.90	£42,905.90
Ballywood	3-7	43	+3.05	£30,670.56	£42,015.56
Dingo Dollar	0-5	-	-5.00	£0.00	£38,969.50
Mahlermade	1-10	10	-3.50	£31,152.00	£38,914.58
Harambe	2-7	29	+0.50	£8,707.32	£29,300.60
Alsa Mix	3-5	60	+10.90	£23,907.90	£24,510.90
Mia's Storm	2-4	50	+2.67	£23,621.50	£24,358.50

Alan King

All runners

	Wins-Runs	%	Win prize	Total prize	£1 level stakes
2018-19	91-499	18	£724,516.87	£1,259,316.08	-156.32
2017-18	58-389	15	£553,491.36	£923,496.4	-133.86
2016-17	104-490	21	£937,375.32	£1,373,269.71	-77.18
2015-16	68-403	17	£742,259.29	£1,044,467.91	-120.54

By course - last five seasons

	Overall			Chases			Hurdles			Bumpers		
	W-R	%	£1	W-R	%	£1	W-R	%	£1	W-R	%	£1
Aintree	6-64	9	-32.58	1-14	7	-1.00	4-36	11	-23.58	1-14	7	-8.00
Ascot	11-87	13	-38.72	2-14	14	-5.25	8-65	12	-28.34	1-8	13	-5.13
Ayr	2-32	6	-16.50	1-10	10	+1.00	1-21	5	-16.50	0-1	0	-1.00
Bangor-on-Dee	19-67	28	-8.75	3-15	20	-5.85	13-39	33	-4.65	3-13	23	+1.75
Cartmel	0-3	0	-3.00	0-1	0	-1.00	0-2	0	-2.00	0-0	-	0
Catterick	4-6	67	+1.74	1-1	100	+0.83	3-5	60	+0.90	0-0	-	0
Cheltenham	19-169	11	-28.17	7-45	16	+6.00	10-109	9	-43.67	2-15	13	+9.50
Chepstow	7-59	12	-32.90	1-8	13	-2.50	6-45	13	-24.40	0-6	0	-6.00
Doncaster	24-115	21	-5.40	9-35	26	+7.48	14-70	20	-5.38	1-10	10	-7.50
Exeter	16-87	18	-21.11	6-24	25	-1.59	9-54	17	-17.52	1-9	11	-2.00
Fakenham	1-11	9	-9.00	0-1	0	-1.00	1-9	11	-7.00	0-1	0	-1.00
Ffos Las	2-14	14	-7.00	0-3	0	-3.00	1-9	11	-6.50	1-2	50	+2.50
Fontwell	19-64	30	+2.22	1-9	11	-6.38	16-47	34	+12.42	2-8	25	-3.83
Haydock	6-46	13	+14.32	2-15	13	+17.50	2-28	7	-14.63	2-3	67	+11.44
Hereford	5-15	33	-0.48	0-1	0	-1.00	5-13	38	+1.53	0-1	0	-1.00
Hexham	1-4	25	-2.56	1-1	100	+0.44	0-3	0	-3.00	0-0	-	0
Huntingdon	23-112	21	-31.69	5-21	24	+0.72	15-70	21	-22.03	3-21	14	-10.38
Kempton	25-178	14	-84.97	4-44	9	-34.70	20-118	17	-44.27	1-16	6	-6.00
Kempton (AW)	1-2	50	+3.00	0-0	-	0	0-0	-	0	1-2	50	+3.00
Leicester	2-19	11	-5.25	1-10	10	-6.25	1-9	11	+1.00	0-0	-	0
Lingfield	1-9	11	-4.50	1-4	25	+0.50	0-5	0	-5.00	0-0	-	0
Lingfield (AW)	3-12	25	-2.68	0-0	-	0	0-0	-	0	3-12	25	-2.68
Ludlow	13-59	22	-13.73	4-11	36	-3.02	8-45	18	-22.72	1-3	33	+12.00
Market Rasen	15-89	17	-14.25	3-23	13	-13.75	11-57	19	-3.50	1-9	11	+3.00
Musselburgh	0-1	0	-1.00	0-0	-	0	0-1	0	-1.00	0-0	-	0
Newbury	20-174	11	-79.72	5-41	12	-16.50	10-103	10	-59.07	5-30	17	-4.15
Newcastle	1-2	50	+1.25	0-0	-	0	1-2	50	+1.25	0-0	-	0
Newton Abbot	10-36	28	-4.58	2-10	20	-5.13	8-23	35	+3.55	0-3	0	-3.00
Plumpton	16-50	32	-10.28	3-10	30	-0.42	13-38	34	-7.86	0-2	0	-2.00
Sandown	12-63	19	+6.71	3-16	19	+13.00	9-44	20	-3.29	0-3	0	-3.00
Sedgefield	1-2	50	0.00	0-0	-	0	1-2	50	0.00	0-0	-	0
Southwell	12-45	27	-12.75	1-7	14	-5.39	9-30	30	-10.36	2-8	25	+3.00
Stratford	13-51	25	-5.81	2-7	29	-0.50	10-37	27	-5.31	1-7	14	0.00
Taunton	6-65	9	-41.07	2-9	22	+2.00	2-47	4	-41.90	2-9	22	-1.17
Towcester	8-32	25	-1.80	0-2	0	-2.00	5-21	24	+0.63	3-9	33	-0.42
Uttoxeter	10-65	15	-21.40	1-17	6	-13.25	7-40	18	-15.15	2-8	25	+7.00
Warwick	31-146	21	-54.44	5-23	22	-7.10	21-92	23	-33.71	5-31	16	-13.62
Wetherby	6-39	15	-20.51	2-7	29	+1.25	3-27	11	-18.38	1-5	20	-3.39
Wincanton	12-81	15	-23.11	3-11	27	+9.00	7-59	12	-37.11	2-11	18	+5.00
Worcester	13-54	24	-13.65	1-11	9	-8.63	9-35	26	-2.23	3-8	38	-2.80

By race type

	Overall			Chases			Hurdles		
	W-R	%	£1	W-R	%	£1	W-R	%	£1
Graded	0-14	0	-14.00	0-0	-	0	0-14	0	-14.00
Handicap	24-211	11	-84.04	11-65	17	-10.73	13-146	9	-73.31
Novice	34-147	23	+4.04	6-27	22	+6.72	28-120	23	-2.68

By jockey

	Overall			Chases			Hurdles			Bumpers		
	W-R	%	£1	W-R	%	£1	W-R	%	£1	W-R	%	£1
Aidan Coleman	22-97	23	-17.71	5-25	20	-6.94	14-60	23	-9.02	3-12	25	-1.75
R Johnson	21-107	20	-24.10	4-22	18	+5.00	15-80	19	-29.85	2-5	40	+0.75
Fergus Gregory	13-47	28	-13.95	0-5	0	-5.00	7-31	23	-10.27	6-11	55	+1.33
Gavin Sheehan	10-22	45	+13.90	5-7	71	+13.73	4-13	31	-0.08	1-2	50	+0.25
Lewis Stones	5-24	21	+6.38	0-0	-	0	4-23	17	-0.63	1-1	100	+7.00
David England	5-47	11	-18.72	1-11	9	-9.09	4-36	11	-9.63	0-0	-	0
A P Heskin	1-1	100	+2.50	0-0	-	0	0-0	-	0	1-1	100	+2.50
Noel Fehily	1-4	25	-1.90	0-1	0	-1.00	1-3	33	-0.90	0-0	-	0
Callum McKinnes	1-7	14	-2.67	0-0	-	0	1-6	17	-1.67	0-1	0	-1.00
Mr Alex Ferguson	1-9	11	-6.90	1-3	33	-0.90	0-5	0	-5.00	0-1	0	-1.00

By month

	Overall			Chases			Hurdles			Bumpers		
	W-R	%	£1	W-R	%	£1	W-R	%	£1	W-R	%	£1
May	6-30	20	+16.71	1-5	20	-2.50	3-22	14	+16.46	2-3	67	+2.75
June	3-30	10	-19.13	1-4	25	-0.75	2-25	8	-17.38	0-1	0	-1.00
July	6-26	23	-2.25	1-5	20	-1.75	3-17	18	-7.75	2-4	50	+7.25
August	9-32	28	+8.37	2-8	25	+11.50	6-21	29	-3.14	1-3	33	0.00
September	4-14	29	+1.15	0-3	0	-3.00	3-9	33	+3.90	1-2	50	+0.25
October	12-38	32	+3.74	4-6	67	+3.73	7-30	23	+0.18	1-2	50	-0.17
November	5-44	11	-27.33	1-5	20	-2.50	2-35	6	-26.00	2-4	50	+1.17
December	12-59	20	-9.34	1-13	8	-1.00	10-41	24	-5.84	1-5	20	-2.50
January	8-43	19	-10.56	3-10	30	+3.91	5-30	17	-11.47	0-3	0	-3.00
February	4-32	13	-16.92	0-8	0	-8.00	2-21	10	-9.00	2-3	67	+0.08
March	7-45	16	-24.09	1-7	14	-5.94	5-35	14	-18.40	1-3	33	+0.25
April	6-38	16	-13.40	1-8	13	-5.90	4-26	15	-7.50	1-4	25	0.00

By horse

	Wins-Runs	%	£1 level stakes	Win prize	Total prize
Thomas Darby	3-6	50	+4.20	£16,692.72	£48,856.72
Itchy Feet	3-6	50	+1.55	£18,082.94	£43,399.44
Brewin'upastorm	1-5	20	-3.17	£5,523.30	£35,656.80
Fiesole	1-4	25	+7.00	£31,280.00	£31,494.60
Yensir	4-5	80	+7.25	£20,793.60	£21,556.80
Knockgraffon	1-3	33	+2.00	£19,494.00	£21,415.28
Angel Of Harlem	3-8	38	-0.81	£13,385.88	£18,055.54
Beau Sancy	3-5	60	+1.85	£13,515.84	£16,042.56
Mon Port	3-7	43	+2.13	£12,021.30	£15,901.10
Skandiburg	3-6	50	+0.19	£11,825.71	£15,228.91
Finawn Bawn	3-5	60	+2.15	£10,461.78	£15,160.78
Let's Get At It	3-9	33	+7.10	£14,479.83	£15,130.34
Motueka	3-5	60	+3.88	£12,216.24	£14,727.28

Olly Murphy

All runners

	Wins-Runs	%	Win prize	Total prize	£1 level stakes
2018-19	82-431	19	£399,059.31	£662,548.89	-93.06
2017-18	47-250	19	£292,047.61	£382,934.59	-61.39

*First runners in July 2017

By course - last five seasons

	Overall			Chases			Hurdles			Bumpers		
	W-R	%	£1	W-R	%	£1	W-R	%	£1	W-R	%	£1
Aintree	0-6	0	-6.00	0-1	0	-1.00	0-5	0	-5.00	0-0	-	0
Ascot	1-4	25	+6.00	0-0	-	0	1-4	25	+6.00	0-0	-	0
Ayr	4-16	25	-6.51	1-5	20	-2.50	1-8	13	-6.17	2-3	67	+2.16
Bangor-on-Dee	3-34	9	-27.92	1-7	14	-4.75	2-24	8	-20.17	0-3	0	-3.00
Carlisle	2-4	50	+2.13	0-0	-	0	1-2	50	+0.63	1-2	50	+1.50
Cartmel	0-8	0	-8.00	0-0	-	0	0-8	0	-8.00	0-0	-	0
Catterick	1-7	14	-2.00	0-1	0	-1.00	1-6	17	-1.00	0-0	-	0
Cheltenham	1-18	6	-11.50	0-2	0	-2.00	1-15	7	-8.50	0-1	0	-1.00
Chepstow	1-7	14	-1.00	0-3	0	-3.00	0-2	0	-2.00	1-2	50	+4.00
Doncaster	2-5	40	-2.03	1-1	100	+0.06	0-2	0	-2.00	1-2	50	-0.09
Fakenham	24-89	27	+13.14	4-14	29	-3.22	19-71	27	+18.52	1-4	25	-2.17
Ffos Las	2-9	22	+1.88	1-2	50	+0.88	0-4	0	-4.00	1-3	33	+5.00
Fontwell	4-22	18	-3.58	2-6	33	+5.75	1-13	8	-7.50	1-3	33	-1.83
Haydock	1-3	33	-1.33	0-0	-	0	1-3	33	-1.33	0-0	-	0
Hereford	1-8	13	-5.50	0-2	0	-2.00	0-5	0	-5.00	1-1	100	+1.50
Hexham	1-2	50	+0.10	1-1	100	+1.10	0-1	0	-1.00	0-0	-	0
Huntingdon	7-23	30	-7.10	0-5	0	-5.00	4-14	29	-5.52	3-4	75	+3.42
Kelso	0-5	0	-5.00	0-1	0	-1.00	0-4	0	-4.00	0-0	-	0
Kempton	1-8	13	-4.50	0-1	0	-1.00	1-7	14	-3.50	0-0	-	0
Leicester	3-7	43	+5.00	0-1	0	-1.00	3-6	50	+6.00	0-0	-	0
Lingfield	2-6	33	+8.00	1-2	50	+5.00	1-4	25	+3.00	0-0	-	0
Lingfield (AW)	0-6	0	-6.00	0-0	-	0	0-0	-	0	0-6	0	-6.00
Ludlow	3-21	14	-14.53	0-3	0	-3.00	3-16	19	-9.53	0-2	0	-2.00
Market Rasen	18-74	24	+6.38	0-11	0	-11.00	18-60	30	+20.38	0-3	0	-3.00
Musselburgh	2-7	29	+2.50	2-5	40	+4.50	0-1	0	-1.00	0-1	0	-1.00
Newbury	0-10	0	-10.00	0-1	0	-1.00	0-8	0	-8.00	0-1	0	-1.00
Newcastle	0-5	0	-5.00	0-0	-	0	0-3	0	-3.00	0-2	0	-2.00
Newcastle (AW)	0-2	0	-2.00	0-0	-	0	0-0	-	0	0-2	0	-2.00
Newton Abbot	7-15	47	+15.95	2-2	100	+11.20	4-12	33	+2.75	1-1	100	+2.00
Perth	0-2	0	-2.00	0-0	-	0	0-1	0	-1.00	0-1	0	-1.00
Plumpton	1-9	11	+2.00	0-3	0	-3.00	1-6	17	+5.00	0-0	-	0
Sandown	0-7	0	-7.00	0-0	-	0	0-7	0	-7.00	0-0	-	0
Sedgefield	2-11	18	-6.77	0-3	0	-3.00	1-4	25	-1.50	1-4	25	-2.27
Southwell	6-49	12	-35.03	1-7	14	-4.13	5-39	13	-27.90	0-3	0	-3.00
Stratford	9-44	20	-11.25	3-8	38	+1.63	5-32	16	-11.13	1-4	25	-1.75
Taunton	2-12	17	-7.93	1-2	50	+0.88	1-10	10	-8.80	0-0	-	0
Towcester	0-10	0	-10.00	0-3	0	-3.00	0-7	0	-7.00	0-0	-	0
Uttoxeter	7-35	20	-7.35	1-5	20	+7.00	4-26	15	-16.10	2-4	50	+1.75
Warwick	4-38	11	+7.88	0-5	0	-5.00	3-28	11	+13.88	1-5	20	-1.00
Wetherby	1-12	8	-9.50	1-2	50	+0.50	0-9	0	-9.00	0-1	0	-1.00
Wincanton	2-6	33	+3.23	1-1	100	+0.73	1-5	20	+2.50	0-0	-	0
Worcester	4-15	27	-2.29	0-2	0	-2.00	4-12	33	+0.71	0-1	0	-1.00

By race type

	Overall			Chases			Hurdles		
	W-R	%	£1	W-R	%	£1	W-R	%	£1
Graded	11-82	13	-1.50	6-48	13	-9.50	5-32	16	+10.00
Handicap	46-384	12	-70.28	31-232	13	-50.66	15-152	10	-19.62
Novice	23-179	13	-60.99	11-86	13	-39.94	12-93	13	-21.05

By jockey

	Overall			Chases			Hurdles			Bumpers		
	W-R	%	£1	W-R	%	£1	W-R	%	£1	W-R	%	£1
Harry Cobden	23-162	14	-1.72	12-77	16	-13.17	11-80	14	+16.45	0-5	0	-5.00
T Scudamore	15-112	13	-25.58	12-65	18	+5.92	3-42	7	-26.50	0-5	0	-5.00
Robbie Power	8-63	13	-10.75	4-25	16	-10.25	4-36	11	+1.50	0-2	0	-2.00
Tom O'Brien	7-43	16	-14.04	3-24	13	-10.67	4-18	22	-2.38	0-1	0	-1.00
Richard Johnson	6-37	16	-9.84	5-26	19	-0.75	1-10	10	-8.09	0-1	0	-1.00
Jonjo O'Neill Jr	3-10	30	+10.41	1-6	17	+0.50	1-2	50	+10.00	1-2	50	-0.09
Harry Kimber	3-16	19	+11.75	0-2	0	-2.00	3-12	25	+15.75	0-2	0	-2.00
Aidan Coleman	3-22	14	-3.25	2-12	17	+4.00	1-8	13	-5.25	0-2	0	-2.00
S Twiston-Davies	2-11	18	-2.27	2-8	25	+0.73	0-2	0	-2.00	0-1	0	-1.00
James Bowen	2-16	13	-10.09	0-5	0	-5.00	0-7	0	-7.00	2-4	50	+1.91

By month

	Overall			Chases			Hurdles			Bumpers		
	W-R	%	£1	W-R	%	£1	W-R	%	£1	W-R	%	£1
May	9-46	20	+39.66	6-23	26	+10.25	2-18	11	+32.50	1-5	20	-3.09
June	4-18	22	+3.25	2-8	25	+7.00	2-10	20	-3.75	0-0	-	0
July	2-22	9	-14.25	2-12	17	-4.25	0-10	0	-10.00	0-0	-	0
August	0-11	0	-11.00	0-9	0	-9.00	0-2	0	-2.00	0-0	-	0
September	2-15	13	-4.50	2-8	25	+2.50	0-7	0	-7.00	0-0	-	0
October	7-53	13	-18.09	6-23	26	+10.00	1-24	4	-22.09	0-6	0	-6.00
November	18-86	21	+13.56	9-42	21	+1.31	8-42	19	+10.25	1-2	50	+2.00
December	9-87	10	-25.80	3-47	6	-23.00	6-37	16	+0.20	0-3	0	-3.00
January	10-73	14	-28.50	7-36	19	-8.00	3-37	8	-20.50	0-0	-	0
February	8-64	13	-18.38	3-27	11	-4.50	5-36	14	-12.88	0-1	0	-1.00
March	3-77	4	-61.25	2-37	5	-25.00	1-34	3	-30.25	0-6	0	-6.00
April	5-48	10	-2.59	2-24	8	-13.50	2-17	12	+16.00	1-7	14	-5.09

By horse

	Wins-Runs	%	£1 level stakes	Win prize	Total prize
Elegant Escape	2-6	33	+2.33	£102,510.00	£188,353.50
Sizing Tennessee	2-2	100	+14.50	£154,396.30	£154,396.30
Lostintranslation	2-6	33	+2.00	£76,088.50	£127,879.66
Native River	0-3	-	-3.00	£0.00	£102,275.00
Vision Des Flos	1-8	13	-3.50	£45,560.00	£83,102.50
Thistlecrack	0-3	-	-3.00	£0.00	£74,645.00
Robinsfirth	1-2	50	+7.00	£56,950.00	£72,977.50
Reserve Tank	3-5	60	+25.75	£65,588.88	£66,294.84
Mister Malarky	3-6	50	+7.25	£37,645.15	£63,898.17
Elixir De Nutz	3-4	75	+8.20	£55,766.40	£58,523.40
West Approach	0-8	-	-8.00	£0.00	£50,675.00
Royal Vacation	1-5	20	+3.00	£31,254.00	£49,904.00
Fox Norton	0-2	-	-2.00	£0.00	£48,105.00

Colin Tizzard

All runners

	Wins-Runs	%	Win prize	Total prize	£1 level stakes
2018-19	77-600	13	£1,021,264.55	£1,888,756.98	-127.89
2017-18	79-536	15	£1,272,104.57	£1,975,899.24	-159.35
2016-17	57-405	14	£1,449,147.45	£2,041,054.55	+8.75
2015-16	50-323	15	£1,147,232.6	£1,443,450.633	-46.75

By course - last five seasons

	Overall			Chases			Hurdles			Bumpers		
	W-R	%	£1	W-R	%	£1	W-R	%	£1	W-R	%	£1
Aintree	14-62	23	+111.49	9-38	24	+66.20	5-23	22	+46.29	0-1	0	-1.00
Ascot	7-72	10	-37.22	4-43	9	-24.56	3-24	13	-7.67	0-5	0	-5.00
Ayr	0-15	0	-15.00	0-12	0	-12.00	0-3	0	-3.00	0-0	-	0
Bangor-on-Dee	2-16	13	-2.09	0-6	0	-6.00	1-6	17	+6.00	1-4	25	-2.09
Carlisle	1-7	14	-2.00	1-6	17	-1.00	0-1	0	-1.00	0-0	-	0
Cartmel	0-2	0	-2.00	0-1	0	-1.00	0-1	0	-1.00	0-0	-	0
Cheltenham	24-244	10	-86.02	13-144	9	-67.27	10-90	11	-12.75	1-10	10	-6.00
Chepstow	20-189	11	-68.13	13-89	15	-13.25	7-79	9	-33.88	0-21	0	-21.00
Doncaster	0-3	0	-3.00	0-3	0	-3.00	0-0	-	0	0-0	-	0
Exeter	33-193	17	-48.94	16-84	19	-22.26	17-96	18	-13.69	0-13	0	-13.00
Fakenham	1-6	17	-2.75	1-4	25	-0.75	0-2	0	-2.00	0-0	-	0
Ffos Las	6-21	29	+22.48	3-9	33	+3.48	3-9	33	+22.00	0-3	0	-3.00
Fontwell	28-132	21	-19.52	16-56	29	+8.58	11-63	17	-19.10	1-13	8	-9.00
Haydock	5-38	13	-11.54	5-25	20	+1.46	0-13	0	-13.00	0-0	-	0
Hereford	1-20	5	-16.25	0-5	0	-5.00	1-13	8	-9.25	0-2	0	-2.00
Huntingdon	3-11	27	+3.13	2-5	40	+6.25	1-4	25	-1.13	0-2	0	-2.00
Kelso	0-1	0	-1.00	0-1	0	-1.00	0-0	-	0	0-0	-	0
Kempton	12-78	15	+20.85	6-43	14	+15.85	6-31	19	+9.00	0-4	0	-4.00
Leicester	0-3	0	-3.00	0-3	0	-3.00	0-0	-	0	0-0	-	0
Lingfield	4-18	22	-4.50	3-13	23	-3.25	1-5	20	-1.25	0-0	-	0
Ludlow	4-35	11	-24.99	0-17	0	-17.00	4-15	27	-4.99	0-3	0	-3.00
Market Rasen	2-10	20	-2.00	0-5	0	-5.00	2-5	40	+3.00	0-0	-	0
Newbury	19-110	17	-10.47	15-62	24	+17.79	3-39	8	-23.25	1-9	11	-5.00
Newcastle	3-8	38	+23.00	1-3	33	+10.00	2-5	40	+13.00	0-0	-	0
Newton Abbot	17-127	13	-36.50	9-61	15	-5.88	7-61	11	-28.63	1-5	20	-2.00
Perth	0-2	0	-2.00	0-2	0	-2.00	0-0	-	0	0-0	-	0
Plumpton	13-79	16	-26.42	6-28	21	-6.29	7-46	15	-15.13	0-5	0	-5.00
Sandown	8-84	10	-50.07	2-50	4	-40.17	6-34	18	-9.90	0-0	-	0
Sedgefield	1-2	50	-0.09	0-0	-	0	0-1	0	-1.00	1-1	100	+0.91
Southwell	2-10	20	+2.00	0-4	0	-4.00	2-5	40	+7.00	0-1	0	-1.00
Stratford	2-15	13	-2.25	1-5	20	-1.25	1-8	13	+1.00	0-2	0	-2.00
Taunton	18-133	14	-19.85	7-47	15	+9.00	11-80	14	-22.85	0-6	0	-6.00
Towcester	0-3	0	-3.00	0-0	-	0	0-1	0	-1.00	0-2	0	-2.00
Uttoxeter	7-52	13	+6.50	4-31	13	+1.50	3-20	15	+6.00	0-1	0	-1.00
Warwick	3-50	6	-36.00	1-21	5	-17.00	2-25	8	-15.00	0-4	0	-4.00
Wetherby	4-15	27	+8.98	2-12	17	+0.25	2-3	67	+8.73	0-0	-	0
Wincanton	36-269	13	-45.76	21-110	19	+8.58	15-129	12	-24.35	0-30	0	-30.00
Worcester	1-23	4	-20.75	0-10	0	-10.00	0-10	0	-10.00	1-3	33	-0.75

By race type

	Overall			Chases			Hurdles		
	W-R	%	£1	W-R	%	£1	W-R	%	£1
Graded	1-10	10	-1.00	0-5	0	-5.00	1-5	20	+4.00
Handicap	40-259	15	-45.49	30-169	18	-17.99	10-90	11	-27.50
Novice	16-68	24	+39.49	4-27	15	-12.16	12-41	29	+51.65

By jockey

	Overall			Chases			Hurdles			Bumpers		
	W-R	%	£1	W-R	%	£1	W-R	%	£1	W-R	%	£1
Sean Bowen	45-210	21	+59.13	30-110	27	+36.10	13-89	15	+24.03	2-11	18	-1.00
James Bowen	15-125	12	-54.50	7-62	11	-27.46	5-55	9	-30.63	3-8	38	+3.58
Mr Peter Bryan	2-7	29	+2.50	0-3	0	-3.00	2-4	50	+5.50	0-0	-	0
Miss J Hughes	1-2	50	+1.75	0-0	-	0	1-2	50	+1.75	0-0	-	0
Richard Johnson	1-2	50	+2.50	0-1	0	-1.00	1-1	100	+3.50	0-0	-	0
Bridget Andrews	0-1	0	-1.00	0-0	-	0	0-1	0	-1.00	0-0	-	0
Lorcan Williams	0-3	0	-3.00	0-2	0	-2.00	0-1	0	-1.00	0-0	-	0
Mr S Morgan	0-3	0	-3.00	0-1	0	-1.00	0-1	0	-1.00	0-1	0	-1.00
Richard Patrick	0-3	0	-3.00	0-0	-	0	0-2	0	-2.00	0-1	0	-1.00
Robert Dunne	0-3	0	-3.00	0-3	0	-3.00	0-0	-	0	0-0	-	0

By month

	Overall			Chases			Hurdles			Bumpers		
	W-R	%	£1	W-R	%	£1	W-R	%	£1	W-R	%	£1
May	7-41	17	-0.21	4-20	20	+1.17	3-18	17	+1.63	0-3	0	-3.00
June	13-39	33	+10.52	7-16	44	+6.52	4-18	22	-1.00	2-5	40	+5.00
July	10-40	25	+56.53	4-21	19	+0.25	5-17	29	+53.95	1-2	50	+2.33
August	5-24	21	-2.96	3-13	23	+1.17	2-11	18	-4.13	0-0	-	0
September	7-25	28	+12.88	3-13	23	+2.88	4-11	36	+11.00	0-1	0	-1.00
October	5-32	16	-7.67	3-18	17	-1.00	2-12	17	-4.67	0-2	0	-2.00
November	3-37	8	-21.50	3-20	15	-4.50	0-16	0	-16.00	0-1	0	-1.00
December	1-34	3	-29.50	1-15	7	-10.50	0-17	0	-17.00	0-2	0	-2.00
January	4-21	19	+0.79	4-14	29	+7.79	0-7	0	-7.00	0-0	-	0
February	1-14	7	-5.00	0-7	0	-7.00	1-6	17	+3.00	0-1	0	-1.00
March	3-28	11	-9.75	2-12	17	+2.50	0-13	0	-13.00	1-3	33	+0.75
April	5-33	15	-14.75	3-16	19	-3.63	1-16	6	-13.63	1-1	100	+2.50

By horse

	Wins-Runs	%	£1 level stakes	Win prize	Total prize
Lord Napier	1-7	14	+2.00	£56,270.00	£70,739.00
More Buck's	3-10	30	+9.75	£52,229.90	£53,056.90
Ontopoftheworld	5-12	42	+0.41	£33,383.88	£43,436.06
Henllan Harri	1-7	14	0.00	£25,024.00	£43,258.18
Beggar's Wishes	2-7	29	+10.00	£37,473.44	£43,017.94
Wells De Lune	4-8	50	+6.92	£39,169.50	£40,734.06
Rolling Maul	3-8	38	+11.50	£31,603.47	£34,173.31
Rons Dream	1-5	20	+5.00	£17,522.25	£33,533.25
Lotus Pond	3-4	75	+2.55	£20,840.76	£21,584.88
Souriyan	3-6	50	+9.80	£17,999.46	£20,197.46
Play The Ace	2-10	20	+3.00	£8,187.48	£19,723.81
Mac Tottie	4-8	50	+3.96	£16,225.38	£18,298.78
Alf 'N' Dor	2-11	18	+1.00	£9,941.94	£18,025.50

Peter Bowen

All runners

	Wins-Runs	%	Win prize	Total prize	£1 level stakes
2018-19	64-368	17	£523,688.84	£717,638.85	-10.62
2017-18	52-293	18	£357,317.72	£517,223.6419	-18.65
2016-17	40-299	13	£319,606.74	£476,682.77	-60.11
2015-16	33-236	14	£217,708.5	£326,520.25	-84.96

By course - last five seasons

	Overall			Chases			Hurdles			Bumpers		
	W-R	%	£1	W-R	%	£1	W-R	%	£1	W-R	%	£1
Aintree	6-72	8	-38.50	2-29	7	-18.00	3-38	8	-24.50	1-5	20	+4.00
Ascot	1-15	7	-11.75	1-9	11	-5.75	0-6	0	-6.00	0-0	-	0
Ayr	1-24	4	-21.00	0-9	0	-9.00	1-12	8	-9.00	0-3	0	-3.00
Bangor-on-Dee	8-51	16	-3.43	2-22	9	-10.13	5-23	22	+9.70	1-6	17	-3.00
Carlisle	3-7	43	+12.75	1-4	25	+1.00	1-2	50	+9.00	1-1	100	+2.75
Cartmel	21-64	33	+26.72	10-34	29	+2.84	11-30	37	+23.88	0-0	-	0
Catterick	0-7	0	-7.00	0-1	0	-1.00	0-5	0	-5.00	0-1	0	-1.00
Cheltenham	2-37	5	-11.00	0-10	0	-10.00	2-26	8	0.00	0-1	0	-1.00
Chepstow	19-122	16	-10.47	9-44	20	+4.30	7-65	11	-15.27	3-13	23	+0.50
Doncaster	1-23	4	-19.00	1-2	50	+2.00	0-20	0	-20.00	0-1	0	-1.00
Exeter	1-28	4	-26.17	0-13	0	-13.00	1-15	7	-13.17	0-0	-	0
Fakenham	3-19	16	-8.00	1-9	11	-6.75	2-9	22	-0.25	0-1	0	-1.00
Ffos Las	39-251	16	-80.05	19-87	22	-6.29	19-136	14	-47.42	1-28	4	-26.33
Fontwell	3-37	8	-25.50	2-19	11	-12.00	1-13	8	-8.50	0-5	0	-5.00
Haydock	6-24	25	+8.53	4-13	31	+10.00	1-10	10	-8.47	1-1	100	+7.00
Hereford	1-6	17	-1.00	1-3	33	+2.00	0-2	0	-2.00	0-1	0	-1.00
Hexham	2-11	18	-5.67	0-4	0	-4.00	1-5	20	-3.67	1-2	50	+2.00
Huntingdon	0-8	0	-8.00	0-5	0	-5.00	0-1	0	-1.00	0-2	0	-2.00
Kelso	1-8	13	-6.43	1-4	25	-2.43	0-4	0	-4.00	0-0	-	0
Kempton	3-15	20	+0.20	1-7	14	0.00	1-6	17	0.00	1-2	50	+0.20
Leicester	0-6	0	-6.00	0-5	0	-5.00	0-1	0	-1.00	0-0	-	0
Lingfield	0-4	0	-4.00	0-3	0	-3.00	0-1	0	-1.00	0-0	-	0
Ludlow	5-29	17	-1.13	3-10	30	+9.00	1-15	7	-9.00	1-4	25	-1.13
Market Rasen	16-84	19	-8.08	7-38	18	-1.38	7-35	20	-0.25	2-11	18	-6.45
Musselburgh	1-4	25	-2.71	1-3	33	-1.71	0-1	0	-1.00	0-0	-	0
Newbury	1-26	4	-22.50	0-15	0	-15.00	1-11	9	-7.50	0-0	-	0
Newcastle	0-1	0	-1.00	0-1	0	-1.00	0-0	-	0	0-0	-	0
Newton Abbot	11-60	18	-5.00	7-28	25	+10.00	4-29	14	-12.00	0-3	0	-3.00
Perth	14-36	39	+17.87	6-19	32	+3.17	6-13	46	+12.20	2-4	50	+2.50
Plumpton	4-37	11	-12.38	2-17	12	-6.25	2-17	12	-3.13	0-3	0	-3.00
Sandown	2-11	18	+39.00	1-7	14	+34.00	1-4	25	+5.00	0-0	-	0
Sedgefield	5-23	22	+3.11	4-13	31	+11.67	1-9	11	-7.56	0-1	0	-1.00
Southwell	12-57	21	+8.36	7-17	41	+20.78	5-30	17	-2.42	0-10	0	-10.00
Stratford	13-61	21	+9.50	10-28	36	+31.08	1-21	5	-16.67	2-12	17	-4.92
Taunton	1-7	14	-3.25	0-2	0	-2.00	0-4	0	-4.00	1-1	100	+2.75
Towcester	1-6	17	+1.00	0-0	-	0	1-5	20	+2.00	0-1	0	-1.00
Uttoxeter	12-106	11	-47.84	5-38	13	-4.00	7-59	12	-34.84	0-9	0	-9.00
Warwick	4-53	8	-30.50	0-14	0	-14.00	3-30	10	-12.00	1-9	11	-4.50
Wetherby	0-3	0	-3.00	0-2	0	-2.00	0-1	0	-1.00	0-0	-	0
Wincanton	1-21	5	-15.50	1-12	8	-6.50	0-8	0	-8.00	0-1	0	-1.00
Worcester	22-105	21	+54.38	9-45	20	+4.25	10-47	21	+53.08	3-13	23	-2.95

By race type

	Overall			Chases			Hurdles		
	W-R	%	£1	W-R	%	£1	W-R	%	£1
Graded	4-64	6	-38.00	2-39	5	-21.50	2-24	8	-15.50
Handicap	39-368	11	-151.32	19-205	9	-93.86	20-163	12	-57.46
Novice	18-128	14	-54.01	7-48	15	-8.50	11-80	14	-45.51

By jockey

	Overall			Chases			Hurdles			Bumpers		
	W-R	%	£1	W-R	%	£1	W-R	%	£1	W-R	%	£1
S T-Davies	38-275	14	-130.87	10-112	9	-67.11	25-144	17	-53.36	3-19	16	-10.40
Tom Bellamy	5-34	15	-5.25	3-24	13	-6.25	2-9	22	+2.00	0-1	0	-1.00
Daryl Jacob	5-43	12	-24.45	2-25	8	-15.25	3-18	17	-9.20	0-0	-	0
Mr Zac Baker	4-16	25	+5.38	2-12	17	-3.13	2-4	50	+8.50	0-0	-	0
Mark Grant	3-15	20	+10.00	3-8	38	+17.00	0-6	0	-6.00	0-1	0	-1.00
Jamie Bargary	3-67	4	-42.00	2-30	7	-11.00	1-32	3	-26.00	0-5	0	-5.00
Callum Bewley	2-4	50	+7.00	2-4	50	+7.00	0-0	-	0	0-0	-	0
Jordan Nailor	2-41	5	-17.75	0-7	0	-7.00	2-30	7	-6.75	0-4	0	-4.00
Mr Jack Savage	1-14	7	-9.00	0-1	0	-1.00	1-13	8	-8.00	0-0	-	0
A P Heskin	0-1	0	-1.00	0-1	0	-1.00	0-0	-	0	0-0	-	0

By month

	Overall			Chases			Hurdles			Bumpers		
	W-R	%	£1	W-R	%	£1	W-R	%	£1	W-R	%	£1
May	1-38	3	-30.00	0-14	0	-14.00	1-21	5	-13.00	0-3	0	-3.00
June	0-6	0	-6.00	0-1	0	-1.00	0-5	0	-5.00	0-0	-	0
July	1-16	6	-13.75	1-9	11	-6.75	0-6	0	-6.00	0-1	0	-1.00
August	1-10	10	-4.00	0-7	0	-7.00	1-3	33	+3.00	0-0	-	0
September	5-22	23	-3.30	1-9	11	-5.25	3-11	27	-0.05	1-2	50	+2.00
October	11-58	19	-14.47	6-30	20	-5.61	5-26	19	-6.86	0-2	0	-2.00
November	8-67	12	-29.45	3-30	10	-8.50	5-36	14	-19.95	0-1	0	-1.00
December	7-79	9	-47.27	2-36	6	-21.50	5-40	13	-22.77	0-3	0	-3.00
January	11-59	19	+0.90	3-23	13	+3.50	6-34	18	-5.20	2-2	100	+2.60
February	6-51	12	-30.63	2-17	12	-9.00	4-31	13	-18.63	0-3	0	-3.00
March	8-72	11	-9.68	4-29	14	-0.63	4-35	11	-1.06	0-8	0	-8.00
April	4-51	8	-39.31	2-22	9	-15.00	2-22	9	-17.31	0-7	0	-7.00

By horse

	Wins-Runs	%	£1 level stakes	Win prize	Total prize
Bristol De Mai	1-4	25	+3.50	£112,540.00	£189,392.50
Blue Flight	3-7	43	+10.50	£51,965.54	£73,752.60
Go Conquer	1-5	20	+4.00	£56,950.00	£72,270.00
Al Dancer	4-5	80	+6.00	£66,283.82	£66,283.82
Ballymoy	3-6	50	+3.33	£53,983.00	£58,380.00
Wholestone	1-6	17	-3.00	£28,152.00	£48,871.00
Cogry	1-5	20	+5.00	£33,791.15	£45,617.15
Ballyhill	1-7	14	-2.50	£11,696.40	£37,201.90
One For Rosie	2-5	40	+1.25	£8,967.24	£33,445.04
Earlofthecotswolds	4-8	50	+3.90	£26,316.90	£30,198.98
Calett Mad	0-5	-	-5.00	£0.00	£29,568.06
Wicked Willy	1-7	14	+14.00	£21,896.00	£28,286.66
Count Meribel	2-4	50	+10.00	£23,684.50	£26,705.00

Nigel Twiston-Davies

All runners

	Wins-Runs	%	Win prize	Total prize	£1 level stakes
2018-19	63-529	12	£738,487.78	£1,257,830.12	-226.95
2017-18	80-527	15	£1,201,080.41	£1,896,192.66	-102.99
2016-17	95-586	16	£950,479.52	£1,582,656.01	-122.54
2015-16	72-482	15	£822,890.08	£1,205,966.19	-79.80

By course - last five seasons

	Overall			Chases			Hurdles			Bumpers		
	W-R	%	£1	W-R	%	£1	W-R	%	£1	W-R	%	£1
Aintree	10-105	10	-49.75	6-60	10	-25.75	4-41	10	-20.00	0-4	0	-4.00
Ascot	4-56	7	-36.50	1-24	4	-17.50	3-28	11	-15.00	0-4	0	-4.00
Ayr	0-21	0	-21.00	0-17	0	-17.00	0-3	0	-3.00	0-1	0	-1.00
Bangor-on-Dee	11-69	16	-18.36	5-28	18	-10.19	3-25	12	-15.67	3-16	19	+7.50
Carlisle	9-25	36	+9.92	3-15	20	+5.00	6-9	67	+5.92	0-1	0	-1.00
Cartmel	1-10	10	-7.25	1-4	25	-1.25	0-6	0	-6.00	0-0	-	0
Catterick	0-1	0	-1.00	0-0	-	0	0-1	0	-1.00	0-0	-	0
Cheltenham	27-263	10	-89.40	13-141	9	-32.17	12-109	11	-59.23	2-13	15	+2.00
Chepstow	19-109	17	+3.27	7-45	16	+2.71	9-50	18	-1.04	3-14	21	+1.60
Doncaster	4-49	8	-15.25	3-21	14	+6.75	1-23	4	-17.00	0-5	0	-5.00
Exeter	4-45	9	-24.75	2-22	9	-13.25	1-21	5	-12.00	1-2	50	+0.50
Fakenham	2-20	10	-9.13	2-12	17	-1.13	0-6	0	-6.00	0-2	0	-2.00
Ffos Las	33-157	21	-11.91	9-46	20	-4.26	20-93	22	-8.91	4-18	22	+1.25
Fontwell	0-7	0	-7.00	0-2	0	-2.00	0-3	0	-3.00	0-2	0	-2.00
Haydock	20-109	18	-15.24	8-58	14	-13.82	12-48	25	+1.57	0-3	0	-3.00
Hereford	4-32	13	-16.75	3-10	30	+0.25	1-16	6	-11.00	0-6	0	-6.00
Hexham	0-3	0	-3.00	0-2	0	-2.00	0-1	0	-1.00	0-0	-	0
Huntingdon	8-78	10	-48.52	3-23	13	-12.45	4-45	9	-28.17	1-10	10	-7.90
Kelso	5-14	36	+7.08	4-10	40	+9.25	1-4	25	-2.17	0-0	-	0
Kempton	12-71	17	-5.89	7-38	18	-4.75	5-29	17	+2.86	0-4	0	-4.00
Leicester	15-65	23	+23.46	9-36	25	+19.33	6-29	21	+4.13	0-0	-	0
Lingfield	8-32	25	+19.58	3-14	21	+16.50	5-18	28	+3.08	0-0	-	0
Ludlow	15-135	11	-79.09	6-51	12	-25.54	9-78	12	-47.55	0-6	0	-6.00
Market Rasen	13-55	24	+8.56	3-19	16	-2.00	9-31	29	+11.56	1-5	20	-1.00
Musselburgh	1-2	50	+4.00	0-1	0	-1.00	1-1	100	+5.00	0-0	-	0
Newbury	8-91	9	-38.09	1-45	2	-38.00	6-35	17	+8.53	1-11	9	-8.63
Newcastle	2-16	13	-7.25	2-11	18	-2.25	0-5	0	-5.00	0-0	-	0
Newton Abbot	9-41	22	-1.43	4-19	21	-0.25	5-19	26	+1.82	0-3	0	-3.00
Perth	18-95	19	-24.38	7-37	19	-11.66	9-51	18	-21.73	2-7	29	+9.00
Plumpton	1-9	11	-2.50	1-1	100	+5.50	0-7	0	-7.00	0-1	0	-1.00
Sandown	12-67	18	+42.96	4-32	13	-7.59	8-35	23	+50.55	0-0	-	0
Sedgefield	1-3	33	-0.80	0-2	0	-2.00	1-1	100	+1.20	0-0	-	0
Southwell	9-53	17	-12.31	4-14	29	+7.25	5-31	16	-11.56	0-8	0	-8.00
Stratford	11-86	13	-36.47	3-32	9	-25.09	8-48	17	-5.38	0-6	0	-6.00
Taunton	5-33	15	-1.00	3-13	23	+3.50	2-19	11	-3.50	0-1	0	-1.00
Towcester	5-52	10	-18.63	2-16	13	+1.38	2-25	8	-16.00	1-11	9	-4.00
Uttoxeter	27-171	16	-35.01	13-70	19	+9.32	13-88	15	-33.43	1-13	8	-10.90
Warwick	19-172	11	-87.31	11-67	16	-19.79	6-81	7	-53.52	2-24	8	-14.00
Wetherby	11-56	20	-16.05	4-26	15	-8.50	6-28	21	-7.05	1-2	50	-0.50
Wincanton	5-42	12	-4.75	4-20	20	+10.75	1-18	6	-11.50	0-4	0	-4.00
Worcester	15-91	16	-10.97	5-27	19	-3.00	7-54	13	-18.88	3-10	30	+10.91

By race type

	Overall			Chases			Hurdles		
	W-R	%	£1	W-R	%	£1	W-R	%	£1
Graded	0-9	0	-9.00	0-4	0	-4.00	0-4	0	-4.00
Handicap	35-380	9	-197.04	14-143	10	-79.00	21-237	9	-118.04
Novice	15-131	11	-76.47	2-40	5	-34.25	13-91	14	-42.22

By jockey

	Overall			Chases			Hurdles			Bumpers		
	W-R	%	£1	W-R	%	£1	W-R	%	£1	W-R	%	£1
Brian Hughes	41-311	13	-160.56	15-123	12	-66.75	24-174	14	-88.81	2-14	14	-5.00
William Kennedy	6-73	8	-43.60	2-18	11	-4.00	3-51	6	-40.10	1-4	25	+0.50
Miss A McCain	5-44	11	-10.90	0-0	-	0	5-42	12	-8.90	0-2	0	-2.00
Lorcan Murtagh	4-52	8	-21.00	0-3	0	-3.00	4-45	9	-14.00	0-4	0	-4.00
Daryl Jacob	2-4	50	+2.43	0-0	-	0	2-4	50	+2.43	0-0	-	0
Harry Stock	2-7	29	+4.63	0-0	-	0	2-7	29	+4.63	0-0	-	0
Harrison Beswick	2-9	22	+9.25	0-1	0	-1.00	2-7	29	+11.25	0-1	0	-1.00
Mr Theo Gillard	1-22	5	-15.50	0-5	0	-5.00	1-17	6	-10.50	0-0	-	0
Brendan Powell	0-1	0	-1.00	0-0	-	0	0-1	0	-1.00	0-0	-	0
Donal McInerney	0-1	0	-1.00	0-0	-	0	0-1	0	-1.00	0-0	-	0

By month

	Overall			Chases			Hurdles			Bumpers		
	W-R	%	£1	W-R	%	£1	W-R	%	£1	W-R	%	£1
May	5-52	10	-32.85	2-17	12	-9.75	3-32	9	-20.10	0-3	0	-3.00
June	0-27	0	-27.00	0-6	0	-6.00	0-20	0	-20.00	0-1	0	-1.00
July	13-41	32	+19.21	4-10	40	+4.38	9-30	30	+15.83	0-1	0	-1.00
August	8-40	20	-6.93	3-13	23	-1.13	5-27	19	-5.81	0-0	-	0
September	3-25	12	-2.50	0-6	0	-6.00	3-19	16	+3.50	0-0	-	0
October	7-57	12	-30.25	3-20	15	-11.00	4-32	13	-14.25	0-5	0	-5.00
November	4-56	7	-30.50	2-17	12	-3.00	2-37	5	-25.50	0-2	0	-2.00
December	10-91	11	-54.68	2-31	6	-20.50	7-52	13	-29.68	1-8	13	-4.50
January	5-50	10	-27.58	1-11	9	-7.75	4-37	11	-17.83	0-2	0	-2.00
February	0-5	0	-5.00	0-2	0	-2.00	0-3	0	-3.00	0-0	-	0
March	5-59	8	-39.67	0-14	0	-14.00	3-43	7	-33.67	2-2	100	+8.00
April	3-54	6	-32.50	0-12	0	-12.00	3-39	8	-17.50	0-3	0	-3.00

By horse

	Wins-Runs	%	£1 level stakes	Win prize	Total prize
Lofgren	2-9	22	-0.25	£20,213.95	£32,242.83
Raise A Spark	3-9	33	-0.38	£26,381.88	£31,919.85
William Of Orange	2-7	29	+14.00	£27,161.64	£29,755.39
Ink Master	3-10	30	+3.38	£13,587.60	£22,911.76
Liva	2-6	33	+0.43	£19,007.96	£22,017.83
Beach Break	3-11	27	-0.25	£14,620.50	£21,343.22
Good Tradition	2-7	29	+4.63	£13,775.76	£16,695.00
Chti Balko	0-5	-	-5.00	£0.00	£14,100.00
The Some Dance Kid	3-4	75	+7.04	£12,671.10	£13,338.90
Lough Derg Jewel	1-5	20	-1.00	£7,342.74	£12,250.86
Sonic	2-8	25	-3.13	£8,187.48	£11,822.22
Wazowski	2-11	18	-3.50	£5,783.22	£11,803.94
Noah And The Ark	2-7	29	+11.25	£11,046.60	£11,666.70

Donald McCain

All runners

	Wins-Runs	%	Win prize	Total prize	£1 level stakes
2018-19	63-557	11	£337,729.88	£627,919.46	-270.25
2017-18	98-539	18	£556,818.155	£838,513.845	-17.29
2016-17	80-573	14	£351,310.49	£578,934.05	-126.20
2015-16	53-497	11	£289,227.76	£430,725.23	-138.27

By course - last five seasons

	Overall			Chases			Hurdles			Bumpers		
	W-R	%	£1	W-R	%	£1	W-R	%	£1	W-R	%	£1
Aintree	3-107	3	-90.67	1-43	2	-33.00	2-56	4	-49.67	0-8	0	-8.00
Ascot	0-4	0	-4.00	0-2	0	-2.00	0-2	0	-2.00	0-0	-	0
Ayr	15-91	16	-35.74	7-40	18	-12.68	7-42	17	-18.57	1-9	11	-4.50
Bangor-on-Dee	63-324	19	+22.80	15-84	18	-16.17	46-210	22	+61.47	2-30	7	-22.50
Carlisle	27-205	13	-53.14	8-60	13	-18.45	17-130	13	-24.14	2-15	13	-10.55
Cartmel	28-134	21	-10.87	7-45	16	-23.38	21-89	24	+12.50	0-0	-	0
Catterick	27-152	18	-19.10	6-41	15	-0.63	19-101	19	-16.73	2-10	20	-1.75
Cheltenham	1-35	3	-26.00	1-20	5	-11.00	0-14	0	-14.00	0-1	0	-1.00
Chepstow	1-18	6	-13.00	0-7	0	-7.00	1-10	10	-5.00	0-1	0	-1.00
Doncaster	7-65	11	-23.50	2-25	8	-9.00	5-38	13	-12.50	0-2	0	-2.00
Exeter	0-7	0	-7.00	0-3	0	-3.00	0-4	0	-4.00	0-0	-	0
Fakenham	2-12	17	-4.00	1-5	20	-2.50	1-7	14	-1.50	0-0	-	0
Ffos Las	0-1	0	-1.00	0-0	-	0	0-0	-	0	0-1	0	-1.00
Fontwell	2-6	33	+1.88	1-4	25	+1.50	1-2	50	+0.38	0-0	-	0
Haydock	14-99	14	-33.97	8-34	24	+5.03	6-61	10	-35.00	0-4	0	-4.00
Hereford	0-11	0	-11.00	0-3	0	-3.00	0-7	0	-7.00	0-1	0	-1.00
Hexham	11-99	11	-69.56	0-14	0	-14.00	11-77	14	-47.56	0-8	0	-8.00
Huntingdon	2-34	6	-21.50	0-7	0	-7.00	2-25	8	-12.50	0-2	0	-2.00
Kelso	25-158	16	-47.84	10-50	20	-7.04	14-101	14	-36.00	1-7	14	-4.80
Kempton	0-8	0	-8.00	0-6	0	-6.00	0-2	0	-2.00	0-0	-	0
Leicester	3-19	16	-5.00	2-9	22	-1.50	1-10	10	-3.50	0-0	-	0
Ludlow	1-64	2	-54.00	1-15	7	-5.00	0-44	0	-44.00	0-5	0	-5.00
Market Rasen	6-87	7	-18.50	2-29	7	-10.00	4-53	8	-3.50	0-5	0	-5.00
Musselburgh	26-135	19	-8.67	7-40	18	-8.00	16-90	18	-7.17	3-5	60	+6.50
Newbury	0-11	0	-11.00	0-3	0	-3.00	0-8	0	-8.00	0-0	-	0
Newcastle	6-71	8	-39.70	2-23	9	-16.13	4-41	10	-16.58	0-7	0	-7.00
Newcastle (AW)	0-3	0	-3.00	0-0	-	0	0-0	-	0	0-3	0	-3.00
Newton Abbot	0-8	0	-8.00	0-2	0	-2.00	0-6	0	-6.00	0-0	-	0
Perth	23-104	22	+12.43	9-38	24	+16.13	12-60	20	-4.07	2-6	33	+0.38
Plumpton	0-2	0	-2.00	0-1	0	-1.00	0-1	0	-1.00	0-0	-	0
Sandown	0-14	0	-14.00	0-8	0	-8.00	0-6	0	-6.00	0-0	-	0
Sedgefield	51-280	18	-44.21	12-63	19	-10.38	35-200	18	-36.34	4-17	24	+2.50
Southwell	1-33	3	-29.50	1-11	9	-7.50	0-22	0	-22.00	0-0	-	0
Southwell (AW)	3-5	60	+1.87	0-0	-	0	0-0	-	0	3-5	60	+1.87
Stratford	11-57	19	+20.88	2-16	13	-3.13	8-37	22	+19.00	1-4	25	+5.00
Taunton	0-4	0	-4.00	0-1	0	-1.00	0-3	0	-3.00	0-0	-	0
Towcester	2-24	8	-10.00	1-8	13	-3.00	1-16	6	-7.00	0-0	-	0
Uttoxeter	10-137	7	-72.13	1-32	3	-28.75	9-93	10	-31.38	0-12	0	-12.00
Warwick	1-23	4	-19.00	1-11	9	-7.00	0-12	0	-12.00	0-0	-	0
Wetherby	8-106	8	-50.00	2-30	7	-12.50	6-68	9	-29.50	0-8	0	-8.00
Wincanton	1-1	100	+3.50	1-1	100	+3.50	0-0	-	0	0-0	-	0
Worcester	12-95	13	-13.07	7-31	23	+18.73	5-58	9	-25.80	0-6	0	-6.00

Top trainers by winners

	All runs			First time out			Horses		
Won	Ran	%	Trainer	Won	Ran	%	Won	Ran	%
205	988	21	Dan Skelton	54	244	22	118	244	48
141	544	26	Nicky Henderson	55	174	32	89	174	51
135	589	23	Paul Nicholls	32	161	20	76	161	47
106	560	19	Philip Hobbs	16	143	11	66	143	46
91	499	18	Alan King	29	139	21	57	139	41
82	431	19	Olly Murphy	27	130	21	53	130	41
77	600	13	Colin Tizzard	22	129	17	51	129	40
64	368	17	Peter Bowen	13	82	16	34	82	41
63	529	12	Nigel Twiston-Davies	16	128	13	43	128	34
63	557	11	Donald McCain	12	140	9	42	140	30
59	421	14	Gary Moore	7	109	6	38	109	35
56	472	12	Jonjo O'Neill	12	125	10	38	125	30
55	206	27	Gordon Elliott	25	120	21	35	120	29
53	217	24	Dr Richard Newland	13	55	24	34	55	62
53	507	10	Evan Williams	4	117	3	36	117	31
52	377	14	Tom George	18	103	17	38	103	37
51	263	19	Kim Bailey	9	79	11	30	79	38
49	409	12	Fergal O'Brien	12	108	11	37	108	34
49	522	9	Neil Mulholland	7	127	6	34	127	27
47	242	19	Harry Fry	12	74	16	30	74	41
45	387	12	Tim Vaughan	10	111	9	28	111	25
44	313	14	Ben Pauling	7	92	8	30	92	33
44	363	12	David Pipe	10	94	11	32	94	34
43	275	16	Philip Kirby	9	66	14	28	66	42
42	222	19	Nicky Richards	6	57	11	28	57	49
42	277	15	Venetia Williams	8	79	10	29	79	37
40	249	16	Neil King	6	39	15	22	39	56
39	211	18	Jeremy Scott	9	53	17	24	53	45
38	178	21	Tom Lacey	11	44	25	25	44	57
38	308	12	Warren Greatrex	8	90	9	22	90	24
37	301	12	Seamus Mullins	8	63	13	26	63	41
36	314	11	Ian Williams	13	94	14	26	94	28
36	364	10	Charlie Longsdon	3	82	4	23	82	28
36	391	9	Lucinda Russell	6	98	6	26	98	27
35	263	13	Emma Lavelle	6	77	8	23	77	30
34	237	14	Oliver Sherwood	11	63	17	24	63	38
34	353	10	Micky Hammond	9	86	10	28	86	33
31	244	13	Jamie Snowden	7	61	11	20	61	33
29	247	12	Sue Smith	3	54	6	19	54	35
28	150	19	Keith Dalgleish	4	45	9	14	45	31
27	205	13	Christian Williams	1	42	2	12	42	29
26	172	15	Iain Jardine	4	40	10	16	40	40
26	192	14	Henry Oliver	2	45	4	14	45	31
25	169	15	Harry Whittington	8	46	17	16	46	35
25	202	12	N W Alexander	4	47	9	17	47	36
23	189	12	Henry Daly	7	47	15	14	47	30
21	161	13	Brian Ellison	4	42	10	17	42	40

Top trainers by prize-money

Total prize-money	Trainer	Win prize-money	Wins	Class 1-3 Won	Class 1-3 Ran	Class 1-3 %	Class 4-6 Won	Class 4-6 Ran	Class 4-6 %
£3,307,172	**Paul Nicholls**	£2,211,224	135	77	398	19	58	191	30
£2,908,080	**Nicky Henderson**	£2,149,853	141	68	326	21	73	218	33
£2,301,457	**Dan Skelton**	£1,516,811	205	61	421	14	144	567	25
£1,888,757	**Colin Tizzard**	£1,021,265	77	41	334	12	36	266	14
£1,409,435	**W P Mullins**	£919,796	8	8	74	11	0	0	—
£1,358,678	**Gordon Elliott**	£1,041,795	55	19	124	15	36	82	44
£1,305,374	**Philip Hobbs**	£905,087	106	45	271	17	61	289	21
£1,259,316	**Alan King**	£724,517	91	35	250	14	56	249	22
£1,257,830	**Nigel Twiston-Davies**	£738,488	63	29	277	10	34	252	13
£902,460	**Tom George**	£456,506	52	22	201	11	30	176	17
£823,437	**Harry Fry**	£604,767	47	27	144	19	20	98	20
£822,908	**Evan Williams**	£420,390	53	16	166	10	37	341	11
£747,096	**Gary Moore**	£498,910	59	23	152	15	36	269	13
£735,010	**Venetia Williams**	£455,895	42	19	136	14	23	141	16
£717,639	**Peter Bowen**	£523,689	64	24	164	15	40	204	20
£710,969	**Emma Lavelle**	£537,543	35	13	108	12	22	155	14
£680,690	**Nicky Richards**	£479,451	42	18	95	19	24	127	19
£662,549	**Olly Murphy**	£399,059	82	5	79	6	77	352	22
£645,005	**Dr Richard Newland**	£464,964	53	23	123	19	30	94	32
£639,240	**Jonjo O'Neill**	£390,041	56	22	190	12	34	282	12
£636,704	**Neil Mulholland**	£364,746	49	11	135	8	38	387	10
£627,919	**Donald McCain**	£337,730	63	16	162	10	47	395	12
£614,859	**Ben Pauling**	£439,781	44	16	100	16	28	213	13
£601,872	**Kim Bailey**	£401,042	51	19	96	20	32	167	19
£583,292	**David Pipe**	£313,813	44	11	122	9	33	241	14
£563,702	**Warren Greatrex**	£282,165	38	12	114	11	26	194	13
£550,654	**Fergal O'Brien**	£311,732	49	18	146	12	31	263	12
£545,005	**Charlie Longsdon**	£320,020	36	18	151	12	18	213	8
£506,416	**Ian Williams**	£296,723	36	16	139	12	20	175	11
£476,562	**Philip Kirby**	£342,160	43	14	72	19	29	203	14
£475,940	**Sue Smith**	£301,811	29	13	98	13	16	149	11
£471,412	**Neil King**	£284,652	40	15	91	16	25	158	16
£428,469	**Mrs John Harrington**	£198,292	4	4	15	27	0	0	—
£413,128	**Lucinda Russell**	£194,984	36	4	78	5	32	313	10
£388,257	**Tim Vaughan**	£215,867	45	4	69	6	41	318	13
£379,506	**Henry De Bromhead**	£253,469	6	6	33	18	0	0	—
£377,918	**Tom Lacey**	£219,400	38	12	74	16	26	104	25
£372,344	**Brian Ellison**	£248,887	21	8	66	12	13	95	14
£357,441	**Jamie Snowden**	£202,955	31	11	80	14	20	164	12
£339,084	**Seamus Mullins**	£185,762	37	3	78	4	34	223	15
£338,718	**Oliver Sherwood**	£189,644	34	7	73	10	27	164	16
£322,273	**Jeremy Scott**	£211,145	39	5	46	11	34	165	21
£309,754	**Christian Williams**	£238,804	27	6	35	17	21	170	12
£308,526	**Gavin Cromwell**	£281,163	6	1	23	4	5	29	17
£307,038	**N W Alexander**	£204,203	25	8	42	19	17	160	11
£302,924	**Micky Hammond**	£162,418	34	4	64	6	30	289	10
£290,482	**Henry Daly**	£158,814	23	10	84	12	13	105	12

Top jockeys

Won	Ran	%	Jockey	Best Trainer	Won	Ran
200	979	20	**Richard Johnson**	Philip Hobbs	53	262
178	745	24	**Harry Skelton**	Dan Skelton	172	696
146	888	16	**Brian Hughes**	Donald McCain	41	311
109	518	21	**Harry Cobden**	Paul Nicholls	84	322
105	681	15	**Sam Twiston-Davies**	Nigel Twiston-Davies	38	275
95	582	16	**Aidan Coleman**	Olly Murphy	22	97
91	593	15	**Sean Bowen**	Peter Bowen	45	210
88	413	21	**Wayne Hutchinson**	Alan King	68	315
86	381	23	**Nico de Boinville**	Nicky Henderson	67	235
82	685	12	**Tom Scudamore**	David Pipe	34	216
78	548	14	**Tom O'Brien**	Ian Williams	22	147
72	481	15	**James Bowen**	Nicky Henderson	20	80
69	411	17	**Gavin Sheehan**	Harry Whittington	15	58
68	553	12	**Paddy Brennan**	Fergal O'Brien	33	228
61	472	13	**Sean Quinlan**	Jennie Candlish	14	125
59	504	12	**Adam Wedge**	Evan Williams	37	306
58	370	16	**Daryl Jacob**	Ben Pauling	13	66
55	334	16	**David Bass**	Kim Bailey	39	180
50	307	16	**Bryony Frost**	Paul Nicholls	18	71
45	377	12	**Jonathan Burke**	Charlie Longsdon	15	175
44	308	14	**Leighton Aspell**	Oliver Sherwood	21	118
43	257	17	**Noel Fehily**	Harry Fry	21	78
41	368	11	**Tom Cannon**	Chris Gordon	19	121
41	416	10	**Robert Dunne**	Neil Mulholland	7	118
39	377	10	**Henry Brooke**	Ruth Jefferson	5	17
37	269	14	**Alan Johns**	Tim Vaughan	27	213
37	318	12	**Danny Cook**	Sue Smith	23	162
36	343	10	**Ross Chapman**	Iain Jardine	13	78
35	150	23	**Barry Geraghty**	Nicky Henderson	15	30
34	376	9	**Jamie Moore**	Gary Moore	27	183
32	187	17	**Rex Dingle**	Jeremy Scott	11	36
31	390	8	**Nick Scholfield**	Jeremy Scott	10	67
30	194	15	**Jonjo O'Neill Jr**	Jonjo O'Neill	15	118
30	310	10	**Kielan Woods**	Graeme McPherson	16	141
28	275	10	**Ben Poste**	Michael Scudamore	8	61
27	194	14	**Charlie Deutsch**	Venetia Williams	25	146
27	256	11	**Ciaran Gethings**	Stuart Edmunds	15	90
26	295	9	**Harry Bannister**	Charlie Mann	10	76
26	314	8	**Richie McLernon**	Ben Haslam	7	36
25	191	13	**Bridget Andrews**	Dan Skelton	22	175
25	243	10	**Charlie Hammond**	Dr Richard Newland	17	51
25	256	10	**Alain Cawley**	Micky Hammond	12	128
24	214	11	**Jeremiah McGrath**	Nicky Henderson	13	79
24	246	10	**Richard Patrick**	Kerry Lee	4	55
22	156	14	**Lorcan Williams**	Paul Nicholls	11	68
22	168	13	**Joshua Moore**	Gary Moore	18	138
21	184	11	**Connor Brace**	Fergal O'Brien	11	85
21	200	11	**Harry Reed**	Tristan Davidson	11	34

Big Race Dates, Fixtures and Track Facts

Perth
Musselburgh
Kelso
Ayr
Hexham
Newcastle
Carlisle
Cartmel
Sedgefield
Catterick
Wetherby
Aintree
Haydock
Doncaster
Bangor
Market Rasen
Southwell
Uttoxeter
Fakenham
Leicester
Ludlow
Worcester
Warwick
Huntingdon
Ffos Las
Hereford
Stratford
Towcester
Cheltenham
Chepstow
Newbury
Ascot
Kempton
Sandown
Lingfield
Folkestone
Taunton
Wincanton
Fontwell
Plumpton
Exeter
Newton Abbot

Fixtures

Key - Flat, **Jumps**

October

1 Tue .... Kempton, Ayr, **Sedgefield**, **Southwell**
2 Wed .... Kempton, Newcastle, Nottingham, **Bangor**, **Huntingdon**
3 Thu .... Lingfield, Chelmsford, Wolverhampton, Salisbury, **Warwick**
4 Fri .... Southwell, Ascot, **Fontwell**, **Hexham**
5 Sat .... Wolverhampton, Ascot, Newmarket, Redcar, **Fontwell**
6 Sun .... **Kelso**, **Uttoxeter**
7 Mon .... Newcastle, Pontefract, Windsor, **Stratford**
8 Tue .... Chelmsford, Brighton, Catterick, Leicester
9 Wed .... Kempton, Newcastle, Nottingham, **Ludlow**, **Towcester**
10 Thu .... Kempton, Southwell, Ayr, **Exeter**, **Worcester**
11 Fri .... Newcastle, Newmarket, York, **Chepstow**
12 Sat .... Wolverhampton, Newmarket, York, **Chepstow**, **Hexham**
13 Sun .... Goodwood, **Newton Abbot**
14 Mon .... Wolverhampton, Musselburgh, Windsor, Yarmouth
15 Tue .... Kempton, Leicester, **Hereford**, **Huntingdon**
16 Wed .... Kempton, Southwell, Bath, Nottingham, **Wetherby**
17 Thu .... Chelmsford, Wolverhampton, Brighton, **Carlisle**, **Wincanton**
18 Fri .... Newcastle, Haydock, Redcar, **Fakenham**, **Uttoxeter**
19 Sat .... Wolverhampton, Ascot, Catterick, **Ffos Las**, **Market Rasen**, ... **Stratford**
20 Sun .... **Kempton**, **Sedgefield**
21 Mon .... Southwell, Pontefract, Windsor, **Plumpton**
22 Tue .... Newcastle, Kempton, Yarmouth, **Exeter**
23 Wed .... Kempton, Wolverhampton, Newmarket, **Fontwell**, **Worcester**
24 Thu .... Chelmsford, Wolverhampton, **Carlisle**, **Ludlow**, **Southwell**
25 Fri .... Newcastle, Doncaster, Newbury, **Cheltenham**
26 Sat .... Chelmsford, Doncaster, Newbury, **Cheltenham**, **Kelso**
27 Sun .... **Aintree**, **Wincanton**
28 Mon .... Kempton, Leicester, Redcar, **Ayr**
29 Tue .... Southwell, Catterick, **Bangor**, **Chepstow**
30 Wed .... Kempton, Wolverhampton, Nottingham, **Fakenham**, **Taunton**
31 Thu .... Lingfield, Chelmsford, Kempton, **Newton Abbot**, **Stratford**

November

1 Fri .... Newcastle, Newmarket, **Uttoxeter**, **Wetherby**
2 Sat .... Chelmsford, Newmarket, **Ascot**, **Ayr**, **Wetherby**
3 Sun .... **Carlisle**, **Huntingdon**
4 Mon .... Kempton, Newcastle, **Hereford**, **Plumpton**
5 Tue .... Southwell, Kempton, Redcar, **Exeter**
6 Wed .... Kempton, Wolverhampton, Nottingham, **Chepstow**, **Musselburgh**
7 Thu .... Chelmsford, Southwell, **Market Rasen**, **Newbury**, **Sedgefield**
8 Fri .... Newcastle, **Fontwell**, **Hexham**, **Warwick**
9 Sat .... Southwell, Doncaster, **Aintree**, **Kelso**, **Wincanton**

10 Sun........ **Ffos Las**, **Sandown**
11 Mon........ **Carlisle**, **Kempton**, **Stratford**
12 Tue........ **Hereford**, **Huntingdon**, **Lingfield**
13 Wed........ **Ayr**, **Bangor**, **Exeter**
14 Thu........ **Ludlow**, **Sedgefield**, **Taunton**
15 Fri........ **Cheltenham**, **Newcastle**, **Southwell**
16 Sat........ Lingfield, Wolverhampton, **Cheltenham**, **Uttoxeter**, **Wetherby**
17 Sun........ **Cheltenham**, **Fontwell**
18 Mon........ Wolverhampton, Southwell, **Leicester**, **Plumpton**
19 Tue........ Kempton, Chelmsford, **Fakenham**, **Lingfield**
20 Wed........ Kempton, **Chepstow**, **Hexham**, **Warwick**
21 Thu........ Newcastle, Chelmsford, **Market Rasen**, **Wincanton**
22 Fri........ Newcastle, **Ascot**, **Catterick**, **Ffos Las**
23 Sat........ Lingfield, Wolverhampton, **Ascot**, **Haydock**, **Huntingdon**
24 Sun........ **Exeter**, **Uttoxeter**
25 Mon........ **Kempton**, **Ludlow**, **Musselburgh**
26 Tue........ Wolverhampton, **Sedgefield**, **Southwell**
27 Wed........ Southwell, Kempton, **Hereford**, **Wetherby**
28 Thu........ Lingfield, Chelmsford, **Taunton**, **Towcester**
29 Fri........ Southwell, Kempton, **Doncaster**, **Newbury**
30 Sat........ Wolverhampton, **Bangor**, **Doncaster**, **Newbury**, **Newcastle**

December

1 Sun........ **Carlisle**, **Leicester**
2 Mon........ Wolverhampton, **Musselburgh**, **Plumpton**
3 Tue........ Wolverhampton, **Lingfield**, **Southwell**
4 Wed........ Lingfield, Kempton, **Haydock**, **Ludlow**
5 Thu........ Southwell, **Leicester**, **Market Rasen**, **Wincanton**
6 Fri........ Newcastle, **Exeter**, **Sandown**, **Sedgefield**
7 Sat........ Wolverhampton, **Aintree**, **Chepstow**, **Sandown**, **Wetherby**
8 Sun........ **Huntingdon**, **Kelso**
9 Mon........ Lingfield, Newcastle, **Musselburgh**
10 Tue........ Wolverhampton, **Fontwell**, **Uttoxeter**
11 Wed........ Lingfield, Kempton, **Hexham**, **Leicester**
12 Thu........ Chelmsford, **Newcastle**, **Taunton**, **Warwick**
13 Fri........ Chelmsford, **Bangor**, **Cheltenham**, **Doncaster**
14 Sat........ Newcastle, Wolverhampton, **Cheltenham**, **Doncaster**, **Hereford**
15 Sun........ **Carlisle**, **Southwell**
16 Mon........ Wolverhampton, **Ffos Las**, **Plumpton**
17 Tue........ **Catterick**, **Fakenham**, **Lingfield**
18 Wed........ Lingfield, Newcastle, **Ludlow**, **Newbury**
19 Thu........ Southwell, Wolverhampton, **Exeter**, **Towcester**
20 Fri........ Southwell, Wolverhampton, **Ascot**, **Uttoxeter**
21 Sat........ Lingfield, **Ascot**, **Haydock**, **Newcastle**
26 Thu........ Wolverhampton, **Fontwell**, **Huntingdon**, **Kempton**,
.... **Market Rasen**, **Sedgefield**, **Wetherby**, **Wincanton**
27 Fri........ Wolverhampton, **Chepstow**, **Kempton**, **Wetherby**
28 Sat........ Lingfield, **Catterick**, **Leicester**, **Newbury**
29 Sun........ Southwell, **Doncaster**, **Kelso**
30 Mon........ Lingfield, **Haydock**, **Taunton**
31 Tue........ Lingfield, **Uttoxeter**, **Warwick**

January

1 Wed.................... Southwell, **Catterick**, **Cheltenham**, **Exeter**, **Fakenham**, ... **Musselburgh**
2 Thu.................... Lingfield, Chelmsford, **Ayr**
3 Fri.................... Wolverhampton, Southwell, **Hereford**, **Musselburgh**
4 Sat.................... Lingfield, Kempton, **Newcastle**, **Sandown**, **Wincanton**
5 Sun.................... Southwell, **Plumpton**
6 Mon.................... Wolverhampton, **Ayr**, **Chepstow**
7 Tue.................... Southwell, **Lingfield**, **Taunton**
8 Wed.................... Newcastle, Kempton, **Ludlow**
9 Thu.................... Newcastle, Chelmsford, **Catterick**, **Leicester**
10 Fri.................... Lingfield, Wolverhampton, **Huntingdon**, **Sedgefield**
11 Sat.................... Lingfield, Chelmsford, **Kempton**, **Warwick**, **Wetherby**
12 Sun.................... Southwell, **Kelso**
13 Mon.................... Southwell, Wolverhampton, **Lingfield**
14 Tue.................... Chelmsford, **Doncaster**, **Exeter**
15 Wed.................... Wolverhampton, Southwell, **Newbury**, **Plumpton**
16 Thu.................... Newcastle, **Ludlow**, **Market Rasen**, **Wincanton**
17 Fri.................... Lingfield, Newcastle, **Chepstow**, **Musselburgh**
18 Sat.................... Lingfield, Chelmsford, **Ascot**, **Haydock**, **Taunton**
19 Sun.................... Wolverhampton, **Ayr**
20 Mon.................... Kempton, Wolverhampton, **Newcastle**
21 Tue.................... Newcastle, **Exeter**, **Leicester**
22 Wed.................... Lingfield, Kempton, **Catterick**, **Warwick**
23 Thu.................... Southwell, Newcastle, **Fakenham**, **Wetherby**
24 Fri.................... Lingfield, Wolverhampton, **Doncaster**, **Huntingdon**
25 Sat.................... Lingfield, Kempton, **Cheltenham**, **Doncaster**, **Uttoxeter**
26 Sun.................... **Fontwell**, **Sedgefield**
27 Mon.................... Wolverhampton, **Kelso**, **Plumpton**
28 Tue.................... Southwell, **Lingfield**, **Newcastle**
29 Wed.................... Kempton, **Hereford**, **Leicester**
30 Thu.................... Southwell, Chelmsford, **Wincanton**
31 Fri.................... Lingfield, Newcastle, **Catterick**, **Chepstow**

February

1 Sat.................... Lingfield, Kempton, **Musselburgh**, **Sandown**, **Wetherby**
2 Sun.................... **Musselburgh**, **Taunton**
3 Mon.................... Wolverhampton, **Carlisle**, **Fontwell**
4 Tue.................... Kempton, **Market Rasen**, **Sedgefield**
5 Wed.................... Southwell, Wolverhampton, **Ludlow**
6 Thu.................... Chelmsford, Newcastle, **Doncaster**, **Huntingdon**
7 Fri.................... Southwell, Chelmsford, **Bangor**, **Kempton**
8 Sat.................... Lingfield, Wolverhampton, **Newbury**, **Uttoxeter**, **Warwick**
9 Sun.................... Southwell, **Exeter**
10 Mon.................... Wolverhampton, **Catterick**, **Plumpton**
11 Tue.................... Newcastle, **Ayr**, **Lingfield**
12 Wed.................... Southwell, Kempton, **Wetherby**
13 Thu.................... Chelmsford, **Fontwell**, **Kelso**, **Leicester**
14 Fri.................... Lingfield, Southwell, **Fakenham**, **Sandown**
15 Sat.................... Lingfield, Newcastle, **Ascot**, **Haydock**, **Wincanton**

16 Sun........ Kempton, **Market Rasen**
17 Mon........ Kempton, **Carlisle**, **Lingfield**
18 Tue........ Southwell, **Bangor**, **Taunton**
19 Wed........ Newcastle, Kempton, **Doncaster**, **Ludlow**
20 Thu........ Southwell, Chelmsford, **Huntingdon**, **Sedgefield**
21 Fri........ Lingfield, Wolverhampton, **Exeter**, **Warwick**
22 Sat........ Lingfield, Chelmsford, **Chepstow**, **Kempton**, **Newcastle**
23 Sun........ **Fontwell**, **Hereford**
24 Mon........ Wolverhampton, **Carlisle**, **Plumpton**
25 Tue........ Lingfield, **Catterick**, **Leicester**
26 Wed........ Southwell, Kempton, **Musselburgh**, **Wincanton**
27 Thu........ Newcastle, Chelmsford, **Ludlow**, **Taunton**
28 Fri........ Lingfield, Newcastle, **Doncaster**, **Newbury**
29 Sat........ Lingfield, Southwell, **Doncaster**, **Kelso**, **Newbury**

March

1 Sun........ **Huntingdon**, **Sedgefield**
2 Mon........ Wolverhampton, **Chepstow**, **Wetherby**
3 Tue........ Southwell, **Exeter**, **Newcastle**
4 Wed........ Lingfield, Kempton, **Catterick**, **Fontwell**
5 Thu........ Southwell, Newcastle, **Carlisle**, **Wincanton**
6 Fri........ Wolverhampton, **Ffos Las**, **Leicester**, **Sandown**
7 Sat........ Wolverhampton, Chelmsford, **Ayr**, **Hereford**, **Sandown**
8 Sun........ **Warwick**, Southwell
9 Mon........ Wolverhampton, **Plumpton**, **Stratford**, **Taunton**
10 Tue........ **Cheltenham**, Southwell, Newcastle, **Sedgefield**
11 Wed........ **Cheltenham**, Lingfield, Kempton, **Huntingdon**
12 Thu........ **Cheltenham**, Chelmsford, **Hexham**
13 Fri........ **Cheltenham**, Lingfield, Southwell, **Fakenham**
14 Sat........ Wolverhampton, **Fontwell**, **Kempton**, **Newcastle**, **Uttoxeter**
15 Sun........ **Carlisle**, **Market Rasen**
16 Mon........ **Hereford**, **Kelso**, **Southwell**
17 Tue........ **Taunton**, **Wetherby**
18 Wed........ **Haydock**, **Ludlow**, **Plumpton**
19 Thu........ **Chepstow**, **Huntingdon**, **Sedgefield**
20 Fri........ Lingfield, Newcastle, **Musselburgh**, **Newbury**
21 Sat........ Lingfield, Southwell, **Bangor**, **Kelso**, **Newbury**
22 Sun........ **Carlisle**, **Exeter**
23 Mon........ Lingfield, Wolverhampton, **Wincanton**
24 Tue........ Southwell, **Hereford**, **Hexham**
25 Wed........ Southwell, Kempton, **Market Rasen**, **Newcastle**
26 Thu........ Lingfield, Wolverhampton, **Ffos Las**, **Warwick**
27 Fri........ Lingfield, Newcastle, **Fontwell**, **Wetherby**
28 Sat........ Doncaster, Kempton, Wolverhampton, **Stratford**, **Uttoxeter**
29 Sun........ Doncaster, **Ascot**
30 Mon........ Bath, Newcastle, **Ludlow**
31 Tue........ Lingfield, Musselburgh, **Southwell**

April

1 Wed........ Lingfield, Wolverhampton, **Market Rasen**, **Wincanton**
2 Thu........ Southwell, Chelmsford, **Aintree**, **Taunton**

3 Fri .... Leicester, Kempton, **Aintree**, **Sedgefield**
4 Sat .... Lingfield, Wolverhampton, **Aintree**, **Chepstow**, **Newcastle**
5 Sun .... **Ffos Las**, **Plumpton**
6 Mon .... Redcar, Windsor, **Kelso**
7 Tue .... Pontefract, **Exeter**, **Southwell**
8 Wed .... Catterick, Nottingham, Wolverhampton, Kempton
9 Thu .... Bath, Chelmsford, **Wetherby**
10 Fri .... Chelmsford, Lingfield, Newcastle
11 Sat .... Kempton, Musselburgh, Wolverhampton, **Carlisle**, **Haydock**, **Newton Abbot**
12 Sun .... Southwell, **Ffos Las**, **Market Rasen**, **Plumpton**
13 Mon .... Redcar, Wolverhampton, **Chepstow**, **Fakenham**, **Huntingdon**, **Plumpton**
14 Tue .... Lingfield, Newmarket, **Warwick**
15 Wed .... Beverley, Newmarket, Kempton, **Cheltenham**
16 Thu .... Newmarket, Ripon, Newcastle, **Cheltenham**
17 Fri .... Newbury, Bath, **Ayr, Fontwell**, **Exeter**
18 Sat .... Newbury, Thirsk, Brighton, Nottingham, **Ayr, Bangor**
19 Sun .... **Stratford**, **Wincanton**
20 Mon .... Pontefract, Windsor, **Hexham**, **Newton Abbot**, **Kempton**
21 Tue .... Yarmouth, Wolverhampton, **Ludlow**, **Sedgefield**, **Southwell**
22 Wed .... Catterick, Epsom, Lingfield, **Perth**, **Taunton**
23 Thu .... Beverley, Chelmsford, **Perth**, **Warwick**, **Exeter**
24 Fri .... Doncaster, Sandown, **Perth**, **Chepstow**
25 Sat .... Haydock, Leicester, Ripon, Doncaster, Wolverhampton, **Sandown**
26 Sun .... Salisbury, Wetherby
27 Mon .... Ayr, Lingfield, Southwell, Thirsk, Windsor
28 Tue .... Brighton, Nottingham, Yarmouth, Ayr, Lingfield
29 Wed .... Ascot, Pontefract, Wolverhampton, Brighton, Chelmsford
30 Thu .... Musselburgh, Redcar, Southwell, Chelmsford, Wolverhampton

May

1 Fri .... Chepstow, Lingfield, Musselburgh, Newcastle, **Cheltenham**
2 Sat .... Goodwood, Newmarket, Thirsk, Doncaster, **Uttoxeter**, **Hexham**
3 Sun .... Hamilton, Newmarket, Salisbury
4 Mon .... Brighton, Nottingham, Windsor, **Kempton**
5 Tue .... Chester, Wolverhampton, **Ayr**, **Fakenham**, **Southwell**
6 Wed .... Chester, Kempton, **Kelso**, **Newton Abbot**, **Fontwell**
7 Thu .... Chester, Chelmsford, **Huntingdon**, **Worcester**, **Wincanton**
8 Fri .... Ascot, Bath, Beverley, Wolverhampton, Ripon, **Warwick**, **Market Rasen**
9 Sat .... Ascot, Lingfield, Nottingham, Thirsk, **Hexham**, **Warwick**, **Haydock (mixed)**
10 Sun .... **Ludlow**, **Plumpton**
11 Mon .... Catterick, Musselburgh, Wolverhampton, Windsor
12 Tue .... Beverley, Chepstow, Ayr, Wetherby, **Sedgefield**
13 Wed .... York, Bath, **Newton Abbot**, **Worcester**, **Perth**
14 Thu .... Salisbury, York, Newmarket, **Perth**, **Fontwell**
15 Fri .... Newbury, Newmarket, York, Hamilton, **Aintree**
16 Sat .... Newbury, Newmarket, Thirsk, Doncaster, **Bangor**, **Uttoxeter**
17 Sun .... Ripon, **Stratford**

18 Mon........ Carlisle, Redcar, Leicester, Windsor
19 Tue........ Lingfield, Nottingham, Wolverhampton, **Hexham**, **Huntingdon**
20 Wed........ Ayr, Yarmouth, Kempton, **Warwick**, **Southwell**
21 Thu........ Lingfield, Wolverhampton, Chelmsford, Sandown, **Market Rasen**
22 Fri........ Bath, Brighton, Haydock, Pontefract, **Worcester**
23 Sat... Beverley, Catterick, Chester, Haydock, Salisbury, **Cartmel**, **Ffos Las**
24 Sun........ **Fontwell**, **Kelso**, **Uttoxeter**
25 Mon........ Chelmsford, Leicester, Redcar, Windsor, **Cartmel**, **Huntingdon**
26 Tue........ Brighton, Leicester, Redcar, Lingfield, **Ludlow**
27 Wed........ Beverley, Hamilton, **Newton Abbot**, **Cartmel**, **Warwick**
28 Thu........ Goodwood, Haydock, Ripon, Carlisle, Sandown
29 Fri........ Carlisle, Goodwood, Yarmouth, Catterick, Haydock, **Stratford**
30 Sat........ Goodwood, Haydock, Newmarket, York, Lingfield, **Stratford**
31 Sun........ Nottingham, **Fakenham**

June

1 Mon........ Wolverhampton, Windsor, Yarmouth, **Southwell**
2 Tue........ Brighton, Lingfield, Newcastle, **Bangor**
3 Wed........ Nottingham, Kempton, Ripon, **Fontwell**, **Newton Abbot**
4 Thu........ Hamilton, Chelmsford, Wolverhampton, **Ffos Las**, **Uttoxeter**
5 Fri........ Catterick, Epsom, Bath, Doncaster, Goodwood, **Market Rasen**
6 Sat........ Doncaster, Epsom, Musselburgh, Chepstow, Lingfield, **Hexham**, ... **Worcester**
7 Sun........ Goodwood, **Perth**
8 Mon........ Ayr, Leicester, Pontefract, Windsor
9 Tue........ Lingfield, Salisbury, Chelmsford, Wetherby
10 Wed........ Haydock, Yarmouth, Hamilton, Kempton, **Fontwell**
11 Thu........ Newbury, Nottingham, Yarmouth, Haydock, **Uttoxeter**
12 Fri........ Chepstow, Sandown, York, Goodwood, **Aintree**, **Newton Abbot**
13 Sat........ Bath, Chester, Sandown, York, Leicester, **Hexham**, **Worcester**
14 Sun........ Doncaster, Salisbury
15 Mon........ Ayr, Thirsk, Nottingham, Windsor
16 Tue........ Royal Ascot, Thirsk, Beverley, Brighton, **Stratford**
17 Wed........ Royal Ascot, Hamilton, Chelmsford, Ripon, **Uttoxeter**
18 Thu........ Royal Ascot, Chelmsford, Ripon, Lingfield, **Ffos Las**
19 Fri........ Royal Ascot, Redcar, Carlisle, Goodwood, Newmarket, ... **Market Rasen**
20 Sat........ Royal Ascot, Ayr, Newmarket, Redcar, Haydock, Lingfield, **Perth**
21 Sun........ Pontefract, **Hexham**, **Worcester**
22 Mon........ Chepstow, Windsor, Wolverhampton, **Southwell**
23 Tue........ Beverley, Brighton, Newbury, **Newton Abbot**
24 Wed........ Carlisle, Salisbury, Bath, Kempton, **Worcester**
25 Thu........ Newcastle, Newmarket, Nottingham, Hamilton, Leicester
26 Fri........ Doncaster, Yarmouth, Chester, Newcastle, Newmarket, **Cartmel**
27 Sat... Chester, Newcastle, Newmarket, Windsor, York, Doncaster, Lingfield
28 Sun........ Windsor, **Cartmel**, **Uttoxeter**
29 Mon........ Pontefract, Windsor, Wolverhampton, **Ffos Las**
30 Tue........ Brighton, Hamilton, Chepstow, **Stratford**

July

1 Wed........ Musselburgh, Thirsk, Bath, Kempton, **Worcester**

2 Thu .... Haydock, Yarmouth, Epsom, Newbury, **Perth**
3 Fri .... Doncaster, Sandown, Beverley, Chelmsford, Haydock, **Newton Abbot**
4 Sat .... Beverley, Chelmsford, Haydock, Leicester, Sandown, Carlisle, Nottingham
5 Sun .... Ayr, **Market Rasen**
6 Mon .... Ayr, Ripon, Windsor, **Worcester**
7 Tue .... Pontefract, Wolverhampton, Brighton, **Uttoxeter**
8 Wed .... Catterick, Lingfield, Yarmouth, Bath, Kempton
9 Thu .... Carlisle, Doncaster, Newmarket, Epsom, Newbury
10 Fri .... Ascot, Newmarket, York, Chepstow, Chester, **Ffos Las**
11 Sat .... Ascot, Chester, Newmarket, York, Hamilton, Salisbury
12 Sun .... **Perth**, **Stratford**
13 Mon .... Ayr, Brighton, Windsor, Wolverhampton
14 Tue .... Bath, Beverley, Chelmsford, **Southwell**
15 Wed .... Catterick, Lingfield, Wolverhampton, Yarmouth, **Uttoxeter**
16 Thu .... Chepstow, Hamilton, Leicester, Epsom, **Worcester**
17 Fri .... Haydock, Newbury, Nottingham, Hamilton, Newmarket, Pontefract
18 Sat .... Newbury, Newmarket, Ripon, Doncaster, Haydock, **Cartmel**, **Market Rasen**
19 Sun .... Redcar, **Newton Abbot**, **Stratford**
20 Mon .... Ayr, Beverley, Windsor, **Cartmel**
21 Tue .... Musselburgh, Chelmsford, Nottingham, **Southwell**
22 Wed .... Bath, Catterick, Lingfield, Leicester, Sandown
23 Thu .... Sandown, Yarmouth, Doncaster, Newbury, **Worcester**
24 Fri .... Ascot, Thirsk, Chepstow, Newmarket, York, **Uttoxeter**
25 Sat .... Ascot, Chester, Newcastle, Newmarket, York, Lingfield, Salisbury
26 Sun .... Pontefract, **Uttoxeter**
27 Mon .... Ayr, Windsor, Wolverhampton, **Newton Abbot**
28 Tue .... Beverley, Goodwood, Yarmouth, **Perth**, **Worcester**
29 Wed .... Goodwood, Redcar, Leicester, Sandown, **Perth**
30 Thu .... Goodwood, Nottingham, Epsom, Ffos Las, **Stratford**
31 Fri .... Goodwood, Wolverhampton, Bath, Musselburgh, Newmarket, **Bangor**

August

1 Sat .... Chelmsford, Doncaster, Goodwood, Newmarket, Thirsk, Hamilton, Lingfield
2 Sun .... Chester, **Market Rasen**
3 Mon .... Kempton, Ripon, Carlisle, Windsor
4 Tue .... Catterick, Ffos Las, Nottingham
5 Wed .... Bath, Brighton, Pontefract, Kempton, Yarmouth
6 Thu .... Brighton, Haydock, Yarmouth, Newcastle, Sandown
7 Fri .... Brighton, Musselburgh, Thirsk, Chelmsford, Haydock, Newmarket
8 Sat .... Ascot, Chelmsford, Haydock, Newmarket, Redcar, Ayr, Lingfield
9 Sun .... Leicester, Windsor
10 Mon .... Ayr, Ripon, Windsor, Wolverhampton
11 Tue .... Chepstow, Nottingham, Lingfield
12 Wed .... Beverley, Salisbury, Kempton, Newcastle
13 Thu .... Beverley, Lingfield, Salisbury, Ffos Las, Yarmouth

14 Fri......... Newbury, Nottingham, Wolverhampton, Chelmsford, Newmarket, Thirsk
15 Sat......... Doncaster, Newbury, Newmarket, Ripon, Bath, **Perth**, **Market Rasen**
16 Sun......... Pontefract, **Southwell**
17 Mon......... Catterick, Lingfield, Windsor, **Bangor**
18 Tue......... Hamilton, Kempton, Carlisle
19 Wed......... Bath, Carlisle, York, Kempton, **Worcester**
20 Thu......... Chepstow, York, Leicester, **Stratford**, **Fontwell**
21 Fri... Musselburgh, Sandown, York, Newcastle, Salisbury, Wolverhampton
22 Sat......... Chester, Sandown, Wolverhampton, York, Chelmsford, Lingfield, **Newton Abbot**
23 Sun......... Brighton, **Worcester**
24 Mon......... Brighton, Chepstow, Ripon
25 Tue......... Yarmouth, Salisbury, **Bangor**
26 Wed......... Catterick, Lingfield, Musselburgh, Kempton, **Stratford**
27 Thu......... Carlisle, Ffos Las, Newbury, **Fontwell**, **Sedgefield**
28 Fri......... Ffos Las, Newmarket, Thirsk, Chelmsford, Goodwood, Hamilton
29 Sat......... Beverley, Chelmsford, Goodwood, Newmarket, Redcar, Windsor, **Cartmel**
30 Sun......... Beverley, Goodwood, Yarmouth
31 Mon......... Chepstow, Epsom, Ripon, Southwell, **Cartmel**

September

1 Tue......... Epsom, Ripon, **Newton Abbot**
2 Wed......... Bath, Lingfield, Hamilton, **Uttoxeter**, **Hexham**
3 Thu......... Haydock, Salisbury, Chelmsford, **Sedgefield**, **Worcester**
4 Fri......... Ascot, Haydock, Newcastle, Kempton, Musselburgh
5 Sat......... Ascot, Haydock, Kempton, Thirsk, Wolverhampton, **Stratford**
6 Sun......... York, **Fontwell**
7 Mon......... Brighton, Windsor, **Newton Abbot**, **Perth**
8 Tue......... Catterick, Goodwood, Leicester, Newcastle
9 Wed......... Carlisle, Doncaster, Wolverhampton, **Uttoxeter**
10 Thu......... Chepstow, Doncaster, Epsom, Chelmsford
11 Fri......... Chester, Doncaster, Sandown, Salisbury
12 Sat......... Bath, Chelmsford, Chester, Doncaster, Lingfield, Musselburgh
13 Sun......... Bath, Ffos Las
14 Mon......... Brighton, Thirsk, Wolverhampton, **Worcester**
15 Tue......... Redcar, Yarmouth, Kempton, **Southwell**
16 Wed......... Beverley, Sandown, Yarmouth, **Kelso**
17 Thu......... Ayr, Pontefract, Yarmouth, Chelmsford
18 Fri......... Ayr, Newbury, Kempton, **Newton Abbot**
19 Sat....... Ayr, Catterick, Chelmsford, Newbury, Newmarket, Wolverhampton
20 Sun......... Hamilton, **Plumpton**
21 Mon......... Hamilton, Leicester, Wolverhampton, **Warwick**
22 Tue......... Beverley, Lingfield, Newcastle, **Warwick**
23 Wed......... Goodwood, Redcar, Kempton, **Perth**
24 Thu......... Newmarket, Pontefract, Kempton, **Perth**
25 Fri......... Haydock, Newmarket, Newcastle, **Worcester**
26 Sat...... Chester, Haydock, Newmarket, Ripon, Chelmsford, **Market Rasen**

27 Sun........Epsom, Musselburgh
28 Mon........Bath, Hamilton, Newcastle, **Newton Abbot**
29 Tue........Ayr, Wolverhampton, **Sedgefield**, **Worcester**
30 Wed........Nottingham, Kempton, **Bangor**, **Huntingdon**

October

1 Thu........Salisbury, Chelmsford, **Southwell**, **Warwick**
2 Fri........Ascot, Newcastle, **Fontwell**, **Hexham**
3 Sat........Ascot, Newmarket, Redcar, Wolverhampton, **Fontwell**
4 Sun........**Kelso**, **Uttoxeter**
5 Mon........Pontefract, Windsor, Wolverhampton, **Stratford**
6 Tue........Brighton, Catterick, Leicester, Southwell
7 Wed........Nottingham, Kempton, **Ludlow**
8 Thu........Ayr, Chelmsford, Southwell, **Exeter**, **Worcester**
9 Fri........Newmarket, York, Kempton, **Chepstow**
10 Sat........Newmarket, York, Chelmsford, **Chepstow**, **Hexham**
11 Sun........Goodwood, **Newton Abbot**
12 Mon........Musselburgh, Windsor, Yarmouth, Wolverhampton
13 Tue........Leicester, Newcastle, **Hereford**, **Huntingdon**
14 Wed........Bath, Nottingham, Kempton, **Wetherby**
15 Thu........Brighton, Chelmsford, Southwell, **Carlisle**, **Wincanton**
16 Fri........Haydock, Redcar, Newcastle, **Fakenham**, **Uttoxeter**
17 Sat........Ascot, Catterick, Wolverhampton, **Ffos Las**, **Market Rasen**,
........**Stratford**
18 Sun........**Kempton**, **Sedgefield**
19 Mon........Pontefract, Windsor, Wolverhampton, **Plumpton**
20 Tue........Newcastle, Yarmouth, Kempton, **Exeter**
21 Wed........Newmarket, Kempton, **Fontwell**, **Worcester**
22 Thu........Chelmsford, Wolverhampton, **Carlisle**, **Ludlow**, **Southwell**
23 Fri........Doncaster, Newbury, Newcastle, **Cheltenham**
24 Sat........Doncaster, Newbury, Chelmsford, **Cheltenham**, **Kelso**
25 Sun........**Aintree**, **Wincanton**
26 Mon........Leicester, Redcar, Newcastle, **Ayr**
27 Tue........Catterick, Southwell, **Bangor**, **Chepstow**
28 Wed........Nottingham, Kempton, **Fakenham**, **Taunton**
29 Thu........Lingfield, Chelmsford, Southwell, **Newton Abbot**, **Stratford**
30 Fri........Newmarket, Newcastle, **Uttoxeter**, **Wetherby**
31 Sat........Newmarket, Wolverhampton, **Ascot**, **Ayr**, **Wetherby**

November

1 Sun........**Carlisle**, **Huntingdon**
2 Mon........Kempton, Wolverhampton, **Hereford**, **Plumpton**
3 Tue........Redcar, Southwell, Newcastle, **Exeter**
4 Wed........Lingfield, Nottingham, Kempton, **Musselburgh**
5 Thu........Chelmsford, Kempton, **Market Rasen**, **Newbury**, **Sedgefield**
6 Fri........Newcastle, **Fontwell**, **Hexham**, **Warwick**
7 Sat........Doncaster, Chelmsford, **Aintree**, **Kelso**, **Wincanton**
8 Sun........**Ffos Las**, **Sandown**
9 Mon........**Carlisle**, **Chepstow**, **Kempton**
10 Tue........**Hereford**, **Huntingdon**, **Lingfield**

11 Wed .... **Ayr**, **Bangor**, **Exeter**
12 Thu .... **Ludlow**, **Sedgefield**, **Taunton**
13 Fri .... **Cheltenham**, **Newcastle**, **Southwell**
14 Sat .... Lingfield, Wolverhampton, **Cheltenham**, **Uttoxeter**, **Wetherby**
15 Sun .... **Cheltenham**, **Fontwell**
16 Mon .... Wolverhampton, Kempton, **Leicester**, **Plumpton**
17 Tue .... Southwell, Newcastle, **Fakenham**, **Lingfield**
18 Wed .... Kempton, **Ffos Las**, **Hexham**, **Warwick**
19 Thu .... Newcastle, Chelmsford, **Market Rasen**, **Wincanton**
20 Fri .... Newcastle, **Ascot**, **Catterick**, **Chepstow**
21 Sat .... Lingfield, Wolverhampton, **Ascot**, **Haydock**, **Huntingdon**
22 Sun .... **Exeter**, **Uttoxeter**
23 Mon .... **Kempton**, **Ludlow**, **Musselburgh**
24 Tue .... Wolverhampton, **Sedgefield**, **Southwell**
25 Wed .... Lingfield, Kempton, **Hereford**, **Wetherby**
26 Thu .... Southwell, Chelmsford, **Taunton**
27 Fri .... Southwell, Chelmsford, **Doncaster**, **Newbury**
28 Sat .... Wolverhampton, **Bangor**, **Doncaster**, **Newbury**, **Newcastle**
29 Sun .... **Carlisle**, **Leicester**
30 Mon .... Wolverhampton, **Ayr**, **Fakenham**

December

1 Tue .... Wolverhampton, **Lingfield**, **Southwell**
2 Wed .... Lingfield, Kempton, **Haydock**, **Ludlow**
3 Thu .... Chelmsford, **Leicester**, **Market Rasen**, **Wincanton**
4 Fri .... Newcastle, **Exeter**, **Sandown**, **Sedgefield**
5 Sat .... Wolverhampton, **Aintree**, **Chepstow**, **Sandown**, **Wetherby**
6 Sun .... **Huntingdon**, **Kelso**
7 Mon .... Wolverhampton, **Musselburgh**, **Plumpton**
8 Tue .... Southwell, **Fontwell**, **Uttoxeter**
9 Wed .... Lingfield, Kempton, **Hexham**, **Leicester**
10 Thu .... Chelmsford, **Newcastle**, **Taunton**, **Warwick**
11 Fri .... Southwell, **Bangor**, **Cheltenham**, **Doncaster**
12 Sat .... Newcastle, Wolverhampton, **Cheltenham**, **Doncaster**, **Hereford**
13 Sun .... **Carlisle**, **Southwell**
14 Mon .... **Ayr**, **Ffos Las**, **Plumpton**
15 Tue .... Wolverhampton, **Catterick**, **Wincanton**
16 Wed .... Lingfield, Kempton, **Ludlow**, **Newbury**
17 Thu .... Southwell, Chelmsford, **Exeter**
18 Fri .... Southwell, Wolverhampton, **Ascot**, **Uttoxeter**
19 Sat .... Lingfield, Wolverhampton, **Ascot**, **Haydock**, **Newcastle**
20 Sun .... Southwell, **Fakenham**
21 Mon .... **Lingfield**, **Musselburgh**
26 Sat ..... Wolverhampton, **Fontwell**, **Huntingdon**, **Kempton**, **Market Rasen**,
.... **Sedgefield**, **Wetherby**, **Wincanton**
27 Sun .... Wolverhampton, **Chepstow**, **Kempton**, **Wetherby**
28 Mon .... Lingfield, **Catterick**, **Leicester**
29 Tue .... Southwell, **Doncaster**, **Kelso**, **Newbury**
30 Wed .... Lingfield, **Haydock**, **Taunton**
31 Thu .... Lingfield, **Uttoxeter**, **Warwick**

Big-race dates

November

2 Wetherby .... Charlie Hall Chase
9 Wincanton .... Elite Hurdle
16 Cheltenham .... BetVictor Gold Cup
23 Haydock .... Betfair Chase
23 Haydock .... Ascot Hurdle
30 Newbury .... Ladbrokes Trophy
30 Newcastle .... Fighting Fifth Hurdle

December

7 Sandown .... Tingle Creek Trophy
7 Aintree .... Becher Chase
14 Cheltenham .... Caspian Caviar Gold Cup
21 Ascot .... Long Walk Hurdle
26 Kempton .... King George VI Chase
27 Chepstow .... Welsh Grand National
28 Newbury .... Challow Novices' Hurdle

January

4 Sandown .... Tolworth Hurdle
11 Warwick .... Classic Chase
18 Ascot .... Clarence House Chase
18 Haydock .... Peter Marsh Chase
25 Cheltenham .... Festival Trials Day

February

8 Newbury .... Betfair Hurdle
15 Ascot .... Ascot Chase
15 Haydock .... Grand National Trial
22 Kempton .... 888Sport Chase

March

7 Sandown .... Imperial Cup
10 Cheltenham .... Champion Hurdle
11 Cheltenham .... Champion Chase
12 Cheltenham .... Stayers' Hurdle
13 Cheltenham .... Cheltenham Gold Cup

April

2 Aintree .... Bowl
3 Aintree .... Melling Chase
4 Aintree .... Randox Health Grand National
13 Fairyhouse .... Irish Grand National
18 Ayr .... Scottish Grand National
25 Sandown .... bet365 Gold Cup

Big-race records

BetVictor Gold Cup (2m4f) Cheltenham

Year	Winner	Age-wgt	Trainer	Jockey	SP	Ran
2009	**Tranquil Sea**	7-10-13	E O'Grady	A McNamara	11-2f	16
2010	**Little Josh**	8-10-8	N Twiston-Davies	S Twiston-Davies (3)	20-1	18
2011	**Great Endeavour**	7-10-3	D Pipe	T Murphy	8-1	20
2012	**Al Ferof**	7-11-8	P Nicholls	R Walsh	8-1	18
2013	**Johns Spirit**	6-10-2	J O'Neill	R McLernon	7-1	20
2014	**Caid Du Berlais**	5-10-13	P Nicholls	S Twiston-Davies	10-1	18
2015	**Annacotty**	7-11-0	A King	I Popham	12-1	20
2016	**Taquin Du Seuil**	9-11-11	J O'Neill	A Coleman	8-1	17
2017	**Splash Of Ginge**	9-10-6	N Twiston-Davies	T Bellamy	25-1	17
2018	**Baron Alco**	7-10-11	G Moore	J Moore	8-1	18

COURSE form is the key factor as 21 of the last 27 winners had previously been successful at Cheltenham and three of the exceptions had been placed at the Cheltenham Festival. That's even more remarkable considering winners tend to be so inexperienced, with 12 of the last 16 being second-season chasers aged five to eight. Splash Of Ginge is the only winner to have had more than 15 chase runs since fellow nine-year-old The Outback Way in 1999 and the last older winner was Clear Cut in 1975. There have been several great weight-carrying performances down the years, most recently Taquin Du Seuil and Al Ferof, but they are the only winners since Exotic Dancer in 2006 to have carried more than 11st.

Betfair Chase (3m1½f) Haydock

Year	Winner	Age-wgt	Trainer	Jockey	SP	Ran
2009	**Kauto Star**	9-11-7	P Nicholls	R Walsh	4-6f	7
2010	**Imperial Commander**	9-11-7	N Twiston-Davies	P Brennan	10-11f	7
2011	**Kauto Star**	11-11-7	P Nicholls	R Walsh	6-1	6
2012	**Silviniaco Conti**	6-11-7	P Nicholls	R Walsh	7-4	5
2013	**Cue Card**	7-11-7	C Tizzard	J Tizzard	9-1	8
2014	**Silviniaco Conti**	8-11-7	P Nicholls	N Fehily	10-3	9
2015	**Cue Card**	9-11-7	C Tizzard	P Brennan	7-4	5
2016	**Cue Card**	10-11-7	C Tizzard	P Brennan	15-8f	6
2017	**Bristol De Mai**	6-11-7	N Twiston-Davies	D Jacob	11-10f	6
2018	**Bristol De Mai**	7-11-7	N Twiston-Davies	D Jacob	13-2	5

FIRST run in 2005, this race has quickly become the first serious port of call for proven top-class staying chasers. Coming so early in the season, most horses will be running first time out, as all five runners were last season, but a prep run is a big help and the previous six winners all had proven fitness on their side, with the Charlie Hall the best guide. Past winners have a remarkable record and the 14 runnings have been shared between just six horses, Kauto Star leading the way with his four victories from 2006 to 2011. Tactical speed is vital at Haydock and class rather than stamina has been the key asset – even before their first win, five of the six winners had already secured a top-two finish at Grade 1 level yet four had never won over 3m, whereas every winner since Kingscliff in the inaugural running had previously won over 2m or 2m1f.

Ladbrokes Trophy (3m2f) Newbury

2009	**Denman**	9-11-12	P Nicholls	R Walsh	11-4f	19
2010	**Diamond Harry**	7-10-0	N Williams	D Jacob	6-1	18
2011	**Carruthers**	8-10-4	M Bradstock	M Batchelor	10-1	18
2012	**Bobs Worth**	7-11-6	N Henderson	B Geraghty	4-1f	19
2013	**Triolo D'Alene**	6-11-1	N Henderson	B Geraghty	20-1	21
2014	**Many Clouds**	7-11-6	O Sherwood	L Aspell	8-1	19
2015	**Smad Place**	8-11-4	A King	W Hutchison	7-1	15
2016	**Native River**	6-11-1	C Tizzard	R Johnson	7-2f	19
2017	**Total Recall**	8-10-8	W Mullins	P Townend	9-2f	20
2018	**Sizing Tennessee**	10-11-3	C Tizzard	T Scudamore	12-1	12

JUST about the most high-quality handicap of the season, won by some very special horses including twice by Denman as well as subsequent Gold Cup and Grand National winners since then. The increasing quality has seen 12 of the last 16 winners carry 11st or more to victory after 16 out of 18 prior to Strong Flow in 2003 had been below that benchmark. Twelve of the 20 winners since 1999 were second-season chasers (including three winners of the RSA Chase) and one of the exceptions, Strong Flow, was a novice, so lack of experience isn't a worry, especially as Be My Royal was also a winning novice in 2002 before being disqualified due to a banned substance. Even last year's winner Sizing Tennessee had been a novice the previous season when becoming the first winner older than nine since Diamond Edge in 1981. The Badger Ales Trophy is best of the traditional trials, although six of the last 13 winners were making their seasonal debuts.

Tingle Creek Trophy (2m) Sandown

2009	**Twist Magic**	7-11-7	P Nicholls	R Walsh	9-4	5
2010*	**Master Minded**	7-11-7	P Nicholls	N Fehily	10-11f	9
2011	**Sizing Europe**	9-11-7	H de Bromhead	A Lynch	11-8f	7
2012	**Sprinter Sacre**	6-11-7	N Henderson	B Geraghty	4-11f	7
2013	**Sire De Grugy**	7-11-7	G Moore	J Moore	7-4jf	9
2014	**Dodging Bullets**	6-11-7	P Nicholls	S Twiston-Davies	9-1	10
2015	**Sire De Grugy**	9-11-7	G Moore	J Moore	10-3	7
2016	**Un De Sceaux**	8-11-7	W Mullins	R Walsh	5-4f	6
2017	**Politologue**	6-11-7	P Nicholls	H Cobden	7-2	6
2018	**Altior**	8-11-7	N Henderson	N de Boinville	8-13f	4

**run at Cheltenham*

THIS changed from a handicap to a Grade 1 conditions event prior to the 1994 renewal and has grown to rank alongside the Champion Chase in terms of quality. Moscow Flyer's epic 2004 win over Well Chief and Azertyuiop was the most memorable running and since then the Irish legend has been matched by Master Minded, Sprinter Sacre, Sire De Grugy, Dodging Bullets and Altior in doubling up at Cheltenham, while Un De

BARACOUDA: the first of three multiple Long Walk winners this century

Sceaux went on to win the Ryanair. As well as going on to big things, winners also tend to have proved themselves already at the highest level as 16 of the last 20 winners had already landed a Grade 1 chase. As a result no winner has returned bigger than 9-1 since the race gained top-flight status.

Caspian Caviar Gold Cup (2m4½f) Cheltenham

2009	**Poquelin**	6-11-8	P Nicholls	R Walsh	7-2f	17
2010	**Poquelin**	7-11-12	P Nicholls	I Popham (5)	16-1	16
2011	**Quantitativeeasing**	6-10-7	N Henderson	B Geraghty	6-1	16
2012	**Unioniste**	4-10-0	P Nicholls	H Derham (5)	15-2	14
2013	**Double Ross**	8-10-8	N Twiston-Davies	S Twiston-Davies	14-1	13
2014	**Niceonefrankie**	8-11-5	V Williams	A Coleman	16-1	12
2015	**Village Vic**	8-10-0	P Hobbs	R Johnson	8-1	14
2016	**Frodon**	4-10-10	P Nicholls	S Twiston-Davies	14-1	16
2017	**Guitar Pete**	7-10-5	N Richards	R Day (3)	9-1	10
2018	**Frodon**	6-11-12	P Nicholls	B Frost	7-1	12

NOT surprisingly, the BetVictor Gold Cup, held at the same venue four weeks earlier, is the most useful guide to this event as eight of the last 14 winners ran in that race. Exotic Dancer was the last horse to do the double in 2006, but three horses – Frodon last year, Quantitativeeasing in 2011 and Poquelin in 2009 – have improved on their second-placed efforts, as did Monkerhostin in 2004. Even compared to the BetVictor, it's a great race for young horses. Four-year-olds Frodon, when winning it for the first time, and Unioniste are the best example and four winners since 2006 were only six, while Double Ross was another successful novice in 2013, whereas Fragrant Dawn was the last winner older than eight in 1993. The race has featured some notable weight-carrying performances and six of the last 12 winners carried 11st 4lb or more.

Long Walk Hurdle (3m½f) Ascot

2009*	**Big Buck's**	6-11-7	P Nicholls	R Walsh	1-2f	8
2010*	**Big Buck's**	7-11-7	P Nicholls	A McCoy	2-13f	6
2011	**Big Buck's**	8-11-7	P Nicholls	R Walsh	3-10f	7
2012	**Reve De Sivola**	7-11-7	N Williams	R Johnson	9-2	7
2013	**Reve De Sivola**	8-11-7	N Williams	R Johnson	9-4	5
2014	**Reve De Sivola**	9-11-7	N Williams	D Jacob	13-2	5
2015	**Thistlecrack**	7-11-7	C Tizzard	T Scudamore	2-1f	8
2016	**Unowhatimeanharry**	8-11-7	H Fry	B Geraghty	6-5f	11
2017	**Sam Spinner**	5-11-7	J O'Keeffe	J Colliver	9-2	8
2018	**Paisley Park**	6-11-7	E Lavelle	A Coleman	8-1	11

**run at Newbury*

THIS is by far the best staying hurdle run before Cheltenham and class tends to come to the fore. Five of the last ten winners went on to win the Stayers' Hurdle, including Big Buck's on three occasions, and the market is a great guide as last year's winner Paisley Park is the biggest-priced at 8-1 since Lough Derg in 2007. Defending champions deserve the utmost respect because ten of the 19 runnings since 2000 have been won by just three horses – Baracouda leads the way with four victories from 2000 to 2004 (he was also second at 4-11 to Deano's Beeno in between), Big Buck's reeled off a hat-trick from 2009 to 2011 and Reve De Sivola did likewise from 2012 to 2014 before finishing second the following year. More recently, many winners have run well in the Long Distance Hurdle at Newbury, with 13 of the last 26 coming via that race and nine doing the double.

King George VI Chase (3m) Kempton

2009	**Kauto Star**	9-11-10	P Nicholls	R Walsh	8-13f	13
2010*	**Long Run**	6-11-10	N Henderson	Mr S W-Cohen	9-2	9
2011	**Kauto Star**	11-11-10	P Nicholls	R Walsh	3-1	7
2012	**Long Run**	7-11-10	N Henderson	Mr S W-Cohen	15-8f	9
2013	**Silviniaco Conti**	7-11-10	P Nicholls	N Fehily	7-2	9
2014	**Silviniaco Conti**	8-11-10	P Nicholls	N Fehily	15-8f	10
2015	**Cue Card**	9-11-10	C Tizzard	P Brennan	9-2	9
2016	**Thistlecrack**	8-11-10	C Tizzard	T Scudamore	11-10f	5
2017	**Might Bite**	9-11-10	N Henderson	N de Boinville	6-4f	8
2018	**Clan Des Obeaux**	6-11-10	P Nicholls	H Cobden	12-1	10

**run in January 2011*

A RACE the best horses often manage to win several times. It's not just the amazing Kauto Star, who landed a fifth win in 2011, as Silviniaco Conti, Long Run, Kicking King, See More Business and One Man are also multiple winners since the days of the legendary Desert Orchid. That also emphasises the importance of experience as 16 of the last 20 winners were in at least their third season of chasing, even the six-year-old Clan Des Obeaux last year – although, staggeringly, Thistlecrack somehow managed to prevail as a novice in 2016. Thistlecrack and Clan Des Obeaux are the only winners not to have previously landed a Grade 1 chase since Teeton Mill in 1998. Kempton's relatively sharp three miles provides slightly less of a stamina test than other major tracks, particularly Cheltenham, and the importance of tactical speed is shown by the fact that 14 of the last

ELEGANT ESCAPE: yet another Welsh National hero with winning course form

16 winners had previously landed a Graded chase from 2m4f to 2m6f. That means those who have just failed to see out the Gold Cup trip often make amends here, such as One Man and Florida Pearl, while Kauto Star was also more vulnerable in March, there were stamina doubts about Kicking King prior to his first win and Edredon Bleu was a 2m performer stepping into the unknown.

Welsh Grand National (3m5f) Chepstow

2009	**Dream Alliance**	8-10-8	P Hobbs	T O'Brien	20-1	18
2010*	**Synchronised**	8-11-6	J O'Neill	A McCoy	5-1	18
2011	**Le Beau Bai**	8-10-1	R Lee	C Poste	10-1	20
2012	**Monbeg Dude**	8-10-1	M Scudamore	P Carberry	10-1	17
2013	**Mountainous**	8-10-0	R Lee	P Moloney	20-1	20
2014	**Emperor's Choice**	7-10-8	V Williams	A Coleman	9-1	19
2015**	**Mountainous**	11-10-6	K Lee	J Moore	9-1	20
2016	**Native River**	6-11-12	C Tizzard	R Johnson	11-4f	20
2017***	**Raz De Maree**	13-11-1	G Cromwell	J Bowen (5)	16-1	20
2018	**Elegant Escape**	6-11-8	C Tizzard	T O'Brien	3-1f	20

**run in January 2011   **run in January 2016   ***run in January 2018*

CHEPSTOW lost a key trial for this race with the Rehearsal Chase moving to Newcastle, but it has basically been replaced by another handicap in early December – aptly named the Welsh Grand National Trial – and course form remains pivotal. Seven of the last 12 winners had previously triumphed at the track, making 14 of the last 21 in all, and the 2017 winner Raz De Maree had finished second in the race 12 months earlier. As with most staying handicap chases run in the mud, horses at the foot of the weights are massively favoured. Only ten winners since 1976 carried more than 11st, with James Bowen's claim taking Raz De Maree below the threshold in 2017, and the last four to to do comprise Gold Cup winners in Synchronised and Native River plus two others who made the first six in that race. Generally punters should not even rule out any horse from out of the handicap, with Mountainous the latest to defy extra weight in 2013, and Kendal Cavalier was as much as 13lb wrong in 1997.

Betfair Hurdle (2m½f) Newbury

2010	**Get Me Out Of Here**	6-10-6	J O'Neill	A McCoy	6-1	23
2011	**Recession Proof**	5-10-8	J Quinn	D Costello	12-1	15
2012	**Zarkandar**	5-11-1	P Nicholls	R Walsh	11-4f	20
2013	**My Tent Or Yours**	6-11-2	N Henderson	A McCoy	5-1f	19
2014	**Splash Of Ginge**	6-10-10	N Twiston-Davies	R Hatch (7)	33-1	20
2015	**Violet Dancer**	5-10-9	G Moore	Joshua Moore	20-1	23
2016	**Agrapart**	5-10-10	N Williams	L Kelly (5)	16-1	22
2017	**Ballyandy**	6-11-1	N Twiston-Davies	S Twiston-Davies	3-1f	16
2018	**Kalashnikov**	5-11-5	A Murphy	J Quinlan	8-1cf	20
2019*	**Al Dancer**	6-11-8	N Twiston-Davies	S Twiston-Davies	5-2f	14

**run at Ascot*

A TOP-CLASS handicap hurdle which has been rewarded for a big increase in prize-money in recent times. Young improvers with Grade 1 potential are preferred to experienced handicappers – the last 12 winners were five or six, eight of the last ten were novices and seven were making their handicap debuts. Eleven of the last 21 winners carried more than 11st, yet Al Dancer was the first to defy a burden in excess of 11st 7lb since Persian War in 1968. Eight of the last 26 winners were officially ahead of the handicapper having had their mark raised since the publication of the weights.

Grand National Trial (3m4½f) Haydock

2010	**Silver By Nature**	8-10-11	L Russell	P Buchanan	7-1	14
2011	**Silver By Nature**	9-11-12	L Russell	P Buchanan	10-1	14
2012	**Giles Cross**	10-10-5	V Dartnall	D O'Regan	4-1f	14
2013	**Well Refreshed**	9-10-0	G Moore	J Moore (3)	9-2f	14
2014	**Rigadin De Beauchene**	9-10-8	V Williams	R Dunne (3)	16-1	14
2015	**Lie Forrit**	11-11-6	L Russell	P Buchanan	8-1	12
2016	**Bishops Road**	8-11-7	K Lee	R Johnson	13-2	8
2017	**Vieux Lion Rouge**	8-11-6	D Pipe	T Scudamore	8-1	13
2018	**Yala Enki**	8-10-11	V Williams	C Deutsch	8-1	8
2019	**Robinsfirth**	10-11-4	C Tizzard	S Bowen	8-1	15

THIS race hasn't lived up to its name as a National trial with the winner finishing no better than fifth at Aintree since 2000 and several running poorly when well fancied, although Neptune Collonges did at least improve on his second place here in 2012. The main reason is that inexperienced horses have fared much better in this race, with none of the last 16 winners having run more than 14 times previously over fences in Britain and Ireland even though five were aged in double figures during that time and none younger than eight – three had run in no more than five chases. This was a graveyard for favourites, with none successful from Frantic Tan in 2001 to Giles Cross in 2012, but six of the last seven winners were priced in single figures.

888Sport Chase (3m) Kempton

2010	**Razor Royale**	8-10-5	N Twiston-Davies	P Brennan	11-1	13
2011	**Quinz**	7-11-0	P Hobbs	R Johnson	8-1	16

2012	**Nacarat**	11-11-8	T George	P Brennan	9-2	10
2013	**Opening Batsman**	7-10-5	H Fry	N Fehily	12-1	13
2014	**Bally Legend**	9-10-12	C Keevil	I Popham	28-1	13
2015	**Rocky Creek**	9-11-11	P Nicholls	S Twiston-Davies	8-1	14
2016	**Theatre Guide**	9-10-6	C Tizzard	P Brennan	6-1	15
2017	**Pilgrims Bay**	7-10-2	N Mulholland	J Best	25-1	13
2018	**Master Dee**	9-11-5	F O'Brien	B Geraghty	8-1	15
2019	**Walt**	8-10-6	N Mulholland	S Twiston-Davies	14-1	10

THIS is the first major handicap chase of the season in which novices have consistently been a big factor as four of them have been successful in the last nine years, with Neil Mulholland's pair Walt and Pilgrims Bay emulating Opening Batsman and Quinz. All four carried 11st or less, but unless coming up against a well-handicapped novice this has been a good race for class acts near the top of the weights and 12 of the last 20 winners were above that threshold including Gungadu, Farmer Jack, Marlborough and Gloria Victis from the top of the handicap. Course form is a handy asset with 11 of the last 20 winners previously successful at Kempton.

Imperial Cup (2m) Sandown

2010	**Qaspal**	6-10-3	P Hobbs	A McCoy	11-4f	23
2011	**Alarazi**	7-10-3	L Wadham	D Elsworth	10-1	24
2012	**Paintball**	5-10-7	C Longsdon	N Fehily	20-1	24
2013	**First Avenue**	8-11-1	L Mongan	N Baker (10)	20-1	19
2014	**Baltimore Rock**	5-10-12	D Pipe	T Scudamore	7-1	14
2015	**Ebony Express**	6-11-7	Dr R Newland	W Kennedy	33-1	23
2016	**Flying Angel**	5-10-10	N Twiston-Davies	R Hatch (3)	9-1	14
2017	**London Prize**	6-11-2	I Williams	T O'Brien	10	13
2018	**Mr Antolini**	8-10-1	N Twiston-Davies	J Bargary (3)	20-1	17
2019	**Malaya**	5-10-2	P Nicholls	H Cobden	7-1	13

THIS falls on the eve of the Cheltenham Festival and, with the sponsors putting up a bonus for horses doubling up, a strong and competitive field is always assured. Unexposed youngsters hold the key as 12 of the last 17 winners were novices – seven having raced no more than four times over hurdles – and ten of the last 22 were five-year-olds, with two of the exceptions aged just four. David Pipe has won three of the last 13 runnings to maintain a strong family tradition as his father Martin also won three of the last five in which he had runners. No winner has carried more than 11st 2lb since 2003.

Supreme Novices' Hurdle (2m½f) Cheltenham

2010	**Menorah**	5-11-7	P Hobbs	R Johnson	12-1	18
2011	**Al Ferof**	6-11-7	P Nicholls	R Walsh	10-1	15
2012	**Cinders And Ashes**	5-11-7	D McCain	J Maguire	10-1	19
2013	**Champagne Fever**	6-11-7	W Mullins	R Walsh	5-1	12
2014	**Vautour**	5-11-7	W Mullins	R Walsh	7-2jf	18
2015	**Douvan**	5-11-7	W Mullins	R Walsh	2-1f	12
2016	**Altior**	6-11-7	N Henderson	N de Boinville	4-1	14
2017	**Labaik**	6-11-7	G Elliott	J Kennedy	25-1	14
2018	**Summerville Boy**	6-11-7	T George	N Fehily	9-1	19
2019	**Klassical Dream**	5-11-7	W Mullins	R Walsh	6-1	16

THIS traditionally gets Ireland off to a flying start at the Cheltenham Festival as the raiders have taken 13 of the last 21 runnings, including three in a row for Willie Mullins from

2013 to 2015. That run reversed the dreadful record of favourites, though Douvan is still the only successful outright market leader since Brave Inca in 2004 and just three of the last 13 horses sent off at 2-1 or shorter came out on top. Among the ten short-priced horses beaten, Cue Card, Dunguib and Cousin Vinny had won the previous year's Champion Bumper so don't be sucked in by winners of that race, with Champagne Fever the only one to follow up since Montelado in 1992. That said, a background in bumpers is much preferred as just two top-four finishers in the last decade had started on the Flat, with Labaik the only winner. Twenty of the last 23 winners had won last time out and 18 had run within the previous 45 days, showing the benefit of recent match practice.

Racing Post Arkle Chase (2m) Cheltenham

2010	**Sizing Europe**	8-11-7	H de Bromhead	A Lynch	6-1	12
2011	**Captain Chris**	7-11-7	P Hobbs	R Johnson	6-1	10
2012	**Sprinter Sacre**	6-11-7	N Henderson	B Geraghty	8-11f	6
2013	**Simonsig**	7-11-7	N Henderson	B Geraghty	8-15f	7
2014	**Western Warhorse**	6-11-4	D Pipe	T Scudamore	33-1	9
2015	**Un De Sceaux**	7-11-4	W Mullins	R Walsh	4-6f	11
2016	**Douvan**	6-11-4	W Mullins	R Walsh	1-4f	7
2017	**Altior**	7-11-4	N Henderson	N de Boinville	1-4f	9
2018	**Footpad**	6-11-4	W Mullins	R Walsh	5-6f	5
2019	**Duc Des Genievres**	6-11-4	W Mullins	P Townend	5-1	12

A TYPICAL Arkle winner tends to be well fancied with proven class over hurdles and plenty of chasing experience for a novice. Nine of the last 13 winners had won a Graded race over hurdles (seven at Grade 1 level) and all but one of the exceptions had been placed, while only Western Warhorse and Simonsig hadn't run at least three times over fences since Well Chief in 2004. Western Warhorse is also the only winner priced bigger than 11-1 since 1989 in the middle of a run of six wins in seven years for odds-on shots, all trained by Nicky Henderson or Willie Mullins, who won the race again with Duc Des Genievres at 5-1 last year. Twelve of the last 13 winners were aged six or seven and no horse older than eight has won since Danish Flight in 1989, which includes several fancied horses such as Ned Kelly, Adamant Approach, Barton, Captain Cee Bee, Overturn, Rock On Ruby and Royal Caviar since 2000 alone.

Ultima H'cap Chase (3m1f) Cheltenham

2010	**Chief Dan George**	10-10-10	J Moffatt	P Aspell	33-1	24
2011	**Bensalem**	8-11-2	A King	R Thornton	5-1	19
2012	**Alfie Sherrin**	9-10-0	J O'Neill	R McLernon	14-1	19
2013	**Golden Chieftain**	8-10-5	C Tizzard	B Powell (5)	28-1	24
2014	**Holywell**	7-11-6	J O'Neill	R McLernon	10-1	23
2015	**The Druids Nephew**	8-11-3	N Mulholland	B Geraghty	8-1	24
2016	**Un Temps Pour Tout**	7-11-7	D Pipe	T Scudamore	11-1	23
2017	**Un Temps Pour Tout**	8-11-12	D Pipe	T Scudamore	9-1	23
2018	**Coo Star Sivola**	6-10-13	N Williams	L Kelly (3)	5-1f	18
2019	**Beware The Bear**	9-11-8	N Henderson	J McGrath	10-1	24

YOUTH has taken over this contest. Fifteen of the last 18 winners were novices (six) or second-season chasers (nine) and The Druids Nephew is the only one to have raced more than 11 times over fences since 2007 hero Joes Edge, whereas just two horses older than ten have even made the frame since 1997. A strong stayer is essential as only three of the last 23 winners lacked previous winning form at 3m or further and all three had been placed over that trip on soft ground. Long-standing trends in favour of those near the bottom of the weights have been turned around in recent years by five of the last six winners carrying more than 11st to victory, although only two have been rated above 150 since 1983. That has also made the race easier to predict, with the last six winners no bigger than 11-1 after three of the previous seven had been 28-1 or bigger.

Unibet Champion Hurdle (2m½f) Cheltenham

2010	**Binocular**	6-11-10	N Henderson	A McCoy	9-1	12
2011	**Hurricane Fly**	7-11-10	W Mullins	R Walsh	11-4f	11
2012	**Rock On Ruby**	7-11-10	P Nicholls	N Fehily	11-1	10
2013	**Hurricane Fly**	9-11-10	W Mullins	R Walsh	13-8f	9
2014	**Jezki**	6-11-10	J Harrington	B Geraghty	9-1	9
2015	**Faugheen**	7-11-10	W Mullins	R Walsh	4-5f	8
2016	**Annie Power**	8-11-3	W Mullins	R Walsh	5-2f	12
2017	**Buveur D'Air**	6-11-10	N Henderson	N Fehily	5-1	11
2018	**Buveur D'Air**	7-11-10	N Henderson	B Geraghty	4-6f	11
2019	**Espoir D'Allen**	5-11-10	G Cromwell	M Walsh	16-1	10

THERE have been four multiple winners since 1998 with Buveur D'Air the most recent, emulating Istabraq, Hardy Eustace and Hurricane Fly. The last-named is perhaps the most notable as he became the first horse to regain the crown since Comedy Of Errors in 1975 and was also unusual as a nine-year-old winner, with younger horses having fared much better in recent times. Nine of the last 11 winners were no older than seven, with Espoir D'Allen even winning as a five-year-old last year after just one success for that age group since 1985. Previous festival form is the key and, as well as the former champions, plenty of horses step up having been placed the previous year, with wins for Hurricane Fly, Binocular, Punjabi and Brave Inca since 2006 after they were third 12 months earlier. Among the other winners in that time, Buveur D'Air, Jezki and Sublimity had top-four finishes in the Supreme, Faugheen and Rock On Ruby were first and second in the Ballymore, Katchit won the Triumph and Annie Power would have won the Mares' Hurdle but for falling at the last.

Ballymore Novices' Hurdle (2m5f) Cheltenham

2010	**Peddlers Cross**	5-11-7	D McCain	J Maguire	7-1	17
2011	**First Lieutenant**	6-11-7	M Morris	D Russell	7-1	12
2012	**Simonsig**	6-11-7	N Henderson	B Geraghty	2-1f	17
2013	**The New One**	5-11-7	N Twiston-Davies	S Twiston-Davies	5-1	8
2014	**Faugheen**	6-11-7	W Mullins	R Walsh	6-4f	15
2015	**Windsor Park**	6-11-7	D Weld	D Russell	9-2	10
2016	**Yorkhill**	6-11-7	W Mullins	R Walsh	3-1	11
2017	**Willoughby Court**	6-11-7	B Pauling	D Bass	14-1	15
2018	**Samcro**	6-11-7	G Elliott	J Kennedy	8-11f	14
2019	**City Island**	6-11-7	M Brassil	M Walsh	8-1	16

MUCH like the Supreme, this has traditionally been a race in which to oppose the short-priced favourite but has seen the picture change in recent years with the success of Irish horses, who horses account for eight of the last 12 winners including favourites Samcro, Faugheen and Mikael D'Haguenet. You have to go back to 2005 for the last winner to have started on the Flat, yet speed is often vital in a race that has proved a fair Champion Hurdle trial and the best horses from around this trip earlier in the season often lack enough toe on quicker ground, with all 17 Challow Hurdle winners to run getting beaten.

In contrast, seven winners since 1998 had won a Grade 1 from 2m-2m2f from just 21 runners. French Holly was the first of those and he is also the only winner older than six since 1974, with 55 beaten subsequently. Seven of the last 20 winners had recorded a top-six finish in one of the big bumpers at Cheltenham, Aintree and Punchestown the previous spring.

RSA Chase (3m½f) Cheltenham

2010	**Weapon's Amnesty**	7-11-4	C Byrnes	D Russell	10-1	9
2011	**Bostons Angel**	7-11-4	Mrs J Harrington	R Power	16-1	12
2012	**Bobs Worth**	7-11-4	N Henderson	B Geraghty	9-2	9
2013	**Lord Windermere**	7-11-4	J Culloty	D Russell	8-1	11
2014	**O'Faolains Boy**	7-11-4	R Curtis	B Geraghty	12-1	15
2015	**Don Poli**	6-11-4	W Mullins	B Cooper	13-8f	8
2016	**Blaklion**	7-11-4	N Twiston-Davies	R Hatch	8-1	8
2017	**Might Bite**	8-11-4	N Henderson	N de Boinville	7-2f	12
2018	**Presenting Percy**	7-11-4	P Kelly	D Russell	5-2f	10
2019	**Topofthegame**	7-11-4	P Nicholls	H Cobden	4-1	12

SIX winning favourites in 13 years have redressed the balance somewhat, but this still justifies its reputation as a race for upsets with plenty of bubbles getting burst. Eight beaten favourites this century had come into the race unbeaten over fences, with only Denman and Don Poli surviving with their records intact. It's worth bearing in mind that many horses in the field will be getting better and better with experience having wasted little time over hurdles as 15 of the last 18 winners had raced no more than once in that sphere outside their novice campaign. It's therefore vital to have had enough runs over fences, with Don Poli the only winner since Florida Pearl in 1998 not to have run in at least three chases and one of only two in more than 50 years not to have run since the

ESPOIR D'ALLEN: only the second five-year-old to win the Champion Hurdle since 1985 but a sad loss to the sport having died during the summer

turn of the year along with Topofthegame. Seven-year-olds have a remarkable record with ten of the last 12 winners, while four of the last eight ran in the previous season's Albert Bartlett. There have been six Irish-trained winners in the last 11 years and four had run big races in the Flogas Novice Chase at Leopardstown.

Coral Cup (2m5f) Cheltenham

2010	**Spirit River**	5-11-2	N Henderson	B Geraghty	14-1	28
2011	**Carlito Brigante**	5-11-0	G Elliott	D Russell	16-1	22
2012	**Son Of Flicka**	8-10-6	D McCain	J Maguire	16-1	28
2013	**Medinas**	6-11-10	A King	W Hutchinson	33-1	28
2014	**Whisper**	6-11-11	N Henderson	N de Boinville (5)	14-1	28
2015	**Aux Ptits Soins**	5-10-7	P Nicholls	S Twiston-Davies	9-1	25
2016	**Diamond King**	8-11-3	G Elliott	D Russell	12-1	26
2017	**Supasundae**	7-11-4	J Harrington	R Power	16-1	25
2018	**Bleu Berry**	7-11-2	W Mullins	M Walsh	20-1	26
2019	**William Henry**	9-11-10	N Henderson	N de Boinville	28-1	25

THIS race has brought pain for punters, with just one winning outright favourite since its outright inception in 1993 and one winner priced in single figures since 2008. Despite William Henry's victory last year, siding with younger, progressive horses should be a good start as ten of the last 14 winners were second-season hurdlers. A light but successful campaign is also key as the last 12 winners had run no more than four times earlier in the season, though not necessarily with an eye on a plot. After all, 14 of the last 17 had managed a victory, nine of them last time out, and this is such a quality race these days that connections being too clever with the handicapper risk not getting a run at all. That has also given those near the top of the handicap a chance, shown by the fact that eight of the last ten winners carried 11st or more including William Henry, Whisper and Medinas under at least 11st 10lb.

Queen Mother Champion Chase (2m) Cheltenham

2010	**Big Zeb**	9-11-10	C Murphy	B Geraghty	10-1	9
2011	**Sizing Europe**	9-11-10	H de Bromhead	A Lynch	10-1	11
2012	**Finian's Rainbow**	9-11-10	N Henderson	B Geraghty	4-1	8
2013	**Sprinter Sacre**	7-11-10	N Henderson	B Geraghty	1-4f	7
2014	**Sire De Grugy**	8-11-10	G Moore	J Moore	11-4f	11
2015	**Dodging Bullets**	7-11-10	P Nicholls	S Twiston-Davies	9-2	9
2016	**Sprinter Sacre**	10-11-10	N Henderson	N de Boinville	5-1	10
2017	**Special Tiara**	10-11-10	H de Bromhead	N Fehily	11-1	10
2018	**Altior**	8-11-10	N Henderson	N de Boinville	Evsf	9
2019	**Altior**	9-11-10	N Henderson	N de Boinville	4-11f	9

THE 2006 hero Newmill is the only winner in more than 25 years sent off bigger than 11-1 and, while it would be wrong to say that was easy to predict, it was nonetheless forecast in the pages of the RFO – Nick Watts tipped Newmill ante-post at 100-1! Newmill is also one of only three winners out of the last 20 to return bigger than 5-1 in a race that generally proves the most predictable of Cheltenham's championship races. The previous year's Arkle is the best pointer as Altior, Sprinter Sacre, Sizing Europe, Voy Por Ustedes, Azertyuiop and Moscow Flyer have all followed up since 2003 and Douvan (injured when a 2-9 shot in 2017) is the only Arkle winner among the last 15 to run the following year not to be at least placed, while Dodging Bullets and Finian's Rainbow were also the highest-placed representatives from the novice championship when victorious.

MASTER MINDED: the only back-to-back Champion Chase winner in more than 20 years until the great Altior came along to match him

Also look at the Tingle Creek as six of the last 15 winners had won the Sandown Grade 1 earlier in the season, including three in a row from 2013 to 2015. However, defending champions have a poor record with Altior only the second to hang on to his crown out of the last 16 to take part.

Weatherbys Champion Bumper (2m½f) Cheltenham

2010	**Cue Card**	4-10-12	C Tizzard	J Tizzard	40-1	24
2011	**Cheltenian**	5-11-5	P Hobbs	R Johnson	14-1	24
2012	**Champagne Fever**	5-11-5	W Mullins	Mr P Mullins	16-1	20
2013	**Briar Hill**	5-11-5	W Mullins	R Walsh	25-1	23
2014	**Silver Concorde**	6-11-5	D Weld	Mr R McNamara	16-1	22
2015	**Moon Racer**	6-11-5	D Pipe	T Scudamore	9-2f	23
2016	**Ballyandy**	5-11-5	N Twiston-Davies	S Twiston-Davies	5-1	23
2017	**Fayonagh**	6-10-12	G Elliott	Mr J Codd	7-1	22
2018	**Relegate**	5-10-12	W Mullins	Ms K Walsh	25-1	23
2019	**Envoi Allen**	5-11-5	G Elliott	Mr J Codd	2-1f	14

BONANZA time for Ireland, winners of 20 of the 27 runnings with nine-time winner Willie Mullins leading the way in style. British trainers have cottoned on to the strength of

Irish bumper form and also now try to buy the best Irish prospects, so in total 17 of the 19 winners this century made their debut in Ireland, with Ballyandy and Cue Card the exceptions. Cue Card is also the only successful four-year-old since Dato Star in 1995 as older horses tend to prove too strong, with the early dominance of five-year-olds now challenged by more and more top-class six-year-olds being held back for the race. Favourites have a poor record with just four winners, while horses who have been off the track since the turn of the year have accounted for seven of the last 18 winners from very few runners.

Pertemps Final (3m) Cheltenham

2010	**Buena Vista**	9-10-4	D Pipe	H Frost (3)	16-1	24
2011	**Buena Vista**	10-10-8	D Pipe	C O'Farrell (5)	20-1	23
2012	**Cape Tribulation**	8-10-11	M Jefferson	D O'Regan	14-1	24
2013	**Holywell**	6-11-4	J O'Neill	R McLernon	25-1	24
2014	**Fingal Bay**	8-11-12	P Hobbs	R Johnson	9-2f	23
2015	**Call The Cops**	6-10-12	N Henderson	A Tinkler	9-1	23
2016	**Mall Dini**	6-10-11	P Kelly	D Russell	14-1	24
2017	**Presenting Percy**	6-11-11	P Kelly	D Russell	11-1	24
2018	**Delta Work**	5-10-10	G Elliott	D Russell	6-1	23
2019	**Sire Du Berlais**	7-11-9	G Elliott	B Geraghty	4-1f	24

THERE'S greater competition to merely get a run in all Cheltenham handicaps these days and that seems to have had a particularly profound effect on this race, especially in giving younger horses much more of a chance. That certainly seems borne out by a run of four six-year-old winners in five years from 2013 to 2017 – the last winner of that age had been in 2005 – followed by the first winning five-year-old since 1988 when Delta Work triumphed in 2017. At the same time, the long-standing dominance of light weights is coming under pressure because, while eight of the last 12 winners carried no more than 10st 12lb, all four exceptions have come since 2013, three of whom lumped at least 11st 9lb to victory. The changes have certainly been good news for punters as three of the last five winners were sent off in single figures after ten in a row had been bigger, including two at 50-1.

Ryanair Chase (2m5f) Cheltenham

2010	**Albertas Run**	9-11-10	J O'Neill	A McCoy	14-1	13
2011	**Albertas Run**	10-11-10	J O'Neill	A McCoy	6-1	11
2012	**Riverside Theatre**	8-11-10	N Henderson	B Geraghty	7-2f	12
2013	**Cue Card**	7-11-10	C Tizzard	J Tizzard	7-2	8
2014	**Dynaste**	8-11-10	D Pipe	T Scudamore	3-1f	11
2015	**Uxizandre**	7-11-10	A King	T McCoy	16-1	14
2016	**Vautour**	7-11-10	W Mullins	R Walsh	Evsf	15
2017	**Un De Sceaux**	9-11-10	W Mullins	R Walsh	7-4f	8
2018	**Balko Des Flos**	7-11-10	H de Bromhead	D Russell	8-1	6
2019	**Frodon**	7-11-10	P Nicholls	B Frost	9-2	12

UPGRADED to Grade 1 status in 2008, this race has got stronger and stronger since its inception just three years earlier. The noticeable pattern over time has been that younger horses have taken over from their older rivals, with second-season chasers winning in five of the last seven years and Un De Sceaux the only winner older than eight since 2011 after five of the first seven winners had been at least old, including three ten-year-olds. Un De Sceaux and Cue Card were notable older failures in 2018, clearing the way for Balko Des Flos, who is one of only two winners not to have already been successful at Cheltenham. In the early days of the race that made the BetVictor Gold Cup and the Caspian Caviar Gold Cup the key guides, as was the case with Frodon last year, but as the race has got classier it's Grade 1 form that is generally required and five of the last ten winners were previous Cheltenham Festival heroes, with Uxizandre also beaten less than a length. Stamina is a more important asset than speed as seven of the last 12 winners had posted their best Racing Post Rating at 3m or beyond and six had been beaten in that season's King George.

Stayers' Hurdle (3m) Cheltenham

2010	**Big Buck's**	7-11-10	P Nicholls	R Walsh	5-6f	14
2011	**Big Buck's**	8-11-10	P Nicholls	R Walsh	10-11f	13
2012	**Big Buck's**	9-11-10	P Nicholls	R Walsh	5-6f	11
2013	**Solwhit**	9-11-10	C Byrnes	P Carberry	17-2	13
2014	**More Of That**	6-11-10	J O'Neill	B Geraghty	15-2	10
2015	**Cole Harden**	6-11-10	W Greatrex	G Sheehan	14-1	16
2016	**Thistlecrack**	8-11-10	C Tizzard	T Scudamore	Evsf	12
2017	**Nichols Canyon**	7-11-10	W Mullins	R Walsh	10-1	12
2018	**Penhill**	7-11-10	W Mullins	P Townend	12-1	15
2019	**Paisley Park**	7-11-10	E Lavelle	A Coleman	11-8f	18

THREE horses – Big Buck's, Inglis Drever and Baracouda – shared nine of the 11 runnings from 2002 to 2012 between them and former winners still deserve more than a second look as all but one defending champion since then has been ruled out. That's largely because 3m form is rarely turned around – horses beaten in the race previously rarely step up, with Derring Rose in 1981 the last to win having finished out of the first two 12 months earlier, and only three winners this century had been beaten in a 3m Graded hurdle earlier in the season. For that reason the market has been a strong guide in this time – 17 of the last 19 winners came from the first four in the betting – with the danger to the defending champion or established form horse coming from those stepping up in trip. In fact a lack of proven stamina shouldn't be considered a negative at all as seven of the last 14 first-time winners were triumphing over 3m for the first time.

Triumph Hurdle (2m1f) Cheltenham

2010	**Soldatino**	4-11-0	N Henderson	B Geraghty	6-1	17
2011	**Zarkandar**	4-11-0	P Nicholls	D Jacob	13-2	23
2012	**Countrywide Flame**	4-11-0	J Quinn	D Costello	33-1	20
2013	**Our Conor**	4-11-0	D Hughes	B Cooper	4-1	17
2014	**Tiger Roll**	4-11-0	G Elliott	D Russell	10-1	15
2015	**Peace And Co**	4-11-0	N Henderson	B Geraghty	2-1f	16
2016	**Ivanovich Gorbatov**	4-11-0	A O'Brien	B Geraghty	9-2f	15
2017	**Defi Du Seuil**	4-11-0	P Hobbs	R Johnson	5-2f	15
2018	**Farclas**	4-11-0	G Elliott	J Kennedy	9-1	9
2019	**Pentland Hills**	4-11-0	N Henderson	N de Boinville	20-1	14

THE juvenile championship has benefited greatly from the advent of the Fred Winter in 2005, with the loss of many of the also-rans helping the cream to rise to the top. Of the 15 subsequent winners, the only winners sent off bigger than 10-1 were subsequent Champion Hurdle third Countrywide Flame and last year's big improver Pentland Hills. Smaller fields also mean experience has become less of a factor, with Pentland Hills and Zarkandar winning after just one outing over hurdles and three of the last six winners never having run on the Flat, which used to be almost guaranteed with 12 of the previous 13 having done so. If still considering one coming via the Flat, bear in mind that Our Conor is the only winner in recent times who hadn't been tried over at least 1m4f. The last six Irish-trained winners had run in the Grade 1 Spring Hurdle at Leopardstown on their previous start, while six of the last 11 British-trained winners had landed the Finesse Hurdle at Cheltenham or the Adonis Hurdle at Kempton. Twenty of the last 26 winners passed the post first on their previous run (Scolardy had been disqualified before winning in 2002).

County Hurdle (2m1f) Cheltenham

2010	**Thousand Stars**	6-10-5	W Mullins	Ms K Walsh	20-1	28
2011	**Final Approach**	5-10-12	W Mullins	R Walsh	10-1	26
2012	**Alderwood**	8-11-1	T Mullins	A McCoy	20-1	26
2013	**Ted Veale**	6-10-6	T Martin	B Cooper	10-1	28
2014	**Lac Fontana**	5-10-11	P Nicholls	D Jacob	11-1	28
2015	**Wicklow Brave**	6-11-4	W Mullins	P Townend	25-1	24
2016	**Superb Story**	5-10-12	D Skelton	H Skelton	8-1	26
2017	**Arctic Fire**	8-11-12	W Mullins	P Townend	20-1	25
2018	**Mohaayed**	6-10-11	D Skelton	B Andrews (3)	33-1	24
2019	**Ch'Tibello**	8-11-5	D Skelton	H Skelton	12-1	24

MUCH like in the Imperial Cup, another fiercely competitive 2m handicap hurdle, young horses have a big edge. Of the last 18 winners, ten were five-year-olds and 16 were novices (six) or had been novices the previous season (ten), although the last winner without handicap experience was Thumbs Up in 1993 with more than 60 having failed since. Irish horses have won eight of the last 13 runnings, four of them having been at least placed in the Coral Hurdle at Leopardstown or the Betfair Hurdle at Newbury with the last two exceptions both being class acts near the top of the weights for Willie Mullins, while Dan Skelton is leading the home defence having sent out three of the last four winners. Just three of the last 15 winners carried more than 11st 1lb, although all three have come in the last five years.

Albert Bartlett Novices' Hurdle (3m) Cheltenham

2010	**Berties Dream**	7-11-7	P J Gilligan	A Lynch	33-1	19
2011	**Bobs Worth**	6-11-7	N Henderson	B Geraghty	15-8f	18
2012	**Brindisi Breeze**	6-11-7	L Russell	C Gillies	7-1	20
2013	**At Fishers Cross**	6-11-7	R Curtis	A McCoy	11-8f	13
2014	**Very Wood**	5-11-7	N Meade	P Carberry	33-1	18
2015	**Martello Tower**	7-11-4	M Mullins	A Heskin	14-1	19
2016	**Unowhatimeanharry**	8-11-5	H Fry	N Fehily	11-1	19
2017	**Penhill**	6-11-5	W Mullins	P Townend	16-1	15
2018	**Kilbricken Storm**	7-11-5	C Tizzard	H Cobden	33-1	20
2019	**Minella Indo**	6-11-5	H de Bromhead	R Blackmore	50-1	20

THOUGH not run as a Grade 1 until 2008, this has always been a level-weights affair since its inception three years earlier. Unowhatimeanharry won as an eight-year-old in 2016 and there have been five winning seven-year-olds, including 33-1 shot Kilbricken Storm in 2018, which is very unusual for a top novice hurdle. The importance of stamina and experience is also shown by the fact that 14 of the 15 winners had run at least three times over hurdles – six of them at least six times, with only 50-1 stunner Minella Indo last year having run just twice – and 12 had already been tried over at least 3m. Seven of

CH'TIBELLO (right): a rare older winner of the County Hurdle last season

the nine non-Irish winners (French-trained Moulin Riche won the inaugural running) had run at least twice at Cheltenham and finished first or second, five of them winning, while Kilbricken Storm had also won his only start at the track.

Cheltenham Gold Cup (3m2½f) Cheltenham

2010	**Imperial Commander**	9-11-10	N Twiston-Davies	P Brennan	7-1	11
2011	**Long Run**	6-11-10	N Henderson	Mr S W-Cohen	7-2f	13
2012	**Synchronised**	9-11-10	J O'Neill	A McCoy	8-1	14
2013	**Bobs Worth**	8-11-10	N Henderson	B Geraghty	11-4f	9
2014	**Lord Windermere**	8-11-10	J Culloty	D Russell	20-1	13
2015	**Coneygree**	8-11-10	M Bradstock	N de Boinville	7-1	16
2016	**Don Cossack**	9-11-10	G Elliott	B Cooper	9-4f	9
2017	**Sizing John**	7-11-10	J Harrington	R Power	7-1	13
2018	**Native River**	8-11-10	C Tizzard	R Johnson	5-1	15
2019	**Al Boum Photo**	7-11-10	W Mullins	P Townend	12-1	16

AS the Gold Cup has increasingly become the be-all and end-all for top staying chasers, winners tend to be proven top-class performers who have been wrapped in cotton wool during the season. Don Cossack is the only winner since Kauto Star in 2007 to have run more than three times earlier in the campaign and even he had been off since early January, while the last 20 winners had already struck at the top level. That's certainly made the race more predictable as eight of the last 17 favourites have won, with 12-1 shot Al Boum Photo only the second winner since 1999 priced bigger than 8-1. Lord Windermere was the other exception, but even he was a solid trends pick having won the previous year's RSA Chase, which has provided five of the last 12 winners with Lord Windermere, Bobs Worth and Denman doing the double. That trio are among a raft of winners for inexperienced horses, with nine of the last 15 in their first or second season over fences, headed of course by the remarkable Coneygree, who was the first winning novice since Captain Christy in 1974. The key races during the season are the King George and the Lexus Chase as 15 of the last 20 winners ran in one of those contests. Horses older than nine struggle, with Cool Dawn the last to win in 1998 and 15 beaten at 8-1 or shorter since then, including four favourites.

Christie's Foxhunter Chase (3m2½f) Cheltenham

2010	**Baby Run**	10-12-0	N Twiston-Davies	Mr S Twiston-Davies	9-2jf	24
2011	**Zemsky**	8-12-0	I Ferguson	Mr D O'Connor	33-1	24
2012	**Salsify**	7-12-0	R Sweeney	Mr C Sweeney	7-1	22
2013	**Salsify**	8-12-0	R Sweeney	Mr C Sweeney	2-1f	23
2014	**Tammys Hill**	9-12-0	L Lennon	Mr J Smyth	15-2	24
2015	**On The Fringe**	10-12-0	E Bolger	Ms N Carberry	6-1	24
2016	**On The Fringe**	11-12-0	E Bolger	Ms N Carberry	13-8f	24
2017	**Pacha Du Polder**	10-12-0	P Nicholls	Miss B Frost	16-1	23
2018	**Pacha Du Polder**	11-12-0	P Nicholls	Miss H Tucker	25-1	24
2019	**Hazel Hill**	11-12-0	P Rowley	Mr A Edwards	7-2f	24

THIS is regarded as a lottery by many punters and six of the last 14 winners were at least 16-1, but with the other eight no bigger than 15-2 it's clearly been kind to plenty. Three horses have won six of the last eight runnings between them, with Pacha Du Polder and On The Fringe retaining their crown as 11-year-olds, but it's generally a wise ploy to rule out any horse older than ten barring these former champions as Hazel Hill was only the second first-time winner aged 11 or older since 1989 and that is often a significant proportion of the field. It's also vital to side with in-form horses rather than formerly classy horses on the downgrade as 25 of the last 33 winners had been successful last time out. Cappa Bleu was very unusual in winning on his debut under rules in 2009, while six of the subsequent ten runnings have gone to Ireland.

Grand Annual H'cap Chase (2m½f) Cheltenham

2010	**Pigeon Island**	7-10-1	N Twiston-Davies	P Brennan	16-1	19
2011	**Oiseau De Nuit**	9-11-6	C Tizzard	S Clements (7)	40-1	23
2012	**Bellvano**	8-10-2	N Henderson	P Carberry	20-1	21
2013	**Alderwood**	9-10-11	T Mullins	A McCoy	3-1f	23
2014	**Savello**	8-11-5	T Martin	D Russell	16-1	23
2015	**Next Sensation**	8-11-2	M Scudamore	T Scudamore	16-1	20
2016	**Solar Impulse**	6-11-0	P Nicholls	S Twiston-Davies	28-1	24
2017	**Rock The World**	9-11-5	J Harrington	R Power	10-1	24
2018	**Le Prezien**	7-11-8	P Nicholls	B Geraghty	15-2	22
2019	**Croco Bay**	12-10-12	B Case	K Woods	66-1	19

CHELTENHAM is one of the few places where you see 2m handicaps run at such a fast and furious pace and those who have excelled at the course before, especially in this race, tend to go well. Eight of the last 12 British-trained winners had previously been successful at Cheltenham and two of the exceptions, Croco Bay and Next Sensation, had been placed in this race, as had Irish pair Rock The World and Tiger Cry with Alderwood also winning a County Hurdle. It takes a strong, mature horse to cope with the demands of the Grand Annual yet you also want one unexposed enough to still be ahead of the handicapper. Eleven of the last 16 winners were eight or older, right up to the 12-year-old Croco Bay at 66-1 last year, even though most of those at the head of the market are younger, including ten favourites in that time. However, just two of the last 18 winners had run more than 12 times over fences.

Betway Bowl (3m1f) Aintree

2010	**What A Friend**	7-11-7	P Nicholls	R Walsh	5-2	5
2011	**Nacarat**	10-11-7	T George	P Brennan	7-2	6
2012	**Follow The Plan**	9-11-7	O McKiernan	T Doyle	50-1	11
2013	**First Lieutenant**	8-11-7	M Morris	T Cooper	7-2	8
2014	**Silviniaco Conti**	8-11-7	P Nicholls	N Fehily	9-4	6
2015	**Silviniaco Conti**	9-11-7	P Nicholls	N Fehily	7-4f	7
2016	**Cue Card**	10-11-7	C Tizzard	P Brennan	6-5f	9
2017	**Tea For Two**	8-11-7	N Williams	L Kelly	10-1	7
2018	**Might Bite**	9-11-7	N Henderson	N de Boinville	4-5f	7
2019	**Kemboy**	7-11-7	W Mullins	R Walsh	9-4f	6

THIS race is Aintree's version of the Gold Cup, but it rarely attracts the winner of the big one and the record of the three who have tried to do the double – Imperial Commander, Desert Orchid and Dawn Run – won't tempt many more to try it as all of them failed to complete. That's part of a wider trend because, of the 23 winners to have come via the Gold Cup, 15 of them finished outside the top four at Cheltenham. Not only were they likely to have avoided a harder race, but Prestbury Park form can always be turned around at this sharp, flat course that, despite being left-handed, has more in common with Kempton. Indeed, form at the Sunbury track seems to be key as 11 of the last 20 winners had been first or second in a King George, with Silviniaco Conti winning both races twice while Might Bite and Cue Card also did the double. Of the exceptions, Tea For Two and Madison Du Berlais had produced their best runs at Kempton and Nacarat had twice won the Racing Post Chase.

Randox Health Grand National (4m2½f) Aintree

2010	**Don't Push It**	10-11-5	J O'Neill	A McCoy	10-1jf	40
2011	**Ballabriggs**	10-11-0	D McCain	J Maguire	14-1	40
2012	**Neptune Collonges**	11-11-6	P Nicholls	D Jacob	33-1	40
2013	**Auroras Encore**	11-10-3	S Smith	R Mania	66-1	40
2014	**Pineau De Re**	11-10-6	Dr R Newland	L Aspell	25-1	40
2015	**Many Clouds**	8-11-9	O Sherwood	L Aspell	25-1	39
2016	**Rule The World**	9-10-7	M Morris	D Mullins	33-1	39
2017	**One For Arthur**	8-10-11	L Russell	D Fox	14-1	40
2018	**Tiger Roll**	8-10-13	G Elliott	D Russell	10-1	38
2019	**Tiger Roll**	9-11-5	G Elliott	D Russell	4-1f	40

THE great Tiger Roll ended a 45-year wait for a back-to-back winner of this great race, but it can hardly be said to have been overdue as past winners, or even those to have run well in the race before, hadn't been knocking on the door at all, most of them handicapped out of future Nationals. In fact, for such a unique challenge, it's remarkable that previous renewals have been such a poor guide to this race – 21 of the last 27 winners had never run in it before and four of the six exceptions failed to complete, with Tiger Roll and Amberleigh House the only winners in this period to have even got round before. The Becher and the Topham over the same fences have thrown up a fair number of winners, but the best guides are other major staying handicaps like the Ladbrokes Trophy, the Welsh National and the Irish National. A light weight used to be the key trend and remains a big help – 65 of the 77 top-11 finishers in the last seven years were below 11st – but the condensing of the handicap in recent years has given class horses more of a chance, with Tiger Roll, Many Clouds, Neptune Collonges, Ballabriggs, Don't Push It and Mon Mome all defying 11st or more in the last nine years after Hedgehunter in 2005

IRIS DE BALME (right): 66-1 win in 2008 rather sums up the Scottish National

had been the first since Corbiere 22 years earlier. Winners still tend to have hidden their ability from the handicapper that season as ten of the last 20 winners hadn't won at all over fences and 17 of them no more than once.

Scottish Grand National (4m) Ayr

2010	**Merigo**	9-10-0	A Parker	T Murphy	18-1	30
2011	**Beshabar**	9-10-4	T Vaughan	R Johnson	15-2	28
2012	**Merigo**	11-10-2	A Parker	T Murphy	15-2	24
2013	**Godsmejudge**	7-11-3	A King	W Hutchinson	12-1	24
2014	**Al Co**	9-10-0	P Bowen	J Moore	40-1	29
2015	**Wayward Prince**	11-10-1	H Parrott	R Dunne	25-1	29
2016	**Vicente**	7-11-3	P Nicholls	S Twiston-Davies	14-1	28
2017	**Vicente**	8-11-10	P Nicholls	S Twiston-Davies	9-1jf	30
2018	**Joe Farrell**	9-10-6	R Curtis	A Wedge	33-1	29
2019	**Takingrisks**	10-10-1	N Richards	S Quinlan	25-1	23

THIS has been a lean race for punters, with 9-1 joint-favourite Vicente the only successful market leader since Paris Pike in 2000 and some real skinners in that time, topped by

66-1 shot Iris De Balme romping to victory in 2008. Vicente had fallen at the first in the Grand National, but in general running at Aintree is a big negative as he is the only winner to come via the National since Little Polveir in 1987. No Cheltenham Festival winner has followed up in more than 30 years either, but previous Scottish Nationals have been a good pointer, with Vicente and Merigo winning four of the last ten renewals between them and Godsmejudge also finishing second 12 months after his 2013 victory. Nine of the last 15 winners carried no more than 10st 4lb, from up to 26lb out of the handicap, and novices have a good record with ten winners in 26 years from small representation.

Irish Grand National (3m5f) Fairyhouse

2010	**Bluesea Cracker**	8-10-4	J Motherway	A J McNamara	25-1	26
2011	**Organisedconfusion**	6-9-13	A Moore	Miss N Carberry	12-1	25
2012	**Lion Na Bearnai**	10-10-5	T Gibney	A Thornton	33-1	29
2013	**Liberty Counsel**	10-9-10	D Love	B Dalton (5)	50-1	28
2014	**Shutthefrontdoor**	7-10-13	J O'Neill	B Geraghty	8-1f	26
2015	**Thunder And Roses**	7-10-6	S Hughes	K Walsh	20-1	28
2016	**Rogue Angel**	8-10-9	M Morris	G Fox (3)	16-1	27
2017	**Our Duke**	7-11-4	J Harrington	R Power	9-2f	28
2018	**General Principle**	9-10-0	G Elliott	JJ Slevin	20-1	30
2019	**Burrows Saint**	6-10-8	W Mullins	R Walsh	6-1f	30

OUR DUKE was a stunning winner of this race in 2017, but that was all the more remarkable because light weights are generally so strongly favoured – 18 of the last 19 winners carried less than 11st. The main reason is that this tends to be a race for lightly raced horses just starting to realise their potential as they step up in trip, with Rogue Angel the only winner since Mudahim in 1998 to have run more than 13 times over fences and last year's winner Burrows Saint in that time carrying novice status. That can also make it a hard race to call, with ten of the last 14 winners sent off 20-1 or bigger. British raiders have traditionally had an awful record, but that's improved slightly in recent times with Shuttthefrontdoor the fourth successful raider in 11 years when he won in 2014.

bet365 Gold Cup (3m5f) Sandown

2010	**Church Island**	11-10-5	M Hourigan	A Heskin (7)	20-1	19
2011	**Poker De Sivola**	8-10-12	F Murphy	T Murphy	11-1	18
2012	**Tidal Bay**	11-11-12	P Nicholls	D Jacob	9-1	19
2013	**Quentin Collonges**	9-10-12	H Daly	A Tinkler	14-1	19
2014	**Hadrian's Approach**	7-11-0	N Henderson	B Geraghty	10-1	19
2015	**Just A Par**	8-10-3	P Nicholls	S Bowen (3)	14-1	20
2016	**The Young Master**	7-11-1	N Mulholland	Mr S Waley-Cohen (3)	8-1	20
2017	**Henllan Harri**	9-10-0	P Bowen	S Bowen	40-1	13
2018	**Step Back**	8-10-0	M Bradstock	J Moore	7-1	20
2019	**Talkischeap**	7-10-11	A King	W Hutchinson	7-1	15

AS in so many staying chases, light weights are favoured – 26 of the last 31 winners carried less than 11st (including The Young Master with Sam Waley-Cohen's 3lb claim) and the best winner of recent times, Tidal Bay, was a rare beast indeed when defying 11st 12lb. However, that knowledge still hasn't helped punters as the race is a graveyard for favourites, with Mr Frisk the last outright market leader to prevail when becoming the only horse to follow up a Grand National victory in 1990. He's one of ten winners to have come via Aintree since 1973 and seven of them had failed to get beyond Becher's on the second circuit. Most winners had run at the Cheltenham Festival – 27 of the last 45 in all – but none of them had won there.

Track Facts

WANT course statistics? Look no further - this section contains all the numbers you'll need for every jumps track in Britain.

Course by course, we've set out five-year trainer and jockey statistics, favourites' records, winning pointers and three-dimensional racecourse maps, plus details of how to get there and fixtures for the new season.

Following this, from page 220, we've got details of course records and standard times for each track. Note that we have been unable to produce standard times in a few cases as there have not been enough recent races over the trip at the track in question.

See also our statistical assessment of last season's records from Britain's top ten trainers in terms of winners (page 119).

Ormskirk Rd, Liverpool,
L9 5AS. Tel: 0151 523 2600

AINTREE

How to get there Road: M6, M62, M57, M58. Rail: Liverpool Lime Street and taxi.

Features The left-handed 2m2f giant triangular Grand National course is perfectly flat. Inside it, the sharp left-handed Mildmay course is 1m4f in circumference.

2019-20 Fixtures
October 27, November 9, December 7, April 2-4

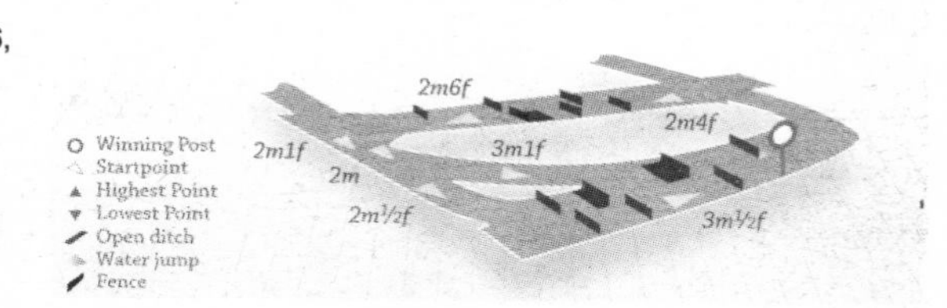

Trainers	*Wins-Runs*	*%*	*Hurdles*	*Chases*	*£1 level stks*
Nicky Henderson	20-106	19	14-62	4-36	-6.40
Dan Skelton	15-106	14	10-63	5-35	+3.05
Colin Tizzard	13-57	23	4-22	9-34	90.49
Paul Nicholls	12-112	11	2-35	8-71	-45.00
W P Mullins	10-53	19	4-22	5-28	-2.16
Tom George	9-71	13	2-19	5-47	+6.00
Nigel Twiston-Davies	9-89	10	3-31	6-54	-36.25
Jonjo O'Neill	7-64	11	5-32	2-29	-16.15
Harry Fry	6-38	16	3-17	3-14	-7.27
Alan King	5-43	12	3-26	1-6	-13.95
Gordon Elliott	5-54	9	3-16	2-36	-17.00
Philip Hobbs	5-61	8	4-32	1-22	-43.55
Ian Williams	4-32	13	3-22	1-8	+14.00

Jockeys	*Wins-Rides*	*%*	*£1 level stks*	*Best Trainer*	*W-R*
Harry Skelton	13-87	15	+16.75	Dan Skelton	13-86
Richard Johnson	11-81	14	+2.64	Philip Hobbs	4-49
Nico de Boinville	10-59	17	-3.84	Nicky Henderson	11-48
Aidan Coleman	9-73	12	-32.83	Jonjo O'Neill	3-22
Sean Bowen	9-80	11	-36.75	Paul Nicholls	4-26
Robbie Power	8-22	36	+52.00	Colin Tizzard	7-13
Noel Fehily	6-38	16	-3.25	Harry Fry	2-15
Daryl Jacob	6-53	11	-21.20	Nicky Henderson	4-20
Barry Geraghty	6-58	10	-23.47	Rebecca Curtis	2-7
Ryan Hatch	5-22	23	+14.50	Nigel Twiston-Davies	5-24
Paul Townend	5-24	21	15.07	W P Mullins	3-14
A P Heskin	5-35	14	+14.50	Tom George	5-29
Sam Twiston-Davies	5-60	8	-35.13	Paul Nicholls	5-43

Favourites

Hurdle 40% 6.53   Chase 28% -6.66   Total 34% -4.25

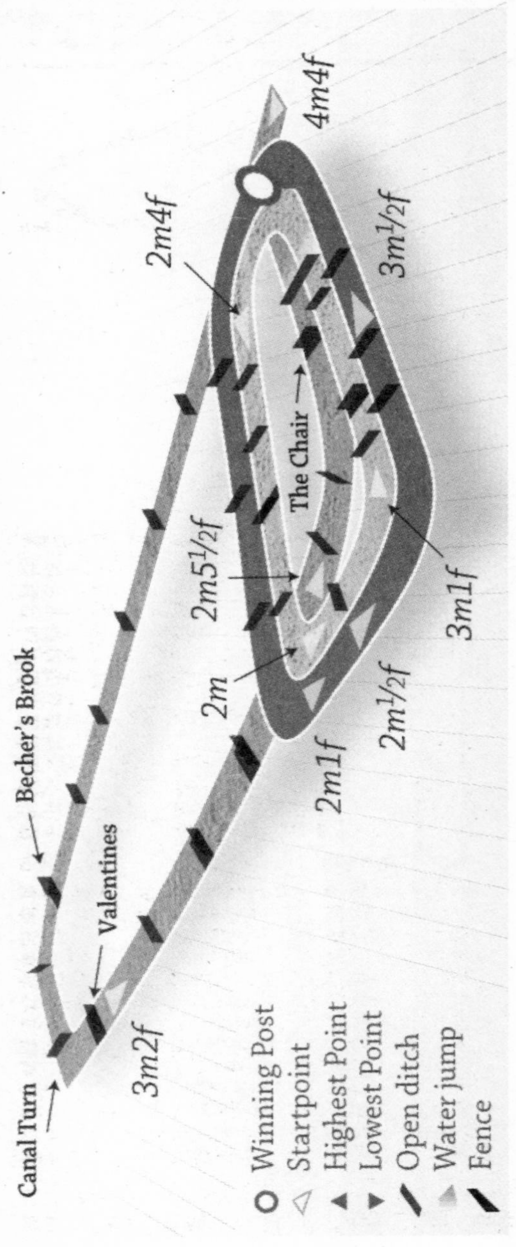

Aintree's Grand National course - used in the Becher Chase, the Grand Sefton Chase, the Topham Chase, the Foxhunters' Chase and the Grand National

ASCOT

Ascot, Berkshire SL5 7JX
0870 7227 227

How to get there Road: M4 junction 6 or M3 junction 3 on to A332. Rail: Frequent service from Reading or Waterloo

Features Right-handed

2019-20 Fixtures November 2, 22-23, December 20-21, January 18, February 15, March 29

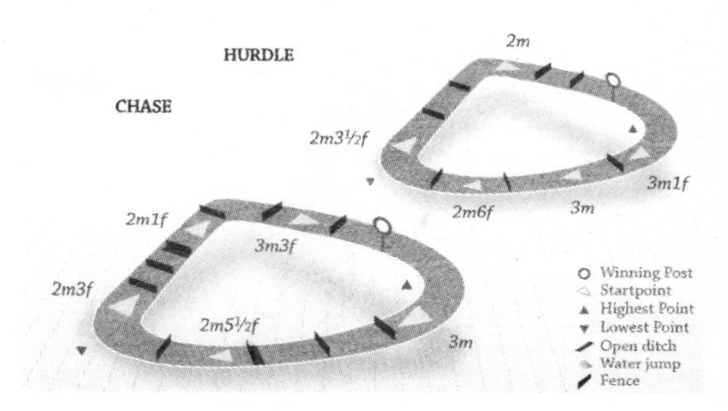

Trainers	Wins-Runs	%	Hurdles	Chases	£1 level stks
Paul Nicholls	35-179	20	12-74	21-95	+22.42
Nicky Henderson	33-158	21	19-100	12-45	-6.26
Harry Fry	17-63	27	13-35	4-22	+6.34
Alan King	11-87	13	8-65	2-14	-38.72
Venetia Williams	10-76	13	3-17	7-57	+12.75
Philip Hobbs	10-90	11	4-40	4-45	-19.59
David Pipe	9-49	18	5-31	3-17	+11.75
Gary Moore	8-92	9	2-43	6-39	-33.50
Colin Tizzard	7-72	10	3-24	4-43	-37.23
Charlie Longsdon	6-51	12	2-20	3-24	+21.00
W P Mullins	5-13	38	2-7	3-5	-5.74
Nick Gifford	4-24	17	3-13	0-8	+16.25
Dr Richard Newland	4-27	15	2-11	2-15	+9.50

Jockeys	Wins-Rides	%	£1 level stks	Best Trainer	W-R
Barry Geraghty	23-87	26	+25.67	Nicky Henderson	9-44
Nico de Boinville	18-66	27	+4.25	Nicky Henderson	14-39
Sam Twiston-Davies	16-90	18	-8.89	Paul Nicholls	11-50
Noel Fehily	14-75	19	-3.36	Harry Fry	6-35
Aidan Coleman	14-91	15	+32.75	Venetia Williams	11-39
Wayne Hutchinson	9-60	15	-13.85	Alan King	8-42
Jamie Moore	9-69	13	+1.50	Gary Moore	8-40
Harry Cobden	8-50	16	+3.15	Paul Nicholls	1-12
Tom Scudamore	8-58	14	-7.75	David Pipe	7-37
R Walsh	7-13	54	+2.75	W P Mullins	5-9
Daryl Jacob	7-49	14	-20.37	Paul Nicholls	2-9
Leighton Aspell	7-50	14	+10.62	Oliver Sherwood	4-22
Richard Johnson	7-82	9	-40.15	Philip Hobbs	8-48

Favourites

Hurdle 36% -8.55 Chase 32% -25.00 Total 34% -39.77

AYR

Whitletts Road, Ayr, KA8 0JE
Tel: 01292 264 179

How to get there Road: south from Glasgow on A77 or A75, A70, A76. Rail: Ayr

Features Left-handed 1m4f oval, easy turns, slight uphill finish

2019-20 Fixtures
October 28, November 2, 13, January 2, 6, 19, February 11, March 7, April 17-18

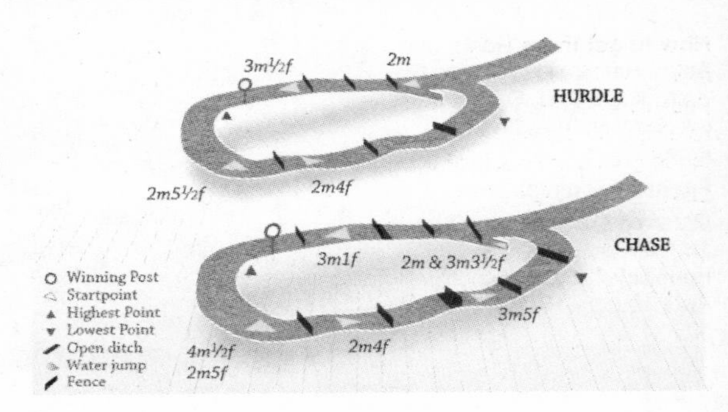

Trainers	*Wins-Runs*	*%*	*Hurdles*	*Chases*	*£1 level stks*
Nicky Richards	43-185	23	20-110	12-49	-3.05
Lucinda Russell	32-299	11	14-156	15-111	-135.37
N W Alexander	28-247	11	15-152	11-76	-58.23
Dan Skelton	15-54	28	6-29	8-23	+5.07
Donald McCain	15-91	16	7-42	7-40	-35.75
S R B Crawford	14-129	11	10-83	2-23	-57.98
Iain Jardine	13-72	18	9-46	2-16	+2.48
James Ewart	13-107	12	7-55	3-23	-25.45
Sandy Thomson	11-68	16	5-30	4-25	-22.65
Martin Todhunter	11-69	16	5-36	6-32	+11.23
Paul Nicholls	10-48	21	4-19	5-27	+12.21
Stuart Coltherd	10-63	16	6-34	4-27	+11.50
Gordon Elliott	9-44	20	6-27	1-10	-16.08

Jockeys	*Wins-Rides*	*%*	*£1 level stks*	*Best Trainer*	*W-R*
Brian Hughes	56-267	21	+3.50	Donald McCain	7-13
Brian Harding	20-113	18	-1.56	Nicky Richards	17-64
Henry Brooke	17-133	13	+4.75	Martin Todhunter	3-24
Derek Fox	17-177	10	-30.08	Lucinda Russell	10-83
Craig Nichol	15-150	10	-38.08	Nicky Richards	8-34
Harry Skelton	14-49	29	+6.07	Dan Skelton	9-36
Ross Chapman	14-70	20	+2.98	Iain Jardine	5-17
Ryan Day	11-59	19	-17.42	Nicky Richards	7-30
Lucy Alexander	11-127	9	-34.00	N W Alexander	7-74
Peter Buchanan	10-56	18	+7.13	Lucinda Russell	12-72
Stephen Mulqueen	9-108	8	-82.39	Nicky Richards	3-6
Callum Whillans	8-46	17	+55.25	Donald Whillans	6-29
Richard Johnson	8-56	14	-27.44	Gordon Elliott	2-5

Favourites

Hurdle	40%	+0.07	Chase	40%	+20.27	Total	41%	+21.46

Bangor-on-Dee, nr Wrexham
Clwyd. Tel: 01948 860 438

BANGOR

How to get there Road: A525. Rail: Wrexham

Features Left-handed, 1m4f round, quite sharp, final fence gets plenty of fallers

2019-20 Fixtures
October 2, 29, November 13, 30, December 13, February 7, 18, March 21, April 18

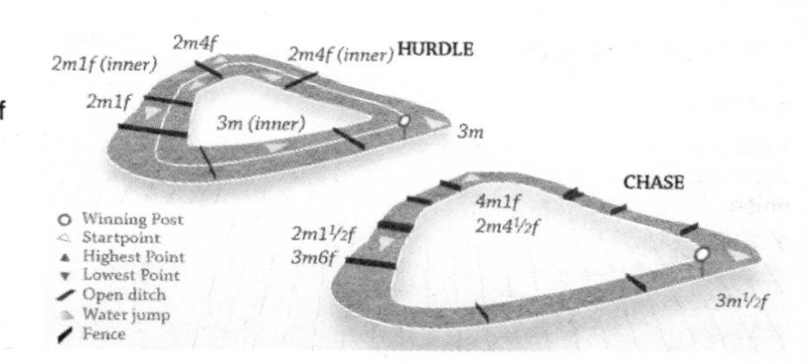

Trainers	Wins-Runs	%	Hurdles	Chases	£1 level stks
Donald McCain	63-324	19	46-210	15-84	+22.80
Dan Skelton	27-106	25	16-70	10-29	-6.82
Alan King	19-67	28	13-39	3-15	-8.75
Henry Daly	14-56	25	9-28	2-14	+50.75
Jonjo O'Neill	14-105	13	5-50	5-48	-20.13
Warren Greatrex	12-50	24	7-30	2-9	-10.36
Kim Bailey	11-55	20	4-26	5-23	-22.19
Charlie Longsdon	11-63	17	6-35	5-23	-8.04
Nigel Twiston-Davies	11-69	16	3-25	5-28	-18.36
Rebecca Curtis	10-55	18	5-24	4-19	-8.67
Jennie Candlish	9-69	13	4-40	5-22	-32.90
Venetia Williams	9-94	10	1-38	8-49	-29.34
David Pipe	8-41	20	4-29	3-10	-8.88

Jockeys	Wins-Rides	%	£1 level stks	Best Trainer	W-R
William Kennedy	25-141	18	+26.92	Donald McCain	20-81
Harry Skelton	22-82	27	+8.73	Dan Skelton	17-53
Richard Johnson	20-99	20	+1.61	Charlie Longsdon	4-6
Brian Hughes	20-102	20	+13.25	Donald McCain	4-6
Gavin Sheehan	14-53	26	+11.37	Warren Greatrex	9-25
Wayne Hutchinson	14-69	20	-27.50	Alan King	12-37
Noel Fehily	12-64	19	-18.95	Charlie Longsdon	5-11
Paddy Brennan	11-46	24	+4.05	Fergal O'Brien	5-16
Sean Quinlan	11-53	21	+8.50	Jennie Candlish	6-43
Tom Scudamore	11-61	18	-16.62	David Pipe	6-18
Richie McLernon	9-58	16	+58.00	George Moore	2-2
Sam Twiston-Davies	9-60	15	-22.17	Donald McCain	2-6
Sean Bowen	8-48	17	+4.00	Peter Bowen	6-27

Favourites

Hurdle	36%	-42.22	Chase	39%	+2.34	Total	37%	-48.15

CARLISLE

Blackwell, Carlisle, CA2 4TS
Tel: 01228 522 973

How to get there Road: M6 Jctn 42. Rail: 2m from Citadel Station, Carlisle

Features Pear-shaped, 1m5f circuit, right-handed, undulating, uphill home straight

2019-20 Fixtures October 17, 24, November 3, 11, December 1, 15, February 3, 17, 24, March 5, 15, 22, April 11

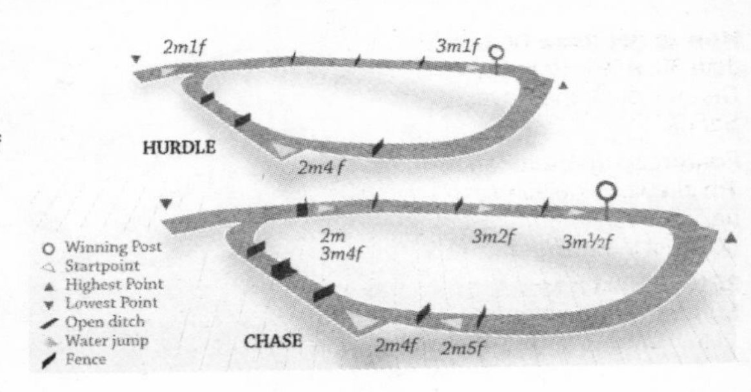

Trainers	Wins-Runs	%	Hurdles	Chases	£1 level stks
Donald McCain	27-205	13	17-130	8-60	-53.14
Sue Smith	20-125	16	3-37	16-79	-21.59
Nicky Richards	19-86	22	12-44	3-35	+30.94
S R B Crawford	14-37	38	7-17	0-7	+10.51
Micky Hammond	13-128	10	7-64	5-54	-34.85
Venetia Williams	11-42	26	4-15	6-23	+15.03
Malcolm Jefferson	10-41	24	1-4	7-28	-2.68
Brian Ellison	10-60	17	5-34	4-19	-28.79
Nigel Twiston-Davies	9-25	36	6-9	3-15	+9.92
Nigel Hawke	9-27	33	5-16	2-7	+5.37
Alan Swinbank	9-29	31	6-19	2-5	+11.28
Jennie Candlish	9-67	13	1-33	8-27	-24.13
Philip Kirby	8-48	17	5-35	3-11	+8.08

Jockeys	Wins-Rides	%	£1 level stks	Best Trainer	W-R
Brian Hughes	41-252	16	-82.89	Malcolm Jefferson	10-42
Danny Cook	19-104	18	-14.38	Sue Smith	10-46
William Kennedy	17-79	22	+23.56	Donald McCain	14-63
Richard Johnson	14-53	26	+5.86	S R B Crawford	2-3
Sam Twiston-Davies	13-34	38	+7.28	Paul Nicholls	4-6
Sean Quinlan	12-94	13	-32.92	Jennie Candlish	5-38
Brian Harding	12-94	13	-27.96	Nicky Richards	14-43
Craig Nichol	12-97	12	-32.75	Rose Dobbin	5-34
Harry Skelton	8-25	32	+12.03	Oliver Greenall	2-2
Paul Moloney	8-28	29	+8.79	Alan Swinbank	7-23
Aidan Coleman	8-34	24	+22.66	Venetia Williams	2-12
Daragh Bourke	7-28	25	+31.25	Maurice Barnes	6-25
James Reveley	7-40	18	+13.08	Philip Kirby	2-5

Favourites

Hurdle 40% -18.16   Chase 34% -26.82   Total 37% -49.93

Grange-over-Sands, Penrith
CA10 2HG. Tel: 01593 536 340

CARTMEL

How to get there Road: M6 Jctn 36, A591. Rail: Cark-in-Cartmel or Grange-over-Sands

Features Tight, left-handed 1m circuit, undulating, half-mile run-in from last (longest in Britain)

2019-20 Fixtures Summer jumping only

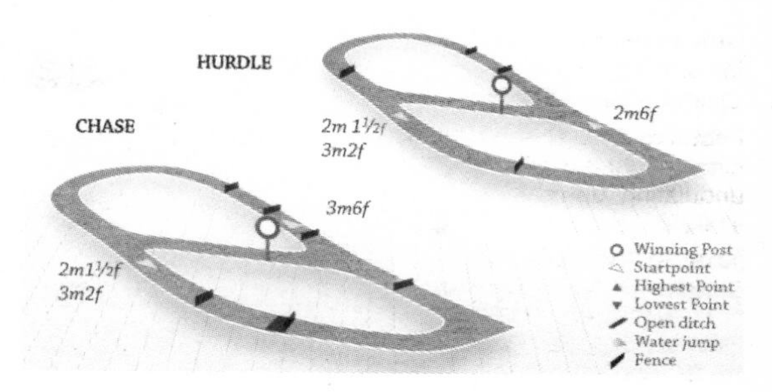

Trainers	*Wins-Runs*	*%*	*Hurdles*	*Chases*	*£1 level stks*
Donald McCain	28-135	21	21-90	7-45	-11.88
James Moffatt	23-218	11	16-161	7-57	-36.88
Peter Bowen	21-64	33	11-30	10-34	+26.72
Gordon Elliott	10-38	26	8-25	2-13	-4.55
Kenneth Slack	9-24	38	9-22	0-2	+52.38
Micky Hammond	9-81	11	2-41	7-40	-26.50
Martin Todhunter	8-55	15	4-30	4-25	-15.63
Dianne Sayer	8-107	7	3-71	5-36	-60.17
Jonjo O'Neill	7-26	27	4-15	3-11	+4.80
Julia Brooke	6-26	23	6-20	0-6	+11.33
Sam England	5-18	28	3-13	2-5	+46.50
Richard Ford	5-20	25	1-8	4-12	+5.87
Neil Mulholland	5-23	22	3-13	2-10	-6.31

Jockeys	*Wins-Rides*	*%*	*£1 level stks*	*Best Trainer*	*W-R*
Brian Hughes	36-211	17	-37.84	James Moffatt	8-59
Henry Brooke	25-143	17	+30.75	Martin Todhunter	5-20
Richard Johnson	21-108	19	-30.23	Gordon Elliott	6-30
Sean Bowen	15-50	30	+8.96	Peter Bowen	8-25
Jonathan England	6-27	22	+38.50	Maurice Barnes	2-6
Tom Scudamore	6-28	21	+1.75	David Pipe	2-6
Brian Harding	6-34	18	+42.23	Pauline Robson	2-4
Sean Quinlan	6-69	9	-37.75	Sue Smith	2-8
A P McCoy	5-15	33	-3.34	Donald McCain	4-9
Robert Hogg	4-15	27	+17.88	Kenneth Slack	2-6
James Cowley	4-17	24	+0.38	Donald McCain	4-18
Harry Reed	4-17	24	+18.83	R Mike Smith	1-1
Sam Twiston-Davies	4-18	22	-2.61	Dr Richard Newland	2-6

Favourites

Hurdle	30%	-30.22	Chase	32%	-20.90	Total	31%	-51.11

CATTERICK

Catterick Bridge, Richmond, N Yorks
DL10 7PE. Tel: 01748 811 478

How to get there Road: A1. Rail: Darlington

Features Left-handed, 1m2f oval, undulating, sharp turns, favours small, handy horses

2019-20 Fixtures
November 22, December 17, 28, January 1, 9, 22, 31, February 10, 25, March 4

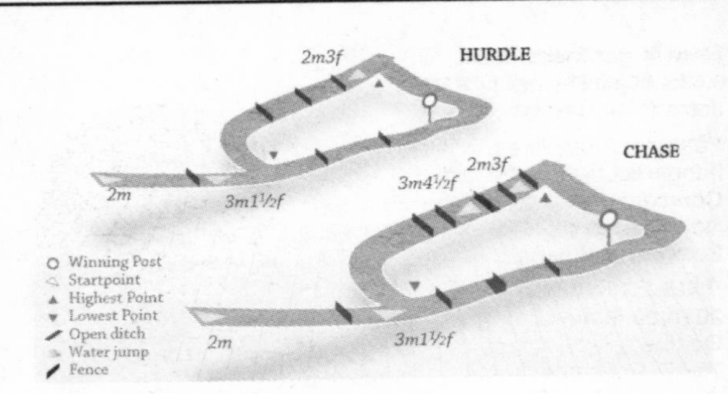

Trainers	Wins-Runs	%	Hurdles	Chases	£1 level stks
Sue Smith	27-90	30	7-40	20-43	+58.83
Donald McCain	27-152	18	19-101	6-41	-19.11
Brian Ellison	15-58	26	9-34	4-19	-16.95
Micky Hammond	12-168	7	6-107	6-52	-58.00
Dan Skelton	8-33	24	5-19	2-12	-11.61
Kenneth Slack	8-37	22	5-25	3-12	+3.25
John Ferguson	7-9	78	5-6	0-1	+11.74
Rebecca Menzies	7-34	21	2-13	4-18	-1.79
John Quinn	6-23	26	6-19	0-2	-4.97
Jamie Snowden	5-11	45	2-6	3-4	+1.32
Sam England	5-25	20	1-9	4-16	-0.75
Alan King	4-6	67	3-5	1-1	+1.73
Pam Sly	4-9	44	3-7	1-2	+10.56

Jockeys	Wins-Rides	%	£1 level stks	Best Trainer	W-R
Danny Cook	27-99	27	+11.74	Sue Smith	16-43
Brian Hughes	26-158	16	-41.65	Malcolm Jefferson	4-31
William Kennedy	12-58	21	-8.47	Donald McCain	7-33
Ross Chapman	10-33	30	+11.00	Kenneth Slack	2-4
Joe Colliver	9-69	13	-2.60	Micky Hammond	6-53
Henry Brooke	9-123	7	-65.13	Donald McCain	3-10
Richard Johnson	8-22	36	+11.80	David O'Meara	1-1
Aidan Coleman	8-25	32	+2.11	John Ferguson	4-5
Sean Quinlan	8-69	12	-27.35	Sue Smith	3-10
Gavin Sheehan	7-19	37	-1.20	Warren Greatrex	2-4
Jonathan England	7-45	16	-3.75	Sam England	3-13
A P McCoy	6-11	55	+6.28	Jonjo O'Neill	4-12
Conor O'Farrell	5-22	23	-1.42	Jamie Snowden	1-1

Favourites

Hurdle 45% -3.96 | Chase 46% +14.44 | Total 46% +19.28

Prestbury Park, Cheltenham,
GL50 4SH. Tel: 01242 513 014

CHELTENHAM

How to get there Road: A435, five miles north of M5 Jctns 9, 10, 11

Features There are two left-handed courses - the Old Course is 1m4f around, the New Course slightly longer. Both are undulating and end with a testing uphill finish

2019-20 Fixtures
October 25-26, November 15-17, December 13-14, January 1, 25, March 10-13, April 15-16

No trainer has been more prolific at Cheltenham in the last five seasons than Nicky Henderson – although he'd love to get one over on Willie Mullins more often!

New Course

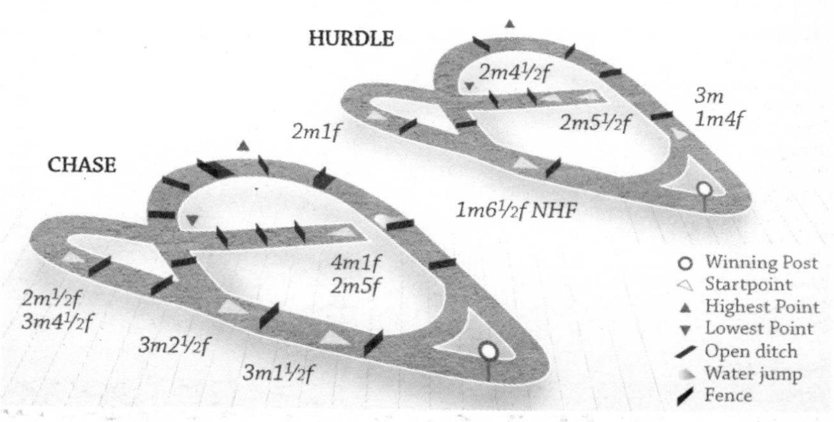

Old Course

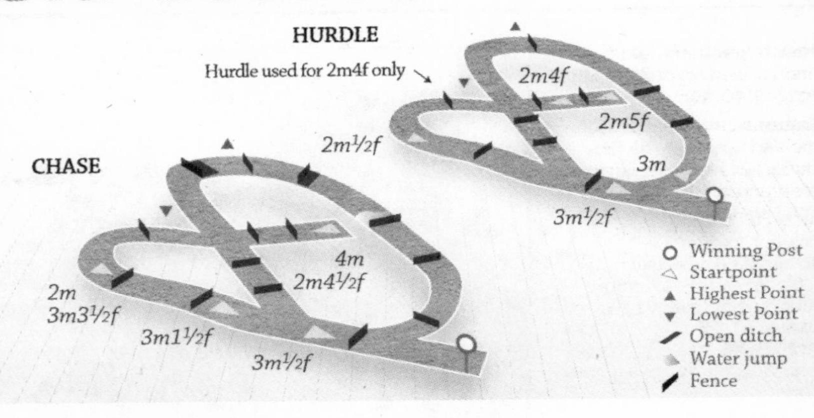

Trainers	*Wins-Runs*	*%*	*Hurdles*	*Chases*	*£1 level stks*
Nicky Henderson	44-378	12	31-239	12-126	-109.87
Paul Nicholls	41-354	12	14-152	24-192	+11.85
W P Mullins	33-300	11	19-188	13-87	-18.74
Philip Hobbs	27-231	12	8-93	16-120	-57.89
Nigel Twiston-Davies	27-263	10	12-109	13-141	-89.40
Gordon Elliott	26-187	14	12-99	12-81	+40.60
Colin Tizzard	24-244	10	10-90	13-144	-86.02
Alan King	19-169	11	10-109	7-45	-28.17
Dan Skelton	19-194	10	14-127	5-61	-40.30
Fergal O'Brien	17-146	12	6-64	7-55	+17.62
David Pipe	13-174	7	4-82	7-86	-89.63
Harry Fry	12-95	13	9-59	2-29	-34.99
Jonjo O'Neill	12-161	7	4-66	8-90	-46.04

Jockeys	*Wins-Rides*	*%*	*£1 level stks*	*Best Trainer*	*W-R*
Barry Geraghty	37-223	17	-53.37	Nicky Henderson	13-98
Richard Johnson	34-276	12	-64.15	Philip Hobbs	25-160
Sam Twiston-Davies	25-268	9	-50.43	Paul Nicholls	15-148
Nico de Boinville	24-125	19	+48.65	Nicky Henderson	14-79
Noel Fehily	23-212	11	-5.73	Neil Mulholland	7-25
Aidan Coleman	21-204	10	-34.71	Martin Keighley	4-15
Paddy Brennan	20-173	12	+7.63	Fergal O'Brien	9-62
R Walsh	19-85	22	-22.43	W P Mullins	22-80
Harry Skelton	17-153	11	-46.80	Dan Skelton	12-109
Tom Scudamore	17-193	9	-82.18	David Pipe	17-134
Harry Cobden	16-107	15	+20.75	Colin Tizzard	5-23
Davy Russell	14-96	15	+18.53	Gordon Elliott	5-21
Daryl Jacob	12-143	8	-95.31	Paul Nicholls	8-48

Favourites

Hurdle 31% -32.37 Chase 30% -41.03 Total 30% -76.40

Chepstow, Gwent, NP6 5YH
Tel: 01291 622 260

CHEPSTOW

How to get there Road: three miles west of Severn Bridge (M4). Rail: Chepstow

Features Left-handed, undulating oval, nearly 2m round, suits long-striding front-runners

2019-20 Fixtures
October 11-12, 29, November 6, 20, December 7, 27, January 6, 17, 31, February 22, March 2, 19, April 4, 13, 24

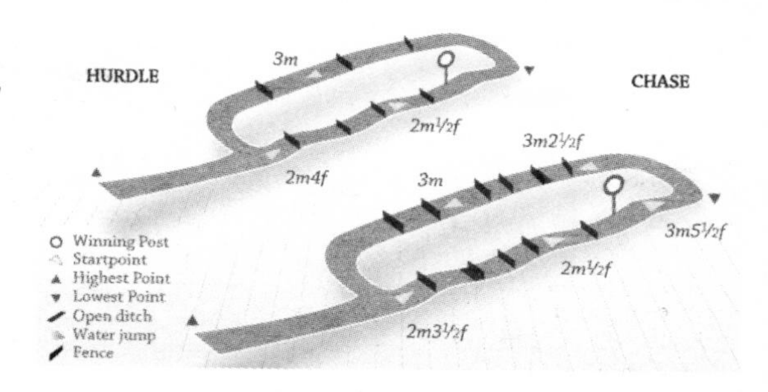

Trainers	Wins-Runs	%	Hurdles	Chases	£1 level stks
Paul Nicholls	35-154	23	20-85	7-52	-23.25
Philip Hobbs	35-167	21	20-82	14-67	-10.06
Evan Williams	34-204	17	23-117	10-77	+77.36
Colin Tizzard	20-189	11	7-79	13-89	-68.13
Nigel Twiston-Davies	19-109	17	9-50	7-45	+3.27
Peter Bowen	19-122	16	7-65	9-44	-10.47
David Pipe	18-113	16	8-68	7-35	-20.55
Venetia Williams	18-130	14	3-55	14-68	-37.32
Tom George	16-80	20	7-42	4-26	-21.04
Jonjo O'Neill	14-120	12	10-69	2-43	-42.99
Matt Sheppard	11-74	15	6-42	5-31	+15.88
Dan Skelton	11-90	12	6-54	3-22	-10.50
Neil Mulholland	11-102	11	7-59	4-37	-37.05

Jockeys	Wins-Rides	%	£1 level stks	Best Trainer	W-R
Richard Johnson	43-183	23	+26.38	Philip Hobbs	15-70
Sean Bowen	28-126	22	+54.48	Peter Bowen	15-57
Tom Scudamore	25-144	17	-14.51	David Pipe	10-56
Sam Twiston-Davies	24-126	19	-38.97	Paul Nicholls	14-59
Adam Wedge	17-129	13	+18.41	Evan Williams	12-66
Harry Cobden	16-92	17	-9.31	Colin Tizzard	3-20
Tom O'Brien	14-102	14	-26.49	Philip Hobbs	5-31
Paddy Brennan	13-80	16	+4.08	Fergal O'Brien	5-24
Stan Sheppard	12-61	20	+17.88	Matt Sheppard	8-39
Paul Moloney	11-69	16	+23.85	Evan Williams	10-55
Aidan Coleman	11-119	9	-56.03	Venetia Williams	3-20
Daryl Jacob	10-60	17	-21.48	Nicky Henderson	2-2
Gavin Sheehan	10-80	13	-35.90	Warren Greatrex	3-22

Favourites

Hurdle 40% +3.91 Chase 33% -4.97 Total 37% -9.56

DONCASTER

Grand Street, Leger Way, Doncaster DN2 6BB. Tel: 01302 320 666/7

How to get there Road: M18 Jctn 3, A638, A18 towards Hull. Rail: Doncaster Central

Features Left-handed, flat, 2m round, run-in of just over a furlong, rarely heavy, favours speed horses

2019-20 Fixtures November 29-30, December 13-14, 29, January 14, 24-25, February 9, 19, 28-29

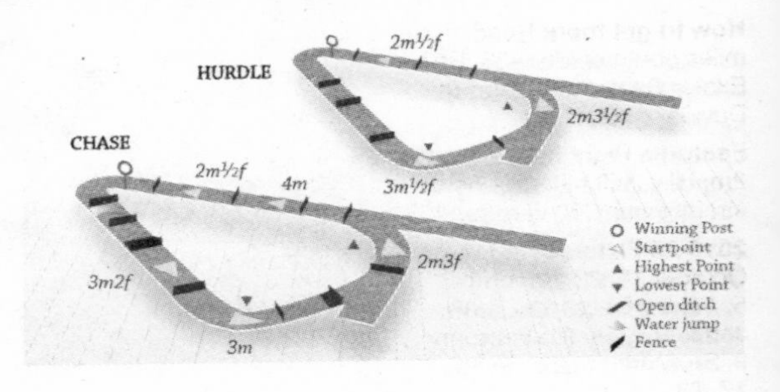

Trainers	Wins-Runs	%	Hurdles	Chases	£1 level stks
Nicky Henderson	26-78	33	17-45	9-24	-1.45
Alan King	24-115	21	14-70	9-35	-5.40
Paul Nicholls	18-70	26	7-29	10-39	-13.95
Ben Pauling	13-52	25	9-33	4-15	+23.15
Emma Lavelle	12-45	27	7-21	2-15	+9.15
Kim Bailey	11-59	19	7-37	3-17	-24.44
Ian Williams	11-74	15	7-51	3-20	-1.83
Dan Skelton	11-82	13	7-54	3-22	-45.29
Charlie Longsdon	11-90	12	4-42	6-42	-18.80
Jonjo O'Neill	11-93	12	4-58	7-33	-21.75
Nicky Richards	9-44	20	4-27	4-13	+25.75
Tom George	8-60	13	4-25	2-30	+25.79
Harry Fry	7-17	41	0-5	5-7	+9.83

Jockeys	Wins-Rides	%	£1 level stks	Best Trainer	W-R
Nico de Boinville	14-54	26	+5.79	Nicky Henderson	10-30
David Bass	14-55	25	-6.87	Kim Bailey	6-29
Aidan Coleman	13-73	18	-20.41	Emma Lavelle	2-8
Leighton Aspell	12-49	24	+3.82	Emma Lavelle	7-16
Nick Scholfield	10-36	28	+23.42	Paul Nicholls	6-20
Wayne Hutchinson	10-49	20	-15.27	Alan King	8-29
James Reveley	10-67	15	+49.83	Keith Reveley	10-78
Brian Hughes	10-131	8	-94.76	Malcolm Jefferson	5-29
A P McCoy	9-26	35	+1.44	Jonjo O'Neill	3-15
Henry Brooke	9-64	14	+19.25	Peter Atkinson	2-4
Noel Fehily	8-39	21	-9.17	Harry Fry	3-9
Daryl Jacob	8-47	17	-28.76	Nicky Henderson	4-5
Harry Skelton	8-50	16	-18.29	Dan Skelton	5-45

Favourites

Hurdle 43% +5.68 Chase 40% -3.30 Total 41% -0.88

Kennford, nr Exeter, Devon
EX6 7XS. Tel: 01392 832 599

EXETER

How to get there Road: five miles south of M5, A38. Rail: Exeter Central or Exeter St Davids

Features Right-handed, 2m, hilly, stiff half-mile home straight with 300-yard run-in

2019-20 Fixtures
October 10, 22, November 5, 13, 24, December 6, 19, January 1, 14, 21, February 9, 21, March 3, 22, April 7, 17, 23

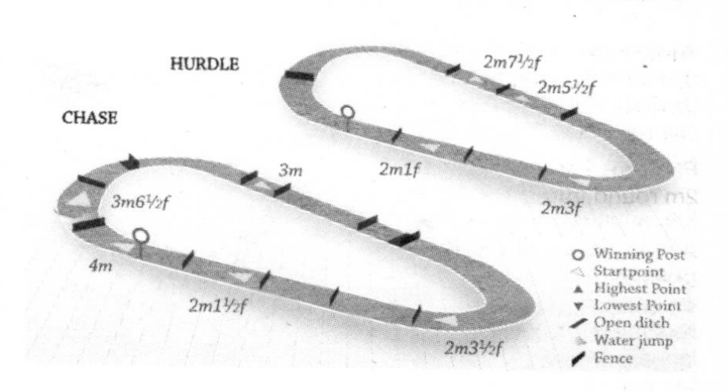

Trainers	Wins-Runs	%	Hurdles	Chases	£1 level stks
Philip Hobbs	51-238	21	33-130	14-91	-49.59
Paul Nicholls	45-142	32	28-81	15-49	-7.69
Colin Tizzard	33-193	17	17-96	16-84	-48.95
Harry Fry	29-79	37	18-52	8-18	+44.79
David Pipe	23-200	12	18-141	3-42	-68.53
Evan Williams	17-76	22	11-45	6-29	+31.63
Alan King	16-87	18	9-54	6-24	-21.11
Venetia Williams	13-89	15	5-36	8-50	-8.47
Sue Gardner	13-130	10	10-97	3-23	-51.38
Victor Dartnall	12-101	12	7-62	4-33	-36.88
Warren Greatrex	10-39	26	7-28	2-8	-6.76
Nick Williams	9-43	21	2-23	7-19	-5.74
Fergal O'Brien	9-49	18	3-28	4-17	+12.80

Jockeys	Wins-Rides	%	£1 level stks	Best Trainer	W-R
Richard Johnson	47-203	23	-50.94	Philip Hobbs	29-118
Noel Fehily	27-116	23	+14.57	Harry Fry	20-47
Sam Twiston-Davies	27-128	21	-26.70	Paul Nicholls	19-62
Tom Scudamore	27-177	15	-62.99	David Pipe	11-96
Nick Scholfield	22-192	11	-72.21	Paul Nicholls	10-29
Harry Cobden	17-94	18	-38.10	Paul Nicholls	4-12
Aidan Coleman	17-112	15	-26.34	Venetia Williams	8-43
Tom O'Brien	16-131	12	-56.73	Philip Hobbs	6-48
James Best	16-191	8	-68.75	Kevin Bishop	4-19
Paddy Brennan	13-68	19	+38.75	Fergal O'Brien	5-21
Lucy Gardner	11-102	11	-39.38	Sue Gardner	13-97
Barry Geraghty	9-32	28	-6.22	Fergal O'Brien	2-2
Tom Bellamy	9-46	20	+19.57	Alan King	2-6

Favourites

Hurdle 42% -5 | Chase 35% -31.72 | Total 39% -48.52

FAKENHAM

Fakenham, Norfolk, NR21 7NY
Tel: 01328 862 388

How to get there Road: A1065 from Swaffham, A148 King's Lynn, A1067 from Norwich. Rail: Kings Lynn, Norwich

Features Left-handed, 1m circuit, undulating, unsuitable for long-striding horses

2019-20 Fixtures October 18, 30, November 19, December 17, January 1, 23, February 14, March 13, April 13

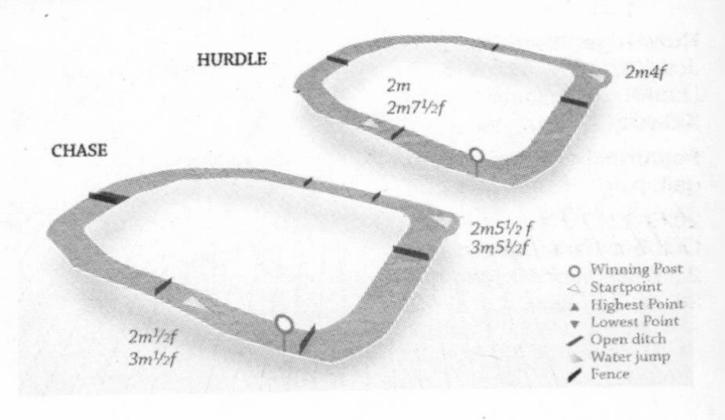

Trainers	Wins-Runs	%	Hurdles	Chases	£1 level stks
Olly Murphy	24-89	27	19-71	4-14	+13.13
Lucy Wadham	20-72	28	11-45	6-19	+18.11
Neil Mulholland	17-51	33	15-37	2-13	+12.76
Dan Skelton	16-72	22	9-46	6-24	-17.42
Nicky Henderson	13-38	34	7-25	2-7	-11.32
Neil King	12-83	14	6-43	5-36	+15.02
Christian Williams	8-23	35	4-10	4-13	+3.19
Stuart Edmunds	8-24	33	6-11	1-4	+30.66
David Pipe	7-15	47	5-10	2-5	+3.31
Charlie Mann	7-28	25	3-11	4-17	+14.00
Alex Hales	7-46	15	4-31	3-15	-4.27
Henry Daly	6-12	50	2-3	4-8	+6.38
Oliver Sherwood	6-26	23	1-14	5-12	+8.50

Jockeys	Wins-Rides	%	£1 level stks	Best Trainer	W-R
Richard Johnson	17-66	26	-10.38	Olly Murphy	7-15
Harry Skelton	16-51	31	+7.88	Dan Skelton	13-40
Tom Scudamore	13-34	38	+11.01	David Pipe	7-13
Leighton Aspell	11-49	22	-1.88	Lucy Wadham	10-31
Jack Quinlan	10-95	11	-41.88	Michael Wigham	2-12
Ciaran Gethings	9-25	36	+35.66	Stuart Edmunds	3-6
Noel Fehily	9-28	32	+1.85	Neil Mulholland	8-16
Harry Bannister	8-27	30	+9.88	Charlie Mann	4-10
James Banks	8-43	19	-0.50	Emma-Jane Bishop	4-13
Kielan Woods	8-67	12	-28.72	Alex Hales	3-16
Fergus Gregory	7-17	41	+21.07	Olly Murphy	4-5
James Bowen	7-20	35	+0.44	Phil Middleton	1-1
Nico de Boinville	7-22	32	-8.18	Nicky Henderson	4-9

Favourites

Hurdle 38% -22.68 Chase 44% -7.35 Total 41% -34.23

Trimsaran, Carmarthenshire
SA17 4DE. Tel: 01554 811 092

FFOS LAS

How to get there Road: M4 Jctn 48, follow A4138 to Llanelli. Rail: Llanelli, Kidwelly, Carmarthen

Features Left-handed, flat, galloping

2019-20 Fixtures
October 19, November 10, 22, December 16, March 6, 26, April 5, 12

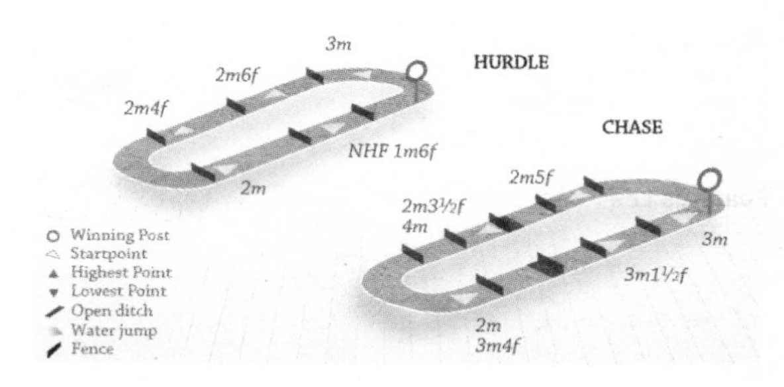

Trainers	*Wins-Runs*	*%*	*Hurdles*	*Chases*	*£1 level stks*
Evan Williams	49-328	15	35-187	9-115	-44.74
Peter Bowen	39-251	16	19-136	19-87	-80.04
Nigel Twiston-Davies	33-157	21	20-93	9-46	-11.92
Rebecca Curtis	29-121	24	12-68	13-36	+12.09
Warren Greatrex	13-51	25	8-32	1-9	-6.84
Nicky Henderson	12-33	36	9-21	1-5	-9.69
Jonjo O'Neill	12-82	15	6-47	5-31	-27.17
Debra Hamer	12-83	14	4-42	8-38	-4.63
Bernard Llewellyn	12-88	14	11-77	1-8	-5.98
David Rees	11-105	10	4-53	7-51	+8.13
David Pipe	10-83	12	6-56	1-14	-37.91
Neil Mulholland	10-85	12	4-45	4-29	+1.37
Tim Vaughan	10-134	7	4-82	6-46	-66.00

Jockeys	*Wins-Rides*	*%*	*£1 level stks*	*Best Trainer*	*W-R*
Sean Bowen	35-174	20	-17.39	Peter Bowen	21-104
Adam Wedge	30-180	17	-15.52	Evan Williams	21-129
Sam Twiston-Davies	24-128	19	-21.67	Nigel Twiston-Davies	22-113
Tom Scudamore	22-132	17	-25.13	David Pipe	11-57
Richard Johnson	18-122	15	-47.92	Tim Vaughan	8-58
Paul Moloney	15-109	14	+2.14	Evan Williams	11-88
David Bass	14-46	30	+39.78	Kim Bailey	7-18
Gavin Sheehan	14-57	25	+0.76	Warren Greatrex	8-31
Noel Fehily	10-52	19	+6.32	Neil Mulholland	3-23
Trevor Whelan	9-63	14	+54.17	Debra Hamer	5-33
Jonathan Moore	8-40	20	-9.69	Rebecca Curtis	8-39
Jamie Moore	8-62	13	-22.00	Peter Bowen	12-54
Robert Williams	7-58	12	-12.86	Bernard Llewellyn	7-49

Favourites

Hurdle 39% -18.77 Chase 34% -19.05 Total 38% -39.64

FONTWELL

Fontwell Park, nr Arundel, W Sussex BN18 0SX. Tel: 01243 543 335

How to get there Road: A29 to Bognor Regis. Rail: Barnham

Features Left-handed, 1m4f circuit, quite sharp

2019-20 Fixtures
October 4-5, 23, November 8, 17, December 10, 26, January 26, February 3, 13, 23, March 4, 14, 27, April 17

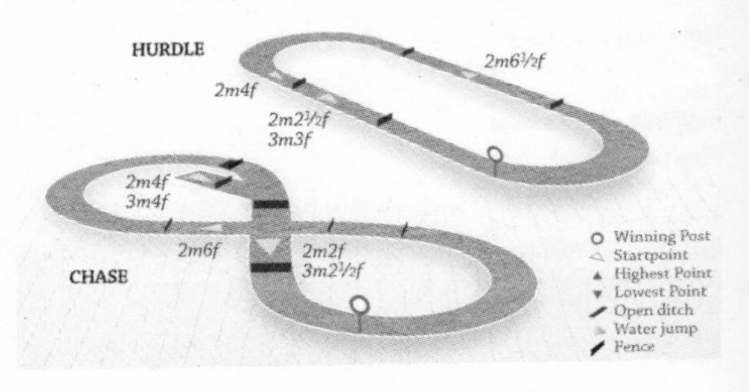

Trainers	Wins-Runs	%	Hurdles	Chases	£1 level stks
Gary Moore	58-361	16	36-235	16-95	-43.43
Chris Gordon	40-263	15	26-175	11-67	-26.33
Neil Mulholland	39-182	21	20-104	14-60	-9.71
Paul Nicholls	37-91	41	12-43	24-45	+8.13
Colin Tizzard	28-133	21	11-63	16-57	-20.52
Anthony Honeyball	27-83	33	14-44	9-27	+26.31
Dan Skelton	22-105	21	9-64	11-27	-20.46
Alan King	19-64	30	16-47	1-9	+2.21
Seamus Mullins	19-163	12	8-88	10-65	-15.92
Philip Hobbs	17-67	25	10-43	6-19	-20.99
Jeremy Scott	15-74	20	7-39	7-32	+1.57
Charlie Longsdon	15-75	20	6-33	6-32	-11.42
Dr Richard Newland	13-38	34	8-29	5-9	+7.37

Jockeys	Wins-Rides	%	£1 level stks	Best Trainer	W-R
Tom Cannon	45-306	15	-61.45	Chris Gordon	28-175
Jamie Moore	44-248	18	-3.73	Gary Moore	31-173
Richard Johnson	36-145	25	+4.94	Philip Hobbs	9-31
Noel Fehily	30-117	26	-18.94	Neil Mulholland	18-61
Aidan Coleman	28-109	26	+29.63	Anthony Honeyball	6-21
Leighton Aspell	24-188	13	-26.86	Oliver Sherwood	8-60
Harry Cobden	22-74	30	+0.26	Colin Tizzard	7-22
Sam Twiston-Davies	20-82	24	-23.27	Paul Nicholls	11-32
Harry Skelton	19-71	27	+7.13	Dan Skelton	14-50
Tom Scudamore	19-85	22	-8.79	David Pipe	6-29
Nick Scholfield	19-127	15	-0.83	Jeremy Scott	6-23
Gavin Sheehan	17-86	20	-8.15	Warren Greatrex	9-24
Joshua Moore	16-142	11	-10.38	Gary Moore	13-108

Favourites

Hurdle	37%	-42.59	Chase	40%	-22.85	Total	38%	-83.58

Newton-Le-Willows, Lancashire
WA12 0HQ. Tel: 01942 725 963

HAYDOCK

How to get there Road: M6 Jctn 23 on A49 to Wigan. Rail: Wigan or Warrington Bank Quay (main line)

Features Flat, left-handed, 1m5f circuit, quarter-mile run-in, chase track much sharper (like hurdles track) since introduction of portable fences

2019-20 Fixtures
November 23, December 4, 21, 30, January 18, February 15, March 18, April 11

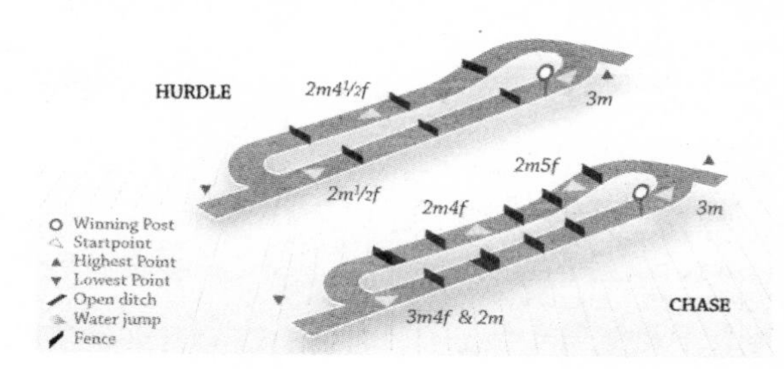

Trainers	Wins-Runs	%	Hurdles	Chases	£1 level stks
Nigel Twiston-Davies	20-110	18	12-49	8-58	-16.25
Paul Nicholls	16-70	23	6-42	10-26	-18.44
Sue Smith	15-117	13	6-42	9-72	-0.39
Donald McCain	14-99	14	6-61	8-34	-33.97
Venetia Williams	13-73	18	4-22	8-48	+58.37
David Pipe	12-66	18	5-34	7-32	+43.00
Nicky Henderson	10-44	23	6-31	3-11	-13.58
Tom George	9-43	21	5-15	3-25	-2.17
Lucinda Russell	7-64	11	5-33	2-30	+15.33
Evan Williams	7-71	10	7-39	0-31	-8.50
Dan Skelton	7-77	9	6-57	1-20	-40.13
Emma Lavelle	6-23	26	5-17	1-6	+23.50
Peter Bowen	6-24	25	1-10	4-13	+8.53

Jockeys	Wins-Rides	%	£1 level stks	Best Trainer	W-R
Daryl Jacob	16-46	35	+44.21	Nigel Twiston-Davies	6-8
Sam Twiston-Davies	13-74	18	-35.87	Nigel Twiston-Davies	8-34
Sean Bowen	12-33	36	+35.20	Peter Bowen	4-9
William Kennedy	12-55	22	-5.62	Donald McCain	11-35
Danny Cook	12-80	15	+12.91	Sue Smith	6-52
Richard Johnson	11-71	15	+1.75	Philip Hobbs	4-32
Paddy Brennan	10-45	22	-4.85	Tom George	4-16
Tom Scudamore	9-67	13	+1.83	David Pipe	7-37
Aidan Coleman	8-60	13	+57.41	Venetia Williams	5-30
Brian Hughes	8-113	7	-65.72	Malcolm Jefferson	5-30
Charlie Deutsch	6-20	30	+11.50	Venetia Williams	3-12
Harry Cobden	6-32	19	+6.50	Paul Nicholls	3-14
Harry Skelton	6-63	10	-30.13	Dan Skelton	5-47

Favourites

Hurdle 34% -11.44 Chase 27% -36.95 Total 32% -45.42

HEREFORD

Roman Road, Holmer, Hereford
HR 4 9QU. Tel 01981 250 436

How to get there Road: A49 1m north of Hereford. Rail: Hereford

Features Right-handed, predominately galloping track with stiffer fences than at many minor courses

2019-20 Fixtures
October 15, November 4, 12, 27, December 14, January 3, 29, February 23, March 7, 16, 24

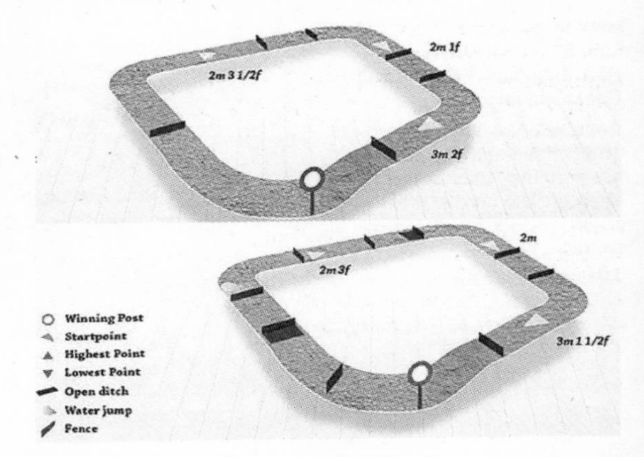

Trainers	*Wins-Runs*	%	*Hurdles*	*Chases*	*£1 level stks*
Venetia Williams	11-56	20	6-37	4-18	+6.23
Warren Greatrex	7-24	29	5-15	1-5	-2.37
Philip Hobbs	6-32	19	3-21	2-8	-13.24
Dan Skelton	6-32	19	3-19	3-11	-2.55
Henry Oliver	6-36	17	3-23	3-11	+13.00
Evan Williams	6-56	11	2-34	4-20	-33.10
Alan King	5-15	33	5-13	0-1	-0.47
Tom George	5-26	19	4-17	1-8	-4.67
Kerry Lee	5-44	11	2-14	3-29	-21.55
Nicky Henderson	4-10	40	3-7	1-3	-1.37
David Rees	4-13	31	1-3	3-8	+12.88
Rebecca Curtis	4-17	24	0-8	3-6	-2.13
Neil Mulholland	4-22	18	2-13	0-5	-7.09

Jockeys	*Wins-Rides*	%	*£1 level stks*	*Best Trainer*	*W-R*
Richard Johnson	10-67	15	-36.88	Philip Hobbs	3-13
Charlie Deutsch	9-36	25	+21.25	Venetia Williams	6-23
Aidan Coleman	7-28	25	+18.63	Tom Symonds	1-1
Wayne Hutchinson	6-17	35	+0.78	Warren Greatrex	1-1
Noel Fehily	6-19	32	-1.60	Harry Fry	3-4
Sean Bowen	6-26	23	+7.00	David Rees	1-1
Sam Twiston-Davies	6-28	21	-4.08	Nigel Twiston-Davies	2-6
Andrew Tinkler	5-19	26	+1.73	Alastair Ralph	1-1
Leighton Aspell	5-20	25	-6.56	Alex Hales	1-1
Tom O'Brien	5-32	16	-3.93	Henry Oliver	1-1
Robert Dunne	5-35	14	+5.30	Dai Burchell	1-6
Gavin Sheehan	4-18	22	-6.32	David Dennis	1-1
Ben Poste	4-40	10	-4.67	Tom Symonds	2-7

Favourites

Hurdle	37%	-12.42	Chase	34%	-6.71	Total	36%	-20.52

High Yarridge, Hexham, Northumberland
NE46 2JP. Tel: 01434 606 881

HEXHAM

How to get there Road: A69. Rail: Hexham

Features Left-handed, 1m4f circuit, very stiff, back straight runs nearly all downhill before steep uphill run from home turn

2019-20 Fixtures
October 4, 12, November 8, 20, December 11, March 12, 24, April 20

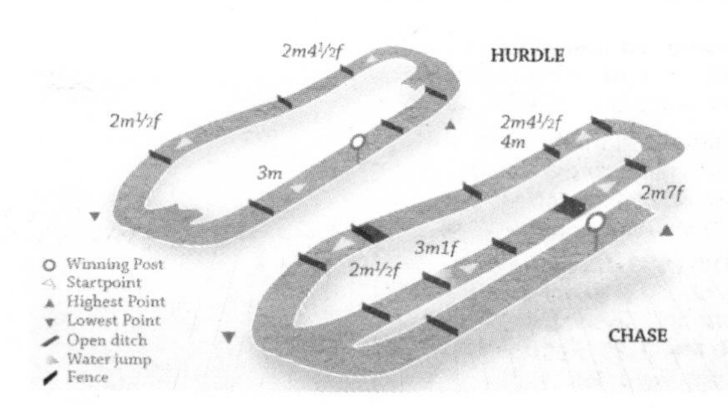

Trainers	*Wins-Runs*	*%*	*Hurdles*	*Chases*	*£1 level stks*
Lucinda Russell	35-236	15	13-123	21-107	+3.06
Maurice Barnes	21-151	14	8-70	13-76	-26.88
Micky Hammond	21-180	12	13-88	8-82	-60.74
Nicky Richards	16-49	33	10-29	6-18	+15.38
Mark Walford	14-72	19	7-40	7-30	+5.77
Brian Ellison	13-66	20	10-51	2-13	-3.18
Stuart Coltherd	12-82	15	4-42	8-40	+21.25
Malcolm Jefferson	11-55	20	5-32	1-9	-25.00
James Ewart	11-59	19	5-27	6-27	+0.25
George Bewley	11-78	14	4-45	7-30	+6.75
Donald McCain	11-99	11	11-77	0-14	-69.56
Jonathan Haynes	10-84	12	9-64	1-14	-2.72
Martin Todhunter	10-84	12	6-47	4-36	-11.88

Jockeys	*Wins-Rides*	*%*	*£1 level stks*	*Best Trainer*	*W-R*
Brian Hughes	44-246	18	-86.17	Malcolm Jefferson	13-50
Thomas Dowson	20-149	13	+24.00	Jonathan Haynes	6-32
Henry Brooke	20-182	11	-13.70	Micky Hammond	3-18
Jamie Hamilton	17-138	12	-3.17	Henry Hogarth	5-13
Dale Irving	16-101	16	-10.90	Maurice Barnes	5-19
Sean Quinlan	13-103	13	-31.76	Sue Smith	3-29
Richard Johnson	12-23	52	+13.88	John C McConnell	2-2
Derek Fox	12-132	9	-67.62	Lucinda Russell	7-53
Danny Cook	11-70	16	-15.60	Brian Ellison	4-17
Jonathon Bewley	11-74	15	+42.25	George Bewley	8-61
Wilson Renwick	10-41	24	-1.81	Donald McCain	4-13
James Reveley	10-44	23	+11.37	Stuart Coltherd	2-5
Craig Nichol	10-115	9	-63.78	Lucinda Russell	6-20

Favourites

Hurdle 37% -55.13 Chase 38% +2.63 Total 38% -48.18

HUNTINGDON

Brampton, Huntingdon, Cambs PE18 8NN. Tel: 01480 453 373

How to get there Road: Follow signs off A14. Rail: Huntingdon

Features Right-handed, flat track, short run-in of around 200 yards

2019-20 Fixtures
October 2, 15, November 3, 12, 23, December 8, 26, January 10, 24, February 6, 20, March 1, 11, 19, April 13

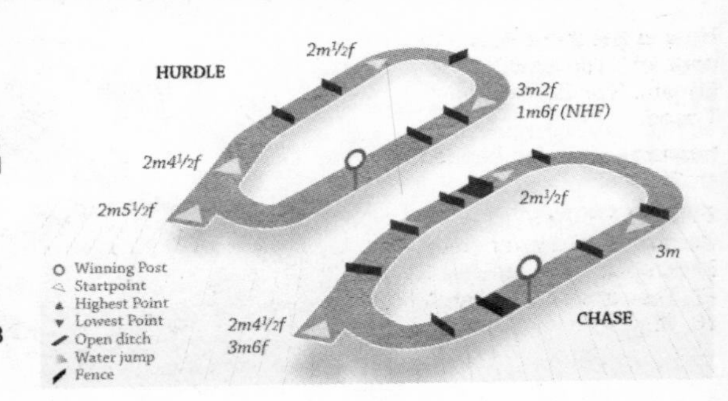

Trainers	Wins-Runs	%	Hurdles	Chases	£1 level stks
Nicky Henderson	31-105	30	21-64	8-19	-21.26
Jonjo O'Neill	24-120	20	14-82	8-33	+4.12
Dan Skelton	24-153	16	16-96	6-36	-55.38
Kim Bailey	23-108	21	12-54	8-38	+25.48
Alan King	23-112	21	15-70	5-21	-31.69
Gary Moore	16-113	14	10-74	6-32	+8.84
John Ferguson	15-29	52	10-21	1-3	+12.11
Ben Pauling	14-75	19	8-49	4-17	+74.15
David Dennis	11-50	22	6-35	5-14	+22.46
Fergal O'Brien	10-45	22	3-24	5-14	+45.46
Ian Williams	10-75	13	5-50	5-19	-25.75
Charlie Longsdon	10-97	10	4-59	6-31	-46.52
Dr Richard Newland	8-24	33	4-15	4-9	+10.10

Jockeys	Wins-Rides	%	£1 level stks	Best Trainer	W-R
Richard Johnson	26-115	23	-1.21	Philip Hobbs	7-27
Noel Fehily	23-84	27	-1.31	Nicky Henderson	5-8
Wayne Hutchinson	19-92	21	-14.61	Alan King	15-65
Sam Twiston-Davies	19-98	19	+15.70	Paul Nicholls	3-12
Aidan Coleman	19-105	18	+7.92	Venetia Williams	7-25
David Bass	17-84	20	+52.37	Kim Bailey	9-43
Leighton Aspell	17-126	13	-42.46	Lucy Wadham	4-27
Harry Skelton	17-128	13	-53.13	Dan Skelton	15-86
A P McCoy	14-29	48	+6.51	Jonjo O'Neill	6-18
Nico de Boinville	14-55	25	+26.93	Ben Pauling	4-9
Paddy Brennan	12-73	16	-2.88	Fergal O'Brien	5-26
Tom O'Brien	12-94	13	-37.58	Paul Henderson	2-12
Ciaran Gethings	11-50	22	-3.25	Stuart Edmunds	4-10

Favourites

Hurdle 37% -29.73 Chase 36% -22.25 Total 37% -59.48

KELSO

Kelso, Roxburghshire.
Tel: 01668 281 611

How to get there Road: 1m north of Kelso on B6461 to Ednam. Rail: Berwick-on-Tweed

Features Tight, left-handed, 1m3f circuit

2019-20 Fixtures
October 6, 26, November 9, December 8, 29, January 12, 27, February 13, 29, March 16, 21, April 6

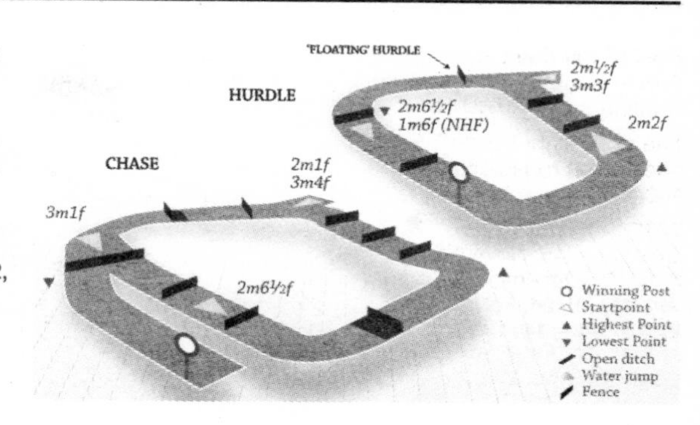

Trainers	Wins-Runs	%	Hurdles	Chases	£1 level stks
Lucinda Russell	37-259	14	17-148	18-98	-46.59
Nicky Richards	31-132	23	18-67	11-52	+14.02
Donald McCain	25-158	16	14-101	10-50	-47.84
N W Alexander	25-189	13	19-116	6-59	-6.86
James Ewart	15-94	16	8-50	6-30	+17.12
Sandy Thomson	15-112	13	6-60	9-50	+40.70
Rose Dobbin	13-129	10	7-83	5-39	-63.06
Malcolm Jefferson	12-56	21	7-25	3-21	-11.09
Keith Dalgleish	11-40	28	8-28	2-6	+29.51
Micky Hammond	10-77	13	4-35	5-38	-24.42
Chris Grant	10-80	13	3-42	6-28	-3.50
Paul Nicholls	9-23	39	3-7	6-16	-1.43
Iain Jardine	9-61	15	2-35	4-15	-21.57

Jockeys	Wins-Rides	%	£1 level stks	Best Trainer	W-R
Brian Hughes	49-273	18	-48.96	Malcolm Jefferson	12-56
Brian Harding	26-130	20	-17.21	Nicky Richards	16-61
Craig Nichol	18-158	11	-65.26	Rose Dobbin	8-56
Lucy Alexander	17-126	13	+3.18	N W Alexander	13-95
Derek Fox	16-137	12	-41.14	Lucinda Russell	10-77
Callum Bewley	15-116	13	+28.17	Keith Dalgleish	3-5
Danny Cook	11-69	16	-4.42	Michael Smith	4-15
Sean Quinlan	11-89	12	-47.02	Jennie Candlish	3-11
Blair Campbell	10-41	24	+34.54	Lucinda Russell	6-18
Peter Buchanan	10-67	15	-14.26	Lucinda Russell	13-81
Ryan Day	9-60	15	-9.40	Nicky Richards	4-23
Jamie Hamilton	9-87	10	-36.04	Malcolm Jefferson	3-10
Sean Bowen	8-18	44	+2.80	Paul Nicholls	2-5

Favourites

Hurdle	39%	-20.95	Chase	35%	-12.36	Total	36%	-45.77

KEMPTON

Staines Rd East, Sunbury-on-Thames TW16 5AQ. Tel: 01932 782 292

How to get there Road: M3 Jctn 1, A308 towards Kingston-on-Thames. Rail: Kempton Park from Waterloo

Features A sharp right-handed track with the emphasis very much on speed

2019-20 Fixtures
October 20, November 11, 25, December 26-27, January 11, February 7, 22, March 14, April 20

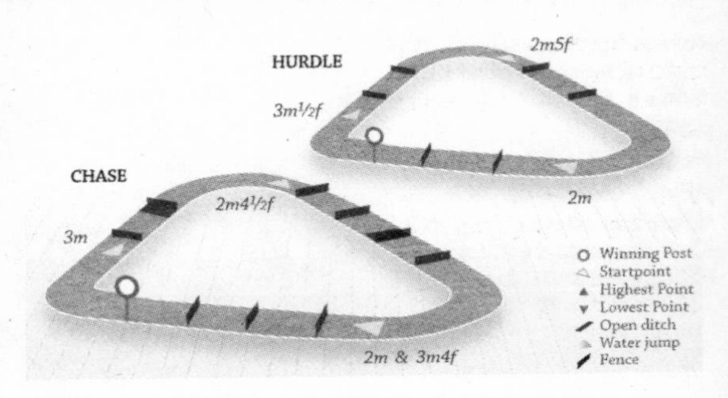

Trainers	Wins-Runs	%	Hurdles	Chases	£1 level stks
Nicky Henderson	64-238	27	36-143	21-69	-25.32
Paul Nicholls	42-196	21	15-91	25-95	-24.28
Alan King	25-178	14	20-118	4-44	-84.97
Harry Fry	12-69	17	10-40	2-22	-29.38
Chris Gordon	12-70	17	4-35	7-32	+18.93
Nigel Twiston-Davies	12-71	17	5-29	7-38	-5.89
Colin Tizzard	12-78	15	6-31	6-43	+20.85
Philip Hobbs	12-100	12	9-54	3-36	-63.53
Tom George	11-70	16	0-10	11-58	-3.00
Dan Skelton	10-133	8	7-87	3-36	-99.46
Charlie Longsdon	9-68	13	2-30	7-37	-6.05
Jonjo O'Neill	9-89	10	6-53	3-34	-46.62
Ben Pauling	8-47	17	6-37	2-8	-10.56

Jockeys	Wins-Rides	%	£1 level stks	Best Trainer	W-R
Nico de Boinville	33-109	30	+9.20	Nicky Henderson	17-60
Sam Twiston-Davies	27-138	20	-27.33	Paul Nicholls	13-86
Barry Geraghty	25-94	27	+0.95	Nicky Henderson	20-67
Noel Fehily	21-138	15	-67.78	Harry Fry	8-38
Richard Johnson	20-128	16	-55.33	Philip Hobbs	9-51
Wayne Hutchinson	19-116	16	-35.63	Alan King	17-92
Tom Cannon	17-95	18	+57.85	Chris Gordon	8-31
Aidan Coleman	17-121	14	-48.45	Jonjo O'Neill	3-23
Harry Cobden	16-68	24	+21.69	Paul Nicholls	4-16
Daryl Jacob	13-97	13	-27.10	Paul Nicholls	4-19
Nick Scholfield	10-73	14	+5.85	Paul Nicholls	7-23
David Bass	9-56	16	+5.50	Kim Bailey	5-24
Paddy Brennan	9-81	11	+8.75	Tom George	6-34

Favourites
Hurdle 42% -9.40   Chase 46% +10.34   Total 44% -2.55

Leicester, LE2 4AL
Tel: 0116 271 6515

LEICESTER

How to get there Road: M1 Jctn 21, 2m south of city centre on A6. Rail: Leicester

Features Right-handed, 1m6f circuit, stiff uphill run-in

2019-20 Fixtures November 18, December 1, 5, 11, 28, January 9, 21, 29, February 13, 25, March 6

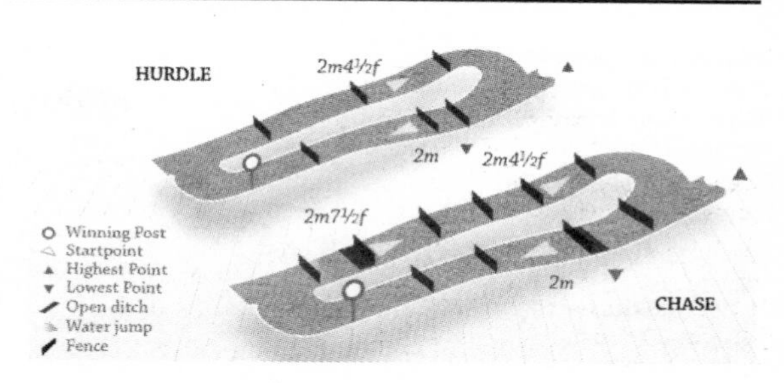

Trainers	*Wins-Runs*	*%*	*Hurdles*	*Chases*	*£1 level stks*
Tom George	17-46	37	2-9	15-37	+27.12
Nigel Twiston-Davies	15-65	23	6-29	9-36	+23.46
Philip Hobbs	12-27	44	7-17	5-10	+14.50
Dan Skelton	12-40	30	5-22	7-18	+12.17
David Pipe	9-29	31	5-18	4-11	+4.89
Caroline Bailey	9-40	23	4-13	5-27	-4.51
Robin Dickin	8-34	24	2-8	6-26	+22.63
Fergal O'Brien	8-40	20	2-13	6-27	+26.13
Gary Moore	7-24	29	3-12	4-12	+1.92
Ian Williams	5-25	20	2-16	3-9	-12.18
Venetia Williams	5-31	16	2-15	3-16	-18.38
Paul Nicholls	4-9	44	1-2	3-7	-0.92
Ali Stronge	4-16	25	3-11	1-5	+12.00

Jockeys	*Wins-Rides*	*%*	*£1 level stks*	*Best Trainer*	*W-R*
Sam Twiston-Davies	16-54	30	+13.88	Nigel Twiston-Davies	12-41
Richard Johnson	12-47	26	-9.27	Philip Hobbs	6-14
Harry Skelton	11-39	28	+14.73	Dan Skelton	4-22
Aidan Coleman	11-51	22	-11.60	Venetia Williams	5-27
Paddy Brennan	10-58	17	+5.25	Tom George	6-24
Tom Scudamore	8-44	18	-8.61	David Pipe	8-22
A P Heskin	7-22	32	+2.54	Tom George	6-18
Tom O'Brien	6-30	20	-11.18	Philip Hobbs	1-2
William Kennedy	5-22	23	-7.31	Ian Williams	4-7
Liam Treadwell	5-24	21	+14.12	Venetia Williams	3-7
Jamie Moore	5-25	20	-6.83	Gary Moore	2-9
Jamie Bargary	5-26	19	+3.38	Nigel Twiston-Davies	3-7
Charlie Poste	5-27	19	+6.50	Robin Dickin	3-15

Favourites

Hurdle 43% +4.98 Chase 40% -10.49 Total 42% -5.5

LINGFIELD

Lingfield, Surrey, RH7 6PQ
Tel: 01342 834 800

How to get there Road: M25 Jctn 6, south on A22. Rail: Lingfield from London Bridge and Victoria

Features Left-handed, 1m4f circuit, hilly

2019-20 Fixtures November 12, 19, December 3, 17, January 7, 13, 28, February 11, 17

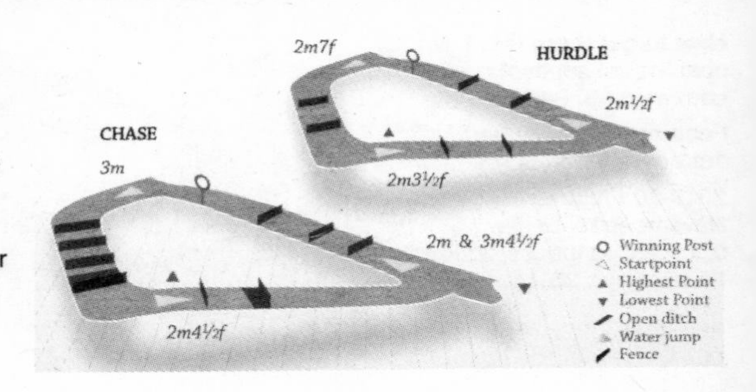

Trainers	*Wins-Runs*	*%*	*Hurdles*	*Chases*	*£1 level stks*
Gary Moore	11-100	11	5-60	6-40	-28.50
Seamus Mullins	9-49	18	5-29	4-20	+17.87
Warren Greatrex	8-25	32	6-18	2-7	-6.66
Nigel Twiston-Davies	8-32	25	5-18	3-14	+19.58
Chris Gordon	8-45	18	4-28	4-17	-15.15
Lucy Wadham	6-16	38	4-11	2-5	+44.75
Dan Skelton	5-17	29	3-13	2-4	+9.00
Martin Keighley	5-18	28	4-13	1-5	+10.17
Anna Newton-Smith	5-26	19	2-12	3-14	+8.50
Nicky Henderson	4-6	67	3-5	1-1	-0.25
Emma Lavelle	4-10	40	2-6	2-4	+11.00
Oliver Sherwood	4-14	29	3-8	1-6	-2.23
Colin Tizzard	4-18	22	1-5	3-13	-4.50

Jockeys	*Wins-Rides*	*%*	*£1 level stks*	*Best Trainer*	*W-R*
Leighton Aspell	12-46	26	+30.25	Oliver Sherwood	3-8
Gavin Sheehan	10-28	36	+5.81	Warren Greatrex	7-16
Tom Scudamore	9-52	17	-15.26	Anabel K Murphy	2-2
Tom Cannon	9-65	14	-25.28	Chris Gordon	7-24
Aidan Coleman	7-28	25	+6.82	Venetia Williams	3-11
Jeremiah McGrath	6-18	33	-0.07	Nicky Henderson	3-4
Jamie Moore	6-54	11	-8.25	Gary Moore	6-37
Paddy Brennan	5-30	17	-8.75	Colin Tizzard	1-1
Harry Cobden	4-14	29	+15.85	Anthony Honeyball	2-2
Sam Twiston-Davies	4-16	25	+3.58	Nigel Twiston-Davies	4-11
Daryl Jacob	4-17	24	-2.90	Dr Richard Newland	2-2
Alan Johns	4-19	21	-9.78	Tim Vaughan	3-17
Andrew Thornton	4-24	17	+14.50	Seamus Mullins	4-15

Favourites

Hurdle	40%	-6.95	Chase	35%	-7.41	Total	38%	-14.36

Bromfield, Ludlow, Shrewsbury, Shropshire. Tel: 01981 250 052

LUDLOW

How to get there Road: 2m north of Ludlow on A49. Rail: Ludlow

Features Flat, right-handed, has sharp turns and a testing run-in of 450 yards

2019-20 Fixtures
October 9, 24, November 14, 25, December 4, 18, January 8, 16, February 5, 19, 27, March 18, 30, April 21

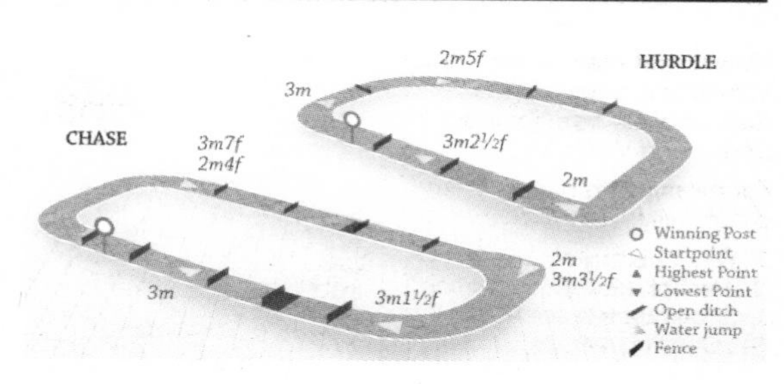

Trainers	Wins-Runs	%	Hurdles	Chases	£1 level stks
Nicky Henderson	31-102	30	16-56	6-23	-12.19
Philip Hobbs	29-115	25	18-65	10-41	+17.87
Dan Skelton	29-129	22	23-93	3-21	-14.76
Evan Williams	28-225	12	13-111	12-98	-82.70
Tom George	21-112	19	4-40	17-67	-17.59
Kim Bailey	20-108	19	11-63	2-29	-15.79
Henry Daly	20-116	17	12-62	6-35	-45.88
Paul Nicholls	15-60	25	6-24	8-32	-15.08
Nigel Twiston-Davies	15-136	11	9-78	6-52	-80.09
Venetia Williams	14-113	12	5-52	9-59	-39.54
Alan King	13-59	22	8-45	4-11	-13.74
Fergal O'Brien	10-59	17	5-29	4-22	+9.37
Jonjo O'Neill	10-94	11	2-41	7-52	-43.13

Jockeys	Wins-Rides	%	£1 level stks	Best Trainer	W-R
Richard Johnson	43-182	24	-35.43	Philip Hobbs	14-68
Paddy Brennan	26-101	26	+20.83	Tom George	13-42
Harry Skelton	25-93	27	+5.24	Dan Skelton	21-81
David Bass	22-77	29	+108.83	Kim Bailey	14-50
Adam Wedge	12-123	10	-47.02	Evan Williams	14-92
Nico de Boinville	11-54	20	-19.38	Nicky Henderson	5-23
Tom O'Brien	11-70	16	+4.50	Ian Williams	4-13
Jeremiah McGrath	10-25	40	+23.07	Nicky Henderson	7-13
Wayne Hutchinson	10-50	20	-25.74	Alan King	9-36
Andrew Tinkler	10-68	15	+0.29	Alastair Ralph	3-6
Paul Moloney	10-76	13	-36.19	Evan Williams	16-89
Aidan Coleman	10-100	10	-49.30	Venetia Williams	6-51
Harry Cobden	9-35	26	-7.81	Colin Tizzard	2-3

Favourites

Hurdle	42%	-15.32	Chase	42%	+31.05	Total	42%	+12.51

MARKET RASEN

Legsby Road, LN8 3EA
Tel: 01673 843 434

How to get there Road: A46 to Market Rasen, course on A631. Rail: Market Rasen (1m walk)

Features Right-handed, easy fences, run-in of 250 yards

2019-20 Fixtures
October 19, November 7, 21, December 5, 26, January 16, February 4, 16, March 15, 25, April 1, 12

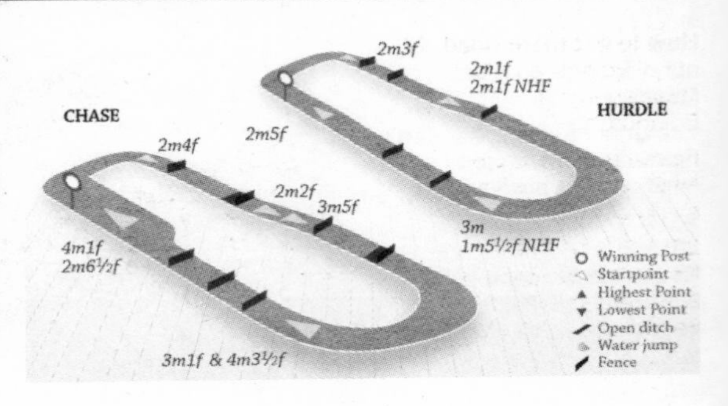

Trainers	*Wins-Runs*	*%*	*Hurdles*	*Chases*	*£1 level stks*
Dan Skelton	57-209	27	33-131	18-60	+18.29
Jonjo O'Neill	31-191	16	15-95	16-88	-49.14
Nicky Henderson	22-73	30	14-47	3-13	-2.38
Brian Ellison	22-145	15	16-94	3-43	-37.12
Dr Richard Newland	20-68	29	13-47	7-21	+24.49
Fergal O'Brien	20-112	18	12-58	6-45	+3.17
Olly Murphy	18-74	24	18-60	0-11	+6.38
Peter Bowen	16-84	19	7-35	7-38	-8.08
Alan King	15-89	17	11-57	3-23	-14.25
Charlie Longsdon	15-122	12	9-58	6-49	-63.60
Nigel Twiston-Davies	13-55	24	9-31	3-19	+8.56
Sue Smith	13-92	14	6-45	7-44	-27.62
David Pipe	12-57	21	5-33	7-21	-11.10

Jockeys	*Wins-Rides*	*%*	*£1 level stks*	*Best Trainer*	*W-R*
Harry Skelton	46-172	27	-8.89	Dan Skelton	33-109
Aidan Coleman	37-191	19	-18.58	Jonjo O'Neill	11-55
Richard Johnson	32-184	17	-77.30	Philip Hobbs	7-28
Paddy Brennan	25-128	20	+15.77	Fergal O'Brien	12-49
Brian Hughes	24-184	13	-51.45	Malcolm Jefferson	12-62
Sam Twiston-Davies	23-102	23	-17.31	Dr Richard Newland	10-36
Tom Scudamore	21-119	18	-22.51	David Pipe	10-39
Sean Bowen	17-93	18	-4.55	Peter Bowen	9-38
Danny Cook	17-104	16	-32.46	Sue Smith	8-34
A P McCoy	16-58	28	-17.34	Jonjo O'Neill	12-51
Noel Fehily	16-80	20	-28.63	Charlie Longsdon	14-42
Gavin Sheehan	15-91	16	-24.07	Warren Greatrex	7-28
Daryl Jacob	14-53	26	+22.24	Emma Lavelle	3-7

Favourites

Hurdle 38% -32.05 Chase 36% -26.84 Total 38% -53.35

East Lothian
Tel: 01316 652 859

MUSSELBURGH

How to get there Road: A1 out of Edinburgh. Rail: Musselburgh from Edinburgh

Features Right-handed, 1m2f circuit, very flat with sharp turns

2019-20 Fixtures November 6, 25, December 2, 9, January 1, 3, 17, February 2-3, 26, March 20

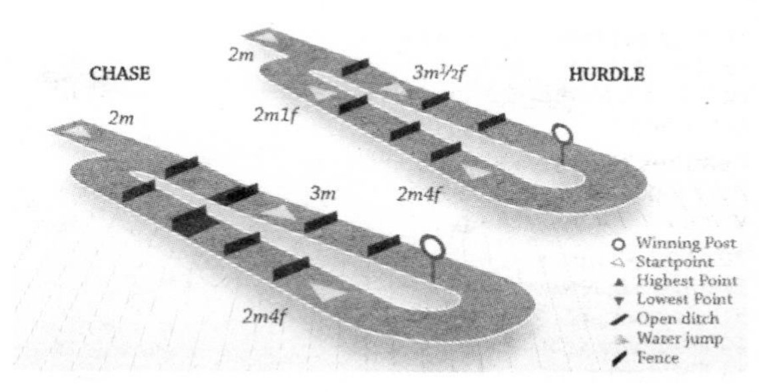

Trainers	*Wins-Runs*	*%*	*Hurdles*	*Chases*	*£1 level stks*
Lucinda Russell	33-255	13	19-146	13-92	-32.07
Donald McCain	26-135	19	16-90	7-40	-8.67
Keith Dalgleish	22-69	32	8-43	9-15	+12.93
Sandy Thomson	16-74	22	8-43	8-29	+27.72
Iain Jardine	12-79	15	11-61	1-13	+4.56
Paul Nicholls	10-26	38	4-16	6-10	+6.72
Tim Vaughan	9-45	20	5-28	4-16	+0.07
Rose Dobbin	9-68	13	1-32	7-33	-15.25
James Ewart	9-76	12	8-51	0-14	-8.95
Jim Goldie	8-85	9	8-80	0-1	-29.59
John Quinn	7-18	39	7-17	0-1	+15.55
Nicky Henderson	7-21	33	7-18	0-2	-5.96
Rebecca Menzies	6-40	15	1-14	5-21	+25.90

Jockeys	*Wins-Rides*	*%*	*£1 level stks*	*Best Trainer*	*W-R*
Brian Hughes	52-223	23	-9.64	Keith Dalgleish	7-11
Derek Fox	16-101	16	-5.63	Lucinda Russell	13-76
William Kennedy	10-48	21	+23.75	Donald McCain	7-28
Craig Nichol	10-100	10	-46.17	Lucinda Russell	5-28
Richard Johnson	9-35	26	-14.75	Gordon Elliott	3-6
James Reveley	9-47	19	+1.49	Jim Goldie	3-13
Danny Cook	9-76	12	-8.54	Sandy Thomson	3-9
Rachael McDonald	8-35	23	+7.17	Sandy Thomson	5-19
Alan Johns	7-27	26	+7.08	Tim Vaughan	4-22
Ryan Day	7-33	21	+19.13	Keith Dalgleish	1-2
Henry Brooke	7-91	8	-34.17	David Thompson	2-2
Daryl Jacob	6-7	86	+13.01	Nicky Henderson	2-2
Peter Buchanan	6-39	15	+26.37	Lucinda Russell	7-50

Favourites

Hurdle	39%	-14.82	Chase	41%	+9.32	Total	40%	-3.78

NEWBURY

Newbury, Berkshire, RG14 7NZ
Tel: 01635 400 15 or 414 85

How to get there Road: Follow signs from M4 or A34. Rail: Newbury Racecourse

Features Flat, left-handed, 1m6f circuit, suits galloping sorts with stamina, tough fences

2019-20 Fixtures
November 7, 29-30, December 18, 28, January 15, February 8, 28-29, March 20-21

Trainers	*Wins-Runs*	*%*	*Hurdles*	*Chases*	*£1 level stks*
Nicky Henderson	42-199	21	33-124	5-46	-39.33
Philip Hobbs	26-144	18	15-71	10-65	+65.76
Paul Nicholls	23-151	15	8-62	14-84	-13.18
Alan King	20-174	11	10-103	5-41	-79.72
Colin Tizzard	19-110	17	3-39	15-62	-10.46
David Pipe	16-93	17	9-59	7-31	+7.02
Ben Pauling	12-63	19	7-40	3-13	+5.36
Harry Fry	12-72	17	7-41	2-20	-20.80
Warren Greatrex	12-76	16	6-45	5-21	-14.75
Dan Skelton	10-91	11	6-65	3-22	-36.63
Nigel Twiston-Davies	8-91	9	6-35	1-45	-38.10
Gary Moore	8-98	8	5-66	3-24	-20.38
Rebecca Curtis	7-62	11	1-24	6-32	-10.67

Jockeys	*Wins-Rides*	*%*	*£1 level stks*	*Best Trainer*	*W-R*
Richard Johnson	36-171	21	+95.84	Philip Hobbs	21-94
Nico de Boinville	23-97	24	+12.42	Nicky Henderson	16-51
Tom Scudamore	21-122	17	+19.40	David Pipe	11-63
Barry Geraghty	20-93	22	-3.60	Nicky Henderson	21-57
Noel Fehily	18-121	15	-20.47	Harry Fry	8-43
Wayne Hutchinson	16-131	12	-48.66	Alan King	11-90
Gavin Sheehan	13-93	14	+22.12	Warren Greatrex	7-41
Sam Twiston-Davies	13-143	9	-66.38	Paul Nicholls	7-74
Harry Cobden	11-53	21	+8.40	Colin Tizzard	4-8
David Bass	9-39	23	+2.97	Ben Pauling	3-10
Aidan Coleman	9-127	7	-91.28	Venetia Williams	5-51
Harry Skelton	8-67	12	-25.13	Dan Skelton	7-40
Paddy Brennan	8-88	9	-50.13	Fergal O'Brien	5-29

Favourites

Hurdle 37% -15.75 Chase 28% -27.93 Total 33% -48.99

High Gosforth Park, Newcastle
NE3 5HP. Tel: 01912 362 020

NEWCASTLE

How to get there Road: Follow signs from A1. Rail: 4m from Newcastle Central

Features Left-handed, 1m6f circuit, tough fences, half-mile straight is all uphill

2019-20 Fixtures November 15, 30, December 12, 21, January 4, 20, 28, February 22, March 3, 14, 25, April 4

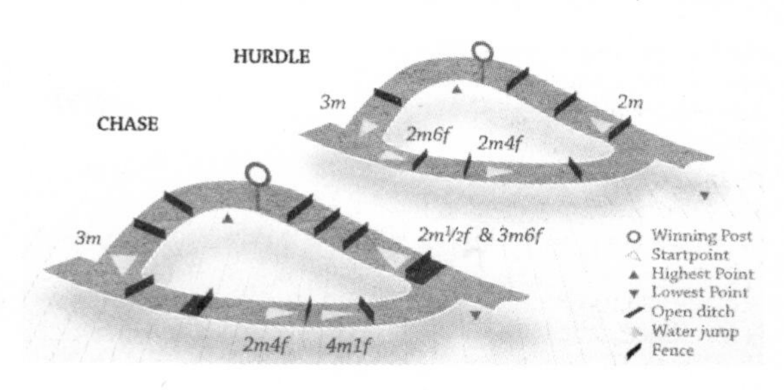

Trainers	Wins-Runs	%	Hurdles	Chases	£1 level stks
Sue Smith	19-113	17	5-42	13-64	-26.26
Nicky Richards	16-69	23	6-27	5-31	-8.62
N W Alexander	16-113	14	7-52	9-52	-19.56
Lucinda Russell	14-121	12	7-61	7-54	-58.47
Micky Hammond	10-83	12	7-36	2-37	-25.62
Philip Kirby	9-49	18	6-33	3-8	-14.83
Malcolm Jefferson	8-26	31	3-6	3-13	-0.53
Keith Dalgleish	8-27	30	2-14	4-8	+14.00
Sandy Thomson	8-42	19	3-19	4-20	-11.47
Brian Ellison	8-46	17	4-22	4-21	-17.19
Nicky Henderson	7-8	88	6-7	1-1	+5.39
Keith Reveley	7-43	16	4-28	2-9	-14.38
Tim Vaughan	6-19	32	4-11	2-7	+14.45

Jockeys	Wins-Rides	%	£1 level stks	Best Trainer	W-R
Brian Hughes	37-170	22	-26.70	Malcolm Jefferson	10-34
Danny Cook	16-90	18	-28.86	Sue Smith	13-47
Brian Harding	12-66	18	-13.86	Nicky Richards	9-34
Craig Nichol	10-96	10	-57.86	Lucinda Russell	3-14
James Reveley	9-55	16	-0.22	Keith Reveley	6-40
Lucy Alexander	9-68	13	-9.25	N W Alexander	8-46
Henry Brooke	9-84	11	-6.51	Donald McCain	2-6
Steven Fox	8-37	22	+16.50	Sandy Thomson	2-8
Alan Johns	7-17	41	+7.33	Tim Vaughan	2-7
Joe Colliver	7-40	18	+3.88	Micky Hammond	6-26
Ross Chapman	7-48	15	+1.41	Alistair Whillans	1-1
Jamie Hamilton	7-72	10	-11.25	Mark Walford	2-7
Gavin Sheehan	6-14	43	+6.72	Brian Ellison	2-2

Favourites

Hurdle 38% -20.60 Chase 38% -7.64 Total 37% -31.84

NEWTON ABBOT

Devon, TQ12 3AF
Tel: 01626 532 35

How to get there Road: On A380 from Newton Abbot to Torquay. Rail: Newton Abbot

Features Tight, left-handed, 1m1f circuit

2019-20 Fixtures
October 13, 31, Aprll 11, 20

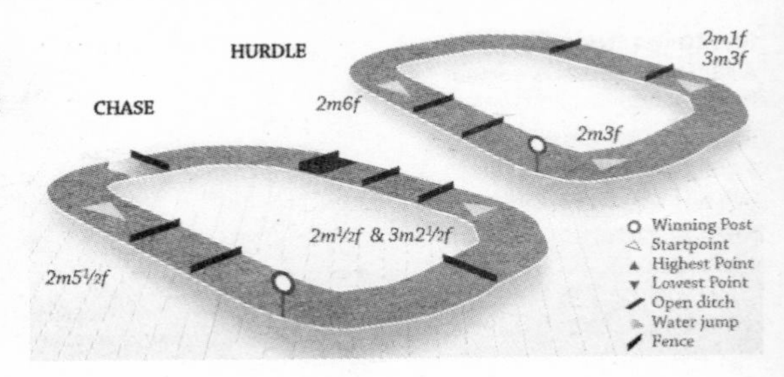

Trainers	Wins-Runs	%	Hurdles	Chases	£1 level stks
Paul Nicholls	43-149	29	18-63	24-81	-45.34
Philip Hobbs	30-143	21	20-83	5-46	-22.16
Jeremy Scott	17-93	18	5-55	12-38	+4.50
Colin Tizzard	17-127	13	7-61	9-61	-36.51
Tim Vaughan	15-86	17	10-59	4-19	+11.79
Evan Williams	14-114	12	8-65	6-45	-53.36
Martin Hill	14-130	11	10-100	3-23	-32.28
Nicky Henderson	13-34	38	9-25	2-6	+6.65
David Pipe	13-135	10	9-96	4-29	-71.77
John Ferguson	12-29	41	8-24	2-3	+10.49
David Bridgwater	12-46	26	4-17	8-27	+0.66
Harry Fry	12-51	24	8-37	2-7	-5.25
Neil Mulholland	12-121	10	9-84	3-32	-25.18

Jockeys	Wins-Rides	%	£1 level stks	Best Trainer	W-R
Richard Johnson	43-210	20	-61.27	Philip Hobbs	17-75
Sam Twiston-Davies	42-173	24	-60.54	Paul Nicholls	30-85
Tom Scudamore	31-206	15	-47.57	David Pipe	10-82
Aidan Coleman	24-95	25	+30.58	John Ferguson	8-13
Tom O'Brien	21-128	16	-34.67	Philip Hobbs	8-27
Nick Scholfield	21-146	14	-30.93	Jeremy Scott	7-32
Noel Fehily	17-87	20	-9.52	Harry Fry	7-21
Daryl Jacob	12-56	21	+23.75	Emma Lavelle	3-7
A P McCoy	11-42	26	-13.99	Jonjo O'Neill	7-32
Paul Moloney	11-66	17	-12.30	Evan Williams	9-43
Harry Cobden	11-82	13	-11.29	Michael Blake	4-10
Bryony Frost	11-99	11	-55.32	Paul Nicholls	7-12
Gavin Sheehan	10-53	19	+5.66	Warren Greatrex	4-11

Favourites

Hurdle 37% -19.49 Chase 38% -21.06 Total 38% -45.12

Scone Palace Park, Perth
PH2 6BB. Tel: 01683 220 131

PERTH

How to get there Road: A93. Rail: Free bus service from Perth

Features Flat, right-handed, 1m2f circuit

2019-20 Fixtures
April 22-24

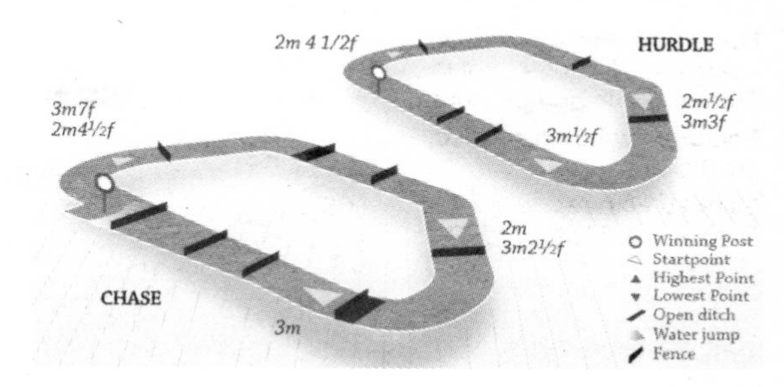

Trainers	*Wins-Runs*	*%*	*Hurdles*	*Chases*	*£1 level stks*
Gordon Elliott	79-275	29	52-163	20-87	-15.20
Lucinda Russell	29-362	8	18-242	10-99	-124.10
Fergal O'Brien	25-90	28	9-40	13-42	+31.00
Donald McCain	23-105	22	12-60	9-39	+11.44
Nicky Richards	23-154	15	13-100	8-44	-10.54
Lisa Harrison	23-174	13	14-110	9-46	-20.59
Nigel Twiston-Davies	18-95	19	9-51	7-37	-24.39
S R B Crawford	15-145	10	7-90	4-31	-68.20
Peter Bowen	14-36	39	6-13	6-19	+17.87
David Pipe	12-23	52	6-14	6-9	+15.61
Rose Dobbin	12-77	16	6-48	5-26	-25.48
Tom George	11-62	18	3-17	8-43	-22.80
Dianne Sayer	10-97	10	9-75	1-21	-34.00

Jockeys	*Wins-Rides*	*%*	*£1 level stks*	*Best Trainer*	*W-R*
Richard Johnson	74-251	29	-28.44	Gordon Elliott	36-145
Brian Hughes	40-280	14	-82.98	Malcolm Jefferson	4-33
Craig Nichol	23-181	13	-59.73	Nicky Richards	7-30
Paddy Brennan	22-113	19	-16.50	Fergal O'Brien	15-47
Sam Twiston-Davies	19-89	21	-11.50	Nigel Twiston-Davies	11-61
Tom Scudamore	17-50	34	+5.77	David Pipe	12-22
Sean Bowen	12-36	33	+26.51	Paul Nicholls	1-3
Derek Fox	12-152	8	-64.64	Lucinda Russell	7-86
Henry Brooke	12-156	8	-71.00	Alistair Whillans	2-9
Ryan Day	11-90	12	-25.17	Lisa Harrison	8-31
William Kennedy	9-24	38	+31.10	Donald McCain	8-17
Tony Kelly	9-56	16	+16.25	Jackie Stephen	6-35
Sean Quinlan	9-65	14	+10.50	Jennie Candlish	4-14

Favourites

Hurdle 40% -17.09 | Chase 29% -60.97 | Total 37% -78.44

PLUMPTON

Plumpton, Sussex
Tel: 01273 890 383

How to get there Road: A274 or A275 to B2116. Rail: Plumpton

Features Quirky, undulating, left-handed 1m1f circuit, uphill straight, has several course specialists

2019-20 Fixtures
October 21, November 4, 18, December 2, 16, January 5, 15, 27, February 10, 24, March 9, 18, April 5, 12-13

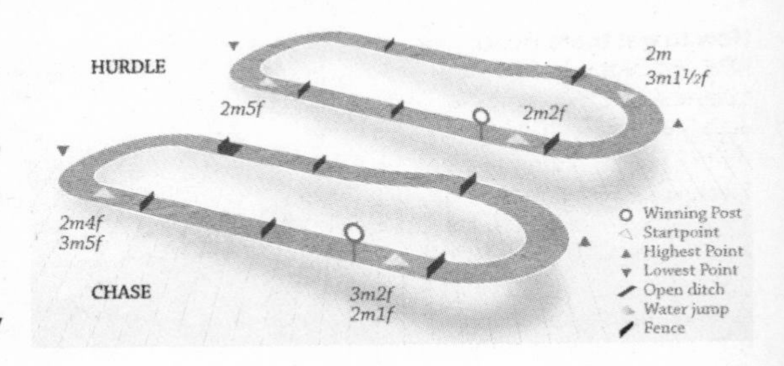

Trainers	Wins-Runs	%	Hurdles	Chases	£1 level stks
Gary Moore	56-321	17	34-208	22-102	-82.27
Chris Gordon	31-175	18	21-125	9-39	+24.09
Alan King	16-50	32	13-38	3-10	-10.28
Anthony Honeyball	16-59	27	8-33	5-17	-8.26
Sheena West	16-90	18	11-74	5-15	+43.08
Seamus Mullins	16-135	12	9-73	7-51	-17.83
David Pipe	14-56	25	8-36	3-11	+16.51
Neil King	14-72	19	7-42	7-29	-18.26
Paul Henderson	13-74	18	5-36	8-38	-11.12
Colin Tizzard	13-79	16	7-46	6-28	-26.42
Suzy Smith	12-56	21	8-38	0-8	+35.38
David Bridgwater	12-81	15	2-34	9-45	-22.47
Charlie Mann	11-37	30	4-20	7-17	+23.77

Jockeys	Wins-Rides	%	£1 level stks	Best Trainer	W-R
Tom Cannon	32-229	14	-9.40	Chris Gordon	18-95
Jamie Moore	28-194	14	-68.54	Gary Moore	23-119
Joshua Moore	26-160	16	-56.91	Gary Moore	28-123
Marc Goldstein	26-191	14	+68.08	Sheena West	13-80
Tom Scudamore	21-102	21	-3.45	David Pipe	10-34
Noel Fehily	18-71	25	-11.42	Neil Mulholland	5-37
Gavin Sheehan	18-79	23	+11.64	Warren Greatrex	9-30
Wayne Hutchinson	17-55	31	-11.38	Alan King	11-30
Tom O'Brien	15-90	17	+19.75	Paul Henderson	6-23
Aidan Coleman	14-75	19	-25.24	Venetia Williams	7-24
Leighton Aspell	12-108	11	-56.37	Oliver Sherwood	7-29
Harry Cobden	11-43	26	+2.60	Colin Tizzard	3-11
Paddy Brennan	11-50	22	+5.70	Paul Henderson	4-13

Favourites

Hurdle 40% -9.70 Chase 42% +5.15 Total 40% -13.54

SANDOWN

Esher, Surrey, KT10 9AJ
Tel: 01372 463 072 or 464 348

How to get there Road: M25 anti-clockwise Jctn 10 and A3, M25 clockwise Jctn 9 and A224. Rail: Esher (from Waterloo)

Features Right-handed, 1m5f circuit, tough fences and stiff uphill finish

2019-20 Fixtures
November 10, December 6-7, January 4, February 1, 14, March 6-7, April 25

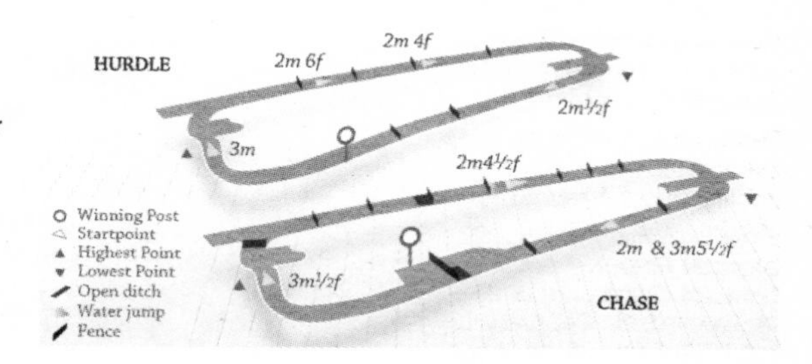

Trainers	*Wins-Runs*	*%*	*Hurdles*	*Chases*	*£1 level stks*
Nicky Henderson	44-161	27	31-108	12-50	+4.83
Paul Nicholls	25-191	13	9-76	16-111	-44.55
Gary Moore	24-142	17	10-83	13-56	+12.23
Philip Hobbs	16-97	16	6-39	10-53	-16.16
Alan King	12-63	19	9-44	3-16	+6.71
Nigel Twiston-Davies	12-67	18	8-35	4-32	+42.96
Fergal O'Brien	8-29	28	4-15	2-8	+23.12
Colin Tizzard	8-84	10	6-34	2-50	-50.07
Venetia Williams	8-97	8	1-34	7-62	-50.00
W P Mullins	7-19	37	4-9	2-8	+18.32
Lucy Wadham	7-44	16	2-19	5-23	-1.67
David Pipe	7-60	12	2-42	5-17	-21.54
Charlie Longsdon	7-65	11	0-17	7-47	+14.25

Jockeys	*Wins-Rides*	*%*	*£1 level stks*	*Best Trainer*	*W-R*
Jamie Moore	23-99	23	+22.77	Gary Moore	15-59
Daryl Jacob	21-82	26	+28.41	Nicky Henderson	7-13
Richard Johnson	17-109	16	-26.57	Philip Hobbs	14-53
Nico de Boinville	16-70	23	-14.37	Nicky Henderson	10-40
Noel Fehily	14-75	19	+0.08	Neil Mulholland	4-12
Sam Twiston-Davies	13-113	12	-10.42	Paul Nicholls	10-71
Barry Geraghty	11-50	22	-4.21	Nicky Henderson	12-41
Joshua Moore	9-59	15	+18.25	Gary Moore	8-39
Tom O'Brien	9-60	15	+7.43	Tom Weston	1-1
Leighton Aspell	9-83	11	-31.25	Lucy Wadham	3-20
Sean Bowen	8-38	21	+49.91	Charlie Longsdon	1-1
Wayne Hutchinson	8-50	16	-5.29	Alan King	7-35
Harry Cobden	8-63	13	-22.25	Paul Nicholls	2-21

Favourites

Hurdle 36% -0.99 Chase 39% +12.87 Total 36% +4.76

SEDGEFIELD

Sedgefield, Cleveland, TS21 2HW
Tel: 01740 621 925

How to get there Road: 2m from A1 on A689. Rail: Stockton, Darlington

Features Left-handed, 1m2f circuit, sharp and undulating, no water jump

2019-20 Fixtures
October 1, 20, November 7, 14, 26, December 6, 26, January 10, 26, February 4, 20, March 1, 10, 19, April 3, 21

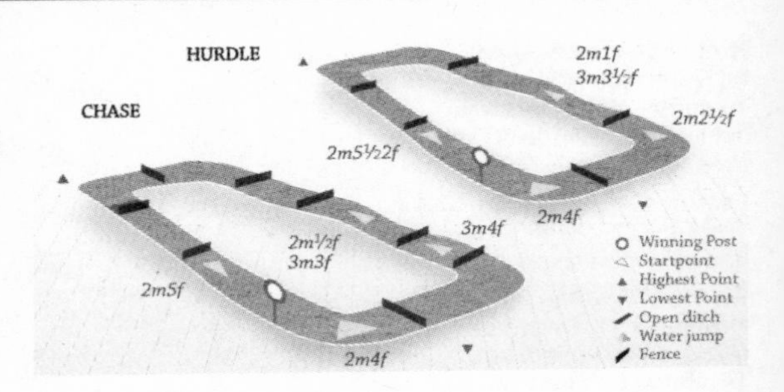

Trainers	Wins-Runs	%	Hurdles	Chases	£1 level stks
Donald McCain	51-280	18	35-200	12-63	-44.22
Brian Ellison	36-160	23	23-101	8-43	-31.78
Micky Hammond	36-276	13	18-162	16-99	-88.37
Sue Smith	23-181	13	13-88	10-85	-63.63
Kenneth Slack	22-77	29	13-55	9-20	+30.38
Malcolm Jefferson	21-85	25	7-43	9-22	-2.50
Neil Mulholland	19-42	45	11-29	7-11	+19.00
Dianne Sayer	19-93	20	17-76	2-16	+31.63
Dan Skelton	17-63	27	12-41	5-18	-11.03
Joanne Foster	14-85	16	3-33	11-52	+31.10
Keith Dalgleish	13-56	23	10-48	2-6	-7.47
Chris Grant	13-154	8	5-97	4-31	-42.53
Sam England	12-70	17	6-38	6-32	-4.35

Jockeys	Wins-Rides	%	£1 level stks	Best Trainer	W-R
Brian Hughes	84-365	23	+35.52	Malcolm Jefferson	25-85
Henry Brooke	35-214	16	-24.01	Kenneth Slack	12-31
Danny Cook	26-143	18	-27.45	Brian Ellison	9-39
Sean Quinlan	20-159	13	-33.21	Sue Smith	6-39
Wilson Renwick	15-66	23	+8.68	Donald McCain	9-28
Joe Colliver	15-82	18	-13.81	Micky Hammond	10-56
William Kennedy	15-128	12	-38.25	Donald McCain	9-71
Richard Johnson	13-41	32	-6.48	Gordon Elliott	2-7
James Reveley	13-46	28	-2.72	Keith Reveley	7-17
Jonathan England	13-89	15	-14.35	Sam England	8-38
Harry Skelton	12-41	29	-1.56	Dan Skelton	11-28
Brian Harding	12-78	15	+10.03	William Amos	4-18
Thomas Dowson	11-128	9	-42.17	Victor Thompson	5-43

Favourites

Hurdle 43% -12.84 Chase 37% -28.77 Total 40% -56.96

Rolleston, nr Newark, Notts
NG25 0TS. Tel: 01636 814 481

SOUTHWELL

How to get there Road: A1 to Newark and A617 to Southwell or A52 to Nottingham (off M1) and A612 to Southwell. Rail: Rolleston

Features Flat, left-handed, 1m2f circuit

2019-20 Fixtures
October 1, 24, November 15, 26, December 3, 15, March 8, 16, 31, April 7, 21

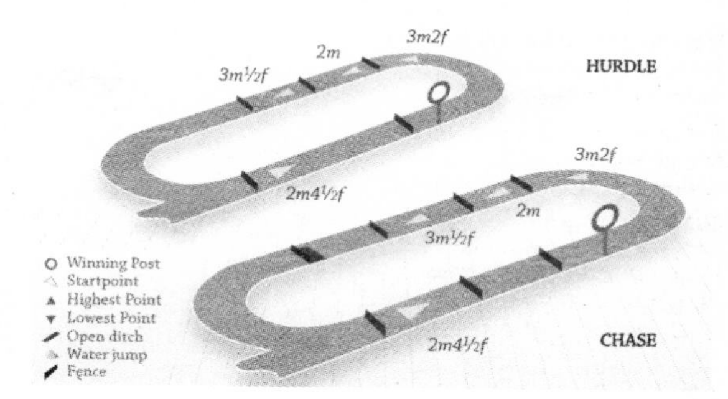

Trainers	*Wins-Runs*	*%*	*Hurdles*	*Chases*	*£1 level stks*
Dan Skelton	37-173	21	20-109	16-41	-32.92
Jonjo O'Neill	26-168	15	11-108	13-50	-40.53
Tom George	22-78	28	16-44	5-23	-0.13
Nicky Henderson	18-55	33	8-31	1-8	-6.32
Caroline Bailey	17-98	17	11-56	6-41	+8.75
Kim Bailey	13-68	19	8-43	4-15	-3.16
Charlie Longsdon	13-86	15	9-49	2-24	-4.71
Tim Vaughan	13-97	13	8-57	5-28	-0.37
Alan King	12-45	27	9-30	1-7	-12.75
Ben Pauling	12-51	24	8-33	1-7	-14.65
Peter Bowen	12-57	21	5-30	7-17	+8.36
Harry Whittington	10-40	25	7-21	1-6	+47.51
Seamus Mullins	10-56	18	4-31	3-19	+21.62

Jockeys	*Wins-Rides*	*%*	*£1 level stks*	*Best Trainer*	*W-R*
Harry Skelton	41-163	25	+9.71	Dan Skelton	20-91
Richard Johnson	35-156	22	-17.57	Tim Vaughan	6-28
Paddy Brennan	24-104	23	+22.11	Tom George	14-39
Nico de Boinville	21-77	27	-8.49	Nicky Henderson	6-17
Aidan Coleman	20-149	13	-55.99	Jonjo O'Neill	6-41
Sean Bowen	19-89	21	+29.86	Peter Bowen	8-37
Sam Twiston-Davies	16-72	22	-4.50	Nigel Twiston-Davies	7-40
A P McCoy	15-43	35	+0.38	Jonjo O'Neill	7-32
Gavin Sheehan	15-66	23	+78.90	Jamie Snowden	3-6
Tom Scudamore	15-95	16	-33.19	David Bridgwater	5-18
Noel Fehily	14-65	22	-8.50	Charlie Longsdon	8-29
Richie McLernon	13-75	17	+4.43	Jonjo O'Neill	7-31
Brian Hughes	13-113	12	-50.75	Mike Sowersby	4-18

Favourites

Hurdle 45% +42.10 Chase 36% -36.04 Total 41% -8.32

STRATFORD

Luddington Road, Stratford
CV37 9SE. Tel: 01789 267 949

How to get there Road: M40 Jctn 15, A3400, B439, A46. Rail: Stratford-Upon-Avon

Features Sharp, left-handed, 1m2f circuit

2019-20 Fixtures October 7, 19, 31, November 11, March 9, 28, April 19

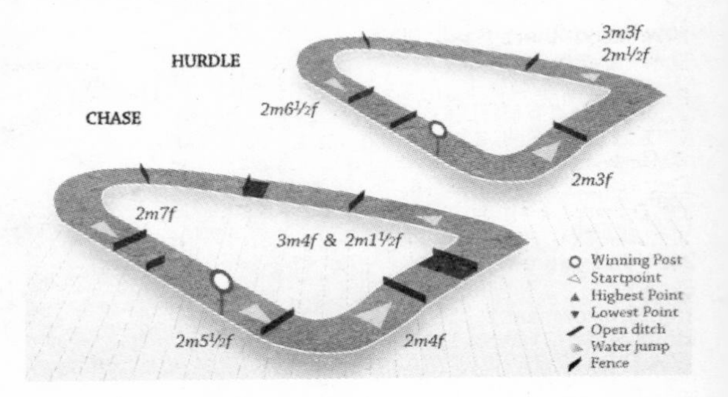

Trainers	*Wins-Runs*	*%*	*Hurdles*	*Chases*	*£1 level stks*
Dan Skelton	29-157	18	17-102	10-44	-58.49
Warren Greatrex	18-64	28	10-39	3-13	+12.24
Tom George	17-68	25	7-22	7-41	+29.57
Philip Hobbs	17-71	24	5-23	12-46	+25.27
John Ferguson	16-30	53	13-25	1-1	+8.01
Neil Mulholland	14-79	18	11-55	2-22	+16.25
Alan King	13-51	25	10-37	2-7	-5.81
Peter Bowen	13-61	21	1-21	10-28	+9.49
Dr Richard Newland	12-41	29	8-29	4-12	-13.98
Donald McCain	11-57	19	8-37	2-16	+20.87
Nigel Twiston-Davies	11-86	13	8-48	3-32	-36.47
Tim Vaughan	11-107	10	5-71	3-25	-40.21
Neil King	10-44	23	5-32	4-10	+9.85

Jockeys	*Wins-Rides*	*%*	*£1 level stks*	*Best Trainer*	*W-R*
Richard Johnson	48-193	25	+15.25	Philip Hobbs	11-37
Aidan Coleman	30-129	23	+17.19	John Ferguson	9-14
Harry Skelton	26-113	23	-29.86	Dan Skelton	20-86
Sam Twiston-Davies	22-126	17	-39.30	Paul Nicholls	6-17
Tom Scudamore	18-127	14	+5.35	David Pipe	9-39
Sean Bowen	13-67	19	-10.86	Peter Bowen	5-23
Tom O'Brien	13-92	14	-2.67	Philip Hobbs	7-20
Wayne Hutchinson	12-50	24	-7.96	Alan King	10-32
Daryl Jacob	12-53	23	+3.58	Emma Lavelle	4-11
Noel Fehily	12-73	16	-20.56	Warren Greatrex	4-4
A P Heskin	11-26	42	+18.46	Tom George	8-19
Gavin Sheehan	11-69	16	-18.65	Warren Greatrex	7-33
Harry Bannister	10-39	26	+18.70	Charlie Mann	5-6

Favourites

Hurdle 41% +0.77 Chase 31% -39.97 Total 36% -56.20

TAUNTON

Orchard Portman, Taunton, Somerset
TA3 7BL. Tel: 01823 337 172

How to get there Road: M5 Jctn 25. Rail: Taunton

Features Right-handed, 1m2f circuit

2019-20 Fixtures October 30, November 14, 28, December 12, 30, January 7, 18, February 2, 18, 27, March 9, 17, April 2, 22

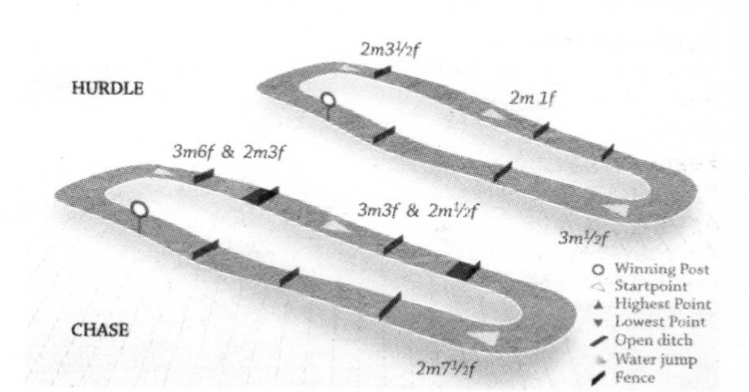

Trainers	*Wins-Runs*	*%*	*Hurdles*	*Chases*	*£1 level stks*
Paul Nicholls	60-194	31	42-128	14-50	-14.91
Harry Fry	19-89	21	15-70	1-7	-29.56
Colin Tizzard	18-133	14	11-80	7-47	-19.85
David Pipe	18-176	10	12-146	5-24	-72.17
Philip Hobbs	17-132	13	13-96	1-25	-63.98
Jeremy Scott	14-68	21	9-47	5-15	+40.48
Evan Williams	13-117	11	10-79	3-33	-41.83
Nicky Henderson	12-36	33	10-30	1-3	+0.62
Dan Skelton	11-63	17	9-53	0-5	-29.53
Anthony Honeyball	10-56	18	8-40	1-11	-11.20
Nick Williams	9-37	24	8-28	1-7	+2.43
Johnny Farrelly	9-82	11	9-71	0-9	-22.38
Neil Mulholland	9-98	9	7-71	2-18	-34.50

Jockeys	*Wins-Rides*	*%*	*£1 level stks*	*Best Trainer*	*W-R*
Sam Twiston-Davies	29-120	24	-2.21	Paul Nicholls	23-73
Harry Cobden	24-85	28	-4.89	Paul Nicholls	5-23
Noel Fehily	17-78	22	-18.54	Harry Fry	10-31
Tom Scudamore	15-130	12	-44.57	David Pipe	9-77
Nick Scholfield	14-108	13	-12.55	Paul Nicholls	11-36
James Best	13-143	9	-57.63	Philip Hobbs	3-9
Aidan Coleman	12-78	15	-34.06	Anthony Honeyball	4-10
David Noonan	12-116	10	-61.22	Anthony Honeyball	4-17
Micheal Nolan	10-74	14	+94.57	Jamie Snowden	3-7
Daryl Jacob	9-43	21	-0.06	Nicky Henderson	2-2
Brendan Powell	9-66	14	-8.75	Johnny Farrelly	5-24
Richard Johnson	9-92	10	-56.20	Philip Hobbs	8-58
Gavin Sheehan	8-44	18	-3.80	Warren Greatrex	3-11

Favourites

Hurdle 41% -0.23 Chase 34% -13.39 Total 39% -13.20

TOWCESTER

Easton Newston, Towcester
NN12 7HS. Tel: 01327 353 414

How to get there Road: M1 Jctn 15a, A43 West. Rail: Northampton (8m) and bus service

Features Right-handed, 1m6f circuit, uphill from back straight

2019-20 Fixtures
October 9, November 28, December 19

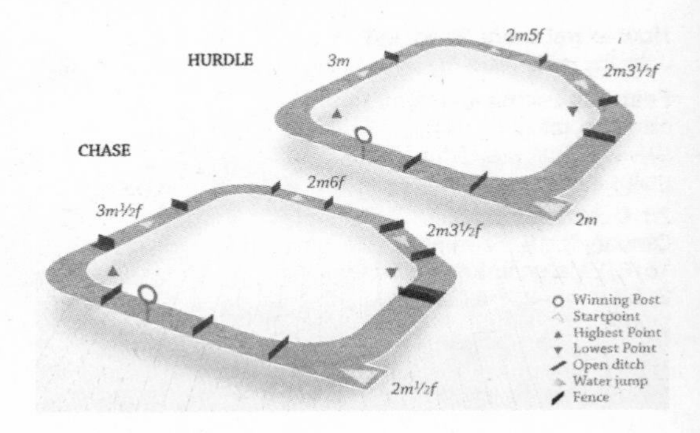

Trainers	*Wins-Runs*	*%*	*Hurdles*	*Chases*	*£1 level stks*
Nicky Henderson	16-37	43	12-20	2-5	+5.33
Kim Bailey	14-57	25	8-30	4-17	-2.04
Henry Oliver	11-36	31	5-23	6-11	+28.50
Fergal O'Brien	11-44	25	9-24	2-13	+6.46
Ben Pauling	11-50	22	5-34	6-14	+25.75
Charlie Longsdon	10-52	19	2-28	7-20	-17.18
Henry Daly	9-32	28	3-18	5-10	+25.60
Dan Skelton	9-37	24	6-25	2-7	-13.39
Alan King	8-32	25	5-21	0-2	-1.79
Neil Mulholland	7-22	32	4-10	2-8	+2.72
Oliver Sherwood	7-34	21	3-18	3-10	-11.73
Martin Keighley	7-52	13	3-29	3-18	-18.75
Gary Moore	6-28	21	4-16	2-9	+4.75

Jockeys	*Wins-Rides*	*%*	*£1 level stks*	*Best Trainer*	*W-R*
Nico de Boinville	11-42	26	-10.30	Nicky Henderson	4-9
Paddy Brennan	11-48	23	+8.38	Fergal O'Brien	12-32
Jeremiah McGrath	10-27	37	+17.43	Nicky Henderson	5-10
David Bass	10-49	20	-4.32	Ben Pauling	6-17
Richard Johnson	7-44	16	-7.34	Henry Daly	4-6
Daryl Jacob	7-45	16	-4.66	Ben Pauling	2-5
Liam Treadwell	6-43	14	-10.60	Venetia Williams	5-20
Jason Maguire	5-9	56	+5.14	Kim Bailey	4-8
A P McCoy	5-14	36	+1.00	Jonjo O'Neill	5-11
Bridget Andrews	5-19	26	+1.69	Dan Skelton	3-10
Joshua Moore	5-26	19	+7.75	Gary Moore	3-12
Gavin Sheehan	5-28	18	0.00	Brian Barr	1-1
Noel Fehily	5-28	18	-10.00	Neil Mulholland	2-8

Favourites

Hurdle	38%	-19.73	Chase	39%	-6.01	Total	38%	-34.01

Wood Lane, Uttoxeter, Staffs
ST14 8BD. Tel: 01889 562 561

UTTOXETER

How to get there Road: M6 Jctn 14. Rail: Uttoxeter

Features Left-handed, 1m2f circuit, undulating with sweeping curves, suits galloping types

2019-20 Fixtures
October 6, 18, November 1, 16, 24, December 10, 20, 31, January 25, February 8, March 14, 28

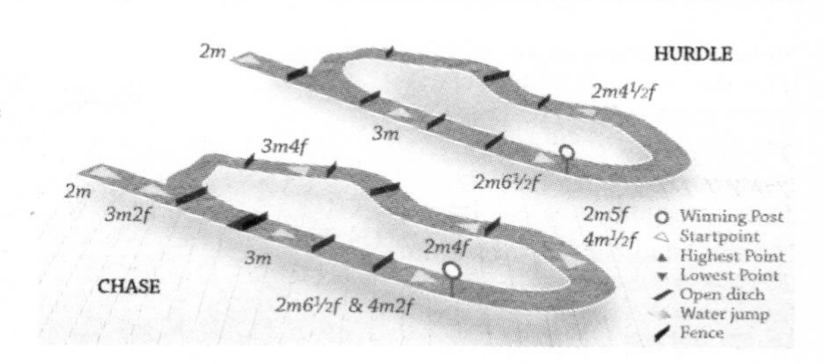

Trainers	*Wins-Runs*	*%*	*Hurdles*	*Chases*	*£1 level stks*
Dan Skelton	68-216	31	46-134	20-68	+46.86
Jonjo O'Neill	33-254	13	18-140	13-103	-82.94
Nigel Twiston-Davies	27-171	16	13-88	13-70	-35.01
Charlie Longsdon	25-126	20	13-62	12-58	-5.27
Dr Richard Newland	22-73	30	19-54	3-19	-5.54
Nicky Henderson	21-75	28	13-43	6-24	-22.51
Warren Greatrex	21-77	27	8-41	3-16	+3.84
Neil King	20-105	19	16-69	2-27	-25.51
David Pipe	20-131	15	8-76	8-41	-15.44
Philip Hobbs	18-111	16	11-64	5-39	-36.96
Evan Williams	17-118	14	10-71	6-39	+30.45
Tim Vaughan	16-152	11	13-119	2-27	-65.37
Fergal O'Brien	15-103	15	6-60	7-33	+0.28

Jockeys	*Wins-Rides*	*%*	*£1 level stks*	*Best Trainer*	*W-R*
Harry Skelton	69-172	40	+111.53	Dan Skelton	24-73
Richard Johnson	46-271	17	-68.16	Philip Hobbs	13-56
Aidan Coleman	42-206	20	+25.90	Jonjo O'Neill	15-58
Sam Twiston-Davies	31-167	19	-17.84	Nigel Twiston-Davies	12-61
Noel Fehily	29-108	27	-0.51	Charlie Longsdon	11-28
Tom Scudamore	29-198	15	-44.45	David Pipe	18-88
Gavin Sheehan	24-113	21	+6.90	Warren Greatrex	14-35
Sean Bowen	20-138	14	-46.22	Peter Bowen	9-46
Tom O'Brien	19-154	12	-50.62	Ian Williams	3-20
Trevor Whelan	16-104	15	-20.30	Neil King	13-72
Paddy Brennan	16-121	13	+0.16	Fergal O'Brien	11-50
A P McCoy	13-54	24	-17.41	Jonjo O'Neill	7-66
Andrew Tinkler	13-93	14	-22.89	Martin Keighley	6-36

Favourites

Hurdle 43% +45.59 Chase 37% -3.11 Total 41% +43.23

WARWICK

Hampton Street, Warwick
CV34 6HN. Tel: 01926 491 553

How to get there Road: M40 Jctn 15 on to A429 and follow signs to town centre. Rail: Warwick

Features Left-handed, 1m6f circuit, undulating

2019-20 Fixtures
October 3, November 8, 20, December 12, 31, January 11, 22, February 8, 21, March 8, 26, April 14, 23

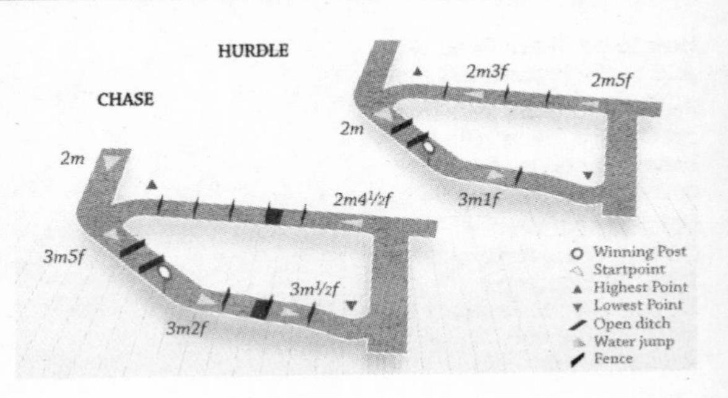

Trainers	Wins-Runs	%	Hurdles	Chases	£1 level stks
Dan Skelton	46-204	23	23-125	17-52	-34.81
Alan King	31-146	21	21-92	5-23	-54.43
Nicky Henderson	28-86	33	16-49	7-10	+17.63
Jonjo O'Neill	27-161	17	14-99	11-49	+60.65
Philip Hobbs	23-109	21	8-54	8-32	-9.04
Nigel Twiston-Davies	19-172	11	6-81	11-67	-87.31
Neil Mulholland	12-52	23	5-30	6-18	+8.42
Paul Nicholls	12-55	22	3-23	8-28	-18.79
Ben Pauling	12-75	16	5-44	0-10	-12.25
Venetia Williams	12-85	14	5-32	6-46	-29.57
Charlie Longsdon	11-112	10	6-65	5-36	-56.51
Warren Greatrex	10-57	18	3-36	1-5	+8.33
Henry Daly	10-67	15	6-36	3-22	-19.88

Jockeys	Wins-Rides	%	£1 level stks	Best Trainer	W-R
Harry Skelton	42-172	24	-14.72	Dan Skelton	28-124
Richard Johnson	39-196	20	-36.29	Philip Hobbs	20-65
Noel Fehily	26-101	26	+22.01	Neil Mulholland	7-24
Aidan Coleman	25-143	17	-38.99	Venetia Williams	10-33
Sam Twiston-Davies	22-130	17	-41.37	Nigel Twiston-Davies	13-62
Nico de Boinville	19-78	24	+21.80	Nicky Henderson	7-20
Wayne Hutchinson	18-109	17	-39.35	Alan King	11-65
Daryl Jacob	15-79	19	-28.67	Nicky Henderson	4-5
David Bass	14-93	15	+2.00	Ben Pauling	6-15
Tom O'Brien	13-96	14	-21.88	Stuart Edmunds	2-2
Gavin Sheehan	12-79	15	-9.79	Warren Greatrex	5-26
Sean Bowen	11-90	12	-46.68	Peter Bowen	3-34
Jamie Moore	10-76	13	+91.75	Richard Lee	3-4

Favourites

Hurdle 38% -46.60 Chase 40% -6.31 Total 39% -50.66

York Road, Wetherby, West Yorks
L22 5EJ. Tel: 01937 582 035

WETHERBY

How to get there Road: A1, A58 from Leeds, B1224 from York. Rail: Leeds, Harrogate, York

Features Long, left-handed circuit (1m4f chases, 1m2f hurdles), suits galloping types

2019-20 Fixtures
October 16, November 1-2, 16, 27, December 7, 26-27, January 11, 23, February 1, 12, March 2, 17, 27, April 9

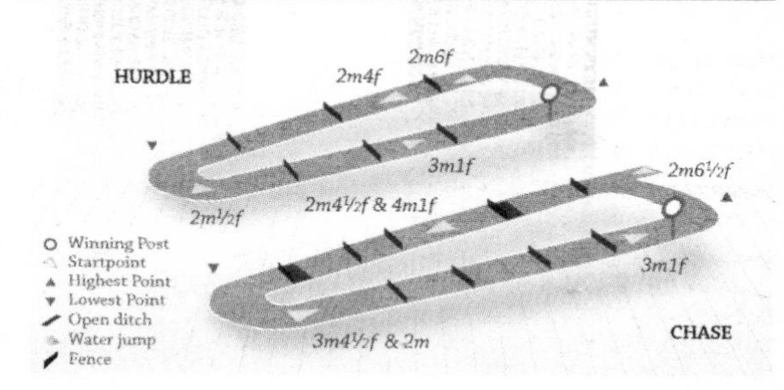

Trainers	*Wins-Runs*	*%*	*Hurdles*	*Chases*	*£1 level stks*
Dan Skelton	37-118	31	22-72	12-37	+9.51
Philip Kirby	26-157	17	21-133	5-10	+28.68
Micky Hammond	26-288	9	16-186	7-87	-25.67
Sue Smith	21-196	11	6-91	14-98	-106.31
Warren Greatrex	19-69	28	15-47	3-11	+2.69
Jonjo O'Neill	15-66	23	11-40	3-23	-7.82
Neil Mulholland	13-39	33	6-23	6-12	+12.32
Kim Bailey	12-41	29	4-21	5-13	+17.07
Brian Ellison	12-98	12	6-57	4-32	-46.05
Nigel Twiston-Davies	11-56	20	6-28	4-26	-16.05
Mark Walford	11-79	14	8-55	3-20	-12.75
Philip Hobbs	10-30	33	6-14	4-16	+4.89
Nicky Richards	10-39	26	5-16	4-17	+54.00

Jockeys	*Wins-Rides*	*%*	*£1 level stks*	*Best Trainer*	*W-R*
Harry Skelton	33-103	32	+2.08	Dan Skelton	25-70
Brian Hughes	30-243	12	-81.78	Malcolm Jefferson	10-70
Danny Cook	22-183	12	-94.60	Sue Smith	14-81
Richard Johnson	21-83	25	+5.05	Philip Hobbs	7-19
Adam Nicol	19-107	18	+30.43	Philip Kirby	10-53
Joe Colliver	14-120	12	+17.58	Micky Hammond	13-94
Gavin Sheehan	13-64	20	-12.97	Warren Greatrex	11-31
Sean Quinlan	13-94	14	+27.00	Jennie Candlish	2-23
David Bass	12-36	33	+24.24	Kim Bailey	6-17
Paddy Brennan	12-37	32	+41.90	Fergal O'Brien	6-9
Craig Nichol	11-70	16	+0.88	Lucinda Russell	4-14
Tom Scudamore	10-44	23	-15.88	David Pipe	4-17
Henry Brooke	10-141	7	-86.82	Rebecca Menzies	1-1

Favourites

Hurdle 40% -24.33 Chase 39% -19.49 Total 39% -54.87

WINCANTON

Wincanton, Somerset
BA9 8BJ. Tel: 01963 323 44

How to get there Road: A303 to Wincanton, course on B3081, 1m from town centre. Rail: Gillingham

Features Right-handed, 1m4f circuit, dries fast

2019-20 Fixtures
October 17, 27, November 9, 21, December 5, 26, January 4, 16, 30, February 15, 26, March 5, 23, April 1, 19

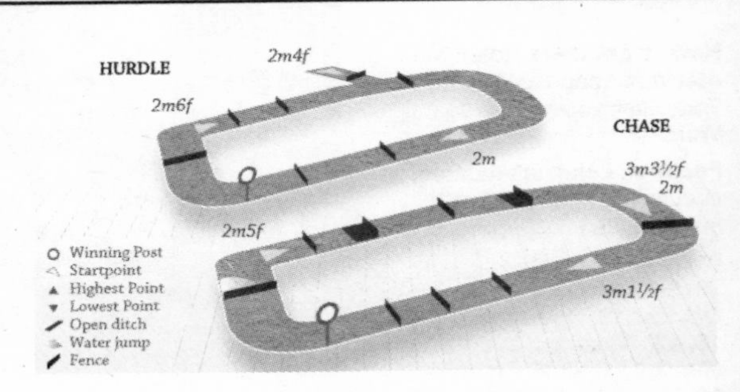

Trainers	Wins-Runs	%	Hurdles	Chases	£1 level stks
Paul Nicholls	99-298	33	62-169	28-94	-5.10
Colin Tizzard	36-270	13	15-129	21-111	-46.77
Philip Hobbs	21-177	12	9-103	8-51	-66.63
Harry Fry	20-100	20	11-66	4-18	-14.19
Neil Mulholland	15-154	10	10-99	4-45	-40.65
Emma Lavelle	14-69	20	8-33	3-26	+41.38
Alan King	12-81	15	7-59	3-11	-23.11
Jeremy Scott	12-109	11	6-63	5-33	-24.13
Warren Greatrex	10-50	20	7-39	2-7	-3.88
Tom George	10-64	16	1-15	8-43	-25.07
Venetia Williams	10-72	14	4-24	6-48	-27.02
Anthony Honeyball	9-67	13	4-40	2-16	-26.68
Nicky Henderson	8-43	19	5-25	3-13	-5.20

Jockeys	Wins-Rides	%	£1 level stks	Best Trainer	W-R
Harry Cobden	49-169	29	+25.47	Paul Nicholls	21-47
Sam Twiston-Davies	37-160	23	-43.57	Paul Nicholls	33-114
Daryl Jacob	22-92	24	+18.64	Paul Nicholls	8-23
Richard Johnson	22-136	16	-20.50	Philip Hobbs	11-75
Nick Scholfield	21-152	14	-19.03	Paul Nicholls	5-29
Noel Fehily	17-103	17	-31.13	Harry Fry	10-44
Tom O'Brien	16-113	14	-33.57	Philip Hobbs	8-41
Gavin Sheehan	14-57	25	+8.71	Warren Greatrex	6-25
Aidan Coleman	12-76	16	-3.20	Anthony Honeyball	4-13
Tom Scudamore	11-99	11	-40.03	David Pipe	10-54
Bryony Frost	10-45	22	+2.66	Paul Nicholls	3-8
Tom Bellamy	10-57	18	-0.88	Alan King	4-10
Adam Wedge	9-45	20	+86.58	Evan Williams	2-13

Favourites

Hurdle 39% -34.89 Chase 37% -26.57 Total 38% -63.28

Pitchcroft, Worcester
WR1 3EJ. Tel: 01905 253 64

WORCESTER

How to get there Road: M5 Jctn 6 from north, M5 Jctn 7 or A38 from south. Rail: Worcester (Forgate Street)

Features Left-handed, 1m5f circuit, prone to flooding

2019-20 Fixtures
October 10, 23

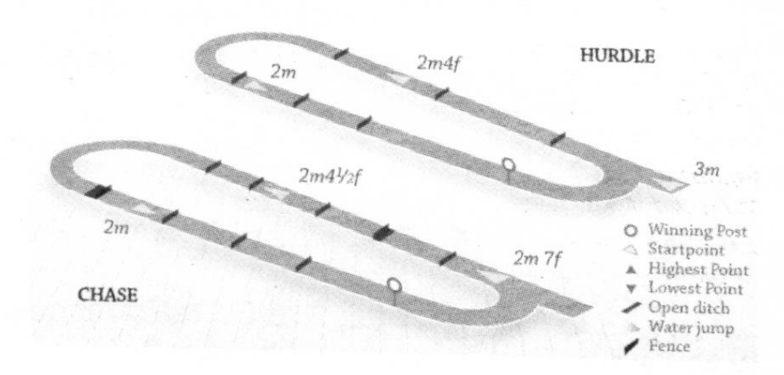

Trainers	Wins-Runs	%	Hurdles	Chases	£1 level stks
Jonjo O'Neill	46-266	17	20-145	24-110	-54.27
Philip Hobbs	34-122	28	20-69	11-46	+54.47
Dan Skelton	34-178	19	20-112	12-53	-34.02
Neil Mulholland	27-174	16	18-112	9-53	-36.81
Nicky Henderson	25-83	30	14-48	5-16	+0.93
Dr Richard Newland	25-83	30	18-60	7-23	-9.19
David Pipe	25-154	16	18-100	3-36	-1.89
Peter Bowen	22-105	21	10-47	9-45	+54.38
Charlie Longsdon	16-104	15	7-51	6-41	+0.68
Paul Nicholls	15-53	28	7-27	7-25	-10.88
Nigel Twiston-Davies	15-91	16	7-54	5-27	-10.97
Kim Bailey	14-61	23	7-34	7-24	+0.29
Tim Vaughan	14-113	12	6-62	8-44	+4.19

Jockeys	Wins-Rides	%	£1 level stks	Best Trainer	W-R
Richard Johnson	59-302	20	-19.56	Philip Hobbs	23-73
Sam Twiston-Davies	40-202	20	-42.73	Nigel Twiston-Davies	14-74
A P McCoy	35-102	34	+18.51	Jonjo O'Neill	23-87
Aidan Coleman	34-224	15	-85.75	Jonjo O'Neill	14-65
Harry Skelton	32-163	20	-4.65	Dan Skelton	18-104
Tom Scudamore	30-241	12	-26.74	David Pipe	18-105
Sean Bowen	26-132	20	+61.63	Peter Bowen	10-49
Noel Fehily	25-138	18	-24.97	Neil Mulholland	12-60
Tom O'Brien	21-141	15	-32.84	Robert Stephens	6-23
Nico de Boinville	17-115	15	-40.62	Nicky Henderson	7-34
Daryl Jacob	15-83	18	+5.35	Paul Nicholls	3-6
Wayne Hutchinson	14-73	19	-11.82	Alan King	7-29
Brendan Powell	13-128	10	+49.46	Brendan Powell	6-38

Favourites

Hurdle 41% -7.32 Chase 34% -19.81 Total 39% -30.35

Record and standard times

Aintree, Mildmay course

2m Ch	Nohalmdun (7 Apr 1990)	3m45.30s	3m49s
2m4f Ch	Wind Force (2 Apr 1993)	4m46.60s	4m48s
3m1f Ch	Cab On Target (2 Apr 1993)	6m03.40s	6m07s
2m½f Hdl	Spinning (3 Apr 1993)	3m44.80s	3m53s
2m1f Hdl	Gabrial The Great (16 May 2014)	4m04.30s	4m00s
	Hawk High (25 Oct 2014)		
2m4f Hdl	Gallateen (2 Apr 1993)	4m37.10s	4m43s
3m½f Hdl	Andrew's First (1 Apr 1993)	5m50.70s	5m54s

Aintree, Grand National course

2m5f Ch	Always Waining (8 Apr 2011)	5m19.30s	5m21s
3m2f Ch	Eurotrek (19 Nov 2006)	6m46.60s	6m38s
4m2½f Ch	One For Arthur (8 Apr 2017)	9m03.50s	9m04s

Ascot

2m1f Ch	Quite By Chance (29 Oct 2016)	3m55.90s	4m04s
2m3f Ch	Master Dee (29 Oct 2016)	4m29.50s	4m34s
2m5f Ch	Princeton Royale (31 Mar 2019)	5m09.28s	5m08s
3m Ch	Exmoor Ranger (29 Oct 2011)	5m49.60s	5m43s
1m7½f Hdl	Brampour (29 Oct 2011)	3m33.30s	3m41s
2m3½f Hdl	Overturn (19 Nov 2011)	4m30.80s	4m28s
2m5½f Hdl	Emmaslegend (19 Nov 2011)	5m10.90s	5m00s
2m7½f Hdl	Heronry (30 Mar 2014)	5m34.10s	5m29s
3m½f Hdl	Unowhatimeanharry (17 Dec 2016)	5m54.30s	5m46s

Ayr

2m½f Ch	Azzuri (13 Apr 2019)	3m45.20s	3m56s
2m4½f Ch	Secret Investor (13 Apr 2019)	4m56.40s	4m58s
2m5½f Ch	Star To The North (9 May 2001)	5m10.20s	5m10s
3m½f Ch	Top 'N' Tale (12 May 1982)	5m57.70s	5m54s
3m3f Ch	Joaaci (15 Apr 2005)	6m50.20s	6m35s
4m Ch	Hot Weld (21 Apr 2007)	7m55.10s	8m02s
2m Hdl	Verdana Blue (13 Apr 2019)	3m39.10s	3m40s
2m5½f Hdl	Cucumber Run (21 Apr 2012)	5m04.70s	5m02s
3m½f Hdl	Nautical Lad (6 Apr 1964)	5m42.00s	5m43s

Bangor

2m1½f Ch	Daulys Anthem (4 Aug 2017)	4m01.80s	4m05s
2m4½f Ch	The Disengager (24 Jul 2012)	4m49.70s	4m49s
3m Ch	Gone Platinum (2 Aug 2019)	5m47.07s	5m43s
3m5½f Ch	Kaki Crazy (23 May 2001)	7m34.10s	7m10s
2m½f Hdl	Andy Rew (24 Apr 1982)	3m44.50s	3m48s
2m3½f Hdl	Captain Peacock (3 Apr 2018)	4m30.80s	4m24s
2m7f Hdl	Silk Run (20 Aug 2018)	5m33.00s	5m20s

Carlisle

2m Ch	Germany Calling (15 Oct 2015)	3m53.70s	3m57s
2m4f Ch	Count Meribel (4 Nov 2018)	4m59.80s	4m57s
2m5f Ch	Amilliontimes (13 Oct 2016)	5m20.90s	5m13s
3m½f Ch	Ripalong Lad (9 Oct 2009)	6m00.70s	6m03s

3m2f Ch	Basford Ben (5 May 2016)	6m38.10s	6m27s
2m1f Hdl (Inner)	Maire Banrigh (25 Oct 2018)	3m59.60s	4m02s
2m1f Hdl (Outer)	Supertop (25 Oct 1997)	4m02.60s	4m04s
2m3½f Hdl (Inner)	Imperial Aura (25 Oct 2018)	4m33.70s	4m39s
2m4f Hdl (Outer)	Gods Law (29 Sep 1990)	4m50.60s	4m45s
3m½f Hdl (Outer)	Maggie Blue (15 Oct 2015)	6m02.30s	5m48s
3m1f Hdl (Inner)	Takingrisks (26 Mar 2016)	6m17.90s	5m50s

Cartmel

2m1½f Ch	Altruism (28 May 2016)	4m05.80s	4m12s
2m5f Ch	Princeton Royale (24 Jun 2016)	5m04.40s	5m12s
3m1½f Ch	Better Times Ahead (28 Aug 1999)	6m13.40s	6m20s
3m5½f Ch	Chabrimal Minster (26 May 2007)	7m12.00s	7m20s
2m1f Hdl	Lisbon (25 May 2013)	3m56.20s	4m02s
2m6f Hdl	Shantou Tiger (19 Jul 2014)	5m10.40s	5m11s
3m1½f Hdl	Portonia (30 May 1994)	5m58.00s	6m03s

Catterick

1m7½f Ch	Preston Deal (18 Dec 1971)	3m44.60s	3m48s
2m3f Ch	Away For Slates (22 Feb 2019)	4m45.10s	4m45s
3m1½f Ch	Clever General (7 Nov 1981)	6m14.00s	6m18s
3m6f Ch	Sharp Response (10 Jan 2019)	7m33.30s	7m25s
1m7½f Hdl	Lunar Wind (22 Apr 1982)	3m36.50s	3m40s
2m3f Hdl	Smadynium (4 Dec 2013)	4m31.50s	4m32s
3m1½f Hdl	Seamus O'Flynn (8 Nov 1986)	6m03.80s	6m08s

AZZURI: wins at Ayr in April on a day when three course records were broken

Cheltenham, New Course

2m½f Ch	Samakaan (16 Mar 2000)	3m52.40s	3m56s
2m4f Ch	Black Hercules (17 Mar 2016)	4m55.20s	4m51s
2m5f Ch	Vautour (17 Mar 2016)	5m05.50s	5m03s
3m2f Ch	Cogry (14 Dec 2018)	6m35.80s	6m26s
3m2½f Ch	Long Run (18 Mar 2011)	6m29.70s	6m37s
4m½f Ch	Hot Weld (16 Mar 2006)	8m33.20s	8m22s
2m1f Hdl	Detroit City (17 Mar 2006)	3m51.20s	3m54s
2m4½f Hdl	William Henry (19 Apr 2017)	4m48.80s	4m47s
3m Hdl	Bacchanal (16 Mar 2000)	5m36.60s	5m41s

Cheltenham, Old Course

2m Ch	Edredon Bleu (15 Mar 2000)	3m44.70s	3m52s
2m4f Ch	Shantou Village (22 Oct 2016)	4m53.30s	4m45s
2m4½f Ch	Dark Stranger (15 Mar 2000)	4m49.60s	4m58s
3m½f Ch	Marlborough (14 Mar 2000)	5m59.70s	5m57s
3m1f Ch	Un Temps Pour Tout (15 Mar 2016)	6m17.80s	6m05s

ANNIE POWER: no horse has run the Champion Hurdle course faster

3m3½f Ch	Rock The Kasbah (17 Nov 2018)	7m01.00s	6m50s
4m Ch	Relaxation (15 Mar 2000)	8m00.60s	7m59s
2m½f Hdl	Annie Power (15 Mar 2016)	3m45.10s	3m51s
2m4f Hdl	Vroum Vroum Mag (15 Mar 2016)	4m45.00s	4m37s
2m5f Hdl	Monsignor (15 Mar 2000)	4m52.00s	4m54s
3m Hdl	Trackmate (18 Oct 2013)	5m46.96s	5m40s
3m1½f Hdl	Rubhahunish (14 Mar 2000)	6m03.40s	6m05s

Cheltenham, Cross-Country Course

3m6f Ch	Balthazar King (13 Mar 2012)	7m51.70s	8m04s

Chepstow

2m Ch	Valseur Du Grenval (2 Nov 2016)	3m53.70s	3m58s
2m3½f Ch	Balder Succes (12 Oct 2013)	4m42.50s	4m45s
2m7½f Ch	Broadheath (4 Oct 1986)	5m47.90s	5m45s
3m2f Ch	Jaunty Jane (26 May 1975)	6m39.40s	6m34s
3m5½f Ch	Elegant Escape (27 Dec 2018)	7m48.21s	6m34s
2m Hdl	Tingle Bell (4 Oct 1986)	3m43.20s	3m47s
2m3½f Hdl	Ballyoptic (8 Oct 2016)	4m37.20s	4m34s
2m7½f Hdl	Chucklestone (11 May 1993)	5m33.60s	5m36s

Doncaster

2m½f Ch	Movie Legend (2 Mar 2019)	3m55.90s	3m57s
2m3f Ch	Buster Thomas (30 Nov 2018)	4m39.00s	4m36s
2m4½f Ch	Kalane (29 Dec 2016)	5m01.70s	4m54s
3m Ch	Rocky's Treasure (15 Dec 2018)	5m53.10s	5m54s
3m2f Ch	Chidswell (2 Mar 2019)	6m29.00s	6m24s
2m½f Hdl	Equus Amadeus (15 Dec 2018)	3m52.80s	3m50s
2m3½f Hdl	Just Milly (29 Dec 2016)	4m32.30s	4m33s
3m½f Hdl	Parish Business (29 Dec 2016)	5m47.50s	5m45s

Exeter

2m1½f Ch	Sir Valentino (1 Nov 2016)	3m57.50s	4m03s
2m3f Ch	West With The Wind (7 May 2013)	4m27.90s	4m30s
3m Ch	Dennis The Legend (13 May 2009)	5m42.80s	5m46s
3m6½f Ch	Thomas Wild (14 Apr 2015)	7m14.70s	7m24s
2m1f Hdl	Remind Me Later (21 Apr 2015)	3m49.20s	3m54s
2m2½f Hdl	Mr Brother Sylvest (18 Oct 2011)	4m14.70s	4m17s
2m5½f Hdl	I'm In Charge (6 Oct 2016)	5m05.20s	5m05s
2m7f Hdl	Very Cool (4 May 2010)	5m26.20s	5m29s

Fakenham

2m½f Ch	Cheekio Ora (23 Apr 1984)	3m44.90s	3m55s
2m5f Ch	Skipping Tim (25 May 1992)	5m10.30s	5m10s
3m Ch	Specialize (16 May 1999)	5m56.90s	5m52s
3m5f Ch	Rebeccas Choice (3 May 2016)	7m24.90s	7m10s
2m Hdl	Cobbet (9 May 2001)	3m45.70s	3m54s
2m4f Hdl	Ayem (16 May 1999)	4m41.20s	4m47s
2m7½f Hdl	Bazarov (22 Apr 2019)	5m42.20s	5m40s

Ffos Las

2m Ch	Teaser (18 Jul 2019)	3m47.20s	3m48s
2m3½f Ch	Cold Harbour (31 May 2011)	4m37.34s	4m40s
2m5f Ch	Putney Bridge (17 Jun 2010)	5m09.70s	5m05s

SIZING TENNESSEE: Fontwell record last year pointed to Ladbrokes Trophy win

3m Ch	Bally Longford (26 Jun 2019)	5m49.20s	5m50s
3m1½f Ch	Backstage (28 Aug 2009)	6m07.10s	6m10s
3m4f Ch	Pobbles Bay (21 Apr 2019)	7m18.00s	6m49s
2m Hdl	Comanche Chieftain (9 May 2017)	3m37.00s	3m36s
2m4f Hdl	Positively Dylan (9 May 2017)	4m40.80s	4m32s
2m6f Hdl	Sizing At Midnight (14 May 2019)	5m11.80s	5m00s
3m Hdl	Chill Factor (21 Aug 2014)	5m39.00s	5m30s

Fontwell

2m2f Ch	Oliver's Hill (7 Oct 2017)	4m23.70s	4m24s
2m5½f Ch	Sizing Tennessee (5 Oct 2018)	5m17.80s	5m23s
2m1½f Hdl	Musical Stardust (29 Aug 2019)	4m11.90s	4m13s
2m5½f Hdl	Haul Away (30 Aug 2018)	5m14.30s	5m14s
3m2f Hdl	Beautiful People (29 Aug 2019)	6m20.80s	6m19s

Haydock

1m7½f Ch	Witness In Court (19 Apr 2014)	3m52.30s	4m00s
2m3f Ch	Barton Knoll (11 May 2019)	4m43.30s	4m45s
2m4½f Ch	Brave Eagle (11 May 2019)	5m12.00s	5m11s
2m5½f Ch	Javert (7 May 2016)	5m20.20s	5m23s

2m7f Ch	No Planning (19 Apr 2014)	5m41.50s	5m51s
3m3½f Ch	Blenheim Brook (19 Apr 2014)	7m07.70s	6m55s
1m7½f Hdl	She's Our Mare (1 May 1999)	3m32.30s	3m40s
2m3f Hdl	Black Mischief (24 Nov 2018)	4m28.20s	4m27s
2m7f Hdl	Whataknight (7 May 2016)	5m28.90s	5m22s

Haydock, Lancashire course

2m½f Ch	Dicosimo (19 Jan 2019)	4m17.50s	4m05s
2m4f Ch	Copper West (20 Apr 2019)	5m00.97s	5m02s
2m5½f Ch	The Bay Birch (20 Apr 2019)	5m28.42s	5m20s
2m6f Ch	Magic Money (15 Apr 2017)	5m47.50s	5m25s
3m4½f Ch	Minella Daddy (20 Apr 2019)	7m24.72s	7m20s

Hexham

1m7½f Ch	Imjoeking (22 Jun 2014)	3m52.80s	3m56s
2m4f Ch	Mr Laggan (14 Sep 2003)	4m55.40s	5m03s
2m6½f Ch	Bobble Hat Bob (4 Jun 2013)	5m48.30s	5m43s
3m Ch	Silent Snipe (1 Jun 2002)	6m07.60s	6m10s
4m Ch	Simply Smashing (18 Mar 2010)	8m34.00s	8m15s
2m Hdl	Francies Fancy (19 June 2005)	3m57.80s	3m55s
2m4f Hdl	Pappa Charlie (27 May 1997)	4m31.50s	4m52s
2m7½f Hdl	Fingers Crossed (29 Apr 1991)	5m45.50s	5m45s

Huntingdon

2m½f Ch	No Greater Love (23 May 2007)	3m53.30s	3m56s
2m4f Ch	Peccadillo (26 Dec 2004)	4m46.40s	4m48s
2m7½f Ch	Ozzie Jones (18 Sep 1998)	5m44.40s	5m45s
3m6½f Ch	Kinnahalla (24 Nov 2001)	8m02.70s	7m40s
1m7½f Hdl	Weather Front (31 Aug 2009)	3m32.70s	3m38s
2m3½f Hdl	Sabre Hongrois (4 Oct 2009)	4m30.20s	4m36s
2m4½f Hdl	Sound Of Laughter (14 Apr 1984)	4m45.80s	4m48s
3m1f Hdl	Orchard King (31 Aug 2009)	5m50.20s	5m56s

Kelso

2m1f Ch	Simply Ned (4 Oct 2015)	3m57.80s	4m02s
2m5½f Ch	Romany Ryme (16 Sep 2015)	5m19.80s	5m01s
2m7½f Ch	Leanna Ban (24 May 2015)	5m40.30s	5m38s
3m2f Ch	Dandy Dan (27 Oct 2018)	6m32.80s	6m16s
4m½f Ch	Seven Towers (17 Jan 1997)	8m07.50s	7m56s
2m Hdl	Life And Soul (26 May 2013)	3m38.90s	3m43s
2m2f Hdl	Croco Bay (26 May 2013)	4m08.70s	4m13s
2m5f Hdl	Waterclock (16 Sept 2015)	4m49.50s	4m50s
2m6½f Hdl	Hit The Canvas (30 Sep 1995)	5m12.20s	5m18s
3m2f Hdl	Dook's Delight (19 May 1995)	6m10.10s	6m12s

Kempton

2m Ch	Special Tiara (27 Dec 2016)	3m46.25s	3m50s
2m2f Ch	Imperial Presence (7 May 2018)	4m19.37s	4m19s
2m4½f Ch	Top Notch (12 Jan 2019)	4m58.80s	4m58s
3m Ch	Tommy Silver (25 Apr 2019)	5m49.20s	5m54s
2m Hdl (Summer)	Hargam (16 Oct 2016)	3m38.20s	3m40s
2m Hdl (Winter)	Southfield Stone (23 Feb 2019)	3m41.60s	3m42s
2m5f Hdl (Summer)	Neverbeen To Paris (6 May 2019)	4m55.40s	4m50s
2m5f Hdl (Winter)	Erick Le Rouge (23 Feb 2019)	5m00.90s	4m55s
3m½f Hdl (Summer)	No Hidden Charges (6 May 2019)	5m52.50s	5m45s

3m½f Hdl (Winter)	Timeforwest (4 Apr 2017)	6m02.10s	5m47s

Leicester

2m Ch	Thankyou Very Much (1 Dec 2016)	3m45.30s	3m51s
2m4f Ch	Oliver's Hill (28 Dec 2016)	4m54.20s	5m01s
2m6½f Ch	Forgotten Gold (27 Nov 2016)	5m37.40s	5m40s
1m7½f Hdl	Tuning Gold (10 Jan 2019)	3m40.30s	3m35s
2m4½f Hdl	Ten Sixty (7 Dec 2016)	4m58.60s	4m45s

Lingfield

2m Ch	Authorized Too (8 Nov 2016)	3m57.80s	3m59s
2m4f Ch	Mr Medic (8 Nov 2016)	4m55.80s	4m59s
2m7½f Ch	Onderun (10 Dec 2016)	6m07.60s	5m48s
2m Hdl	Bobble Emerald (8 Nov 2016)	3m46.20s	3m50s
2m3½f Hdl	Phobiaphiliac (8 Nov 2016)	4m36.80s	4m40s
2m7f Hdl	Geordie B (4 Jan 2019)	6m01.40s	5m27s

Ludlow

2m Ch	Pearl King (5 Apr 2007)	3m47.30s	3m53s
	Bullet Street (10 May 2015)	3m47.30s	
2m4f Ch	Handy Money (5 Apr 2007)	4m47.30s	4m54s
3m Ch	Braqueur D'Or (11 Oct 2017)	5m54.70s	5m44s
3m1½f Ch	Moving Earth (12 May 2005)	6m17.30s	6m12s
2m Hdl	Leoncavallo (13 May 2018)	3m32.80s	3m38s
2m5f Hdl	Templehills (5 Oct 2016)	4m55.80s	4m56s
3m Hdl	Dark Spirit (9 Oct 2013)	5m33.30s	5m38s

Market Rasen

2m1f Ch	Mister Wiseman (7 Jul 2013)	4m13.60s	4m14s
2m3f Ch	Bocciani (10 May 2013)	4m41.40s	4m45s
2m5½f Ch	Vintage Vinnie (24 Sep 2016)	5m17.40s	5m16s
3m Ch	Allerlea (1 May 1985)	6m01.00s	5m46s
3m3½f Ch	Carli King (26 Dec 2014)	7m26.10s	6m46s
2m½f Hdl	Dino Velvet (17 Feb 2019)	3m55.50s	3m55s
2m2½f Hdl	Attaglance (19 Feb 2012)	4m26.10s	4m25s
2m4½f Hdl	Fiulin (19 Feb 2012)	5m03.70s	4m47s
2m7f Hdl	Let's Get At It (20 Mar 2019)	5m35.70s	5m39s

Musselburgh

2m Ch	Monsieur Co (28 Feb 2019)	3m46.60s	3m45s
2m1f Ch	Wishfull Dreaming (10 Mar 2019)	4m07.70s	4m00s
2m4f Ch	Bohemian Spirit (18 Dec 2005)	4m44.50s	4m41s
3m Ch	Snowy (18 Dec 2005)	5m47.70s	5m40s
3m2½f Ch	Present Flight (6 Nov 2015)	6m47.10s	6m20s
4m1f Ch	Dancing Shadow (4 Feb 2017)	8m28.60s	7m50s
1m7½f Hdl	Superb Story (1 Jan 2017)	3m35.00s	3m35s
2m½f Hdl	Manamite (27 Feb 2019)	3m49.80s	3m48s
2m3½f Hdl	Strongpoint (9 Dec 2013)	4m34.70s	4m30s
2m6f Hdl	Dizoard (7 Nov 2018)	5m23.00s	5m05s
3m Hdl	Jet Master (1 Jan 2019)	5m45.70s	5m32s
3m2f Hdl	El Bandit (5 Feb 2017)	6m26.90s	6m05s

Newbury

2m½f Ch	Valdez (30 Nov 2013)	3m57.34s	4m02s

VALDEZ: Newbury record-breaker in 2013 and still going strong at the age of 12

2m2½f Ch	Highway Code (29 Nov 2013)	4m31.87s	4m22s
2m4f Ch	Espy (25 Oct 1991)	4m47.90s	4m49s
2m6½f Ch	Pepite Rose (24 Mar 2012)	5m28.93s	5m25s
2m7½f Ch	Long Run (17 Feb 2012)	5m42.53s	5m40s
3m2f Ch	Ikorodu Road (24 Mar 2012)	6m22.86s	6m31s
2m½f Hdl	Dhofar (25 Oct 1985)	3m45.20s	3m48s
2m3f Hdl	Songsmith (24 Mar 2012)	4m26.70s	4m26s
2m4½f Hdl	Argento Luna (21 Mar 2009)	4m48.63s	4m49s
3m Hdl	Lansdowne (25 Oct 1996)	5m45.40s	5m45s

Newcastle

2m½f Ch	Greenheart (7 May 1990)	3m56.70s	3m59s
2m4f Ch	Snow Blessed (19 May 1984)	4m46.70s	4m53s
2m7½f Ch	Even Swell (30 Oct 1975)	5m48.10s	5m44s
4m½f Ch	Domaine Du Pron (21 Feb 1998)	8m30.40s	8m21s
2m½f Hdl	Padre Mio (25 Nov 1995)	3m40.70s	3m41s
2m4½f Hdl	Mils Mij (13 May 1989)	4m42.00s	4m44s
2m6f Hdl	Bygones Of Brid (28 Nov 2009)	5m24.90s	5m13s
3m Hdl	Withy Bank (29 Nov 1986)	5m40.10s	5m37s

Newton Abbot

2m½f Ch	Shantou Rock (13 Oct 2017)	3m49.70s	3m57s
2m5f Ch	The Unit (6 Aug 2018)	5m01.00s	5m08s

3m2f Ch	No Loose Change (8 Jul 2013)	6m09.50s	6m24s
2m1f Hdl	Windbound Lass (1 Aug 1988)	3m45.00s	3m50s
2m2½f Hdl	Rum And Butter (22 Aug 2013)	4m15.20s	4m17s
2m5½f Hdl	Virbian (30 Jun 1983)	4m55.40s	5m00s
3m2½f Hdl	Veneaux Du Cochet (1 Jul 2016)	6m09.90s	6m20s

Perth

2m Ch	Go West Young Man (15 Jul 2018)	3m41.70s	3m51s
2m4f Ch	Strobe (14 Jul 2013)	4m48.20s	4m52s
3m Ch	Problema Tic (9 Jun 2013)	5m46.20s	5m42s
3m6½f Ch	Laertes (24 Apr 2009)	7m43.70s	7m30s
2m Hdl	Court Minstrel (22 Aug 2015)	3m40.20s	3m42s
2m4f Hdl	Valiant Dash (19 May 1994)	4m41.20s	4m44s
3m Hdl	Imtihan (2 Jul 2009)	5m41.60s	5m35s
3m2½f Hdl	Noir Et Vert (28 Apr 2006)	6m37.20s	6m11s

Plumpton

2m1f Ch	Pearls Legend (17 Apr 2017)	4m04.40s	4m08s
2m3½f Ch	Dead Or Alive (10 May 2009)	4m42.80s	4m44s
3m1½f Ch	Sunday Habits (19 Apr 2003)	6m23.50s	6m15s
3m4½f Ch	Ecuyer Du Roi (15 Apr 2002)	7m19.80s	7m06s
2m Hdl	Royal Derbi (19 Sep 1988)	3m31.00s	3m38s
2m1½f Hdl	Arthington (24 Sep 2017)	4m08.50s	4m05s
2m4½f Hdl	Urban Warrior (21 Sep 2008)	4m46.80s	4m48s
3m1f Hdl	Listen And Learn (18 Sep 2016)	5m49.80s	5m57s

Sandown

1m7½f Ch	Dempsey (28 Apr 2007)	3m43.40s	3m46s
2m4f Ch	Coulton (29 Apr 1995)	4m57.10s	4m57s
2m6½f Ch	Menorah (29 Apr 2017)	5m41.40s	5m26s

YOUNEVERCALL: won at Sandown in a record time at the season finale

3m Ch	Arkle (6 Nov 1965)	5m59.00s	5m58s
3m5f Ch	Cache Fleur (29 Apr 1995)	7m09.10s	7m15s
2m Hdl	Olympian (13 Mar 1993)	3m42.00s	3m45s
2m4f Hdl	Oslot (28 Apr 2007)	4m35.70s	4m37s
2m5½f Hdl	Younevercall (27 Apr 2019)	5m16.30s	5m00s
2m7½f Hdl	Rostropovich (26 Apr 2003)	5m39.10s	5m35s

Sedgefield

2m½f Ch	Mixboy (27 Sep 2016)	3m49.90s	3m50s
2m3½f Ch	The Backup Plan (27 Aug 2015)	4m38.80s	4m32s
2m5f Ch	Degooch (1 Sep 2016)	5m10.50s	4m58s
3m2½f Ch	Running In Heels (30 Aug 2018)	6m29.00s	6m30s
3m5f Ch	Buachaill Alainn (27 Oct 2016)	7m20.40s	7m14s
2m1f Hdl	Snookered (5 Sep 2019)	3m44.80s	3m50s
2m4f Hdl	Grams And Ounces (27 Aug 2015)	4m32.80s	4m32s
2m5f Hdl	Palm House (4 Sep 1992)	4m46.30s	4m52s
3m3f Hdl	Pikestaff (25 Jul 2005)	6m19.70s	6m20s

Southwell

1m7½f Ch	Unify (27 Sep 2016)	3m53.70s	3m58s
2m4½f Ch	Gentleman Anshan (17 May 2011)	5m06.60s	5m04s
3m Ch	Best Boy Barney (22 Jul 2014)	6m10.10s	6m04s
3m1½f Ch	Sumkindofking (22 May 2019)	6m55.50s	6m26s
1m7½f Hdl	Dealing River (22 Jul 2014)	3m44.30s	3m42s
2m4½f Hdl	Red Not Blue (17 May 2011)	4m57.30s	4m57s
3m Hdl	Jawaab (22 Jul 2014)	5m55.40s	5m50s

Stratford

2m1f Ch	One For Billy (15 Jul 2018)	3m54.00s	4m02s
2m3½f Ch	Comanche Chieftain (2 Aug 2018)	4m31.70s	4m40s
2m5f Ch	Spare Change (16 Sep 2007)	4m56.60s	5m01s
2m6½f Ch	Monbeg Legend (8 Sep 2018)	5m19.30s	5m25s
3m3½f Ch	Mossey Joe (7 Jun 2013)	6m38.30s	6m40s
2m½f Hdl	Chusan (7 May 1956)	3m40.40s	3m46s
2m2½f Hdl	Lostock Hall (24 Aug 2016)	4m17.30s	4m21s
2m6f Hdl	Broken Wing (31 May 1986)	5m06.80s	5m10s
3m2½f Hdl	Burren Moonshine (11 Jun 2006)	6m13.10s	6m17s

Taunton

2m Ch	I Have Him (28 Apr 1995)	3m49.50s	4m00s
2m2f Ch	Wait No More (28 Mar 2012)	4m24.90s	4m35s
2m5½f Ch	Howlongisafoot (12 Nov 2015)	5m31.80s	5m21s
2m7f Ch	Glacial Delight (24 Apr 2006)	5m39.80s	5m45s
3m2½f Ch	Copperfacejack (1 Nov 2017)	6m51.00s	6m30s
3m4½f Ch	No Buts (27 Apr 2017)	7m21.70s	7m09s
2m½f Hdl	Indian Jockey (3 Oct 1996)	3m39.40s	3m50s
2m3f Hdl	Prairie Spirit (2 Apr 2009)	4m19.70s	4m27s
3m Hdl	On My Toes (15 Oct 1998)	5m30.20s	5m33s

Towcester

2m Ch	Pinkie Brown (5 Oct 2016)	3m51.90s	3m52s
2m4f Ch	Rakaia Rosa (4 May 2017)	4m53.40s	4m49s
2m5½f Ch	Midnight Shot (4 May 2017)	5m14.30s	5m16s
3m½f Ch	Lucky Luk (29 May 2009)	5m52.60s	5m53s
1m7½f Hdl	Moonday Sun (5 Oct 2016)	3m42.60s	3m43s

2m3f Hdl	Ballygrooby Bertie (19 May 2014)	4m31.50s	4m36s
2m5f Hdl	Plantagenet (11 Oct 2017)	4m58.60s	4m55s
3m Hdl	Dropshot (25 May 1984)	5m44.00s	5m40s

Uttoxeter

2m Ch	Festive Affair (2 Jul 2017)	3m45.70s	3m48s
2m4f Ch	Javert (23 Sep 2018)	4m51.90s	4m49s
2m6½f Ch	Just A Feeling (19 May 2018)	5m36.90s	5m25s
3m Ch	Angel Of Harlem (11 Sep 2019)	5m54.20s	5m50s
3m2f Ch	Drop Out Joe (26 Jun 2016)	6m23.10s	6m18s
2m Hdl	Mountainside (26 Jun 2016)	3m42.20s	3m39s
2m4f Hdl	Chicago's Best (11 Jun 1995)	4m39.10s	4m39s
2m7½f Hdl	Princeton Royale (4 Oct 2015)	5m36.60s	5m29s

Warwick

2m Ch	Wells De Lune (20 Sep 2016)	3m51.00s	3m51s
2m4f Ch	Templehills (4 Oct 2018)	4m55.10s	4m49s
3m Ch	Urcalin (1 Oct 2015)	5m52.60s	5m48s
3m1½f Ch	Laurium (25 Sep 2018)	6m10.80s	6m09s
3m5f Ch	Impulsive Star (12 Jan 2019)	7m16.10s	7m04s
2m Hdl (Inner)	Nylon Speed (25 Sep 2018)	3m37.90s	3m38s
2m3f Hdl (Outer)	One For Rosie (22 Feb 2019)	4m32.20s	4m26s
2m3f Hdl (Inner)	Kristal Hart (25 Sep 2018)	4m19.10s	4m21s
2m5f Hdl (Outer)	Bendomingo (13 May 2017)	4m57.10s	4m50s
2m5f Hdl (Inner)	Beakstown (12 Jan 2019)	4m50.20s	4m50s
3m1f Hdl (Inner)	The Tourard Man (24 Apr 2017)	5m56.40s	5m45s
3m2f Hdl (Outer)	Braventara (4 Nov 2016)	6m18.50s	6m03s
3m2f Hdl (Inner)	Dreamsoftheatre (25 Sep 2018)	6m02.90s	5m57s

Wetherby

1m7f Ch	Theflyingportrait (17 Oct 2018)	3m37.20s	3m43s
2m3½f Ch	Lough Derg Spirit (17 Oct 2018)	4m40.90s	4m45s
2m5½f Ch	Rosquero (4 May 2016)	5m17.60s	5m14s
3m Ch	Definitly Red (3 Nov 2018)	5m58.00s	5m57s
2m Hdl	Lightening Rod (31 Oct 2014)	3m43.20s	3m45s
2m3½f Hdl	Mustmeetalady (14 Oct 2015)	4m40.90s	4m34s
2m5½f Hdl	Kaysersberg (15 Oct 2014)	5m02.10s	4m56s
3m Hdl	Nautical Nitwit (3 Nov 2018)	5m43.20s	5m48s

Wincanton

1m7½f Ch	Kie (13 Apr 2014)	3m37.90s	3m50s
2m4f Ch	Meldrum Lad (23 Apr 2017)	4m54.20s	4m56s
3m1f Ch	Swansea Bay (8 Nov 2003)	6m09.70s	6m15s
3m2½f Ch	Gullible Gordon (24 Oct 2010)	6m37.20s	6m40s
1m7½f Hdl	Cliffs Of Dover (14 Oct 2016)	3m22.60s	3m31s
2m4f Hdl	Deserter (14 Oct 2016)	4m28.30s	4m31s
2m5½f Hdl	San Satiro (23 Apr 2017)	4m53.10s	4m52s

Worcester

2m½f Ch	Mercian King (12 Oct 2017)	3m51.60s	3m52s
2m4f Ch	Rene's Girl (12 Oct 2017)	4m39.90s	4m48s
2m7f Ch	Go Another One (1 Sep 2019)	5m21.40s	5m35s
2m Hdl	Moonday Sun (30 Aug 2016)	3m37.30s	3m40s
2m4f Hdl	Doubly Clever (1 Sep 2019)	4m37.90s	4m44s
2m7f Hdl	Net Work Rouge (14 Oct 2015)	5m28.10s	5m22s

NAUTICAL NITWIT: popular gelding enjoyed his finest hour at Wetherby

Win - free form!

THIS YEAR'S QUIZ could hardly be more simple and the prize should prove invaluable to our lucky winner. We're offering a free subscription to The Jumps Form Book 2019-20, the BHA's official form book – every week up to April 2020, you could be getting the previous week's results in full, together with notebook comments highlighting future winners, adjusted Official Ratings and Racing Post ratings.

All you have to do is this: identify the three horses pictured on the following pages. And here's a clue – they were the first three in the market in last season's Champion Hurdle yet all failed to make the first three in the race.

Send your answers along with your details on the entry form below to:

2019-20 Jumps Annual Competition, Racing & Football Outlook, Floor 7, Vivo Building, South Bank Central, 30 Stamford Street, London, SE1 9LS.

Entries must reach us no later than first post on December 12. The winner's name and the right answers will be printed in the RFO's December 17 edition.

Six runners-up will each receive a copy of last year's form book.

Name...

Address...

....

Town...

Postcode...

In the event of more than one correct entry, the winner will be drawn at random from the correct entries. The Editor's decision is final and no correspondence will be entered into.

BETTING CHART

ON	ODDS	AGAINST
50	Evens	50
52.4	11-10	47.6
54.5	6-5	45.5
55.6	5-4	44.4
58	11-8	42
60	6-4	40
62	13-8	38
63.6	7-4	36.4
65.3	15-8	34.7
66.7	2-1	33.3
68	85-40	32
69.2	9-4	30.8
71.4	5-2	28.6
73.4	11-4	26.6
75	3-1	25
76.9	100-30	23.1
77.8	7-2	22.2
80	4-1	20
82	9-2	18
83.3	5-1	16.7
84.6	11-2	15.4
85.7	6-1	14.3
86.7	13-2	13.3
87.5	7-1	12.5
88.2	15-2	11.8
89	8-1	11
89.35	100-12	10.65
89.4	17-2	10.6
90	9-1	10
91	10-1	9
91.8	11-1	8.2
92.6	12-1	7.4
93.5	14-1	6.5
94.4	16-1	5.6
94.7	18-1	5.3
95.2	20-1	4.8
95.7	22-1	4.3
96.2	25-1	3.8
97.2	33-1	2.8
97.6	40-1	2.4
98.1	50-1	1.9
98.5	66-1	1.3
99.0	100-1	.0.99

The table above (often known as the 'Field Money Table') shows both bookmakers' margins and how much a backer needs to invest to win £100. To calculate a bookmaker's margin, simply add up the percentages of all the odds on offer. The sum by which the total exceeds 100% gives the 'over-round' on the book. To determine what stake is required to win £100 (includes returned stake) at a particular price, just look at the relevant row, either odds-against or odds-on.

RULE 4 DEDUCTIONS

When a horse is withdrawn before coming under starter's orders, but after a market has been formed, bookmakers are entitled to make the following deductions from win and place returns (excluding stakes) in accordance with Tattersalls' Rule 4(c).

	Odds of withdrawn horse	*Deduction from winnings*
(1)	3-10 or shorter	75p in the £
(2)	2-5 to 1-3	70p in the £
(3)	8-15 to 4-9	65p in the £
(4)	8-13 to 4-7	60p in the £
(5)	4-5 to 4-6	55p in the £
(6)	20-21 to 5-6	50p in the £
(7)	Evens to 6-5	45p in the £
(8)	5-4 to 6-4	40p in the £
(9)	13-8 to 7-4	35p in the £
(10)	15-8 to 9-4	30p in the £
(11)	5-2 to 3-1	25p in the £
(12)	100-30 to 4-1	20p in the £
(13)	9-2 to 11-2	15p in the £
(14)	6-1 to 9-1	10p in the £
(15)	10-1 to 14-1	5p in the £
(16)	longer than 14-1	no deductions

(17) ....When more than one horse is withdrawn without coming under starter's orders, total deductions shall not exceed 75p in the £.

**Starting-price bets are affected only when there was insufficient time to form a new market.*

Feedback!

If you have any comments or criticism about this book, or suggestions for future editions, please tell us.

Write

Nick Watts/Dylan Hill
2019-20 Jumps Annual
Racing & Football Outlook
Floor 7, Vivo Building, South Bank Central
30 Stamford Street
London SE1 9LS

email rfo@rfoutlook.co.uk

Horse index

All horses discussed, with page numbers, except for references in the big-race form and novice sections (pages 79-118), which have their own indexes